TRANSGRESSIONS: CULT
Volume 70

Series Editor:
Shirley R. Steinberg, *McGill University, Canada*

Founding Editor:
Joe L. Kincheloe (1950–2008) *The Paulo and Nita Freire International Project for Critical Pedagogy*

Editorial Board
Jon Austin, *University of Southern Queensland, Australia*
Norman Denzin, *University of Illinois, Champaign-Urbana, USA*
Rhonda Hammer, *University of California Los Angeles, USA*
Nikos Metallinos, *Concordia University, Canada*
Christine Quail, *McMaster University, Canada*
Ki Wan Sung, *Kyung Hee University, Seoul, Korea*

This book series is dedicated to the radical love and actions of Paulo Freire, Jesus "Pato" Gomez, and Joe L. Kincheloe.

To Jenn:
All the very best to you!
Val

TRANSGRESSIONS: CULTURAL STUDIES AND EDUCATION

Cultural studies provides an analytical toolbox for both making sense of educational practice and extending the insights of educational professionals into their labors. In this context *Transgressions: Cultural Studies and Education* provides a collection of books in the domain that specify this assertion. Crafted for an audience of teachers, teacher educators, scholars and students of cultural studies and others interested in cultural studies and pedagogy, the series documents both the possibilities of and the controversies surrounding the intersection of cultural studies and education. The editors and the authors of this series do not assume that the interaction of cultural studies and education devalues other types of knowledge and analytical forms. Rather the intersection of these knowledge disciplines offers a rejuvenating, optimistic, and positive perspective on education and educational institutions. Some might describe its contribution as democratic, emancipatory, and transformative. The editors and authors maintain that cultural studies helps free educators from sterile, monolithic analyses that have for too long undermined efforts to think of educational practices by providing other words, new languages, and fresh metaphors. Operating in an interdisciplinary cosmos, Transgressions: Cultural Studies and Education is dedicated to exploring the ways cultural studies enhances the study and practice of education. With this in mind the series focuses in a non-exclusive way on popular culture as well as other dimensions of cultural studies including social theory, social justice and positionality, cultural dimensions of technological innovation, new media and media literacy, new forms of oppression emerging in an electronic hyperreality, and postcolonial global concerns. With these concerns in mind cultural studies scholars often argue that the realm of popular culture is the most powerful educational force in contemporary culture. Indeed, in the twenty-first century this pedagogical dynamic is sweeping through the entire world. Educators, they believe, must understand these emerging realities in order to gain an important voice in the pedagogical conversation.

Without an understanding of cultural pedagogy's (education that takes place outside of formal schooling) role in the shaping of individual identity–youth identity in particular–the role educators play in the lives of their students will continue to fade. Why do so many of our students feel that life is incomprehensible and devoid of meaning? What does it mean, teachers wonder, when young people are unable to describe their moods, their affective affiliation to the society around them. Meanings provided young people by mainstream institutions often do little to help them deal with their affective complexity, their difficulty negotiating the rift between meaning and affect. School knowledge and educational expectations seem as anachronistic as a ditto machine, not that learning ways of rational thought and making sense of the world are unimportant.

But school knowledge and educational expectations often have little to offer students about making sense of the way they feel, the way their affective lives are shaped. In no way do we argue that analysis of the production of youth in an electronic mediated world demands some "touchy-feely" educational superficiality. What is needed in this context is a rigorous analysis of the interrelationship between pedagogy, popular culture, meaning making, and youth subjectivity. In an era marked by youth depression, violence, and suicide such insights become extremely important, even life saving. Pessimism about the future is the common sense of many contemporary youth with its concomitant feeling that no one can make a difference.

If affective production can be shaped to reflect these perspectives, then it can be reshaped to lay the groundwork for optimism, passionate commitment, and transformative educational and political activity. In these ways cultural studies adds a dimension to the work of education unfilled by any other sub-discipline. This is what Transgressions: Cultural Studies and Education seeks to produce—literature on these issues that makes a difference. It seeks to publish studies that help those who work with young people, those individuals involved in the disciplines that study children and youth, and young people themselves improve their lives in these bizarre times.

Cold Breezes and Idiot Winds

Patriotic Correctness and the Post-9/11 Assault on Academe

Valerie Scatamburlo-D'Annibale
University of Windsor

SENSE PUBLISHERS
ROTTERDAM/BOSTON/TAIPEI

A C.I.P. record for this book is available from the Library of Congress.

ISBN: 978-94-6091-407-2 (paperback)
ISBN: 978-94-6091-408-9 (hardback)
ISBN: 978-94-6091-409-6 (e-book)

Published by: Sense Publishers,
P.O. Box 21858,
3001 AW Rotterdam,
The Netherlands
www.sensepublishers.com

Printed on acid-free paper

DEDICATION

This book is dedicated to my husband, John D'Annibale

In the words of Bon Jovi, Thank you for loving me

TABLE OF CONTENTS

ACKNOWLEDGMENTS

My gratitude to the late Joe Kincheloe who embraced this project from the get-go and to his partner, Shirley Steinberg, who helped it come to fruition after his untimely passing.

Thanks to two wonderful graduate students, Jennifer Budinsky and Crystal Kotow, for reviewing various parts of the manuscript. I owe a debt of gratitude to my very creative colleague, Min Bae, for his work on the cover design. Thanks also to my other colleagues, Jyotika Virdi, James Winter and Irv Goldman for their friendship and support.

I must also acknowledge my dear friends from Pennsylvania, Gary and Lauri Centolanza for many, many lively political discussions, accompanied with fine red wine, over the years.

To my wonderful in-laws, Fernand and Marguerite D'Annibale–thanks for raising such a fine son. My deepest appreciation goes to my parents, Renato and Pierina Scatamburlo, for being a constant source of love and encouragement.

Finally, to John: thanks for being with me every step of the way. I appreciate your love, support, understanding and patience more than I can ever express.

Valerie Scatamburlo-D'Annibale
LaSalle, Ontario, August 2010

INTRODUCTION

Liberal Hunting in the Promised Land

Liberal Hunting Permit: No Bag Limit—Tagging Not Required. May be used while under the influence of alcohol. May be used to Hunt Liberals at Gay Pride Parades, Democrat Conventions, Union Rallys, Handgun Control Meetings, News Media Association, Lesbian Luncheons and Hollywood Functions. May Hunt Day or Night With or Without Dogs. *{sic}*

When contemplating college liberals, you really regret once again that John Walker is not getting the death penalty. We need to execute people like John Walker in order to physically intimidate liberals, by making them realize that they can be killed, too. Otherwise, they will turn out to be outright traitors.[1]

If you're against the president and his policies, you're unpatriotic and rooting against America.[2]

The bumper sticker "permit" quoted here has been around for quite some time—circulating, for the most part, among the fringes of the far right. Yet, the odium that animates such sentiments has, for some time, been making its way to a broader mass audience. One need only sample the diatribes authored by conservative "luminaries"—including Ann Coulter's *Treason: Liberal Treachery from the Cold War to the War on Terrorism*; Sean Hannity's *Let Freedom Ring: Winning the War of Liberty over Liberalism* and *Deliver Us From Evil: Defeating Terrorism, Despotism and Liberalism*, Bill O'Reilly's *Culture Warrior* and Glenn Beck's *Arguing with Idiots: How to Stop Small Minds and Big Government*—to see the hateful rhetoric at work.

This type of rabid anti-liberalism is the lifeblood of a right-wing media/culture apparatus that has been established over the last 30–40 years. Over the airwaves, millions of "Dittoheads" delight in Rush Limbaugh's tirades against "femi-Nazis," "long-haired dope smoking peace pansies," wimpy "limousine liberals" and "leftist terrorist sympathizers" whose sordid politics allegedly crystallized during the murky mayhem of the 1960s. Others rely on the likes of Laura Ingraham and Michael Savage for their daily dose of talk-radio liberal-bashing; Savage has called liberalism a "mental disorder" and written books rebuffing the liberal/left "assault" on the nation's schools, faith and military.

On the Fox News Channel, smear merchant Bill O'Reilly routinely entertains his sycophants with Banshee-like screeching about loony leftists and berates, with autocratic homilies, those few guests he does invite on his show who prove to be formidable opponents as was the case when he warned Port Authority worker Jeremy Glick to "get out of my studio before I tear you to fucking pieces." Glick, whose father perished in the 9/11 attacks, had criticized O'Reilly for continually invoking "9/11" to rationalize everything from domestic plunder to imperialist aggression.[3] Combining his trademark self-congratulatory belligerence and Stygian anger, O'Reilly often offers smug sermons about "girly men" and "immoral" liberals—this even after he narrowly escaped becoming "the Pee Wee Herman of the Right" by settling a lawsuit filed by a co-worker who alleged that he "harassed her with conversations of masturbation, vibrators, and invitations to participate in pornographic sex."[4] And Glenn Beck, the grand poobah of paranoid conspiracy theorists, has assumed a professorial persona, complete with chalkboard in tow, in order to "educate" citizens about the ills of liberalism and the dangers associated with American universities that, according to Beck, "teach garbage."[5]

One may be inclined to dismiss the bumper-sticker bile and quasi-fascistic rants of the aforementioned authors and their ilk as symptoms of unstable minds. And, at some level, that is perhaps the case. However, such a flippant stance is somewhat naïve given the frosty climate that emerged in the United States in the aftermath of 9/11. Although not all conservatives agreed with Ann Coulter's outrageous call to physically intimidate college liberals (an invitation that came as no shock to anyone remotely familiar with her; after all, some have suggested that if she "had been around for the Third Reich Ice-Cream Social, Eva Braun wouldn't have stood a chance"), after 9/11 far too many on the right-wing of the political spectrum were quick to dub liberals (let alone leftists) as unpatriotic scoundrels who were jeopardizing the very foundations of the 'American way of life.'[6] While they may not have advocated threatening their liberal and left opponents, many actively lobbied for their symbolic eradication and the silencing of their dissident voices. For conservatives, "liberal" has become an epithet—the approximate counterpart to the godless communist of an earlier era; anti-liberalism has replaced anti-communism as the rallying cry of the right.[7]

This truculent posturing was not limited to the aforementioned bevy of bellicose blowhards; it was apparent in the uppermost echelons of the no less bellicose Bush administration which employed a rhetorical strategy that was both opportunistic and mendacious for it essentially cast its critics as terrorist supporters as the quote from former Vice-President Dick Cheney cited above demonstrates. Such posturing was also on display in 2005 in Midtown Manhattan courtesy of Karl Rove—also known as Turdblossom and Bush's brain—who insinuated that those who disagreed with the President's impetuous cowboy foreign policy were giving comfort to the "enemy."[8] Speaking at a fundraiser for the Conservative Party of New York State, Rove claimed that:

> Conservatives saw the savagery of 9/11 and the attacks and prepared for war; liberals saw the savagery of the 9/11 attacks and wanted to prepare indictments and offer therapy and understanding for our attackers. In the wake of 9/11, conservatives believed it was time to unleash the might and power of the United States military against the Taliban; in the wake of 9/11, liberals believed it was time to submit a petition ... Conservatives saw what happened to us on 9/11 and said: We will defeat our enemies. Liberals saw what happened to us and said: We must understand our enemies.[9]

Rove's message was unequivocal—liberals are pantywaists, incapable of the moral clarity needed to combat the "enemy" and protect the "homeland," and weak in the face of "evil." Rove's incendiary remarks were, of course, designed to score political points and they created a mild furor among many Democrats, some of whom demanded an apology. Not surprisingly, right-wing columnists lavished Rove with praise for speaking the "truth" while others shrugged off his comments as merely partisan. But Rove's anti-liberal rhetorical flourishes were more than partisan tripe for they represented a reincarnation of a style of politics that was eerily reminiscent of McCarthyism. Although columnist E.J. Dionne Jr. characterized Rove's version as a "kinder, gentler" form of McCarthyism, his assessment would be much too charitable particularly if applied to the tactics that Rove's fellow conservatives employed in other contexts. Nowhere were these egregious tactics more visible than on the campuses of American universities.

In April 2005, the editors of *The Nation* astutely noted that

[t]he suppression of ... dissent, a disconcerting feature of political life since the Bush administration took power, has been most sharply felt on college campuses ... Not since the McCarthy era have American campuses felt such a cold breeze—make that an idiot wind. And the new campus McCarthyism is made of much of the same ingredients: thuggish intimidation, the circulation of specious rumors and ... that least venerable of American traditions, anti-intellectualism.[10]

Examples of the "cold breeze," some of which are explored up in the following chapters, were plentiful across the country post-9/11. They ranged from efforts by right-wing student groups to suppress campus dissent, attempts to introduce legislation that would police the content of courses offered in universities and target professors critical of U.S. foreign policy (especially in the Middle East), to calls for the outright dismissal of faculty members who failed to robotically sanction Bush's "war on terror." These and other examples unmistakably revealed that the idiot wind spawned a new form of PC—patriotic correctness.

The notion that 9/11 "changed everything" became an oft-repeated and widely circulated cliché and there is little doubt that the events of that day had a dramatic and immediate impact on the political landscape. Yet, one thing that did *not* really change was the right's long-standing contempt for the "liberal/left" professoriate. Conservative criticisms of the academy as a citadel of radicalism are, after all, hardly new. They have a long and ignoble history in the United States, dating back to nineteenth century attacks launched by religious zealots and the anti-communist witch-hunts undertaken in the 1920s, 1930s, and most famously in the 1950s under the auspices of Joe McCarthy who led the government inquisition that resulted in the firing and blacklisting of dissident intellectuals both in and out of the academy.[11] In 1964, Ronald Reagan was pontificating about the long-hairs at Berkeley; twenty-seven years later, George H.W. Bush was chastising the 'political correctness' of tenured radicals in an infamous University of Michigan address.

The public perception of universities as bastions of 'political correctness' where conservative views are marginalized and/or censored was burnished in the public mind in the early 1990s at the height of the "culture wars" as right-wing custodians of the "Western tradition" and media cognoscenti managed to paint a picture of campus life reminiscent of Hieronymus Bosch's vision of hell. Back then, it was asserted that left-wing vigilantes and burned-out Sixties hippies-turned-academics were running amok at the nation's universities. The Left—a catch-all phrase that encompassed feminists, multiculturalists, deconstructionists, postmodernists, and others—was vilified as a coterie of propagandists; as Orwellian dragoons of group-think intent on silencing free expression and imposing the diktats of ideological correctness. In a paradoxical shift, it was claimed that those who had once marched for the right to free speech were vigorously creating mini 'ministries of truth' that were springing up like noxious weeds and choking out the flowers of free expression on campuses. As an ideological code, "political correctness" operated as a device that mediated perception in the relations of public discourse—progressive intellectuals were cast as social oddballs, elements of a radical fringe, and politically threatening extremists.

Of course, the brouhaha over "political correctness" eventually subsided, the headlines waned, and assaults on liberal/left scholars were, for a time, consigned to opinion columns penned by conservative garrisons such as Thomas Sowell, professional academe-basher George Will, and the pages of right-wing academic "journals." Nonetheless, the broader "culture war" bluster persisted and, in many ways, informed the attacks on the Clinton White House. Clinton—hardly a man of the 'left'—was projected as the Sixties personified, a product of that decade who smoked pot, dodged the draft and whose wife Hillary evidently represented the epitome of feminism gone awry. During the Clinton presidency, rightist rage was mainly focused on "Slick Willie's" libido and his indiscretions that were, of course, routinely attributed to his "liberal" promiscuity. As a result of the obsession with various "gates," Monica Lewinsky, cigars and a blue dress, academe itself was *temporarily* spared.

However, after the September 11 attacks, a motley crew of right-wing rabble-rousers, religious firebrands, and militant neoconservatives donned their culture war armor, capitalized on widespread angst for "national security," and found a scapegoat in the serious domestic "threat" posed by liberal/left professors. This posse sanctimoniously summoned Bush's bromidic binarism, "you are with us or against us;" the "war on terror" quickly gave way to a war on dissent and the academy was once again thrust into the spotlight. Many of the same tiresome themes and hackneyed charges that were bandied about in the early 1990s were simply repackaged for post-9/11 America; rightists, draped in the Stars and Stripes, seized the moment to resuscitate the "culture wars," thwart any criticism of the Bush administration, U.S. foreign policy and imperialist military aggression and, especially, the nobility of American capitalism. James Pbierson, a contributor to the *Weekly Standard*, captured the right's post-9/11 sentiment quite well when he groused about academics who were "both anti-American and anticapitalist."[12] Predictably, many of the same personalities, right-wing foundations, and think tanks that helped to popularize and finance the backlash against political correctness were once again at the center of post-9/11 efforts to liken legitimate dissent to treason.

What *was* different and profoundly more disturbing was that the hyperbole was ratcheted up significantly. The liberal/left professoriate was no longer just a post-modern, deconstructionist nuisance; it was identified as a subversive "fifth column."

Moreover, the tactics employed by conservatives who called for the figurative heads of those who strayed from the patriotically correct line which they espoused went well beyond those used in the 1990s. Long before the talking heads on the Fox News Channel made former University of Colorado professor Ward Churchill their poster-boy for intellectual repression and coercion, the right used the American Council of Trustees and Alumni (ACTA)—an organization co-founded by former Second Lady Lynne Cheney—to launch a crusade against rebellious academics who were described as barbarians hell-bent on dismantling "Western civilization" itself. Not long after the attacks, ACTA produced a report that documented more than 100 examples of "anti-Americanism" on college campuses and posted it online. The hit list included the names and affiliations of academics that were, according to ACTA, insufficiently patriotic and averse to teaching students about the "virtues" of the Western political order. The document was rife with inaccuracies, distortions, and outright fallacies but the stench of McCarthyism was irrefutable.

Then there was the right's favorite red diaper baby—David Horowitz—who created a website exhorting students to complain about licentious liberal professors and leftist lunatics who were presumably trying to poison their young minds with anti-American ideologies. And through his vast empire, he amassed a brigade of collegians who were dispatched as shock troopers to intimidate (sometimes physically) campus liberals from coast to coast. Horowitz, who literally drips with the ooze of blacklisting, even went so far as to claim that universities were a base for terrorism.[13]

In 2005, at the University of California, Los Angeles, Andrew Jones, a former campus Republican operative and one-time protégé of Horowitz tried to garner support for patriotic correctness by offering to pay UCLA students to surveil professors critical of the Bush administration. He subsequently led the charge in creating a website "exposing" the "Dirty Thirty"—a list of liberal/left educators who were supposedly, among other things, collaborating with radical Muslims to undercut the war on terror. These are just a few of the more flagrant examples of rightist efforts to coerce campus progressives; many more are explored throughout this treatise.

The "right-wing efforts and demands to reform higher education" that emerged after the terrorist attacks took a decidedly dangerous turn that "far exceeded the threat posed by the previous "culture wars."[14] Arguably, the post-9/11 campaign against the academy was even more serious than the one witnessed during the McCarthy era for it reached directly into the classroom. In contrast to the McCarthy era, powerful private organizations and corporate-funded think thanks, rather than the government, were behind the attempts to "quarantine dissent," dominate the "framing of public discourse" and "rechannel the flows of knowledge production."[15] In the "name of establishing intellectual diversity," forces on the right tried to "impose outside political controls over core educational functions like personnel decisions, curricula, and teaching methods." Such interference not only endangered the "faculty autonomy that traditionally protects academic freedom," it also threatened the very "integrity of American higher education."[16] It is therefore necessary to consider the forces that advanced patriotic correctness as a strategy to intimidate the liberal/left and devalue critical thought. However, before doing so, it is necessary to define how the phrase "patriotic correctness" is being used in this context.

PATRIOTIC CORRECTNESS

Patriotic correctness (hereafter PC), refers to a multifaceted and multileveled discourse that was promoted as a form of public pedagogy after 9/11 by an ideological coalition of religious fundamentalists, militant neoconservatives and think tank mandarins. Given the enormity of the tragedy and its overwhelming impact on the collective consciousness of the country, culture war veterans, opportunistic demagogues and right-wing campus tyros worked to produce a set of unambiguous and implied rules for what constituted "acceptable" forms of thought, speech and deed. The moral panic surrounding the meaning of patriotism in post-9/11 America produced much confusion that was easily leveraged by proponents of PC who sought to control the 'bounds of the expressible' and advance a very specific worldview—one that emphasized, among other things, notions of American "exceptionalism" and innocence, the "Christian" foundations of the nation, the supremacy of the American "free market" and the perils of "liberalism." Of course, many of these ideas existed prior to 9/11 but afterwards they coalesced into a "grand narrative" of sorts—one that was militaristic, hyper-masculinist and intensely anti-intellectual.

Patriotism is an abstract concept that has taken different forms over the course of the nation's history and there is no doubt that a *general* patriotic mood did in fact sweep the country after the attacks. However, PC advanced what could arguably be called "superpatriotism" which suggested that uncritical assent to governmental authority was synonymous with loving 'freedom' and that dissent was tantamount to supporting terrorism. Superpatriotism also rests on the "dubious assumption that the United States is endowed with superior virtue" and that it has a "unique history and special place in the world."[17] Thus, the belief in America's "exceptionalism" was at the heart of PC. Of course, this exceptionalism has a long history; it is deeply rooted in the "discourse of early American preachers" and has powered many "citizens' visions of manifest destiny, which animated the U.S. history of expansion and imperial vision."[18] But, after 9/11 it manifested itself in new and particularly powerful ways. Exceptionalism defines America as a "model" for the rest of the world and is rooted in the conviction that the U.S. is a benevolent entity in world affairs that is motivated not by avarice and power but by the greater global good; that American military force is directed only towards noble purposes and laudable goals and that American foreign policy is a civilizing force for the benefit of dispossessed and disenfranchised people throughout the world. Stemming from these beliefs, PC also implied that the military embodied all that was "good" and "righteous," that war-making abroad was ordained by the Almighty as inherently just and that it had to be supported unquestioningly. Allegiance to the homeland was demanded at all costs, regardless of the facts.

Many of these convictions were epitomized in the declaration made by George W. Bush on May 1, 2003 when he issued a decree in honor of Loyalty Day, a legal American holiday that was established in 1958.[19] In his proclamation, Bush said:

> Today, America's men and women in uniform are protecting our Nation, defending the peace of the world, and advancing the cause of liberty. The world has seen again the fine character of our Nation through our military as

they fought to protect the innocent and liberate the oppressed ... [t]heir service and sacrifice ... are a testament to their love for America ... [and] reaffirms our Nation's most deeply held beliefs: that every life counts, and that all humans have an unalienable right to live as free people. These values must be imparted to each new generation. Our children need to know that our Nation is a force for good in the world, extending hope and freedom to others. By learning about America's history, achievements, ideas, and heroes, our young citizens will come to understand even more why freedom is worth protecting.[20]

This particular statement was one among many that captured the pedagogical vision preferred by the right—one that imparts a sanitized version of history and obfuscates from view the "value system disorder" that lies at the heart of American empire including "US logistical and financial support of death-squads, terrorist networks and so-called "wars of liberation" that systematically fomented chaos around the globe, long before the thundering collapse of the Twin Towers.[21] In this sense, PC evoked an "amnesiac claim of political innocence, a guise of national blamelessness" that philosopher Cornel West referred to as America's "Peter Pan complex."[22]

Typically, in times of war, themes of sacrifice are common in presidential orations and Bush undoubtedly drew on them when speaking about military service. However, more pronounced was the way in which he and other conservative politicians such as Rudy Guiliani encouraged what could be called free market patriotism. For example, the importance of an orderly restoration of trading was repeatedly accentuated; panic was deemed unpatriotic as Americans were told that if they ceased to work or lost faith in the market that this would signal a victory for the terrorists. Those who fought terror through pledging allegiance to the market were assimilated as heroic foot soldiers in the emblematic war against evil at home. By late September 2001, Bush was being dispatched to press events across the country to tell people to "get on board," to do their patriotic duty by traveling and going shopping. In identifying consumption as a panacea for all that ailed a traumatized nation and as a way to "fight back" against the nation's enemies, the Bush administration was coaxing citizens to find solace in the world of goods and to display their patriotism through the purchase of clip-on symbols and kitschy artifacts. After 9/11, "citizens were patriots, and patriots were consumers" and individuals were beseeched, especially by the corporate media, to buy assorted paraphernalia to express their love of country; consumerism "became both a public act of patriotism and a symbolic act to thwart the terrorists."[23]

Among the objects that Americans purchased en masse in the first week or two after 9/11 were flags, which quickly sold out across the country, and which were prominently displayed on cars, SUVs, trucks and homes. T-shirts, many of which were, ironically, made in China, emblazoned with the stars and stripes and others sporting the phrase "Never Forget" added to the super-patriotic imagery that flooded the visual landscape; teddy bears were also ubiquitous as part of the kitsch culture that emerged. The "kitschification" of 9/11, allowed for, if not facilitated, the means by which the tragedy was "exploited for particular political agendas and incorporated into a continuum of kitsch political discourse." Kitsch objects address "consumers within a particular emotional register" (including sympathy, sadness, and comfort). On one level, these objects "skirt anger, since they are couched in terms of empathy and reassurance" but these forms of consumer culture also "enable a political acquiescence, in which consumers signal their 'categorical agreement' through the purchase of tokens." When tokens such as teddy bears are "circulated as 'universal' symbols of comfort," the teddy bears essentially say "we are innocent, and, by extension, the nation is innocent too."[24]

Sturken notes that this melding of consumerism and patriotism discouraged people from thinking critically about the attacks and what may have precipitated them. Kitsch consumerism and its concomitant commoditization of grief is deeply connected to a sense of national identity and a version of American history that is fundamentally based on a "disavowal of the role played in world politics by the United States not simply as a world power, but as a nation with imperialist policies and aspirations to empire."[25] Such consumptive practices functioned to reinforce the concept of American innocence and were useful to opportunists seeking to cultivate a culture of compliance and conceal the involvement of the U.S. "in the troubled global strife of the world."[26] American innocence, a central trope of PC, was promoted so as to avoid "any discussion of what long histories of U.S. foreign policies had done to help foster a terrorist movement specifically aimed at the United States."[27] Moreover, this comfort, kitsch culture had significant political repercussions insofar as it made possible the propagation and acceptance of "beautifying lies"— i.e. "a 'spread of democracy' that often bolsters its opposite, a 'march of freedom' that often liberates people to death, a 'war on terror' that is often terroristic, and a trumpeting of 'moral values' often at the cost of civil rights."[28]

Manufacturing consent for imperial military misadventures involved multifarious maneuvers that encouraged not only the consumption of patriotic artifacts but the consumption of spectacles as well. Two months after the attacks, Karl Rove summoned forty of the top television and movie executives to the swanky environs of the Beverly Hills Peninsula Hotel to explore how the entertainment industry could assist the administration in making war more palatable to the American public. Rove, with a power point presentation on hand, asked the Hollywood moguls to consider how they might contribute to "educating" the public about the virtues of the war on terror and helping to boost morale at home. In mid-December 2001, the industry unveiled its "first response on more than ten thousand movie screens—a quarter of all American cinemas—and in classrooms across the country."[29]

The Spirit of America, a 3-minute film, featured clips from 110 American movies that its creator, Oscar-winning director Chuck Workman, felt captured and celebrated the essence of the country. Befitting the presidency of George W. Bush, whose favorite prop was his Texas ranch where he was often photographed clearing brush, the film began and ended with scenes from John Ford's 1956 classic western *The Searchers* that starred none other than America's quintessential cowboy and symbol of masculinity, John Wayne. This was hardly surprising since talk about the 'return' of John Wayne had been circulating among the conservative chattering class months before the film was released. "Welcome Back, Duke" was the title of an article authored by former Reagan speechwriter Peggy Noonan wherein she gushed about "a certain style of manliness" that was rising from the ashes of the Twin Towers and the "rubble of the past quarter century."[30] This thrilled Noonan who had been saddened by Wayne's metaphorical death at the hands of "feminists," "peaceniks," "leftists," and "intellectuals."[31] Post-9/11 was no time for girly men and nerdy professors who would rather "talk about everything and do nothing."[32]

PC was steeped in the sort of hyper-masculinity that had Noonan swooning like a twelve year-old girl at a Justin Bieber concert as rightists viewed the post-9/11 atmosphere as an opportunity for cultural remasculinization. PC reflected the "tough guy" talk of George W. Bush who had claimed that "terrorist attacks" were not caused by the "use of strength" but rather were "invited by the perception of weakness" while at the same time renewing one of the right's most redundant themes—liberal spinelessness.[33] The age of Reagan's rugged sentimentalism introduced the country to "war wimps" and ever since liberal lily-liveredness has been a prominent motif in conservative political discourse; however, with the rise of the Bush gang, the bully boy behavior reached unprecedented heights. Many on the right (including David Horowitz) insinuated that Bill Clinton was to blame for the attacks because he had not been punitive enough in dealing America's adversaries and after 9/11, Bush, Cheney, Rove and Rumsfeld's various attempts to cast critics of their war-mongering as inferior were often couched in a feminized discourse. Liberal pansies were simply too impotent for the cowboy masculinity necessary to undertake the war on terror. What's more, virtually all other subsidiary criticisms that emanated from the patriotically correct right—whether they were targeted at social programs (they keep individuals dependent on the teat of big government), environmental protections and taxes (manifestations of the nanny state) tended to exploit traditional gender stereotypes and reinforce the theme of liberal wimpery.

In the discourse of PC that brimmed with bravado, American might equaled right; obtrusive, intimidating tactics were valorized as displays of moral fortitude and cries for old-fashioned ass-kicking (in the words of country music star Toby Keith) courtesy of the red, white and blue were preferred over rational political dialogue. The right-wing celebration of "manly men" eventually found its way into mainstream popular culture as *People Magazine* named Donald Rumsfeld one of the sexiest men alive in 2002—a gesture which amounted to saluting the post-9/11 spirit of patriarchal vitality. As a poster boy for PC, Rumsfeld embodied the ultimate union of militarism and macho. In the *People Magazine* spread, quotations from media outlets such as the *Wall Street Journal* describing Rumsfeld as a "virtual rock star" and a "beltway babe magnet" were particularly telling as was President Bush's reference to the former Secretary of Defense as "Rumstud." Linking the studly septuagenarian's perverse national sex appeal to the fact that he exercised absolute, raw, ruthless power and "enjoyed" it, the article noted that Rumsfeld "with his worn brown shoes and rumpled grey suits" had put a new spin on Henry Kissinger's maxim: "Power is the ultimate aphrodisiac."[34]

In press conferences covering the Iraq war—the neocons' ultimate wet dream—Rummy, with a backdrop of visuals demonstrating the awesomeness of American weaponry, spoke orgasmically about U.S firepower and military capacity to wreak havoc on the "enemy" like an advertisement for a pornographic film—in effect amending Kissinger's phrase to read: "Inflicting death is the ultimate aphrodisiac." In associating the power to orchestrate the death and destruction of countless lives with mass sexual arousal, the raping of Iraq and its resources was depicted as a cause for celebration—a sign of potent manhood.[35] Eros and Thanatos were dressed in stars and stripes jumpsuits and united in the sublime service of imperial spectacle.

Bush's main handler, Karl Rove, made hyper-masculinity pivotal to the construction of the president's public persona which bristled with an almost cartoonish machismo. Indeed, one need only be reminded of Bush's impersonation of the fictional character Pete "Maverick" Mitchell, immortalized on screen by Tom Cruise in *Top Gun*, on the day of his "Mission Accomplished" propaganda spectacle that was jarringly evocative of Leni Riefenstahl's *Triumph of the Will*. With a mass of sailors who had been lined up like an assembly of tin soldiers, Bush swaggered across the flight deck of the *USS Abraham Lincoln* after a choreographed tail hook landing in what was arguably the mother of all photo-ops.[36] In a snug fitting flight suit; his tautened groin accentuating straps strung salaciously between his legs, Bush displayed a distinctly bulbous crotch that had conservatives salivating. The presidential appendage became an object of adulation among those discussing his manly attributes after the carefully contrived exhibition. In an interview on MSNBC's *Hardball*, host Chris Matthews and guest Gordon Liddy were absolutely giddy and the latter could hardly contain his admiration for Bush's padded panache:

> And here comes George Bush. You know, he's in his flight suit, he's striding across the deck, and he's wearing his parachute harness. You know, and I've worn those because I parachute—and it makes the best of his manly characteristic… You know all those women who say size doesn't matter – they're all liars…check that out…what a stud.[37]

Even though the president's "military drag performance" was in obvious contrast to his real personal history as he had never "scuffed his snakeskin boots in combat," Bush's phallic photo-op was widely revered on the right primarily because it signified an "unstoppable hypermasculine empire" that had long been the fantasy of neconservatives.[38]

This phallic fascination was also evidenced by the rapid selling of George W. Bush action figures manufactured by *Talking Presidents*. The 12" doll came complete with a visor, goggles, oxygen mask and an anatomically, exaggerated penis underneath its little flight suit. The penis was constructed from a life-like silicone material making it clear that the company realized that Americans needed to know that the president was not a genitally-challenged Ken doll but rather a leader with *cajones* who was only too happy to brandish his big stick on the world stage.

However, perhaps most deserving of a patriarchal prize for over-the-top patriotically correct paeans to revivified manhood was a special issue of *The American Enterprise* (a publication associated with the "scholarly" institute discussed in chapter two) entitled "Real Men: They're Back" published in September 2003. A "delirious right-wing strut fest" that defied "parody," included "inspirational articles such as 'The Return of Manly Leaders and the Americans Who Love Them,' 'Why We Need Macho Men,' 'The Car and the Man,' 'Me Man, Me Hunt' and

'The Manliness of Men.'"[39] The issue also contained a "research" article that compared the "manliness of Republican and Democratic male members of Congress" and which ultimately concluded that "GOP=GUY."[40] The hyper-masculinity of PC was not merely symbolic; it reflected the kind of governance long favored by the right and think tanks such as the AEI—a lean, mean authoritarian state that would do away with any last vestiges of New Deal liberalism and an aggressive foreign policy hatched by neoconservatives to spread free market fundamentalism to every corner of the globe.

Undoubtedly, a large majority of American citizens consider themselves Christians; however, PC was, and is, rooted in a right-wing interpretation of Christianity that is more of a political ideology than a religion. It is therefore necessary to distinguish between the Christian faith as a whole and the authoritarian, even fascistic, impulses of Christian nationalism which glorifies the white male power structure, fancies the dissolution of church and state, conflates patriotism and "American-ness" with Christianity, and which fiercely perpetuates the historical myth of America as God's chosen agent and messianic savior of the planet. For many on the religious right, the history of the U.S. is deeply providential and they see themselves as moral stewards of a country preordained by God to save humanity. This form of religious fundamentalism despises secularism and is fervidly anti-liberal. Armies of flag-waving Christians view themselves as soldiers in a war against America's enemies; the enemies are both foreign and domestic but an emphasis is placed on neutralizing the alleged destructive tendencies of the home-grown threat. The true locus of evil, according to PC, is represented by the kind of liberalism that engendered the New Deal, government regulation of corporate excess, the civil rights and feminist movements, the anti-war protests of the 1960s, and environmental protections, among other things. The liberal media and the liberal academy are both culprits for the role they have played in fostering moral corruption, denigrating the Judeo-Christian foundations of the nation, and preaching anti-capitalism.

PC forges a bond between social conservatism and neoliberalism insofar as it favors a form of unbridled capitalism that has been promulgated by generations of Milton Friedman acolytes—something that is explored in more detail in Chapter One. The Christian right's influence is far-reaching, in part, because of its ties to American corporate power and its unwavering commitment to the so-called free market.[41] And, the appropriation of Christianity in the service of the American imperialist/ globalization project was particularly evident in the Bush administration. In the post-9/11 context, proponents of PC peddled an ideologically-laden narrative which suggested that free market capitalism was the best economic system in world history and that countries around the world should all fall in line with the "Washington consensus." Indeed, on September 20, 2001, U.S. Trade Representative Robert Zoellick announced that the Bush administration would seek to counter "terror with trade" and in the name of "fighting terror," he called for the "passage of a series of corporate globalization agreements—including negotiations to expand the WTO and Fast Track authority—which had already been the topic of serious Congressional debate and conflict."[42] The agreements were designed to expand the rights of multinational corporations and lessen regulation in accordance with the Friedman free market bible. Such enthusiasm for the magic of the market, however, ignored the negative effects of neoliberalism and the fact that for millions of people around the world the real source of "terror" was, and continues to be, American-led globalization as Eduardo Galeano has convincingly argued.[43]

PC also implied that the mantra 'there is no alternative' (TINA) should be read as 'there is no alternative to American empire;' it embraced the views of warmongers who promoted the idea that the world's only choice was between their version of *Pax Americana* and the axis of 'evildoers.' And since the United States was apparently called upon to defend the 'hopes of all mankind,' the saving grace of all humanity was presumably to be found in the religion of neoliberalism and a commitment to American economic hegemony. In short, the only alternative was to embrace the manic logic of American capitalism dipped in the patina of "democratic" platitudes. The 'war on terror' also provided ideological cover for the Bush administration to pursue, even more vigorously, the Friedman trinity of privatization, deregulation and skeletal social spending at home; in effect it amounted to domestic 'shock and awe' in the service of a corporate agenda and wealthy interests.

PC both operated in, and reflected, a landscape dominated by a military-industrial-media complex whose main function was to serve up spectacles that reinforced the Manichaeanism favored by neocons and domestic ayatollahs. Perhaps most insidious was that PC preferred image and spin to 'reality;' it discouraged people from thinking, from asking too many questions, and from looking beyond the surface of the manufactured images. It dealt in powerful tools of fiction; in images that both pleased and deceived. It was a world of dramatic visual effects, counterfeit emotions, and preconceived spontaneity. Appearances were preferred over reality and "truth" was that which could be sold by PR hucksters and image consultants. In the post-9/11 context, the "big lie" was able to circulate all the more freely, often without contestation as the "collapse of the distinction between truth and fiction" opened the "way to totalitarian occupation of consciousness."[44] Drawing comparisons between old and new forms of totalitarianism, McMurty argued that,

> in the old totalitarian culture of the Big Lie, the truth is hidden. In the new totalitarianism, there is no line between the truth and falsehood to embarrass the lies. The truth is what people can be conditioned to believe. In a cultural field where corporate symbols and roles, commodities, ads and PR campaigns dominate, what used to be called 'lies' are no longer an issue. Ronald Reagan is a cultural icon of this *fin de siecle* politics ... Reagan's media triumphs for eight years set the stage of the new culture of no line left between truth and falsehood.[45]

Arguably, the former Bush administration took stagecraft and image politics to a level unimaginable to even the savviest of Reagan's spin doctors. In fact, one of Bush's presidential aides once spoke sarcastically of the "reality-based community" to author Ron Suskind. The aide, in typical Rovean fashion, added that a "judicious study of discernible reality" was "not the way the world" really worked anymore and explained that since the U.S. was an "empire," the Bush White House could create its "own reality."[46] In a cultural environment inundated by manufactured visual imagery, issues of truth and falsity are relegated to the sidelines in favor of assessments that hinge upon whether the images presented are likeable or not (i.e. aesthetically pleasing). The realm of logic is superseded by the realm of PR-driven aesthetics; all of life becomes nothing more than a media show, a spectacle to be consumed rather than contemplated. In such a world, the precepts of rational inquiry—so central to academe—are rendered superfluous and anti-intellectualism is idolized. Sophistry is valued over pedagogical rigor and reason; acceptance of feel-good images, sound bites and spectacles by large gullible audiences is the goal. The right-wing populism that provides ideological scaffolding for PC depends precisely on such forms of anti-intellectualism.

The concept of "liberal" dominance or bias, particularly in the media and institutions of higher learning, is vital to PC. Part of the right's strategy to "take back" the academy was based on the myth of the liberal campus—a narrative that paralleled the myth of the liberal media which has become one of the most enduring and influential fictions in modern American history and one which has empowered conservatives to frame and control debate in the United States.[47] For years, rightists have reveled in telling harrowing tales about the bias of the media. From the pages of the late William F. Buckley, Jr.'s *National Review* and William Kristol's *Weekly Standard* to the reactionary rants of Rush Limbaugh, Ann Coulter, and Bernard Goldberg, complaints of the mainstream media's liberal slant and its attendant suppression of conservative viewpoints abound.

Such assertions, however, are not supported by the evidence garnered through various studies that have shown that most journalists consider themselves "centrist" on social issues with many more describing their views as conservative on economic issues.[48] Moreover, the very notion that the media's messages can be boiled down to the personal biases of individual journalists is profoundly reductionist for it ignores the fact that the media system is composed not merely of individuals but also of institutions, organizational structures, and economic interests. Beyond personal preferences, when the very structures of the media and the many and varied factors which impinge upon the *creation* of the news are considered; when we acknowledge that the almighty profit motive often determines the content of the news, the idea of a liberal media reveals itself to be that which it is—a myth. If anything, mainstream media have an in-built corporate bias which is attributable to their concentrated ownership by mammoth conglomerates and wealthy tycoons, something which Ben Bagdikian has chronicled in five editions of his book *The Media Monopoly* dating back to 1983. And, in reality, "most media are owned by Republican conservatives."[49]

What's more, an honest survey of the contemporary American mediascape clearly demonstrates the existence of a rabidly right-wing communications apparatus comprised of the Fox News Channel, the *Wall Street Journal*, and the *Washington Times* among others. Additionally, conservatives are "extremely well represented in every facet of the media"—including outlets that are not as fiercely partisan as those mentioned above. Even the so-called liberal media, whose leading beacon is apparently the *New York Times* (the *NYT* basically led the charge to the war in Iraq) are "not so liberal" and they are certainly "no match—either in size, ferocity, or commitment—for the massive conservative media structure that, more than ever, determines the shape and scope of our political agenda."[50] David Brock alerts us to the fact that even dyed-in-the-wool right-wingers acknowledge this:

> The 'liberal media' mantra aside, if one looks and listens closely to what the right wing says when it thinks others may not be paying attention, there should be no doubt that it has made potent political gains not despite the media but *through* it. Rush Limbaugh says his program has 'redefined the media' and refers to the 'Limbaugh echo chamber syndrome,' by which messaging originating on his show drives the twenty-four-hour news cycle. 'The radical Left,' he says, is 'furious that liberals no longer set the agenda in the national media' ... Conservative *New York Times* columnist David Brooks has written that the conservative media have 'cohered to form a dazzlingly efficient ideology delivery system that swamps liberal efforts to get their ideas out' ... Commenting on the media while interviewing Ann Coulter about her book *Reason: Liberal Treachery from the Cold War to the War on Terrorism*, right-wing radio host Sean Hannity crowed, "We've basically taken over!" Coulter, who had made millions off the charge of 'liberal media bias' while maintaining a career as perhaps the most biased right-wing voice in the media, laughed in agreement.[51]

Long before the likes of Limbaugh, Brooks, Hannity and Coulter began boasting about the right-ward shift of media, William Kristol practically admitted that the liberal media claim was little more than a rhetorical strategy employed by conservatives to move national discourse even more to the right and to make the media more hospitable to movement conservatism.[52] At its very core, the liberal media "campaign" was "a political battering ram to make the regular media more conservative."[53] And it was indeed a campaign—one abundantly funded by right-wing foundations and think tanks for decades. Though little, if any evidence was ever adduced to support the charge of the liberal media, it was a Big Lie that not only took hold but one which was internalized—even by many "liberals" and the mainstream media.[54]

The claim of liberal bias in the academy is principally a fiction based on the same sort of ideological contrivances, selective and questionable analyses; this is not to suggest that liberal professors and campuses do not exist for they do—as do conservative professors and campuses—but as I note in subsequent chapters, studies that purportedly demonstrate academe's liberal/left leanings tend to focus disproportionately on the humanities and the social sciences and more particularly on women's studies, ethnic studies, and sociology departments where more progressive oriented thinkers tend to be housed. Rightists are generally not interested in exploring the political dynamics of economics or business departments which tend to be inherently conservative. For example, a recent article from *The Nation* clearly demonstrates the stranglehold that Milton Friedman's laissez-faire philosophy continues to have on the field of economics. Critics of neoliberalism and unfettered free markets within the discipline are marginalized as are those who challenge the very foundations of Friedman's formulations. One "heterodox" economist, Michael Perelman described the mainstream members of his profession as a "mafia," which vigorously attempts to police the parameters of allowable discourse with regard to economic theory and policy.[55] This form of orthodoxy, however, does not seem to trouble conservatives; nor are they particularly concerned with studying "the political orientation of engineering professors or biogeneticists."[56]

It is also the case that universities are generally chartered corporations ruled, like other corporations, "by a self-appointed, self-perpetuating board of trustees composed overwhelmingly of affluent and conservative businesspeople" who have a great deal of influence on matters pertaining to funding, investment, budgets and even "the academic curriculum."[57] Moreover, the corporatization of the academy that John Dewey warned about in the 1940s has only accelerated as the tenets of neoliberalism, which have permeated the top administrative ranks of the university, and the commercialization of knowledge work in tandem to create a "culture of conformity" which is "decidedly hostile to the university's traditional role as a haven for informed social criticism."[58]

PLAN OF THE BOOK

The post-9/11 blitzkrieg on democracy was supported by an alliance of Christian nationalists, intransigent free-market fundamentalists, and assorted ideological mullahs who were determined to impose a campus culture where critical faculties could be lulled into slumber and where anti-intellectualism and mind-numbing conformity could reign supreme. Although a new round of culture wars may have been precipitated by the events of 9/11 and while PC may have represented a more combative, updated brand of "cultural conservatism," the most recent assault on the academy is indubitably the product of a four-decade-long campaign undertaken by a network of right-wing think tanks, campus organizations, policy institutes and media outlets to delegitimize scholarly contemplation, silence voices of dissent and create an environment that is less and less hospitable to the kind of rational, informed dialogue that is central to a properly functioning democracy.

The groups that were, and are, still involved in efforts to "take back" the university are not ideologically homogeneous; nor are they of one mind when it comes to strategy. However, the conservative, patriotically correct among us all tend to share an intense hatred for the so-called liberal/left elite. Moreover, they are all generously funded, very well-organized, politically connected and unified in their attempts to protect capitalism and shield conservative hegemony from the threat posed by critical thought. The ultimate aim of this alliance is to effect lasting political change that limits freedom of speech to ensure a rigid social and moral order; a conformist atmosphere in which the boundaries of expression are demarcated in accordance with an ideological barometer that ranges from the right to the far right.

Each of the following chapters addresses the malevolent attacks on the academy, the reactionary right-wing agenda, and the ideological infrastructure that has been constructed to advance PC, in overlapping ways. The first chapter briefly examines the broader pre-9/11 political climate—a time in which the country was deeply divided after the rancorous 2000 election and a time in which the embattled President's right-wing, pro-corporate policies were being challenged on numerous fronts—in order to better contextualize the post-9/11 milieu and the way in which the "culture of fear," engendered by the tragedy, fueled by the Bush administration, and amplified in the corporate media, enabled the opportunistic forces of PC to enact their radical agenda on both the foreign and domestic fronts under the guise of the "war on terror."

Chapter Two provides an historical account of movement conservatism with a focus the right's "sugar daddies," namely four foundations (Scaife, Olin, Bradley and Smith-Richardson), often referred to as the "four sisters" that have funded myriad missions targeting the liberal/left professoriate and, liberalism more generally, for decades. The labyrinth of think tanks, campus student organizations and media outlets that have long fed at this trough and which used foundation lucre to portray the post-9/11 academy as a sanctuary for unpatriotic malcontents is explored as are the links between these groups. Some of the more recent patriotically correct, anti-democratic campaigns are also discussed.

Chapter Three charts the emergence of David Horowitz's empire and the way in which he used his assortment of disinformation outlets to exploit 9/11 and peddle a particularly pernicious brand of pitch-fork anti-intellectualism; he enlisted armies of right-wing student mercenaries to carry out a war designed to "smoke out" opposition to the Bush administration and the radical right in general. His attempts to exile critical intellectuals and quash dissent through mechanisms such as the Academic Bill of Rights and the Student Bill of Rights are fodder for this chapter as are his more current Tea-Partying and "teach-in" activities. ACTA's history and its various McCarthy-esque crusades to vilify academics, weed out "subversive" thought, and intervene in university affairs are also taken up in this chapter.

Chapter Four begins by appraising the Bush era media environment and the ways in which it imperiled democratic principles. It then elaborates on the role that right-wing media played in boosting PC by disseminating to mass audiences hysterical anecdotes of leftist indoctrination and fables about professors who provided intellectual cover for American-hating ne'er-do-wells. Specific attention is paid to the Fox News Channel (FNC) and some of its most prominent spokespeople including Sean Hannity and Bill O'Reilly who, contrary to Fox's "fair and balanced" slogan, essentially served as ideological ventriloquists for the right and helped to popularize the backlash against the academy. But more than this, these media attack dogs not only provided succor to the well-orchestrated campaigns of Horowitz, ACTA and others, they themselves were part of the broader alliance seeking to re-define America according to the edicts of PC. Indeed, the high-octane anti-liberalism and antediluvian nostalgia for an America dominated by white, conservative Christian males that is the hallmark of the FNC is central to the ongoing efforts to "mainstream" PC and demonize liberalism. Far from being a reputable news network, the FNC is a pillar of the right's ideological infrastructure.

To a certain degree, the more brazen assaults on academe have abated as the right has recently set it sights on sabotaging the presidency of Barack Obama (who is hardly a leftist!). Now that the cannons of conservative calumny have been redirected to the 'socialist,' 'closet' Muslim in the White House, it appears as though the ivory tower has been granted a temporary reprieve. No longer subjected to the white-hot glare of the media spotlight it would be easy for progressive intellectuals to retreat to their seminar rooms, comfortable in the fact that right-wing witch-hunters have seemingly refocused their wrath. They would do so at their own risk; the campus project for "cultural conservatism" is very much alive. It lives on in Horowitz's new "teach-in" campaign, the "9/11 Never Forget Project" started by the Young America's Foundation, and the 2009 unveiling of the overtly racist "Youth for Western Civilization" to name just a few initiatives. As such, retreat cannot be an option; the struggles to defend academic freedom, civil liberties and critical thought must not be abandoned.

Moreover, increasingly perilous strains of anti-intellectualism are contaminating the larger body politic. While many heralded Obama's election as a decisive turning point in American politics and suggested that his overwhelming victory signaled the death knell of conservatism, the broader based campaign for PC has, arguably, intensified since he took office. Aspects of PC continue to play a significant role in the nation's public dialogue and are, in fact, contributing to its increased toxicity. Its characteristic disdain for rational debate, exaltation of white patriarchy and right-wing Christianity, and its allegiance to big business principles informs most—but not all—members of the contemporary Republican Party, animates the Tea Party "movement" and the right-wing media machine. Its venomous anti-liberalism, channeled through talk radio, the FNC and a network of think tanks, has contributed to the dramatic rise in right-wing hate groups and the reemergence of anti-government militias since 2008.

The patriotically correct are fuelling fear, paranoia, racism and nativism in the aftermath of another tragedy which has affected more lives than the events of 9/11—the economic meltdown precipitated by corporate greed and the runaway capitalism that they themselves have championed for decades. As people lose their jobs, homes and life savings, the anger on the ground is palpable but many unscrupulous rightists are redirecting that understandable rage so that liberals and minorities are made the fall-guys for a mess that was created by the very economic philosophy that conservatives doggedly pushed for more than forty years—often under the guise of "culture wars."

We must remind ourselves that the foundations, right-wing research factories, campus organizations, media outlets and pressure groups of various kinds which have led the charge against the liberal/left academy and liberalism in general are guided by two main objectives—to dismantle any remaining traces of the New Deal and to extinguish, once and for all, the heritage of democratic openness and social reform that dates back to the 1960s. For these reasons, this apparatus and its reactionary agenda must be exposed, confronted and vigorously contested.

THE LAND OF OPPORTUNISM

9/11 had its benefits.[59]

The story of terrorism is written by the state and is therefore highly instructive. The spectators must certainly never know everything about terrorism, but they must always know enough to convince them that, compared with terrorism, everything else must be acceptable, or in any case more rational and democratic.[60]

The slaughter of 2,976 innocents on September 11, 2001 offered a dramatic example of a perverse and malevolent assault on human life and dignity. Yet, amidst the rubble and destruction, the light of humanism shone through. It was evident in the scores of workers and ordinary citizens who flocked to the site where the Twin Towers once stood to sift through the wreckage in search of victims and to offer medical aid to those who were bloodied and battered. The light of humanism glimmered in the candles that burned along the sidewalks of Manhattan illuminating notes of thanks to the heroic firefighters, Port Authority workers, emergency personnel, and other public employees—many of whom sacrificed their own lives trying to save others. The nightly news was full of tales and images of strangers, in New York and elsewhere, coming together to console those who had lost loved ones and to keep hope alive for those awaiting news of missing family members and friends. These were displays of courage, compassion, and civilian good will.

Approximately two months after the unspeakable tragedy, the ever eloquent and thoughtful Bill Moyers penned an article for *The Nation* which asked a rather simple question: "Which America Will We Be Now?"[61] In it, Moyers expressed his admiration for the valiant deeds of public servants and citizens. He reflected on how the soul of democracy might be revitalized after years of "drowning in a rising tide of big money" and the cesspools of corruption—how the Hobbesian world view that denigrated any notion of the common good might be overcome. He hoped that the events of 9/11 would restore the public's faith in the role of government after years of being undermined by neoconservatives who advocated that the government should be shrunk, in the words of Friedmanite think-tanker and ultra-right tax reform crusader Grover Norquist, to a size where it could be drowned in a bathtub.[62] In that very same essay, Moyers registered his disdain for the "wartime opportunists,"—"the mercenaries of Washington" including lobbyists, politicians, pundits, and corporate marauders who were already lurking about trying to think up ways to exploit the tragedy for their own private political and pecuniary gain. It did not take long for opportunism to rear its ugly head; in fact, it was evident weeks before Moyers even posed his question.

Before considering the shameful opportunism exhibited post-9/11, it is necessary to recall the conditions that existed prior to that day's disturbing events. Months earlier, the United States of America, the world's foremost 'superpower,' had struggled to elect a new leader. Commentators in several other countries and citizens at home had questioned the very legitimacy of the American electoral system. Still reeling from the acrimonious 2000 election, many regarded George W. Bush as an illegitimate president as evidence of Republican election shenanigans continued to surface and as the actions of what Vincent Bugliosi deemed the "felonious five" of the Supreme Court continued to outrage large segments of the domestic populace.[63]

Despite his dubious road to the White House and the divided nation he faced, Bush was intent on pursuing one of the most radical right and corporate-friendly agendas in American political history. This agenda embodied an economic and government philosophy that the conservative movement had long embraced—one inspired by Milton Friedman and his hallmark trinity of privatization, deregulation, and limited government. This mode of governance views the "state as a perversion and considers the market the ideal nexus of human society."[64] Although the complexion of the conservative movement had changed over the years, it remained steadfast in its commitment to core principles including a laissez-faire approach to the economy meaning minimal government interference in the so-called free market, a blatant contempt for workers and unions, and hostility toward civil liberties that enabled citizens to challenge the excesses of corporate avarice. Anything remotely resembling, in Friedman's words, an "irrational attachment to a socialist system"—i.e. public schools, social security, welfare, government programs designed to assist the less fortunate—was ripe for the chopping block in a Bush administration.[65] While Reagan had made significant progress in dismantling many remnants of the New Deal and forging American military dominance there was, according to neo-conservatives, still considerable work to be done and Bush was their man.

On the day of his January 20, 2001 inauguration, Bush's Chief of Staff Andrew Card announced a sixty-day moratorium halting all safety, environmental, and health regulations that had been issued in the waning days of the Clinton administration.[66] This was a result of a request Bush made, during his transition to the White House, to the right-wing Heritage Foundation to review all the executive orders put in place by Clinton and recommend which ones should be overturned.[67] In typical conservative fashion, Bush targeted labor. In February 2001, he put forth an executive order that would limit the funds that unions could use to engage in political action and then proposed repealing the *Davis-Bacon Act* that required the payment of prevailing wage rates, as determined by the Department of Labor, to those working on large federal construction projects. One month later Bush signed the first-ever congressional repeal of an Occupational Safety and Health Administration (OSHA) worker protection rule that outlined ergonomics standards (that had been initiated by his father) designed to protect workers from repetitive stress injuries.[68] And, as is now well known, Bush will likely go down in history as one of the most anti-worker presidents to ever occupy the White House.

Pandering to the religious zealots who had been disillusioned by his father's failure to deliver on their patriarchal quest to dismantle women's rights and save the nation from the follies of feminism, George W., the born-again evangelical also saw fit to target women. On the twentieth-eighth anniversary of *Roe vs. Wade*, he reinstated the Reagan-era "global gag rule" that blocked U.S. funding to international family planning groups and non-governmental organizations (NGOs) that offered family planning counseling abroad. This represented more than just a wink and a nod to many of the Christian right organizations that had financed his presidential campaign. Just weeks before he was anointed president, ultra-conservatives had called upon Bush to use his executive powers to severely restrict reproductive rights both at home and abroad. Others bizarrely suggested that ceasing support for contraception in other nations could help to restore and strengthen American foreign policy.[69] The global gag was just a first step in the administration's "war on women." Others included the closing of the White House Office on Women's Initiatives and Outreach; stripping federal employees of contraceptive coverage in his first budget; redefining the legal status of a fetus in the "Unborn Victims of Violence Act" in ways that could have rendered *Roe* moot; and nominating numerous anti-women's rights candidates for positions in the nation's court system.[70] We should also remember that Bush subsequently appointed a fellow evangelical Christian, Dr. W. David Hager, to the Advisory Committee for Reproductive Health Drugs in the Food and Drug Administration. In addition to being a staunch opponent of emergency contraception, reproductive rights, and premarital sex, Hager had engaged in an extramarital affair with a Bible-study classmate and sodomized his wife—without her consent—on several occasions before their divorce.[71]

In keeping with the dominionist theology of his fundamentalist supporters, Bush launched his Office of Faith-Based and Community Initiatives that paved the way for millions of federal funds to be channeled to religious right organizations such as National Right to Life and other church-based welfare and abstinence programs. This move led Barry Lynn, executive director of Americans United for Separation of Church and State, to state unequivocally that Bush's plan was the single greatest assault on the church-state separation in modern American history.[72] In another one of his first actions as President, Bush halted all federal funding for embryonic stem cell research.

The pre-9/11 administration also took the hatchet to environmental protections. In March 2001, at the behest of business interests Bush abandoned his presidential campaign pledge to regulate carbon dioxide emissions from power plants. And on May 17, 2001 Vice President Dick Cheney announced a sweeping National Energy Policy that was centered on decimating then-existing environmental restrictions on the drilling and refining of oil, the use of coal, and the construction of new nuclear plants and that called for enormous subsidies for the oil, gas, coal and nuclear power industries. The policy also discouraged the use of new technologies that would have increased fuel efficiency in automobiles. Additionally, it deregulated the electricity market and diluted regulations that protected consumers from price gouging. The White House also put industrialists in environmental posts, assuring that the air and water would grow dirtier and Bush, of course, backed out of the Kyoto treaty on global warming.

It should also be noted that prior to 9/11, neoliberalism itself was under fire. Just two years earlier, the battle against corporate globalization and the Friedmanite policies that made it possible made a dramatic appearance in Seattle during World

Trade Organization (WTO) week. Activists and workers from around the world were calling for more regulation of the global economy, more corporate accountability, and stricter labor and environmental protections. They were also calling for less American-led corporate rule. Many of those very same activists took to the streets during Bush's inauguration. As the President's motorcade crept through the largest inaugural protests since the Nixon-Vietnam era, demonstrators denounced the electoral platform on which he had run and the lack of democratic process that had marred the election itself.

Amidst growing public fear of how Bush's radical agenda was unfolding, his un-popular faith-based policies and proposals, an economy that was already showing signs of weakness, and a growing tide of home-grown activism aimed precisely at the economic philosophy that Bush epitomized, the President's poll numbers began to plummet. His hard-right stance was so disconcerting that even fellow Republicans began to jump ship. The defection of Vermont Senator Jim Jeffords in May 2001 gave Democrats a slim edge in Congress that would enable them to block many of Bush's proposed programs and policy initiatives. Other moderate Republicans began to express their uneasiness with many of the administration's extreme plans and some political observers claimed that the President was losing control of the policy agenda.

Bush responded to the changed Beltway environment and his dwindling poll numbers by retreating to the creature comforts of his Crawford, Texas ranch. His first summer vacation—at the time the longest presidential vacation in 32 years—extended from August 4 to August 31. Nothing, not even an August 6 presidential daily briefing stating that Osama Bin-Laden was poised to strike the U.S., could wrest Bush away from the privileged life of leisure to which he had grown accustomed. The spoiled frat boy and former cheerleader went about his brush-cutting and rock-clearing business in Texas as some back in Washington openly questioned his ability to lead.[73] On September 10, *Newsweek* released its September 17 edition to newsstands with an article by David Kaplan entitled "The Accidental President" which called into question not only the legitimacy of Bush's presidency but also his level of competence and commitment. A poll taken from September 5–9, 2001 showed his approval rating hovering at 45%.

Then came 9/11.

Suddenly, the bitter partisanship that had marked the early days of his presidency virtually diminished as a wave of patriotism swept the country. Foreign observers who had openly mocked the American president's lack of intelligence and curiosity were proclaiming, in the words of the French daily newspaper *Le Monde*, that all the world's citizens were "Americans." There was a new enemy—even though it was not really *that* new—and Sheriff Bush assumed the mantle of global warlord with his posse in tow. Opportunity, as they say, had come a-knocking and the administration was ready to pounce.

While most people undoubtedly felt that the events of September 11 were an utter tragedy, Bush and his cronies described 9/11—or at least the political climate it engendered—as an "opportunity." Bush had spent the morning of September 11 at a pre-planned photo-op reading *The Pet Goat* with children at an elementary school in Sarasota, Florida. After hearing about the attacks, he flew around the country from Louisiana to Nebraska before heading back to Washington. Yet, according to Bob Woodward, just hours later in a meeting with key advisors, Bush declared that 9/11 was "a great opportunity" and directed his staff to think of it as such.[74] That very night, he wrote in his diary that "the Pearl Harbor of the 21st century took place today."[75] On October 3, 2001 Bush told a group of business leaders in New York to "seize" the "fantastic opportunity" afforded by the catastrophe.[76]

It is important to note that the events of September 11, 2001 crystallized at least two long-term processes. First was the emergence of the United States as a virtually uncontested global economic and military power. As Arundhati Roy made chillingly clear,

> [f]or the first time in history, a single empire with an arsenal of weapons that could obliterate the world in an afternoon has complete, unipolar, economic and military hegemony. It uses different weapons to break open different markets. There isn't a country on God's earth that is not caught in the cross-hairs of the American cruise missile and the IMF checkbook ... Poor countries that are geopolitically of strategic value to Empire, or have a 'market' of any size, or infrastructure that can be privatized, or God forbid, natural resources of value—oil, gold, diamonds, cobalt, coal—must do as they're told or become military targets.[77]

Second, was the domestic "political triumph of a highly ideological coalition of evangelical religious fundamentalists, militant nationalists, and neoconservatives" that "dominated the presidency, the Congress, and the top civilian ranks of the Pentagon."[78] In many ways, 9/11 fortified a variety of conservative forces that were already in place in American society and provided a new dynamism for this coalition to pursue, even more assertively, a wide-ranging agenda that included American unilateralism and imperialism abroad as well as domestic shock and awe at home—namely "dismantling the New Deal society, reversing the gains of the various civil-rights and environmental movements, and blurring the line between church and state."[79]

With the vivid images of smoldering debris and the putrid stench of death still fresh, many politicos, ideologues, and media pundits attempted to make "sense" of the appalling acts that had been perpetrated on American soil and to offer their "advice" on how the situation should best be handled. Over at the *National Review*'s website, right-wing rabble-rouser Ann Coulter ranted that the U.S. should invade the hijackers' countries, "kill their leaders and convert them to Christianity."[80] Not to be outdone, the ever pugnacious Bill O'Reilly pontificated from his perch at Fox about the need to "bomb the Afghan infrastructure to rubble." In an exchange broadcast on the Christian Broadcasting Network (CBN) on September 12th, domestic ayatollahs Jerry Falwell (since deceased) and Pat Robertson blamed feminists, gays and lesbians, and liberal groups such as People for the American Way (among others) for inviting the Almighty's wrath as a result of their secularist agendas.[81] In Falwell and Robertson's delusional minds, the explanation for 9/11 was summarized as follows: God was pissed at liberals and gays, women's rights advocates, and indeed

"America" for tolerating the "pagans" and abortionists in our midst. What the United States needed was more Christianity—or at least a particular brand of Christianity—one that condoned both torture and imperialism.

Those on the right also tended to privilege Samuel Huntington's "clash of civilizations" thesis, which was hardly surprising since conservative foundations had generously funded his work long before the attacks. Written in 1996, *The Clash of Civilizations and the Remaking of World Order* suggested that the future would be marked by a series of clashes between "the West and the rest" based on religion, which Huntington maintained was the core of civilization. Speaking on the Fox News Network, the late Jeane Kirkpatrick—a rabid anti-communist, former UN ambassador and Reagan administration apologist who, for years legitimated that administration's alliances with insalubrious fascists and terrorists in the name of eradicating the Evil Empire—presented a simplified variation on the clash of civilizations motif arguing that the nation was at war with Islam and should do all it could to defend "Western civilization." A day after the tragedy, she joined "cultural values" commissar and inveterate gambler William Bennett in calling on Congress to issue a formal declaration of war against a network of Islamic fundamentalists.

In the context of such religious rhetoric, it is imperative to recall a perspicacious observation made by Alexander Cockburn almost twenty years ago at the height of the "culture wars." He argued then that the right's attempts to couch their agenda as part of defending "Western civilization" masked it's real ideological intent—namely to shape minds "deadened to reason and history to allow the capitalist project to reproduce itself from generation to generation."[82] Arguably, his comments were entirely applicable to the post-9/11 landscape as Christians such as Bennett linked the defense of civilization to support of the neoconservative worldview. Christian rightists often invoke a cult of traditionalism that they cleverly wed to the idea that the unfettered free market should serve as the guiding beacon for all social, political, and economic decisions. After all, any government oversight of the market is viewed as reminiscent of godless communism. As Moyers has observed, Christian conservatives are actually "foot soldiers in a political holy war financed by wealthy economic interests."[83] This American variant of militant faith adheres to and is committed to a belligerent U.S. imperial expansionism.[84] And when it comes to matters of business, economics, wealth, the tendency of the religious right—which is composed of both followers of Jesus and Milton Friedman—is to "oppose regulation and justify wealth and relative laissez-faire."[85] The kind of right-wing Christianity that the Bush administration embraced and from which it garnered so much loyalty aggressively "supports capitalism in all its forms and effects."[86] Amidst all the apocalyptic culture war and clash of civilization narratives, the Bush administration was plotting to accomplish what it had only dreamed of doing before 9/11: pursuing the aims of two mutually reinforcing ideologies, neoliberalism and neoconservatism both on the foreign and domestic fronts.[87]

WHY DO "THEY" HATE "US"?

After 9/11, George W. Bush, hardly a paragon of nuanced thought, told the public that the country was terrorized because it was the "brightest beacon of freedom and opportunity in the world" and because the assailants were "evil" folks.[88] The press, in response to the question "Why Do They Hate Us?" essentially parroted Bush's simplistic Manichaeanism. On September 16, 2001, the lead analysis in the so-called "liberal" *New York Times* concluded that the "perpetrators acted out of hatred for the values cherished in the West—values such as freedom, tolerance, prosperity, religious pluralism and universal suffrage." That same day, the *Boston Globe* claimed that Bin Laden and his followers hate who "we are," the fundamental values of American society, and its prosperity. And so it went. The hymn of freedom-hating miscreants who hate "our way of life" became a chorus refrain that Bush repeated in his September 20th speech to a joint session of Congress:

> Americans are asking, why do they hate us? They hate what they see right here in this chamber—a democratically elected government ... They hate our freedoms—our freedom of religion, our freedom of speech, our freedom to vote and assemble and disagree with each other.[89]

Of course, that the Bush regime was ever "democratically elected" in the first place was still a matter of considerable debate at the time. It is also likely that the "freedom to vote" rhetoric rang hollow for the countless citizens who were effectively disenfranchised in the 2000 elections through various means.[90] As for religious freedom, one could clearly see from the vitriol spouted by the likes of Falwell and Coulter that many on Bush's rightist evangelical flank did not share the enthusiasm for that principle. Moreover, the swift passage of the Orwellian named Patriot Act would eventually cast a pall on dissent and "freedom of speech" as would Ari Fleischer's ominous warning to Americans to watch what they say and do. As the President was delivering his sermon about "freedom," there were already plans afoot to curtail the civil liberties of American citizens.

The "they hate us because we're free" mantra became the dominant narrative within the mainstream media as networks, particularly those of the 24-hour cable variety, tried to outdo one another in the patriotism department. Chest-thumping nationalism, discourses of American "superiority," and waving the flag took precedence over reasoned discussion and rational debate. About a month after Bush's September 20th speech, former CBS-TV anchor Dan Rather (a once respected newsman who was reduced to blubbering on the *David Letterman Show* shortly after 9/11), appeared on CNN's now-defunct show *Crossfire* with the perpetually bow-tied Tucker Carlson and Bill Press. Rather's reply to the query "why do they hate us" was quick, to the point, and was expressed in what can only be described as a sophomoric idiom. He said, "They hate us because they are losers." Bill Press, the "liberal" on the show, replied to Rather's remark in an equally juvenile fashion by saying: "Guess that sums it up, doesn't it? We are the winners. They are the losers."

Such sentiments, which amounted to what Arundhati Roy aptly dubbed the "Idiots Guide to Anti-Americanism," presented a comforting picture to a devastated domestic population but they were at variance with historical reality.[91] Absent in such a jingoistic climate was any measured dialogue that might have insinuated that the suicidal assassins of 9/11 had attacked not "America" but rather American foreign policy which had wreaked havoc in the Middle East and elsewhere for decades.

Roy argued that, "if people in the United States" wanted a "real answer" to the question of "why do they hate us," they could have read Noam Chomsky's writings on "U.S. military interventions in Indochina, Latin America, Iraq, Bosnia, the former Yugoslavia, Afghanistan, and the Middle East." Had they done so, the question may have been framed a little differently. Perhaps "it would be: 'Why don't they hate us more than they do?'"[92] As retired lieutenant-colonel of the US Air Force, Robert Bowman, suggested in the alternative news publication *North Coast Xpress*, Americans are often "hated because our government has done hateful things."[93]

With respect to the Middle East, this has included decades of American economic domination and exploitation of the region's people and resources, particularly oil; the U.S. government's seemingly endless supply of advanced weaponry and aid to the state of Israel that has been used in brutish fashion against the Palestinian people; a 1949 CIA-backed coup in Syria that overthrew the elected government and established a military dictatorship and another in Iran in 1953 that replaced the Mossadeq government—after it nationalized British holdings in Iran's vast oilfields—with the Shah whose twenty-five year reign of terror included the torture, killing, and imprisonment of his political opponents; American support for reactionary client states throughout the region; the killing of hundreds of thousands of Iraqis during "Operation Desert Storm" and the subsequent imposition of sanctions that contributed to hundreds of thousands civilian deaths, most of them children. This is merely a partial list of the kinds of activities that American governments of both political stripes have engaged in over the years—interventions that date back to at least the 1920s.[94] However, the sordid underbelly of American history is rarely, if ever, accorded serious attention for our governments, political leaders, schools, and media continue to burnish the false notions of American benevolence and moral superiority into our collective consciousness.

The Bush administration, the cowered press, the conservative talking heads who dominated the media coverage after 9/11, and Democratic collaborationists left no room for any attempts to contextualize the events in relation to U.S. foreign policy. Amid the swashbuckling discourse, the nobility of American "values" and the government's political motives were off-limits. Any discussion of America's historical entanglement with atrocity and terror—its history of sponsoring repressive regimes and undermining democratically elected governments in other parts of the world, was, at best swept away as "inappropriate" for a country at war and at worst, deemed treasonous. Anyone who dared to stray from the patriotically correct orthodoxy risked the charge of conspiring with the terrorists and being "un-American." You were either with "us" or against "us."

Undoubtedly, such coverage served the President well. By elevating the simplistic good versus evil explanation to the status of sacrosanct truth, the media helped to paint Bush as the only hope for salvation—you were either with Bush the "good" or with the "bad" terrorists. By extension, anything that the White House proposed to do in response to the attacks was just and necessary to protect "us" from evil. Amid the post-9/11 fear and anxiety that the media dutifully fueled, the administration was given free reign to refashion the world and the country as it saw fit.

On October 7, 2001, under the guise of "Operation Enduring Freedom," 25,000 cluster bombs rained down on the parched terrain of Afghanistan in a so-called humanitarian effort to "free" the Afghan people from the tyrannical rule of the Taliban. Shortly thereafter, the U.S. began to supervise the construction of an oil pipeline across Afghanistan and Pakistan.

Of course, a main target of the war was not terror but Iraq. The neoconservative warmongers in Bush's cabinet wasted no time in making political hay while the proverbial getting was good. In fact, it did not take long for the neocons occupying the star chambers of U.S. foreign policy to use the catastrophe as a springboard to launch an aggressive political and military agenda that had been crafted years *prior* to 9/11. Within hours of the attacks, Donald Rumsfeld was "ordering his staff to find something that could be used to pin the blame on Iraq" and Condoleeza Rice instructed her staff to "consider the opportunities 9/11 provided" in order to "justify the vigorous extension of U.S. hegemony."[95] While the White House hawks subsequently presented the attack on Iraq as an extension of the "war on terrorism," neoconservatives had been clamoring for a confrontation with that nation for quite some time—long before the events of September 11th. To confirm this, one need only be reminded of the now defunct Project for the New American Century (PNAC) to see the roots of the agenda for American global dominion.

PNAC was established in 1997 as "a non-profit educational organization whose goal was to promote American global leadership."[96] It should be noted that PNAC has since been replaced by the Foreign Policy Initiative (FPI) which was unveiled in early 2009 by William Kristol after he and his neoconservative brethren determined that PNAC had become "over-identified with the Iraq debacle" and because so many of its members had played major roles in advancing that war.[97] As a result it was necessary to shut PNAC down and "reboot it as FPI." For all intents and purposes, FPI is "basically a re-branded" PNAC.[98] Although PNAC's original self-proclaimed mission sounded rather benign, the organization was closely aligned with right-wing think tanks, particularly the American Enterprise Institute, and was funded heavily by conservative foundations—including the Bradley, Olin and Scaife foundations whose histories and agendas are explored in chapter two.[99] PNAC was also stacked with followers of Leo Strauss, often referred to as the philosopher of deception and for whom democracy was considered an "act against nature [that] must be prevented at all costs."[100] Strauss, a harsh critic of liberalism, "endorsed Machiavellian tactics in politics—not just lies and the manipulation of public opinion but every manner of unscrupulous conduct necessary to keep the masses in a state of heightened alert, afraid for their lives ... willing to do whatever was deemed necessary for the security of the nation" and willing to obediently accept whatever their leaders might tell them.[101] For Strauss, the constant threat of a common enemy was needed to ensure the public's complicity with the agenda of the ruling elite.

PNAC essentially provided the blueprint for Bush's establishment of *Pax Americana* in a report entitled *Rebuilding America's Defenses: Strategy, Forces and Resources for a New Century*, authored in September 2000 by a cabal of far-right intellectuals and think tank mandarins. The plan called for, among other things, regime change in Iraq and the events of 9/11 were quickly pressed into service towards that aim. In short, the attacks on the World Trade Center and the Pentagon provided needed justification for adopting and implementing the plan detailed in the document. Prior to 9/11, PNAC (which was chaired by arch conservative William Kristol and whose staunchest supporters included Donald Rumsfeld, Cheney, Richard Perle, John Bolton, and Paul Wolfowitz) hypothesized that the United States could not attempt to conquer the globe without some "catastrophic and catalyzing event, like a new Pearl Harbor." As 'luck' would have it, 9/11 was the Pearl Harbor they had hoped for. On September 20, 2001, PNAC sent a letter to George W. Bush encouraging the removal of Saddam Hussein from power "even if evidence" did "not link Iraq directly to the attack."[102] The efforts to falsely implicate Saddam Hussein and Iraq in the September 11 tragedy prompted some observers to compare American neoconservatives to Nazis: "Not since Hitler and the Nazis dressed up storm troopers as Polish soldiers and staged 'attacks' on German positions in 1939" had there "been such a flagrant and cynical effort to manufacture a casus belli."[103]

The PNAC report also emphasized unilateral military action, preemptive strikes and permanent U.S. military and *economic* domination of every region of the globe. It was a clarion call for empire building and the marriage of two worldviews that had deep roots in the Bush administration—those of Leo Strauss and Milton Friedman, both of whom taught at the University of Chicago. The drive towards global empire, or what neoconservatives called "the American hegemon," spelled out in the document did not constitute a classical imperial mission in the sense of direct control over another territory. It was not necessarily about establishing a set of colonies around the globe. However, it clearly reflected the use and projection of political and military power on behalf of a radical, pro-corporate, anti-government, free market fundamentalism—which had been hatched at the University of Chicago's Economics Department in the 1950s by Milton Friedman—that would mainly benefit the global activities of multinational corporations all the while cloaked in the palatable rhetorical garb of "democracy."

Neoconservatives were intent on targeting Iraq not because it posed a security threat to the U.S. but because they believed that the country could serve as a laboratory for implementing Friedmanite policies in the Middle East. Since the "entire Arab world could not be conquered all at once, a single country needed to serve as a catalyst."[104] The plan was to have the military bomb Iraq, a country already weakened by years of sanctions, to smithereens, then funnel American taxpayers' money to corporate contractors to rebuild it—not as it was before a war, but rather as a shiny showroom for laissez-faire economics. It was believed that turning Iraq into one "giant free-trade zone" would set off "a series of democratic/neoliberal waves throughout the region."[105] As time has proven, as with most things, the neoconservatives were dead wrong. While a handful of companies and major Republican donors did profit quite handsomely from the war in Iraq, the citizens of that beleaguered nation have not.

The goal of American global economic domination had been announced within days of the 9/11 attacks when then-U.S. Trade Representative Robert Zoellick proclaimed that the Bush administration would seek to counter terror with trade—in other words, American-led corporate globalization applied in tandem with America's military forces. Eventually, most of the strategies delineated in the PNAC report were echoed in the September 2002 National Security Strategy document (otherwise known as the Bush Doctrine) as Bush offered "two policies, war and free trade, as twin solutions to virtually all of the world's problems" and "as the means to achieving a better world." Juhasz argues that within the

> Bush agenda, 'freer trade for a freer world' refers to specific economic policies designed especially to support key U.S. multinational corporations that are used as veritable weapons of war, both in the war on terror and in the administration's broader struggle to spread its vision of a freer and safer world ... Free trade is shorthand for a number of economic policies that expand the rights of multi-national corporations and investors to operate in more locations, under fewer regulations.[106]

While advocates contend that such deregulation spurs economic growth and creates wealth that eventually trickles down to all members of society that has not been the case. Although the economic policies that steer corporate globalization

> do generate vast wealth for certain multinational corporations and investors, those benefits rarely spread throughout a society. Instead, governments are restricted from using policies proven to benefit small local business, workers, consumers, or the environment, while being required to expand policies that benefit multinational corporations. The result is increased economic inequality both within and between nations, and greater economic and political insecurity, including job loss, poverty, and even disease. While the policies *free* multinational corporations from government regulation, they *cost* the rest of society a vast amount of economic and social security.[107]

The 'freer' and 'safer' world envisioned by the Bush regime was ultimately "one of an ever-expanding American empire driven forward by the growing powers of the nation's largest multinational corporations and unrivaled military."[108] In his first State of the Union address following 9/11, the opportunistic Bush—a servant to wealthy interests—called upon Congress to pass his corporate globalization agenda "in the spirit of recovery from 9/11."[109] According to Bush, free markets and free trade were synonymous with freedom and he was quite clear that he was willing to spread this version of "freedom" through the use of military force. What used to be called gunboat diplomacy was rewritten as a diplomatic and literal gunning down of any and all opposition to the unfettered flow of finance capital in and out of new markets. It was "pure imperial ambition, which the advocates of the Bush agenda had been waiting for decades to implement."[110]

It would be misleading, however, to attribute the imperial quest solely to Bush's belligerent band of PNAC allies or to far-right crackpots. Consider the hubristic musings penned by the relatively sane (and so-called liberal) journalist Thomas Friedman who has been one of the most ardent cheerleaders for corporate globalization:

> We Americans are the apostles of the Fast World, the prophets of the free market and the high priests of high tech. We want "enlargement" of both our

values and our Pizza Huts. We want the world to follow our lead and become democratic and capitalistic, with a Web site in every pot, a Pepsi on every lip.[111]

But of course,

[t]he hidden hand of the market will never work without a hidden fist—McDonald's cannot flourish without McDonnell Douglas, the builder of the F-15. And the hidden fist that keeps the world safe for Silicon Valley's technologies is called the United States Army, Air Force, Navy and Marine Corps ... Without America on duty, there will be no America Online.[112]

Friedman's manifesto that starkly spelled out, in bone-chilling explicitness, the program for a new imperialism was the featured article in a March 1999 edition of the *New York Times Magazine*. Its cover displayed a colossal clenched fist festooned in the stars and stripes motif of the American flag above the words "What the World Needs Now: For globalization to work, America can't be afraid to act like the almighty superpower it is." The phrase "what the world needs now" was reminiscent of a tune famously belted out by chanteuse turned psychic network spokeswoman Dionne Warwick. The lyrics of that classic song suggested that what the world needed was "love, sweet love." There was no mention of Pepsi or Pizza Huts or the use of military force to buttress the profit margins of American multi-national corporations. Nonetheless, that is what it came down to in the post-9/11 world. No longer was there any pretence about the fist being hidden—it was paraded out in plain view.

Thomas Friedman, like so many other neoconservatives and neoliberals, conflates the term democracy with free market "capitalism." Yet it is important to acknowledge that while free trade has been offered up as a weapon in the war against terrorism, for many of the world's inhabitants who have suffered under corporate globalization, the real source of terror *is* the "market" as are governments and institutions that have forced poor nations "to accept ruinous trade deals and usurious loans."[113] In fact, Galeano refers to the globalized economy as the "most efficient expression of organized crime" and bluntly asserts that American-led globalization, assisted by bodies such as the International Monetary Fund and the World Bank that essentially serve corporate interests, "practice international terrorism against poor countries, and against the poor of all countries, with a cold-blooded professionalism that would make the best of the bomb throwers blush."[114] In a similar vein, Katsiaficas identifies the true "axis of evil" as composed of the World Trade Organization, the World Bank, and the International Monetary Fund whose policies have led to more poverty for nations on the periphery of the world system.[115]

Given that such sentiments are quite widespread in many parts of the world, one could reasonably conclude that the reason why so many people hate the U.S. is that its governments—both Republican and Democratic—have aided and abetted forms of 'economic terrorism.' For decades, Milton Friedman and his disciples inflicted misery around the globe in their crusade to advance his economic agenda. Their efforts to "liberate" world markets were, more often than not, accompanied by violence, coercion, coups, torture and slaughter. As Naomi Klein brilliantly documents in her book *The Shock Doctrine: The Rise of Disaster Capitalism*, in country after country, Friedmanites exploited tragedy and fear (foreign equivalents of 9/11) to benefit wealthy corporate interests with privatization and deregulation schemes that left large swathes of the populations destitute and without basic services such as water and electricity. Despite all the fanfare surrounding the promises of free markets, it remains the case that both advanced and developed countries have been traumatized by the corporate globalization championed by Friedman and his acolytes. In virtually every country of the world, the era of free market fundamentalism has ushered in more and more forms of social disintegration as revealed by a rise in abject poverty, inequality, un- and underemployment and devastating environmental destruction. But, of course, there were a select few who made out like bandits.

DOMESTIC SHOCK AND AWE

In the weeks following the attacks, Bush appeared in countless photo-ops with firefighters, rescue workers and other unionized civil employees that the "modern conservative movement had devoted itself to destroying."[116] He went on a "grand tour of the public sector," mugging for the cameras in "public schools, firehouses, and memorials" and embracing "civil servants for their contributions and humble patriotism."[117] As a result, some opined that Bush was having an ideological change of heart—from a man dedicated to radical free market economic philosophy to one who was ready to embrace Franklin D. Roosevelt and Keynesian economics, given the "twin demands of a sagging economy and an urgent new war on terrorism."[118] Others implied that we might witness, at the very least, a resurgence of military Keynesianism on the domestic front.

Military Keynesian, traditionally understood, refers to government attempts to pump up the military sector through increased spending. It is believed that such spending, even if financed through deficits, can boost the economy. The Keynesian aspect of the policy used to relate to "the issue of full employment and rising wages."[119] During previous wars (i.e. the Korean War), such a policy had room for unions and benefited the domestic working class since "virtually all major military contractors and subcontractors" operated with "the cooperation of union workers in a high-wage, labor-intensive environment."[120] However, in the contemporary era of "global-neoliberal militarism," the objectives of raising wages and contributing to workers' economic security are no longer considerations as they "were in the days of military Keynesianism."[121] Under Bush, the government did intervene with a gigantic military build-up and 9/11 forced the administration to recognize the need for government programs and federal funds to assist in rebuilding New York City and improving security at vulnerable airports. However, the White House never intended to embrace Keynesianism—military or otherwise. In addition to serving as a rationale for promoting corporate globalization around the world, September 11 provided the Bushies with a golden, if not blood-drenched, opportunity to advance Friedman's gospel, create a privatized national security state, and drive a stake through whatever was left of New Deal liberalism at home:

> Public pronouncements and photo ops aside, Bush and his inner circle had no intention of converting to Keynianism. Far from shaking their determination

to weaken the public sphere, the security failures of 9/11 reaffirmed their deepest ideological (and self-interested) beliefs—that only private firms possessed the intelligence and innovation to meet the new security challenge. Although it was true that the White House was on the verge of spending huge amounts of taxpayer money to stimulate the economy, it most certainly was not going to be on the model of FDR. Rather Bush's New Deal would be exclusively with corporate America, a straight-up transfer of hundreds of billions of public dollars a year into private hands … The Bush team, Friedmanite to the core, quickly moved to exploit the shock that gripped the nation to push through its radical vision of a hollow government in which everything from war fighting to disaster response was a for-profit venture … It was the pinnacle of the counterrevolution launched by Friedman. For decades, the market had been feeding off the appendages of the state; now it would devour the core. Bizarrely, the most effective ideological tool in this process was the claim that economic ideology was no longer the primary motivator of U.S. foreign or domestic policy. The mantra "September 11 changed everything" neatly disguised that for free-market ideologues and the corporations whose interests they serve, the only thing that changed was the ease with which they could pursue their ambitious agenda.[122]

September 11, 2001 enabled free market neoconservatives to unleash Friedman-omics on the American population with unprecedented vigor. An ideology developed in "American universities and fortified in Washington institutions finally had its chance to come home."[123]

William Greider has argued, rightfully in my opinion, that the conservative movement's Friedman-inspired ambition has been to literally "roll back the twentieth century" by defenestrating the federal government (with exceptions, of course, for 'homeland security,' spying, and military spending) and reducing its scale and powers "to a level well below what it was before the New Deal's decentralization." This project consisted of rescuing old American virtues of "self-reliance and individual autonomy" (i.e. personal responsibility) from the so-called clutches of "collective action and 'statist' left-wingers." Movement conservatives, he noted, also envisioned a society where authority and resources would be diverted from Washington and returned to "local levels and also to individuals and private institutions," especially corporations and religious institutions.[124]

The assault on the governing order established by twentieth-century liberalism was pursued in three successive waves—first by Reagan's ascent to the presidency in 1980, sparked, no doubt, by the massive and well-funded mobilization of conservatives after Barry Goldwater's resounding defeat in 1964. The second took hold in the mid-1990s as Newt Gingrich led the Republican revolution in 1994 and secured his party's control of Congress for the first time in two generations. And, in Greider's estimation, George W. Bush set in motion the third and most powerful wave after the Supreme Court installed him as president. As previously noted, the Bush administration's commitment to a radical right, pro-corporate agenda was already apparent before 9/11 but after the tragedy, the proverbial gloves came off.

Bush stated that 9/11 signalled a "cultural shift toward personal responsibility" in America that would make his administration better able to "deal with those who could be left behind." He added that it was his job to "seize" the "opportunity" to foster its impact on the culture.[125] Of course, "personal responsibility" has long been a coded phrase among conservatives and free market holy-rollers who despise government social programs and who champion a culture of the strong against the weak and an unrelenting pursuit of the power to dominate others, especially the most vulnerable. Bush's faith-based initiatives were animated by the gospel of privatization as a way to shift responsibility for social welfare from the government to the private and religious sectors. The perspective of Bush and other right-wing evangelicals constituted an "unwholesome stew of libertarian economics and religious orthodoxy," that exalted "church and corporation over the modern democratic state," and condemned "democratic initiatives to constrain corporate power or regulate economic activity."[126] It defined "the wealthy as God's elect, even if, like George W. Bush," they inherited the "wealth and power" that made their lives easy.[127] Personal responsibility is a euphemism for a war against those government programs—welfare, Medicaid, and food stamps—that, according to rightists, corrupt generations of the poor. Naturally, those very same right-wing sages never seem to fret that "inheriting millions of tax-free dollars might encourage idleness, dependency, and indulgence among the children of the rich."[128] Hence, while Moyers believed that 9/11 could serve as a catalyst for a restored faith in government, the public sector, and some notion of the collective good, the Bush administration, not missing an opportunistic beat, saw 9/11 as a chance to advance their own brand of mean-spirited free market fundamentalism in the good old U.S.A.

Amid the public trauma after 9/11, the White House pushed through, with the aid of an acquiescent House of Representatives, its domestic version of "Shock and Awe." At a time when citizens were unlikely to oppose "their" president, Bush cut taxes for large corporations and moved to cut individual income taxes for the well-to-do. He subsequently sought a rollback of the estate tax that benefited the wealthiest sectors of American society. In addition to massive tax cuts for the rich, the Bush agenda favored capital freed from government restraints, deregulation, privatization and cuts in public services, a systematic dismantling of labor rights and environmental protections. The frontal assault on civil liberties that ensued was icing on the cake.

In the most fundamental sense, Bush and his right-wing minions sought nothing less than the total obliteration of the New Deal and any remaining vestiges of the social safety net. The Bush administration; however, much to the chagrin of tax-cut fanatics and old-school conservatives actually presided over the largest deficits in American history and one of the most significant expansions of the federal government in recent memory. Yet there is little doubt that it targeted programs intended to assist the disadvantaged and the working classes while seeking to make corporate power both morally and politically unaccountable. The very idea of the Great Society and its emphasis on collective responsibility and basic social provisions for all was displaced by the PR-friendly notion of the "ownership" society—a pleasant-sounding euphemism for privatization and the concomitant transfer of wealth from the public to the private sector—that is, to the real corporate owners of our society.[129]

To the historically uninitiated, Bush's economic and cultural rollback agenda may have seemed radically new but it had a lengthy trajectory. The Bushite alliance of right-wing religious zealots and free market fundamentalists harkened back to the presidency of William McKinley which had "a consummate passion to serve corporate and imperial power" above all else.[130] Giroux reminds us that McKinley ruled at a time (1897–1901) when the values of corporate robber barons were paramount—a time when big government "served the exclusive interests of the corporate monopolies."[131] Interestingly enough, "big government" only became a threat to the economic liberalism favored by wealthy industrialists and financiers when it eventually yielded some ground to the demands made by popular movements and unions in light of the crises engendered by the Great Depression. In short, "big government" was seen as the enemy when viewed in the context of its *social* component. It is therefore scarcely shocking to learn that those who had profited the most from the arrant disparities of wealth and power during America's reign of the robber barons angrily opposed the period of state intervention and regulation ushered in by Franklin D. Roosevelt who railed against "private autocratic powers" as well as "dulled conscience, irresponsibility, and ruthless self-interest."[132] Sadly, as the above examples suggest, the kind of ruthless self-interest that Roosevelt once lamented and the opportunism that Moyers feared were fully on display.

After 9/11, there were few willing to question the President's radical agenda; the majority of Democrats (even the more "liberal" ones) tended to cower in fear of being labeled anti-American and insufficiently supportive of the administration at a "time of war." The mainstream media, taking a cue from the fervent flag-waving right-wing media apparatus, shied away from any substantive criticism of the White House's policies lest they be subjected to howls of manufactured protest about their liberal bias. There were, however, spaces in the culture where such critiques were being articulated—at teach-ins, anti-war protests and peace rallies—many of which took place on the nation's college campuses. Of course, that posed a problem for the rightist alliance that was demanding acquiescence and something had to be done. As such, on the intellectual front, a similar and equally disturbing form of opportunism reared its ugly head.

Following Bush in exploiting 9/11 to maximal effect and taking more than a few pages from McCarthy's playbook, right-wing culture warriors pounced on the opportunity to breathe new life into their campaign for "cultural conservatism;" they upped the ante and identified domestic enemies that were corrupting youth, weakening the nation at a time of war, and providing comfort to terrorists. These enemies were to be found on the nation's campuses so a game plan was developed to "take back" the academy. The right declared war on academic freedom and the liberal-left professoriate and rounded up its armies which consisted of an array of intemperate demagogues, campus proto-fascists, alumni associations, and media outlets. It is to them that I now turn.

MONEY AND IDEAS MATTER

The F(o)unding Fathers and Families of the Conservative Movement

PLANTING THE SEEDS

Many accounts of the conservative movement and the origins of its philanthropic base tend to point to two prominent figures—William F. Buckley, Jr. and Lewis Powell. Indeed, Buckley is often referred to as the father of modern conservatism and Lewis Powell is credited with mobilizing big business to the cause of fighting "liberal" orthodoxy and reinvigorating free-market ideology in the early 1970s.[133] Undoubtedly, these two men have been quite influential as noted below; however, it is also necessary to acknowledge the role played by an individual some have referred to as the "forgotten man of the right"—Albert Jay Nock.[134]

Before the 1960s became the bête noir of the right, the thorn in the sides of conservatives and corporate marauders was, as previously alluded to, New Deal liberalism. Nock's book, *Our Enemy, The State*, published in 1935 reflected his scorn for the liberal state and his legendary pessimism about the possibility of containing the "beast" that had been unleashed by the egalitarian impulses of the New Deal era. Just as modern day conservatives characterize critiques of the excessive greed of the capitalist class and the gross inequality that flows from it as a form of "class warfare," Nock believed that the New Deal was a "coup d'état" that enabled the "economic exploitation of one class by another." Presumably, Roosevelt's policies represented a capitulation to the demands of the working classes whom Nock regarded as lesser species. According to Nock, the state, if it deserved any credence at all, should represent the interests of business rather than those of the indolent masses.[135] His worldview would eventually have a profound influence on the conservative model of governance.

In an essay entitled *Isaiah's Job*, first published in 1936 in *Atlantic Monthly*, Nock bemoaned the success of Roosevelt's New Deal, the creation of the "welfare" state, and "collectivism." He mourned the contemporaneous state of conservative politics and described what he called the conservative "remnant"—an obscure, un-organized, and inarticulate world view which, nonetheless, could "come back and build a new society" with the appropriate amount of nurturing.[136] What kind of citizens would constitute this new society? They would love "tradition" but loathe the state, believe in radical freedom while never doubting the fixity of human nature and natural laws. They would be elitist and anti-democratic yet despise elites (read: liberals) in power and they would unflinchingly defend the principles of economic "freedom."[137] Nock believed that such an "ideal" society could be achieved if only there was a "prophet" who could lead the remnant out of its cloisters.

That prophet, as some have contended, was the late William F. Buckley, Jr. And, not surprisingly, Buckley once identified Nock as a seminal influence on his own personal and intellectual formation.[138]

After being commissioned as a second lieutenant in the US army in 1944, Buckley enrolled in Yale University in 1945 where he was actively involved with the Conservative Party and the Yale Political Union. He was also a member of the furtive Skull and Bones society and "maintained cordial relationships with New Haven FBI agents" while a student.[139] In 1951, Buckley was recruited into the Central Intelligence Agency (CIA) and was trained as a secret agent in Washington before being dispatched to Mexico City presumably to monitor the burgeoning student movement there. His stint with the CIA was rather short-lived as he served for less than a year.

That same year, Buckley published *God and Man at Yale: The Superstitions of "Academic Freedom"* in which he chastised the idea of academic freedom (at least for liberals and leftists) and the independent academy. Buckley lamented the "atheism" and "secularism" of the professoriate and recommended that universities should embrace one value system and seek to inculcate it in their students. The value system advocated by Buckley was one that would extol the virtues of capitalism and Christianity. Jacoby notes that Buckley's book "can be situated as a salvo in the McCarthyite attack on the universities" and given Buckley's predilection, it is hardly surprising that three years later, in 1954, he and his brother-in-law Brent Bozell penned *McCarthy and His Enemies*, a defense of the Wisconsin Senator's career and activities.[140] If this sounds remotely familiar, it should, for it is the coalition of economic conservatives and the Christian right which has promulgated contemporary forms of patriotic correctness and neo-McCarthyism.

Like Nock, Buckley expressed his disdain for what he perceived to be collectivist and liberal orthodoxy in both American public life and higher education. Slowly but surely, Buckley began to sow the seeds of a conservative "counterrevolution"— an enterprise whose legacy continues to mould the minds of those seeking to castrate intellectual dissent on campuses to this very day. Like the prophet Nock longed for, Buckley was, without a doubt, a visionary. What was needed, in Buckley's opinion, was a publication that would provide a forum for the articulation of a conservative world view.[141] Initially, Buckley attempted to purchase *Human Events*, but was turned down. He subsequently forged a relationship with Willi Schlamm, an ex-communist editor of *The Freeman* (Nock's publication), and began to raise funds to start their own weekly magazine. With a $100,000 donation from his father, a Texas-born oil wildcatter and lawyer, and additional monies raised Buckley published the first issue of *National Review* (*NR*) in 1955.

While *NR* shared some affinities with previous publications like *The Freeman*, Blumenthal has noted that the *NR* was "wholly new" in its approach and represented the views of "free-marketers, ex-Communists and cultural conservatives."[142] In short, it epitomized the "fusionist" ideology which conservatives had forged. Sara Diamond argues that:

> Fusionism, simply put, was the historical juncture at which right-wing activists
> and intellectuals focused, diversely, on the libertarian, moral- traditionalist,

and emerging anticommunist strains of conservative ideology, recognized their common causes and philosophies, and began to fuse their practical agendas.[143]

Before Buckley's emergence as the Svengali of conservatism, there was no "common designation for people on the right."[144] This is not to suggest that American conservatism did not exist before the 1950s, for it did; however, it was during that decade that conservatives painstakingly took up the task of reconstructing their ideology and building a long-term strategy and movement to gain political power. It was also the first time they agreed on the label "conservative" to identify themselves and their agenda. As Blumenthal maintains:

> National Review ... was largely responsible for giving the believers an identity as "conservatives" ... the conservative label enabled conservatives to gloss over their incoherence by providing a convenient rubric under which to file everything. Identification as "conservative" also gave the conservatives a self-consciousness as a movement aspiring to power.[145]

In addition to providing a central outlet for those of a rightist persuasion to debate among themselves and expound their views to the unconverted, NR provided an instrument to unite what had been a disparate ensemble of "remnants" and provided a center from which to delineate a more coherent brand of conservative philosophy. Taken together, Buckley's ability to articulate a vision for what would eventually be labelled conservatism and the establishment of NR helped to plant the seeds for the right-wing revolution.

From the onset, NR projected itself as a renegade publication, one designed to combat the hegemony of "liberalism" and pull mainstream thinking in a conservative direction. It was also a journal where the protracted struggle against the Soviets abroad and the dissidents at home was a recurring theme. In many cases rehashing the arguments from McCarthy and His Enemies, Buckley used the magazine as a vehicle for propagating his rabid anticommunism, his contempt for liberalism and freedom of expression. But in addition to that, Buckley was adamant about the need for conservatives to think strategically and urged his comrades to engage in systematic propagation of anti-liberal ideology. To that end, they were encouraged to, among other things, attack the following: (i) the "growth of government;" (ii) the "cultural menace" of "conformity of the intellectual cliques" in education (rhetoric which sounds strikingly familiar to that in circulation today); (iii) the communist threat; (iv) "politically oriented unionism"; (v) "the United Nations ... and internationalism" (this contempt for the UN was quite evident within the Bush administration particularly after 9/11).[146]

Buckley was also instrumental, along with one of his mentors Frank Chodorov (another Nock disciple), in creating the Intercollegiate Society of Individualists which was eventually renamed the Intercollegiate Studies Institute (ISI)—the first national conservative organization of its kind—in 1953.[147] Buckley served as the first president of the ISI which was dedicated to conveying "to successive generations of college youth an appreciation for the values and institutions that sustain a free and virtuous society." These values and institutions included limited government, individual liberty, personal responsibility, a free market economy, and moral norms derived from the Judeo-Christian tradition.[148]

Buckley and his *NR* and ISI colleagues belonged to the "first generation" of conservatives—a generation that exuded a sort of Burkean and Nockean reverence for yesteryear and "tradition." They saw themselves more as the intellectual guardians of a romanticized cultural past than as political activists. Diamond notes that the seeds of the movement were essentially sowed by a cadre of "conservative intellectuals," rather than a "grassroots-based echelon of activists," who were disturbed by the "expansion of the welfare state" and "seemingly related trends" including "racial minorities' nascent demands for civil rights" and the "spread of secularism."[149] For the most part, however, this first generation was more inclined to philosophize rather than organize. But, by the late 1950s and early 1960s, the ISI had successfully introduced clubs on dozens of college campuses and had helped to establish a "loose confederation of student conservatives, groups, and individuals" which would eventually provide a foundation for student organizing.[150]

Among the major consequences of that organizing was the creation of the Young Americans for Freedom (YAF)—an organization whose 1960 founding meeting was held at Buckley's Great Elm estate in Sharon, Connecticut and whose stated intent was to mobilize support among American youth for conservative political candidates and policy initiatives. At that meeting of about ninety student activists, the YAF drafted its manifesto—the Sharon Statement—which, among other things, chastised government intervention in the economy, advocated free market ideology, and avowed the group's commitment to fighting the menace of Communism.[151] In many ways, the establishment of the YAF marked a definitive shift in conservatism, from a focus on abstract economic and legal theory to one in which more populist and moralistic themes were emphasized. The organization was also dedicated to concrete forms of political activism and one of its major projects was garnering support for Barry Goldwater's run for the presidency. In fact, YAF itself contends that Goldwater's run for the White House "catalyzed YAF more than any other event in its history."[152]

Goldwater had begun his ascent to national prominence by speaking all across the United States between 1954 and 1960. While initially reluctant to run for political office, his book *Conscience of a Conservative*, ghost-written by Buckley's brother-in-law Brent Bozell in 1960, made him wildly popular among young rightists and he assumed the unofficial leadership of the conservative movement. Goldwater, of course, suffered a crushing defeat in the 1964 election—a loss many attributed to Goldwater's "radical" and "reactionary" views on everything from the New Deal to civil rights and his conservative political fundamentalism (which some subsequently likened to the fundamentalism of George W. Bush).[153] Nonetheless, the Goldwater campaign energized grass-roots activists, set the stage for the age of Reaganism, and helped to lay the foundations for the "new" right. Indeed, the campaign produced a noteworthy base of conservative activists with the know-how necessary for coalition building and provided training in political mobilization and fundraising tactics to a new generation.[154] It also inspired an unprecedented wave of conservative philanthropy which is discussed below.

Confounded and deeply distressed by Goldwater's devastating defeat, many rightists channeled their efforts into waging what has been called the "war of ideas."[155] Throughout the 1960s and 1970s, they worked diligently to construct a network to disseminate their beliefs. As Covington notes, conservatives "built new institutional bastions; recruited, trained, and equipped their intellectual warriors; forged new weapons as cable television, the Internet, and other communications technologies evolved; and threw their resources into policy and political battles" in an attempt to promote "market theology."[156] One of the early goals of movement foot soldiers was to enlist support and funding from major business executives who were disgruntled about New Deal inspired social policy and the democratic and egalitarian thrust of the 1960s. Their efforts were undoubtedly bolstered by a 5,000 word memo penned by Lewis Powell, a prominent corporate lawyer, just months before he became a Supreme Court Justice under Richard Nixon.[157]

Prior to joining the Supreme Court, Powell worked as an attorney for the tobacco industry and in that capacity he toiled diligently to protect tobacco companies from government regulation. Given his background, the content of his infamous communiqué is hardly surprising in its defense of the central tenets of economic liberalism, including an aversion to any form of regulation—even if that regulation was intended to benefit the public interest. In a 1971 memo—circulated under the heading *Confidential Memorandum: Attack on the American Free Enterprise System*—directed to Eugene Sydnor, Jr. of the U.S. Chamber of Commerce, Powell summarized what he perceived to be a liberal "attack" on the free enterprise system and outlined how all sectors, both public and private, needed to actively resist the 'threat.' While the attack allegedly emanated from a number of quarters including neo-Marxist faculty members (i.e. Herbert Marcuse), for Powell, the *real* threat came not from what he called the Communists or New Leftists, but rather from what he termed "the respectable elements of society" including college campuses, the media, and scholarly journals. Powell urged American business to challenge the "dissenting voices and to fund an organized, coordinated, long-range plan" directed against liberals and leftists that would be "amply financed and implemented through united action and national organizations." Among his suggestions: situating conservative scholars within universities, increasing dialogue with schools of business, monitoring the media and using it to promote conservative ideology, evaluating textbooks to ensure that America and free-market principles were portrayed in a positive light, and publishing both popular and scholarly journals championing "traditional" views.[158]

It is worth emphasizing that Powell was particularly adamant about targeting institutions of higher education for he believed that liberal and leftist professors (especially in the social sciences) were wielding "enormous influence" and radicalizing their students "to the point of being revolutionaries." Similar to the contemporary rhetoric espoused by David Horowitz, organizations such as ACTA, and a variety of other institutes and think tanks (many of which are subsequently examined), Powell lamented a "conspicuous" absence of conservative voices on campus. While he cautioned against outright attacks on academic freedom, he nonetheless encouraged rightists to appeal to alumni associations and boards of trustees to correct what he perceived to be an ideological imbalance in many faculties and hostility directed toward free market capitalism.[159] The Powell memo remained largely under wraps as it had been distributed exclusively to members of the Chamber of

Commerce but it surfaced publicly after it was leaked to syndicated columnist Jack Anderson who cited it as a reason to question Powell's legal objectivity. In fact, Anderson warned that Powell "might use his position on the Supreme Court to put his ideas into practice ... in behalf of business interests."[160] For the right, the memo quickly became a manifesto for all things neoliberal and it attracted considerable attention from various corporations and business groups.[161]

Powell's clarion call to corporations to begin funding the right's intellectual infrastructure was heeded. Eventually, conservatives received a big boost from the business community that began to mobilize in the "mid-1970s in response to a crisis it saw as political and ideological as much as economic."[162] Part of the corporate community's response was to initiate ideological warfare through an unprecedented funding blitz of conservative policy think tanks in the hopes of influencing public opinion and the media. Together with various rightist foundations, they launched an all-out effort to promote free market ideology and a favorable image of big business but often used hot-button "cultural" issues as ideological cover. Levitas has argued that the conservative attempt to control the cultural sphere has long been motivated by economic concerns.[163] In fact, the backbone of conservative ideology is rooted in notions such as personal responsibility, individualism, and unfettered free markets; however, as Gramsci perceptively noted many years ago, the creation of consent (or willing assent) to a particular ideology or socio-political vision is often played out in the cultural terrain.[164] For conservatives, culture and economics are inextricably intertwined, since their correlation is necessary for both the efficient functioning of capitalism and the hegemony of white, patriarchal ideology.

These sentiments have been echoed by Thomas Frank who makes the following observations about the "Great Backlash," a form of conservatism that "first came snarling onto the national stage" in response to the protests and activities of the late sixties:

> While earlier forms of conservatism emphasized fiscal sobriety, the backlash mobilizes voters with explosive social issues ... which it then marries to pro-business economic policies. Cultural anger is marshaled to achieve economic ends. And it is these economic achievements—not the forgettable skirmishes of the never-ending culture wars—that are the movement's greatest monuments ... In fact, backlash leaders systematically downplay the politics of economics. The movement's basic premise is that culture outweighs economics as a matter of public concern—that *Values Matter Most*, as one backlash title has it. On those grounds it rallies citizens who would once have been reliable partisans of the New Deal to the standard of conservatism. Old-fashioned values may count when conservatives appear on the stump, but once conservatives are in office the only old-fashioned situation they care to revive is an economic regimen of low wages and lax regulations. Over the last three decades they have ... generally facilitated the country's return to a nineteenth-century pattern of wealth distribution ... The leaders of the backlash may talk Christ, but they walk corporate.[165]

While some have criticized Frank for downplaying the effect which the culture wars have had on specific constituencies (i.e. women and minorities) and for valorizing economic concerns, it is difficult to deny that the "corporate wing of the Republican Party (which is to say the dominant wing, ideologically and financially) sees the religious right as a key constituency that is essential to a winning coalition and useful for such purposes as providing a moral rationale for laissez-faire policies." From Reagan to Bush the father and son, "cultural issues have indeed been a handy demagogic tool rather than a serious priority."[166] As Frank has more recently noted, in America

conservatism has always been an expression of business. Absorbing this fact is a condition to understanding the movement; it is anterior to everything else has been over the years. To try to understand conservatism without taking into account its grounding in business thought—to depict it as, say, the political style of an unusually pious nation or an extreme dedication to the principle of freedom—is like setting off to war with maps of the wrong country ... yes, the conservative coalition has changed over the years, but through it all a handful of characteristics have remained steadfast: a commitment to the ideal of *laissez-faire*, meaning minimal government interference in the marketplace, along with hostility to taxation, regulation, organized labor, state ownership, and all the business community's other enemies.[167]

The increased involvement of the corporate community in the 1970s spawned what came to be called the "new right," as conservatives themselves began to use the designation to describe aspects of their movement. While there was nothing particularly novel about the ideology inspiring the movement, what was new was the greatly enlarged resource base that it was enjoying. A large part of the lucre that helped to fund the war of ideas and which has continued to fuel the contemporary right-wing crusade to "take back the university" was derived from several prominent conservative philanthropies.

THE RIGHT-WING'S SUGAR DADDIES

For decades, conservative philanthropy has undoubtedly played an influential role in moving many public policy discourses to the right on a wide array of social issues and it has aggressively pushed the larger economic agenda of neoliberalism. Behan contends that the sea change in our public life and the dismantling of democratic gains is primarily the result of the efforts of twelve "archconservative philanthropic foundations," which he calls the diligent dozen, that set out to advance free market theology forty years ago.[168] In what follows, I do not claim to cover the entire spectrum of conservative philanthropy and the full extent to which a "cadre of ultraconservative and self-mythologizing millionaires" undertook a program to rescue the country "from the hideous grasp of Satanic liberalism."[169] Nor do I present a comprehensive portrait of the right's financial base and political strategies. Rather, the focus is on the far reaching and well coordinated conservative movement on college and university campuses that has been largely financed by what some have called the "four sisters"—foundations that have been especially active in the culture wars, the right-wing attack on higher education and the campaign for PC.[170]

These foundations, Scaife, Bradley, Olin, and Smith Richardson—all part of Behan's diligent dozen—have lavishly financed a number of right-wing research factories, think tanks, social advocacy groups, media outlets and pressure groups of various kinds which, taken together, constitute perhaps the most potent "institutionalized apparatus ever assembled in a democracy to promote one belief system."[171] This apparatus includes, but is not limited to, the aforementioned Intercollegiate Studies Institute and its Collegiate Network, the Heritage Foundation, the American Enterprise Institute, the now defunct Madison Center for Educational Affairs, David Horowitz's Freedom Center (formerly named the Center for the Study of Popular Culture), Lynne Cheney's ACTA, the National Association of Scholars (NAS), the Leadership Institute, Young America's Foundation and others—many of which are subsequently discussed. Some of these organizations played an integral role in the anti-political correctness campaign of the early 1990s and have, more recently, been at the forefront in pushing the agenda of PC on campuses.

The Scaife Foundations

Richard Mellon Scaife has been alternatively described by friends and foes as a press-shy introvert, a conspiracy theory buff with a mean, vindictive streak, the archconservative godfather of the right, a gutter drunk, a fine public-spirited individual, and even a hero.[172] Although a generally aloof man known to shun the media spotlight, he nonetheless became the focus of several news reports in the mid-to-late 1990s for the financial largesse he bestowed upon numerous anti-Clinton activities.[173] Among them was the notorious Arkansas Project in which $2.4 million of his money was funneled through the *American Spectator* magazine to dig up dirt on the former president.[174] Not surprisingly, the Clinton White House and its allies identified Scaife as one of the central movers and shakers of the "vast right-wing conspiracy" which dogged the Clinton presidency.[175]

Scaife's network was not necessarily the command center of "the vast right-wing conspiracy," however, the funding which he provided was crucial in "sustaining anti-Clinton conspiracism, especially around the case of Clinton's aide Vince Foster, whose suicide early in the Clinton administration was widely regarded as suspicious on the "hard right."[176] Indeed, Scaife once suggested to the late John F. Kennedy Jr., former owner and publisher of *George* magazine, that up to sixty people associated with Clinton had died mysteriously.[177] More recently, Scaife's name was linked to a controversial and factually-challenged docudrama (some dubbed it a crocudrama) that attempted to lay blame for the terrorist attacks on the World Trade Center and the Pentagon squarely at the doorstep of Bill Clinton. *The Path to 9/11*, which aired on ABC in fall 2006 to commemorate the fifth anniversary of the attacks, was directed by David Cunningham who has long been associated with a "secretive evangelical religious right" group committed to battling the liberal bias that presumably permeates the Hollywood establishment. This group, in turn, has ties to David Horowitz whose Freedom Center has benefited quite handsomely from Scaife funding over the years.[178]

Max Blumenthal reports that Horowitz has labored tirelessly to facilitate the establishment of a network of politically active conservatives in Hollywood through his "Wednesday Morning Club, a weekly meet-and-greet session for Left Coast conservatives." The Club was set up the morning after Clinton's electoral triumph in 1992—hence the name—by Horowitz to open the Hollywood front in his war against the left. Almost immediately after 9/11, Horowitz was at the vanguard of the right-wing effort to accord culpability for the attacks on the Clinton administration and the left in general for undermining America's security and opening the door for sinister terrorist assaults on American soil. *The Path to 9/11* was, more or less, a faithful adaptation of Horowitz's anti-Clinton jeremiads.[179] Given their shared and deeply rooted hatred of all things Clintonian, Scaife's support of Horowitz's various projects comes as no surprise although Scaife is certainly not Horowitz's only sugar daddy.[180] While Scaife gained a certain degree of unwanted publicity for his bankrolling of the Arkansas Project and, to a lesser extent, for his indirect funding of the aforementioned crocudrama, his real influence lies in helping to establish the modern conservative movement in the United States more than forty years ago. Indeed, he has been deemed the "most generous donor to conservative causes in American history."[181]

The billionaire conservative was born July 3, 1932 in Pittsburgh, Pennsylvania to Alan Scaife, a descendant of one of Pittsburgh's upper-crust families, and Sarah Mellon, the wealthy heir of the Mellon empire.[182] From the time he was a teenager attending Deerfield Academy in Massachusetts, Richard Mellon Scaife earned the reputation of a bully and a hard drinker.[183] In his freshmen year at Yale he was expelled after he rolled a keg of beer down a flight of stairs and broke the legs of a classmate in an alcohol-induced haze. At the age of 22 he caused a serious, near-fatal car accident which injured five members of a family. As a result, the family won a large settlement.[184] Scaife eventually attended the University of Pittsburgh, where his father was chairman of the board of trustees, and earned a bachelor's degree in English in 1957.

Unlike his mother, a well-known philanthropist who had established various trusts and foundations dedicated to causes including family planning and the environment, Scaife was much more interested in bankrolling conservative initiatives. Beginning in 1962, he provided monetary assistance to groups with "educational missions on conservative themes" including "education against communism."[185] In 1963 he began funding the American Enterprise Institute (AEI) formerly known as the American Enterprise Association (AEA) and became an enthusiastic supporter and financial backer of none other than Barry Goldwater in 1964. After his mother died in 1965 Scaife and his sister Cordelia assumed control of the family's considerable trusts. Judis reports that from 1965 to 1973, the two siblings battled over the direction of the family's philanthropic efforts. While Cordelia wanted to spend the foundations' money on causes that had been dear to her mother's heart, including the arts, family planning and population control, her brother had other visions.

When Scaife became chairman of the Sarah Mellon Scaife Foundation in 1973, he had a freer hand in controlling the family funds which he in turn used to back right-wing causes, organizations and publications.[186] Not surprisingly, Scaife helped to launch the Heritage Foundation with beer magnate Joseph Coors. Although Coors was commonly credited as Heritage's chief financial patron, Scaife was, in essence, a silent partner in that enterprise. In fact, Scaife contributed $900,000 to Coors' $250,000, for the establishment of the foundation. At Heritage the joke was, "Coors gives six-packs; Scaife gives cases."[187] Today, the Heritage Foundation, founded by right-wing activist Paul Weyrich, continues to be a main recipient of Scaife's largesse.

Scaife's philanthropic empire is comprised of three foundations—the Sarah Scaife Foundation, the Carthage Foundation, and the Allegheny Foundation. Over the years, they have contributed hundreds of millions of dollars to the development of an immense and interconnected institutional apparatus dedicated to recruiting, nurturing, and funding a cadre of conservative journalists, economists, and academics to preach what one observer calls "the right-wing gospel."[188] Between 2005 and 2008, the Scaife Foundations' collectively paid out $94,146,200 in grants with more than $73 million coming from the Sarah Scaife Foundation alone.[189] Among the major beneficiaries were the Heritage Foundation ($2,700,000); Free Congress Research &Education Center/Foundation ($1,385,000); ISI ($1,450,000); AEI ($2,000,000); David Horowitz's Freedom Center ($1,400,000); Collegiate Network, Inc. ($1,270,000); National Association of Scholars ($1,000,000); and ACTA ($200,000). The Foundation for Individual Rights in Education (FIRE), a major proponent of the "intellectual diversity" movement that aims to confront the so-called liberal bias of higher education received $437,500.

Lynde and Harry Bradley Foundation

The Lynde and Harry Bradley Foundation is currently the wealthiest and most influential organization of its kind in the United States. Like its other "three sisters," it supports free market ideology, limited government, "traditional" values and a belief system modeled on Judeo-Christian principles. It is also apparently dedicated to American imperialism having given almost $2 million to help fund the Project for the New American Century (PNAC), the prominent neoconservative group that had advocated for an invasion of Iraq since it was founded in 1997. Additionally, it provided financing for Samuel P. Huntington's *The Clash of Civilizations and the Remaking of the World Order*, a tome that arguably "brought the domestic culture wars to the global stage."[190] It should also be noted that Huntington's widely read, and highly disputed, texts on the "clash of civilizations" reflect the views championed by Bernard Lewis—the right's poster boy of patriotically correct (read: pro-Israel, anti-Palestine) Middle East scholarship. In fact, the very phrase—clash of civilizations—was derived from a 1990 essay Lewis wrote for *Atlantic Monthly*.[191]

The late Lynde and Harry Bradley brothers were members of one of Milwaukee's most well-known families. Their maternal grandfather, William Pitt Lynde, was one of Wisconsin's first two congressmen. He also served as the state's U.S. attorney and mayor of Milwaukee. In 1903, Lynde and Harry established a business in Milwaukee that grew to become the Allen-Bradley company—a major manufacturer of radio and electronic components. By 1942, the brothers had created the Allen-Bradley Foundation which, while granting funds to rightist groups, was essentially dedicated to local philanthropic efforts.

Perhaps one of the earliest indications of the Bradley foundation's eventual political leanings was Harry's early embrace of and financial support for, the John Birch Society, one of the country's most notorious far-right organizations based in

Appleton, Wisconsin. The idea of the John Birch Society was first introduced by Robert Welsh, a candy manufacturer, at a meeting of twelve "patriotic and public-spirited" men convened in Indianapolis on December 9, 1958.[192] The first chapter of the society was founded just a few months later in February 1959 and was militantly anti-communist. Welsh was a frequent speaker at Allen-Bradley sales meetings and Harry Bradley regularly circulated Birchite literature at the company. Like Welsh, the burrs in Harry's britches at the time were "World Communism and the U.S. federal government, not necessarily in that order."[193]

Generally prone to conspiracy theories, the John Birch Society maintained that "internationalist 'insiders' with a collectivist agenda" were out to undermine "national sovereignty and individualism." Liberals, they contended, "consciously encourage the graduate process of collectivism" and as such are "secret traitors whose ultimate goal is to replace the nations of Western civilization with a one-world socialist government." Despite its self-proclaimed, and seemingly benign, commitment to "less government, more responsibility, and—with God's help—a better world," the Birch Society essentially promotes a "culturally defined White Christian ethnocentrism as the true expression of America."[194] Hardly surprising is the fact that it is hostile to the Department of Education and valorizes home-schooling, and private and parochial schools rooted in the teachings of 'Judeo-Christian' style civilization and the 'values of America.'

Goldberg has argued that today's rampant Christian nationalism and many of its fixations can be traced to the obsessions of the John Birch Society, particularly a "fearful loathing of secular liberals." Indeed, Tim LaHaye, co-author, with Jerry B. Jenkins, of the apocalyptic Christian fundamentalist *Left Behind* book series (which predicts the end-times and which casts Baghdad as Satan's headquarters), was a member of the group and even ran training seminars on behalf of the society in the 1960s and 1970s. LaHaye's indebtedness to Birchite teachings were most readily apparent in he and David Noebel's 2000 paranoid polemic entitled *Mind Siege* in which they argued that the United States was being ruled by a small but influential cabal of committed humanists who were determined to "turn America into an amoral, humanist country ripe for merger into a one-world socialist state."[195]

Given Harry Bradley's long-time affiliation with the Birch society, one could have certainly predicted that the foundation's current pattern of funding (especially of Christianist and culturally conservative programs) would reflect the right-wing legacy of its founder. But, it is also important to note that like other founding families of the conservative movement, the Bradley's were particularly disturbed by New Deal liberalism and the constraints it presumably imposed on big business. While the Allen-Bradley Foundation quietly provided financing for a variety of rightist causes throughout the 1960s and 1970s, its profile was raised quite drama-tically in 1985 when the company was sold to Rockwell International, a leading defense and aerospace conglomerate, for $1.651 billion. After the company's sale, the foundation saw its assets skyrocket virtually overnight from less than $14 million to more than $290 million. At around the same time, in an effort to publicly separate the foundation from the company, the Allen-Bradley Foundation was renamed the Lynde and Harry Bradley Foundation.[196]

With the influx of money derived from the sale of the company, the foundation's trustees quickly acknowledged the need to hire a high profile administrator in order to expand the foundation's philanthropic efforts beyond the local and state levels. For that they turned to Michael Joyce. Joyce, who died in 2006, was named as "one of the three people most responsible for the triumph of the conservative political movement" by *Atlantic Monthly* magazine and was hailed by neoconservative guru Irving Kristol as "the godfather of modern philanthropy."[197] Prior to joining the Bradley Foundation in 1985, Joyce served on Ronald Reagan's presidential transition team in 1980 as well as a host of other Reagan-Bush advisory boards and task forces in subsequent years. He also toiled at the Institute for Educational Affairs (a neoconservative outfit started by Irving Kristol and William Simon) and the John M. Olin Foundation (see below).[198]

While working at the Olin Foundation, Joyce was instrumental in launching the Federalist Society (also a recipient of Scaife and Smith Richardson Founda-tions' munificence), the rather secretive conservative legal association devoted to "restricting privacy rights and reproductive freedoms, rolling back civil rights gains, and thwarting the authority of government to regulate industry in the public interest."[199] With Joyce's ongoing support the society fostered the development of ultra-conservative legal scholars and politicians. Among its current and former members are ex-Attorney General, statuary clothier, and Crisco aficionado John Ashcroft (also a darling of the John Birch society),[200] disgraced torture-loving former Attorney General Alberto Gonzales, Clinton-hunter Kenneth Starr and Supreme Court Justices Antonin Scalia, Clarence Thomas, and Samuel Alito. Current Chief Justice John Roberts, a Federalist Society favorite, denied any affiliation with the group during his confirmation process despite the fact that he was once listed in its leadership directory.

Joyce was also largely responsible for providing a more focused and sophisticated approach to the Bradley Foundation's philanthropy making it one of the premiere right-wing establishments in the United States. Under his guidance, the foundation purposefully funded the authors and writers who could set the terms for national debate on key issues of public policy, the think tanks that could develop specific programs, the activist organizations that could implement those programs, and the legal offices that could defend those programs in court, as well as carry out legal offensives against other targets.[201]

The Bradley Foundation's grant-giving apparatus reflects its commitment to "limited government, free enterprise, a strong national defense and international democratic capitalism."[202] Critics, however, describe the foundation's agenda much more harshly. As Wilayto contends:

> Bradley envisions the return to a pre-1935 form of laissez-faire capitalism, free from the concessions forced from the property-owning class by the labor movement of the 1930s and the social movements of the 1960s. The means to this goal are the privatization of government services, deregulation of business, and the entrenched social stratification of society by class, race, and gender.[203]

Given the Bradley's family and corporate history, it is rather difficult to deny Wiyalto's assertions. For decades, women working at Allen-Bradley were not paid the same as men for operating the same machinery. That changed when a group of women sued the company in 1966 and a federal judge ruled in their favor. Its record on labor is equally unsettling. Although employees of Allen-Bradley had been unionized since 1937, the company was adamantly opposed to a closed or union shop. After a 76-day strike in 1970, management reluctantly agreed to allow payroll deductions for union dues. The company was also one of Milwaukee's last bastions of a racial segregation—in 1968, of its more than 7,000 member work force, only 46 employees were either Black or Latino. The Bradley clan, long-recognized opponents of civil rights, finally capitulated to public and legal pressure in 1968 after the federal government expressed its support of a discrimination suit that had been filed.[204]

The Bradley's hostility to civil rights however, lives on. Beneficiaries of Bradley's generosity include Charles Murray and the late Richard Herrnstein who penned the controversial *The Bell Curve*, Dinesh D'Souza (see below), and a variety of groups and organizations that have actively lobbied for anti-affirmative action legislation including the National Association of Scholars and Ward Connerly's deceptively named American Civil Rights Institute. The foundation has also used Wisconsin—and particularly Milwaukee's black community—as a "kind of social laboratory for its right-wing experiments" in everything from welfare restructuring to school "reform" (i.e. privatization and vouchers) initiatives and faith-based programs designed to bolster the "influence of conservative religious groups in communities of color as a means of social control."[205]

In fact, sponsoring "faith-based" organizations and programs designed to foster the privatization and deregulation of social programs and erase any remaining vestiges of the New Deal, has been one of Bradley's pet causes. It is therefore no surprise that Michael Joyce, who ended his sixteen-year tenure as the foundation's president in 2001, eventually went to work for the Bush administration in an attempt to bolster the president's then-floundering faith-based initiative. The current president of the Foundation, Michael Grebe, who replaced Joyce, describes the fundamental principles animating Bradley-supported faith-based programs as follows: "Individual citizens should be viewed as persons who are capable of running their own affairs and who are personally responsible for their actions. These programs were developed in response to our uncertainty that government assistance programs as they were then constituted were truly effective in helping citizens." Grebe, a long-time Republican Party operative, also added that he was confident that the social programs of faith-based organizations were often more effective than those of their non-faith-based counterparts.[206] Of course, one may be inclined to question Grebe's certitude about the efficacy of faith-based programs since there was little, if any, oversight of such programs while Bush was in office and some have charged that such programs generally helped the former president's political base rather than the poor.[207]

In addition to attacks on public education and concomitant support of privatization and school vouchers, the Bradley Foundation has provided abundant financial backing to the same institutes, groups and associations (AEI, ISI, David Horowitz Freedom Center, ACTA, FIRE, etc.) dedicated to countering the perceived "liberal bias" on college campuses and promoting patriotic correctness.[208] The foundation has also taken its philanthropy a step further by rewarding Bradley prizes of $250,000 to individual scholars who sanction and advance ideas (read: pro-free market, unfettered capitalism and unabashed support of all things conservative) congruent with the foundation's mission. As well, the foundation also bankrolls conservative programs and a Bradley Graduate and Postgraduate Fellowship Program at several esteemed academic institutions including Harvard and the University of Chicago.

The Bradley Foundation's conservative penchants are quite obvious, but perhaps what should be unsettling to most level-headed adults is the fact that it has also provided substantial funding to Encounter for Culture and Education—to the tune of $5,500,000 from 2004–2008—which publishes books by extremists including Ann Coulter.[209] In the immediate aftermath of the 9/11 attacks Coulter, we should be reminded, infamously suggested that the U.S. government should invade Muslim countries, kill their leaders, and convert them to Christianity. And as previously noted, she expressed regret that John Walker (the so-called "American Taliban") was not sentenced to death since she believed he could serve as a physically intimidating example to college liberals by making them realize that they could be killed were they to criticize the Bush administration's actions in the "war on terror." One of her post-9/11 forays into the culture wars was *Treason*, a paean to Senator Joe McCarthy whom she painted as a beloved figure in the annals of American history. At a February 2005 Conservative Political Action Conference (an annual right-wing wingding), the dyspeptic Coulter recommended that right-wingers take a page "from McCarthy's handbook and persecute left-leaners the way the good senator sniffed out commie pinkos."[210] In a speech that *Time* magazine deemed "part right-wing stand-up routine" and part "bloodcurdling agitprop," Coulter called for nothing less than a "new McCarthyism" on campuses.[211]

The Bradley Foundation is certainly not alone in financing right-wing causes (including the now defunct radical right National Empowerment Television) and personalities but the fact that it boasts the most assets coupled with its national outreach makes it one of the leading movers and shakers in the conservative movement. Some of its main beneficiaries from 2004 to 2009 included the usual cast of institutes and characters— the AEI ($2,985,000), the Heritage Foundation ($1,913,500), the ISI ($1,190,000), the Collegiate Network ($580,000), ACTA ($800,813), that National Association of Scholars ($470,000), FIRE ($555,000) and the odious David Horowitz ($2,025,000).[212]

J.M. Olin Foundation

John Merrill Olin, who once graced the cover of *Sports Illustrated* dressed in a three-piece suit and brandishing a gun, was born in 1892 in Alton, Illinois to a family of emerging capitalists. In that same year, his father, Franklin W. Olin, a Cornell-educated engineer founded the Equitable Powder Company in East Alton, Illinois. A predecessor of Olin Industries, Equitable Powder provided blasting materials to Mid-Western coal fields and eventually began making bullets. Thus was born the Western Cartridge Company in 1898 where John started his career in 1913 as a chemical engineer after having received a B.Sc. degree in chemistry from Cornell.

The father and son worked together to build a manufacturing behemoth that sold 15 billion rounds of ammunition during World War II and subsequently expanded its business to make cellophane, metals, rocket fuel, and pharmaceuticals. John eventually became president of the Olin Industries chemical and munitions empire and the fortune amassed in the family business enabled him to launch his foundation in 1953.

A stalwart institution of the conservative movement, the J.M. Olin Foundation officially shuttered its doors on November 29, 2005 after decades of bankrolling the right's "counterintelligentsia" to the tune of almost $400 million. The foundation was established after Olin determined that it was necessary to vigorously promote American capitalism and ward off what he perceived to be an encroaching socialist threat. In a 1977 interview, Olin claimed that he created his foundation in an effort to "see free enterprise re-established" in America and contended that business and the public had to be reawakened to "the creeping stranglehold that socialism" had gained in the U.S. since World War II.[213] It should also be noted, however, that Olin had other motivations as well. In a fawning tribute *A Gift of Freedom: How the John M. Olin Foundation Changed America*, John J. Miller, a conservative writer for *National Review* stated quite unapologetically that events of the 1960s were also of grave concern to Olin. In particular, he was troubled by the influx of minority students into the nation's prestigious universities which Olin viewed as a "recipe for trouble."[214]

The foundation made its first donation of $18,000 to Cornell University in 1954 but it was relatively dormant until 1969 when a building takeover by student protesters at Olin's alma mater incited him to action.[215] He began allocating large sums of money as well as his own time to the organization. Like its conservative siblings, Olin provided financing for Washington institutes devoted to lowering taxes and minimizing government regulation (i.e. the Heritage Foundation, AEI) but once the late William E. Simon, a former Secretary of the Treasury under presidents Nixon and Ford, became its president in 1977, the foundation swiftly set its sights on so-called intellectual elites.[216]

In his 1978 publication, *A Time for Truth*, Simon declared that the country was going to hell in a hand basket because of an "assault on America's culture and its historic identity" that was emanating mainly from the incorrigibly left-leaning intelligentsia. He called for

> nothing less than a massive and unprecedented mobilization of the moral, intellectual and financial resources which reside in those ... who are concerned that our traditional free enterprise system ... is in dire and perhaps ultimate peril ... [and] those who see a successful United States as the real "last best hope of mankind."[217]

To remedy the deplorable state of affairs, Simon offered the following three-point plan:

1) Funds generated by business ... must rush by multimillions to the aid of liberty ... [and] funnel desperately needed funds to scholars, social scientists, writers and journalists who ... [would] dissent from a dominant socialist-statist-collectivist

orthodoxy which prevails in much of the media, in most of our large universities, among many of our politicians and, tragically, among not a few of our top business executives;

2) Business must cease the mindless subsidizing of colleges and universities whose departments of economics, government, politics and history are hostile to capitalism;

3) Finally, business money must flow away from the media which serve as megaphones for anticapitalist opinion and to media which are ... at least professionally capable of a fair and accurate treatment of procapitalist ideas, values and arguments.[218]

For Simon then, nothing less than the creation of a "counterintelligentsia" would suffice to further the rightist agenda—the key for Simon was to redirect the grant making apparatus of the foundation in order to achieve explicit partisan political results.[219]

Through the years, the foundation has supported right-wing think tanks including Heritage, which has benefited the most from Olin money, and the AEI. Olin, it should be noted, actually suspended funding to the latter in 1986 due to a perception that the AEI had shifted to the political center; it resumed its funding to AEI in 1987. According to the National Committee for Responsive Philanthropy's 2004 report, *Axis of Ideology*, the Olin Foundation ranks third (behind Sarah Scaife and Lynde and Harry Bradley) in providing public policy grants to conservative organizations.[220] It has also funneled hundreds of millions of dollars to some of the nation's top universities—particularly to law and economics programs—including Harvard, the University of Chicago, Yale, Columbia, Stanford, Cornell and UCLA. Olin has also filled the financial trough for a whole host of conservative scholars including the late Allan Bloom who received more than $3 million in grants and donations, mainly from the Olin Foundation, to write *The Closing of the American Mind* (published in 1987) which many agree was the opening salvo in a concerted campaign to sabotage the public's faith in higher education and which established the tone for many subsequent attacks on the academy and the bogeyman of political correctness in the early 1990s. In fact, Bloom's right-wing cultural manifesto in which he condemned the Sixties and critical philosophy for the decline of nothing less than Western civilization arguably started the trend towards the corporate funded "intellectual" diatribes that have become popular within the mainstream.

In addition to providing the capital that has helped to build a network of research institutions and academic fellowships, Olin also financed more arcane pursuits including the *New Criterion*, a literary journal founded in 1982 by art critic Hilton Kramer and currently co-edited by Roger Kimball. According to its website, the journal is a self-described defender of high culture and an "articulate scourge of artistic mediocrity and intellectual mendacity wherever they are found: in the universities, the art galleries, the media, the concert halls, the theater, and elsewhere."[221] Kimball, of course, was the author of the much talked about harangue *Tenured Radicals*—a book which appeared at the height of the anti-political correctness frenzy of the early 1990s.

Kimball's tract—a pastiche of essays that had already been published in the journal—was an unmistakably unscholarly and transparently idiosyncratic critique of higher education based on anecdotal evidence and the much-vaunted methodology, otherwise known as tourism, carried out by attending academic conferences. *Tenured Radicals*, which was charitably supported by the Olin Foundation and the Institute for Educational Affairs, purported to describe the horrors of political correctness on campuses and the plague of Marxism, postmodernism and deconstruction. Far from providing a sophisticated critique of theories and methods which he held in such low regard, Kimball's self-proclaimed "report from the front" read more like a petulant log book in which he offered blow-by-blow descriptions of the "wars" allegedly being waged against Western civilization at conferences and in college classrooms. For someone ostensibly dedicated to challenging mediocrity and mendacity, Kimball's patchy tome was rife with fallacies, over-exaggerations, and in some cases, outright lies. In the aftermath of 9/11, he channeled his consider-able energies into attacking what he and other conservatives saw as a pervasive anti-Americanism among liberal and left intellectuals.[222]

Olin's philanthropy has undoubtedly facilitated a variety of projects (including the aforementioned Federalist Society) but perhaps the foundation's most noteworthy legacy was in helping to establish the very edifice of a conservative "counter-culture" on college campuses through its sponsorship of notoriously right-wing student publications like the *Dartmouth Review* which have served as breeding grounds for the conservative talking heads industry. Greene notes that funding "conservative student publications not only served to increase the voice of conservatives on campus, it provided students with the skills and connections to continue in punditry and activism upon graduation."[223] Indeed, some of the most notorious right-wing mouthpieces including David Horowitz, Ann Coulter, and Laura Ingraham, have "all been associated with Olin-funded organizations or publications."[224] While both Horowitz and Coulter are accorded additional attention in parts of this book, it is worth detouring off the main path to comment on Ingraham.

A graduate of Dartmouth College (and ex-speechwriter in the Reagan adminis-tration and former law clerk to U.S. Supreme Court Justice Clarence Thomas), Ingraham is one among a bevy of blonde bloviators who have parlayed right-wing extremism into a profitable media career. Famously known for her feline fashion finery, Ingraham is a nationally syndicated talk radio host and author who Eric Alterman once referred to as "more full of shit" than just about anyone he had ever known.[225] Before she stormed the airwaves, she plied her trade writing for the *Dartmouth Review* in the mid-1980s. While at Dartmouth, she secretly attended meetings of the Gay Students Association for the sole purpose of outing its members in the newspaper. After covertly taping one of the sessions, she published the transcript identifying gay students by name and castigating them as "sodomites."[226]

Her 2003 indignant screed, *Shut Up and Sing: How Elites from Hollywood, Politics, and the UN are Subverting America*, published by the right-wing Regnery company, was an indictment of liberal celebrities, media personalities, and academics whom she demonized as godless, un-American, French-loving, socialist, anti-democratic miscreants. During the 2006 election, she exhorted her sycophants to jam the phone lines of 1-888-DEM-VOTE (which she ridiculed as 1-888-DUMB-VOTE), a voter assistance hotline sponsored by the Democratic Party. That someone who openly attempted to thwart efforts to get out the vote could—with a straight face—scold others for being anti-democratic is merely another example of right-wing hubris and duplicity.

As noted above, the Olin Foundation was disbanded in 2005 based on the directives of its founder who feared that if it existed in perpetuity, it might stray from the principles that animated its existence. Olin is, undoubtedly, resting comfortably in his grave for the foundation did indeed stay true to its aims in its concerted attempts to reverse the hard-fought democratic gains engendered by sixties campus activism and roll back the 20th century.

Smith-Richardson Foundation

According to a grandiose hagiography available on the foundation's website, Henry Smith Richardson was born in 1885 to Lunsford Richardson and Mary Lynn Smith and was virtually reared in his father's small-town drug store. Lunsford, as is now well known, went on to invent Vicks VapoRub and the fortunes accrued from the family business eventually enabled Henry and his wife Grace Jones Richardson to establish their foundation in 1935. The Richardson clan is estimated by Forbes magazine to have a net worth approaching $900 million making it one of the nation's wealthiest families. And like Olin, Bradley and Scaife, the Richardsons have used their considerable riches to line the coffers of right-wing think tanks and organizations.

For the most part, Richardson lucre began to flow most aggressively when Randolph, scion of Henry, assumed the presidency of the foundation in 1973. The Smith-Richardson Foundation made its mark as an enthusiastic and early supporter of intellectual movements that championed supply-side and monetarist economics and neoconservatism in general. The appointment of Leslie Lenkowsky as director of research in 1976 paved the way for directing a large portion of the foundation's budget to the support of supply-side theory, which became a central theme in the Reagan administration. As Reagan began his ascent to political power, conservatives saw and seized their opportunity to make "trickle-down" policies all the rage. Arguing that large tax cuts would stimulate the economy (much like the Bush administration did to ruinous effect), the neophytes of neoconservatism and neoliberalism set in motion economic legislation that helped to create what were then unprecedented federal deficits. These deficits were then, in turn, used as a political bludgeon to rationalize a frontal assault against any semblance of the democratic state and the very notion that the government had any obligation to promote the common good and the general welfare of its citizens.

The late Canadian-born political economist James Galbraith was one among many who endeavored to discredit the right's trickle-down economic policies as both reactionary and deeply far-fetched by arguing that they were derived from the abstract theory spawned by Milton Friedman and his disciples. Friedman, who died in November 2006 just six months after the death of Galbraith—his primary intellectual antagonist—was instrumental in stimulating a major rethinking of Keynesian economic theory and monetary policy. Before his death, Friedman was a chief mascot and guiding spirit of fiscal conservatism (in the tradition of Friedrich von Hayek who attacked Keynes and Roosevelt's New Deal) and his thinking influenced public policy not only in the United States but in most Western countries including Britain and Canada.[227] As an unwavering cheerleader of unfettered free markets and minimalist government, Friedman helped to establish the University of Chicago's economics department as a powerhouse of neoliberalism and played a central role in popularizing free market theology via books and television. Educationalists may well recognize Friedman as the originator of, and staunch advocate for, school vouchers—something which has been robustly funded by the "four sisters" and vigorously promoted by the contemporary right.

The Smith-Richardson Foundation has systematically funded rightist causes in addition to contributing to CIA-linked media projects and training programs for CIA and Defense Department personnel.[228] In November of 1983, Reagan nominated Lenkowsky to be deputy director of the U.S. Information Agency but the Senate Foreign Relations Committee rejected his nomination amidst allegations that he had blacklisted "liberals" including Walter Cronkite and Coretta Scott King from speaking on behalf of the agency.[229] Lenkowsky's ideological rigidity was obviously appealing to George W. Bush who named him chief executive officer of the National and Community Service where he basically sabotaged the Americorps, a national volunteer program originally established during the Clinton administration. Lenkowsky's mis-management of Americorps, a program largely despised by conservatives in the first place, eventually led to two separate government investigations.

More important for purposes here, however, is a conservative plan to infiltrate campuses, a strategy which was spelled out in a confidential memo written by Roderic R. Richardson for the Smith-Richardson Foundation in 1984. The memo outlined two potential anti-left tactics at the university level: deterrence activism and high-ground activism, also termed 'idea marketing.' According to Richardson, deterrence activism existed purely as a response to left-wing agendas and was not very interesting as a proactive strategy. Rather than deterrence activism, Richardson preferred high-ground activism which he defined as

> the attempt to steal one or another highground away from the left, by ... doing things like insisting on rigorous discussion and debates, setting up political unions ... Student journalism is a highground approach. It is ... an approach geared to long run success.[230]

Richardson further recommended that the right "mimic left-wing organization" by forming "regional resource centers," and faculty networks, aimed at setting up a permanent infrastructure to "defuse the left, to grab the highground" and to "change the atmosphere on campuses." Richardson's insistence on the significance of actively cultivating conservative campus journalists ultimately became a centerpiece of the right's long-term strategy and it has proven effective as noted below. Richardson, like many of his contemporaries, clearly recognized that funding for various forms of youth activism and journalism was an investment that would help to sustain the rightist movement both on and off campuses.

According to figures amassed from its annual reports, the Smith-Richardson Foundation disbursed $153,815,243 between 2001 and 2008.[231] In addition to Yale and Harvard (two of the top beneficiaries of the foundation's generosity), the AEI has also been heftily sponsored ($6,072,044 from 2001–2008). Of the $1.16 million which the foundation gave to AEI in 2000 alone, $125,000 went toward a study of U.S. foreign entanglement conducted by John Bolton—the United Nations-hating American diplomat who was appointed by George W. Bush, in a recess appointment no less, to serve as the U.S. ambassador to that same body.[232] Bolton, it should also be noted, was a member of PNAC when he received the Richardson funding so one could have easily surmised—without the benefit of the 'study'—what his views on American foreign entanglement might entail.[233]

Several reports indicate that members of the Richardson clan were embroiled in an internecine family feud and legal battle from 1990 to 2002. As a partial result of the imbroglio, Peter Richardson (nephew of R. Randolph) assumed the presidency of the foundation in 1992 while a lesser entity—The Randolph Foundation (TRF)—was established that same year by R. Randolph Richardson and his daughter Heather Richardson Higgins. Under Higgins leadership, the TRF has sponsored a number of organizations including the Independent Women's Forum (IWF) where Higgins also serves as Chairman of the Board of Directors. The IWF, funded by Randolph (as well as by Bradley and Scaife), was apparently established to combat the women-as-victim, pro-big-government ideology of radical feminism. Co-founded in 1992 by the late Barbara Olson (wife of Theodore Olson who represented George W. Bush in Bush v. Gore during the 2000 election fiasco), the IWF grew out of an ad hoc group, Women for Judge Thomas (Clarence).[234]

The IWF claims to be non-partisan but it mainly houses and supports conservative media personalities (i.e. the aforementioned Laura Ingraham had ties to the IWF) and Republican spokeswomen. And, in keeping with the right's preferred imperialist, pro-corporate, and anti-equality agenda, the IWF claims as its mission the task of rebuilding civil society by advancing, among other things, economic liberty, personal responsibility, respect for limited government and free markets, strong families, and a powerful foreign policy.[235] Directors emeritae include former Second Lady and culture wars veteran Lynne Cheney, Katie O'Beirne and Midge Decter. O'Beirne, a former Vice President of the Heritage Foundation, is an antifeminist pundit and a Washington editor of *NR*.[236] One of her most recent tirades against progressive values, *Women Who Make the World Worse: and How Their Radical Feminist Assault is Ruining Our Schools, Families, Military and Sports*, essentially takes second-wave feminism to task and blames the feminist movement for everything from the breakdown of the family to the feminization of society and a weakened military. Long on right-wing rhetoric and short on evidence to substantiate her claims, the treatise is a laundry list of the most tiresome, monotonous, and erroneous arguments against feminism, feminists like Gloria Steinem, and political targets like Hillary Clinton.

Midge Decter, spouse of Norman Podhoretz (one of the pioneering figures of neoconservatism and long-time editor of *Commentary*, a publication of the American Jewish Committee), is a member of the Heritage Foundation's Board of Trustees and a founding member of PNAC. Decter was a co-chair, with Donald Rumsfeld, of the now defunct Committee for a Free World, a pro-free market organization that was essentially devoted to American hegemony on the world stage. Its original funders included Scaife, Olin, and Smith-Richardson. While it was still in operation, its board of directors was comprised of a veritable "who's who" of the conservative movement including Irving Kristol, and newspaper columnist and culture warrior George F. Will. One of Decter's contributions to the literary lexicon of the right is *Rumsfeld: A Personal Portrait*, a sycophantic paean to the former Secretary of Defense who became the Bush administration's first casualty after the 2006 mid-term elections. Given that the chorus demanding Rumsfeld's resignation became deafening in the months before he finally stepped down (including voices from his own party and the military brass) and given his role as a principal architect in the Iraq war debacle, Decter's fervent defense of him and his policies actually comes across as comically naïve.[237]

While George W. Bush was in office, the IWF solidified its power within the administration and also became actively involved in campus politics post-9/11 as part of the larger "intellectual diversity" campaign. In keeping with the right's strategy of cultivating and nurturing a base among college youth, in the late 1990s the organization turned its attention to "recruiting college women to conservatism" in an attempt to combat what it saw "as feminism's hegemony on the nation's college campuses." One of its first initiatives was to provide guidance and financial support to a fledgling group at Georgetown University—the Georgetown Women's Guild. The Guild produced a "guide" ostensibly about women's campus life which, echoing the anti-feminism of the IWF, contended that the fight for women's equality was largely a relic of the past, that rape and eating disorders were exaggerated problems and that feminism was irrelevant to the lives of contemporary women.[238] Not surprisingly, the guide also featured columns by Laura Ingraham and anti-feminist AEI resident scholar Christina Hoff Sommers whose books *Who Stole Feminism? How Women Have Betrayed Women* (1994) and *The War Against Boys: How Misguided Feminism is Harming our Young Men* (2000) have been roundly and soundly criticized both in the alternative and mainstream media for shoddy research and misrepresenting the scholarly literature on gender while concomitantly advancing conservative talking points on such issues as school vouchers and standardized testing.[239] Sommers also joined the ranks of vocal pundits who alleged that liberal bias was rampant on American campuses.[240] In 2000, the IWF launched a webzine for college women entitled SheThinks.org which was teeming with attacks on both feminism and political correctness and in 2004, the IWF created an advertising campaign on college campuses (including Columbia, Harvard, Princeton, and UCLA) to raise awareness of "left-wing bias among college professors." It was also active in the right-wing "take back the campus" initiative presumably designed to promote "intellectual diversity" and "academic freedom."[241]

The four sisters are certainly not alone in financing the culture wars. Nor are they alone in seeking to advance the complementary agendas of neoliberalism and neoconservatism. Other prominent players of the axis of conservative ideology include the Castle Rock Foundation which is funded by the Coors family fortune, the Shelby Cullom Davis Foundation, and the Richard and Helen DeVos Foundation whose money is derived from the family's Amway empire. Nonetheless, the Scaife,

Bradley, Olin, and Smith-Richardson foundations have arguably had the most impact on efforts to undermine the critical function of higher education, dismantle many of the democratic gains of the 1960s, further the corporatist agenda, and inhibit participatory and deliberative democracy through their sponsorship of the think tanks and organizations that are explored below.

THE CONSERVATIVE LABYRINTH: NOT QUITE A CONSPIRACY, BUT SOMETHING LIKE IT

The resurgent culture wars resound with an apodictic familiarity reminiscent of the frenzied apex of the anti-political correctness campaign of the early 1990s. In this sense, the post-9/11 attempts to undermine the autonomy of the professoriate and the integrity of the academy as a public sphere dedicated to independent thought and critical inquiry uncorrupted by vested economic and political interests did not represent a radical departure into unfamiliar political territory. These collective efforts, rather, were merely another manifestation of a project that was set in motion decades ago by a diverse and ever-expanding network of rightist institutes and organizations. More than twenty-five years ago, John Saloma, a moderate Republican, described the apparatus driving this project as a "conservative labyrinth" that represented a major new presence in the American political landscape. And he warned that, if left unchecked, the labyrinth would push the country sharply to the right.[242] Today, that labyrinth is even larger, more sophisticated and better funded and has grown even more influential in the post-9/11 era. More ominously, its politics have become more authoritarian and they threaten the very foundations upon which democratic institutions are built.

The members of this coalition are not homogeneous in terms of their foci or their strategies. However, the degree of interconnectedness within this network is quite considerable. For example, many personalities, "scholars" and even media pundits associated with the aforementioned foundations have affiliations (be it as board members, spokespersons, etc.) with the think tanks and groups discussed below. Moreover, regardless of their differences, all of the entities explored herein are politically connected, extremely well-funded, supremely well-organized—particularly in terms of "message discipline," and most had a symbiotic, if not incestuous relationship with the former Bush administration. As stewards of PC, these organizations and think tanks also share at least four discernible commonalities in that they all seek to cultivate and train conservative student activists; they aggressively support right-wing student publications and activities (including funding for conservative speakers and national and regional conferences); they exist to indoctrinate and nurture the next generation of culture warriors; and they are committed to revealing the so-called liberal/leftist hegemony on college campuses. After 9/11, they manufactured the drumbeat against "academic bias" that only grew more intense and cacophonous as the Bush years wore on.

American Enterprise Institute for Public Policy Research

The American Enterprise Association (AEA) started in 1938 as a loose coalition of business executives from companies including Bristol-Meyers, General Mills and

Chemical Bank and prominent policy intellectuals who were generally appalled by the New Deal programs established by Franklin D. Roosevelt between 1933 and 1937.[243] The group vowed to open a Washington office in an effort to revitalize free-market ideology and hence the AEA, founded in 1943 by Lewis Brown, was formally established. Following Brown's death, William Baroody Sr. assumed the presidency of the AEA in 1954 and renamed it. Baroody Sr.'s decision to change the name was in part due to the fact that he wanted the organization to sound less like a "trade association and more like an intellectual centre"[244] for he clearly understood, in a perversion of Lenin's famous dictum, that without conservative theory there would be no conservative movement. For the most part, however, the AEI, functioned in relative obscurity until the 1970s when it put into place an aggressive and immensely successful formula for attracting money and garnering influence by courting conservative "scholars" who felt alienated in "liberal" academia and by forcefully advocating for economic deregulation.[245]

Under the leadership of William Baroody Jr., the AEI underwent a major change in reputation as Baroody Jr. (who took over after his father's death) used the public relations skills he had honed while working for the Nixon and Ford administrations to transform the persona of the institute from that of a "pro-corporate lunatic fringe" to that of a "mainstream" conservative think tank.[246] Soon after, corporations and conservative foundations began to fund the institute's free-market research. By the late 1970s, more than 200 corporations were helping to bankroll AEI's $5 million budget with the list growing to 600 corporate sponsors by 1981, at which point the institute boasted a budget of $10 million, sponsorship of four journals, and a monthly television show. By 1985, this organization, which had started out as little more than letterhead, had a budget of $12.6 million, a staff of 176 and ninety adjunct scholars, thanks to corporate benevolence, the fundraising ventures of neoconservative icons like Irving Kristol, and the largesse of right-wing foundations.[247]

Today, the AEI is the single most influential think tank in the United States.[248] According to its 2009 Annual Report, the institute had revenues of $41 million in 2008 derived from a mix of corporate, individual, and foundations' donations. In addition to monies provided by the four sisters, corporate donors have included Amoco, Kraft, General Electric, and AT&T. Its Washington, D.C. headquarters employs approximately 175 people, lists 100 adjunct "scholars" and fellows and it claims that the work of those individuals is cited more frequently and published more often in "leading" American newspapers and public affairs magazines than is the work of scholars housed at all other national think tanks combined. The *Daily Beast*, a popular "news-aggregator site," reports that AEI "crushes the competition, liberal and conservative, in racking up bylines."[249]

While AEI boasts about such an accomplishment, it should certainly not be read as an indication of the scholarship's merit. Indeed, like other right-wing think tanks and research factories, AEI is essentially a platform that has been used to "float scholarly-sounding" ideas that have "not passed academic muster" but which nonetheless have informed conservative and Republican policy since at least the Reagan era.[250] Cultural rightists and neoconservatives have essentially used corporate sponsored think tanks to produce "expert" knowledge that they could perhaps not generate from within the academy. They have done so by "conflating 'expertise' as it pertains to knowledge produced by scholarly methods and 'expertise' as pertains to the aura of authority surrounding those who produce this knowledge." In this sense, think tanks have "constituted an 'academicized' aura of authority upon which conservatives have capitalized to advance their political agenda."[251]

As I note below, conservative think tanks, in general, operate in a world devoid of scholastic rigor, mechanisms of peer review, basic rules of conduct, and penalties for bad scholarship. Nonetheless, the AEI itself confuses media exposure, which is the result of its remarkable public relations infrastructure, with credible scholarship. This is hardly surprising given the institute's history—it was one of the first think tanks to gain access to the mainstream media by hiring ghostwriters for scholars to produce op-ed articles which were then sent out to newspaper outlets that were, in turn, more than willing to oblige the AEI by publishing them. In addition to its media outreach, the institute sponsors hundreds of conferences in any given year, supports large internships for undergraduate and graduate students as well as post-graduates in order to disseminate its "research." It also operates a publishing press and churns out *The American Enterprise*, a magazine which examines issues related to politics, business, and culture and that regularly features attacks on higher education.

The AEI is the nation's foremost bastion of neoconservatism and has been credited for facilitating the election of Ronald Reagan.[252] The AEI's close ties to the former George W. Bush administration bordered on the incestuous. In fact, when Bush took office in 2001, dozens of AEI alumni either assumed key positions in his administration or served on various policy panels and commissions. In addition, Dick Cheney is an alumni and his wife Lynne is an AEI Senior Fellow. Richard Perle, former deputy Secretary of Defense, and one of the primary architects of the Iraq war through his involvement with PNAC is listed among AEI's scholars and fellows. Paul Wolfowitz, also affiliated with PNAC, is a former member of AEI's Council of Academic Advisors and is currently listed as a visiting scholar. Others that have associated with the institute include David Frum who coined the infamous "axis of evil" phrase[253] and the late Kenneth (Kenny Boy) Lay of Enron notoriety.

John Yoo, a Berkeley law professor, received more than $114,000 in grants from the Olin Foundation and is also a revered member of AEI's flock of visiting scholars. While working for the Justice Department's Office of Legal Counsel between 2001 and 2003, Yoo authored an unconscionable memo in which he argued that terrorism suspects were not covered by the War Crimes Act or the Geneva Conventions. In that memo and others, he also "spelled out the fundamentals of a secret emergency Constitution" under which former President Bush's inherent powers in the 'war on terror' were essentially said to be unlimited.[254] An August 2002 legal opinion (which was eventually repudiated) widely referred to as the "torture memo" basically provided the Bush administration with legal justification to subject terrorist detainees to harsh interrogations, including water boarding.[255] More recently, Yoo was named as one of the "Bush Six" who are being targeted by prosecutors in Spain for war crimes. When asked by the *Orange County Register* in an interview published March 3, 2009 if he rued his decisions, Yoo suggested he had no regrets and blamed his damaged reputation on "hippies, protesters, and left-wing activists."[256]

In effect, the AEI was home to the engineers of the Iraq war and its major cheer-leaders. It served as the "intellectual" hub of a closely knit network of activists and interest groups that were closely aligned with the most unilateralist and pro-Likud elements in the former Bush administration. Prior to the 9/11 attacks, the AEI and its associates were advocating a number of radical foreign policy proposals. Among them was the military ouster of Saddam Hussein which AEI contended would be a catalyst for transforming and "democratizing" the entire Middle East. Prior to the Iraq war, scholars, policy wonks, and researchers linked to the think tank repeatedly proclaimed, among other things, that the American military would be greeted as liberators by Iraqi citizens, that the war would be a "cakewalk" that would not require a large number of ground troops, that weapons of mass destruction (WMD) would be found, that Iraqi oil would pay for the war, and that civil war in Iraq was unlikely.

AEI has even supported individuals who have sought to provide religious justifica-tions for pre-emptive, unilateral wars and American corporate-led globalization. For example, neoconservative Catholic Michael Novak has, in various books, argued that "the government has a Christian imperative to cut taxes."[257] A steadfast supporter of unbridled capitalism, Novak has spent more than two decades working to build a "new" American Catholicism—one that counters the "religion's traditional mission of social justice and service to the poor"[258] and which attempts to use Catholicism as "window dressing to promote an economic system based solely on self-interest."[259] In *The Spirit of Democratic Capitalism*, Novak calls for a "theology of the corpora-tion" and condemns those who argue for a more equitable distribution of wealth and the world's resources. For his efforts, he has received more than $1.5 million in grants from foundations including Olin and Bradley which have helped to sustain his program on Religion, Philosophy and Public Policy according to Media Trans-parency, a website dedicated to revealing the money behind the conservative move-ment. In February 2003, Novak was dispatched to Rome by James Nicholson, then the U.S. ambassador to the Vatican (and former National Chairman of the Republican Party), to make the Bush administration's case for a "just war" in Iraq and pre-emptive military action in general. For that, he earned the ire of dozens of prominent American Catholics who passionately declared that Novak was hardly representative of their views.[260] And, of course, the Vatican has consistently maintained an anti-war stance.

Despite various attempts to justify war, AEI's neocons were egregiously wrong on all counts as the still unfolding debacle in Iraq demonstrates. Weapons of mass destruction were never found—as many on the left had predicted—and it is now commonly accepted, except among the most delusional of right-wingers, that the Bush White House purposely misled the nation into war. American troops were never really greeted as liberators and the continued occupation in the country further fueled anti-American sentiment not only in Iraq but throughout the Arab world. The war itself—at least in terms of the initial military offensive (i.e. Shock and Awe)—was, by most counts, a cakewalk of sorts but the manufactured images of Iraqis dancing in the streets quickly gave way to pictures of chaos, looting and pillage. And, far from a cakewalk the current situation in Iraq can be much more appropriately characterized with a much different set of descriptors—unmitigated disaster. The claim that Iraqi oil revenues would fund the war has also proven to be nothing more than a fantasy concocted by rightist war-mongers. The total cost of the Iraq war that was initiated by Bush and that is still ongoing under the Obama administration is approximately $732 billion and rising. And another $281 billion has been spent thus far in the war in Afghanistan.

Since the AEI was so dramatically off-the-mark in terms of Iraq, one might have expected the Bush administration to distance itself from the think tank and its hawkish denizens but it did not. On the contrary, Bush's 2007 revamped Iraq policy which called for a "surge" in troop numbers was, in large part, the brainchild of AEI fellow and op-ed writer for the right-wing *Weekly Standard* Frederick Kagan. In fact, the majority of the seventeen contributors to the plan called "Choosing Victory: A Plan for Success in Iraq" were also AEI associates. Although the mainstream media often refer to Kagan as a military expert, he really is nothing of the sort. Neither is he an expert on insurgency, civil war, stability operations or the Middle East for that matter. While he earned a doctoral degree in history, his focus was on the 19th century Russian military. His major scholarly treatise was on the topic of Napoleon, 1801–1805 and he has not published in any refereed history or political science journals in over a decade. Despite the fact that the Iraq Study Group (which was co-chaired by Bush family *consigliere* James Baker) and virtually every reasonable analyst in the foreign policy establishment had suggested that the solution to the Iraq fiasco was political, not military and despite the fact that even active duty military personnel had called on Congress to bring the troops home—Bush relied on the "expertise" of pseudo-scholars, who helped to plot the catastrophic path to war in the first place, to devise his surge strategy which many now agree did little to quell the violence in Iraq.

Given its predilection for warfare, even the grossly ill-advised kind, it is hardly shocking that the AEI, like many of the think tanks and organizations examined in this context, also provided spirited support for the war on the academy. In a September 2002 cover story that appeared in its *American Enterprise* magazine, the AEI claimed to provide incontrovertible evidence of the left's stranglehold on American campuses. Karl Zinsmeister reported on a "painstakingly" conducted study (assisted by David Horowitz's then-named Center for the Study of Popular Culture) in which student volunteers were dispatched to boards of election to search out the party registrations of more than 1800 college teachers at 21 institutions. For the purposes of the "study," Democrats, Greens and Working Family registrants were categorized under "L" for "parties of the left" while Republicans and Libertarians were filed under "R" for "parties of the right." Independents were completely ignored. The study revealed a dramatic discrepancy between the "L's" and the "R's"—those affiliated with "parties of the right" were presumably outnumbered by a ratio of 11-to-1. The results, according to Zinsmeister, unmistakably illustrated that colleges and universities were "virtual one-party states, ideological monopolies" that were "hostile environments for economic and cultural conservatives."[26] Shortly after the findings were released, conservative media pundits kicked their rhetoric into overdrive.

George Will remarked to his ABC *This Week*'s sidekick Cokie Roberts that parents should bypass sending their children to college and instead "cut out the middle men and send their money directly to the Democratic Party." Will added that college campuses were "intellectually akin to North Korea."[262] Just a few days later, *The Wall Street Journal* chimed in with a piece entitled "One Faculty Indivisible: Even the Press Corps Isn't This Uniformly Liberal." The article claimed that the findings about the "uniformity of political allegiance in major university faculties" were "positively breathtaking" particularly in light of the fact that the ideal of "diversity" is propounded with "fervor" on the nation's campuses.[263]

While the figures looked compelling at first glance, they hardly held up to scrutiny. Plissner notes that the methodology itself was "slapdash" and that the sampling process was skewed. He cites the example of the University of Texas where 28 of the 94 teachers that constituted the "test group" came from women's studies while none of the 94 came from the "university's huge schools of engineering, business, law or medicine." Nor for that matter were there any representatives "from any of the sciences." Given the selective parameters of the sample culled exclusively from the humanities and social sciences, bias was built in from the onset. Similar biases were evident in the samples from other institutions.[264] The study was merely another example of the kind of specious research churned out by right-wing tanks to bolster their contention that universities are the ideological fiefdoms of the left.

Russell Jacoby observes that while "conservatives claim that studies show an outrageous number of liberals on university faculties and increasing political indoctrination or harassment of conservative students," only "a very few studies have been made, and each is transparently limited or flawed."[265] He goes to suggest that

> the most publicized investigations amateurishly correlate faculty departmental directories with local voter registration lists to show a heavy preponderance of Democrats. What this demonstrates about campus life and politics is unclear. Yet these findings are endlessly cited and cross-referenced as if by now they confirm a tiresome truth: leftist domination of the universities.[266]

Putting aside the false premise that party affiliation and/or professorial voting habits have something to do with teaching practices, Zinmesiter and his ilk would also have us believe that professors who registered as Democrats are wild-eyed leftists. This is simply an untenable position based on a false equivalency for there is no simple correlation between the two. Being a registered Democrat does not a radical make—one need only look to the example of John Silber cited by Susan Searls-Giroux. Silber, who served as the president of Boston University from 1971 to 1996 was not only a registered Democrat, he even ran (unsuccessfully) for governor of Massachusetts—as a member of that party—in 1990. Despite his official political membership, Silber was one of the "most radically conservative influences not only at Boston University ... but also on educational administration and policy across the nation."[267]

But more than this, there is no simple cause and effect relationship between students being exposed to "liberal" professors and ideas and then in turn becoming more liberal or voting Democratic as George Will and others imagine. Indeed, even studies referenced in the rightist on-line magazine, *Campus*, contradict such assertions. In a December 2006 feature article, a self-described conservative student gleefully reported that "while liberal professors may dominate college campuses, attending such universities does little to instill liberal values into most students." The author cited a University of Michigan National Election Study which showed that "people who attend college are more likely to vote Republican than those who do not." Moreover, "young adults from Republican households are 11 percent more likely to vote like their parents" while "young adults from Democratic households are 11 percent less likely to vote Democratic if they have gone to college than if they have not." Although the student contended that increasing the number of conservative professors in academia would be desirable, he concluded that contrary to what some "pundits have asserted the overwhelming majority of liberal professors do not brainwash their students over the four years they spend at college." In a similar vein, another conservative student opining on the topic of the professoriate claimed that "colleges' reputation for producing far more liberals than conservatives is misguided if not completely wrong." In fact, "colleges convince slightly more Democrats to become Republicans than the other way around."[268]

Additionally, the findings of two recent research studies clearly indicate that the conservative charges of a gross ideological balance on campuses are vastly overblown if not utterly misleading. First, an analysis of professorial politics published in *Public Opinion Quarterly* noted that while college faculties are generally populated with more liberals than conservatives, the most noteworthy trend over time *for most disciplines* was a shift toward a "centrist" position.[269] The study also revealed that there are disciplines where conservative faculty members constitute a clear majority including influential scholarly areas such as business, technical/vocational fields (i.e. engineering), health, and computer sciences—yet these are fields largely ignored by the kinds of ideologically-driven studies funded and/or conducted by pseudo-scholars affiliated with right-wing think tanks. Moreover, the authors also found a shift toward conservatism in the social sciences which rightists have repeatedly insisted are fortresses of liberalism and political correctness.

Other results from the study also contradicted the propagandistic poppycock routinely circulated by partisan political hacks. For example, while conservatives accuse liberal faculty members of shoving their values down students' throats, there is little actual evidence other than the most anecdotal sort to support such assertions. Ironically, the researchers found that it was conservative academics that were most likely to identify the "shaping" of students' values as an important goal of higher education and less likely to support important components of academic freedom including the "free exchange of ideas in the classroom." The study also revealed that liberal faculty were more "committed to what can best be described as the *traditional* goals of higher education" including an appreciation of literature and the arts, creative thinking and the free exchange of ideas.[270]

A second study sponsored by the American Federation of Teachers and conducted by John Lee also yielded conclusions that directly undermine declarations about conservative viewpoints being systematically excluded from the professoriate and curricula and suggestions that students who disagree with their "liberal" professors are subjected to various forms of harassment and/or punishment including lower grades. Lee analyzed eight reports/studies (including some that have attracted considerable attention)—two that were produced by ACTA—*How Many Ward*

Churchills? and *Intellectual Diversity: Time for Action*; two studies that were set to be published in *Academic Questions*, a journal published by the right-wing National Association of Scholars (NAS); another co-authored by David Horowitz and conducted under the auspices of his formerly named Center for the Study of Popular Culture; one by Stephen Balch from the NAS; another by a husband and wife team—April Kelly and Matthew Woessner—who have contributed to Horowitz's FrontPage Magazine; and finally, a report published in the on-line journal *Forum*. Two of the three authors of the last study, Stanley Rothman (a former president of the NAS) and Robert Lichter (a paid consultant to the Fox News Channel), head organizations—the Center for the Study of Social and Political Change and the Center for Media and Public Affairs respectively—funded by Scaife, Olin and other conservative foundations. These various analyses, while by no means indistinguishable, did share two broadly construed themes—namely that faculty members are overwhelming liberal and that their liberal proclivities are significant in considering their academic performance.

In order to test the validity of the studies in question, Lee wanted to ensure that the standards he used could not be considered partisan. He therefore used criteria derived from a 2006 statement by the Bush White House Office of Management and Budget on the concept of research objectivity. Based on that statement, Lee applied the following five questions to his examination of the eight aforementioned studies:

1) Can another researcher with a different perspective replicate the results using the information provided by the author?
2) Are the definitions used in the studies clear enough?
3) Does the research eliminate alternative explanations for the results?
4) Do the conclusions follow logically from the evidence?
5) Has the author guarded against assumptions that could introduce systematic bias into the study?

Utilizing this framework, Lee gave the studies failing grades for all eight fell far short in meeting minimum research standards that would allow a reader to accept the results. He also concluded that

> [t]he authors of the studies cited here have a clear agenda—to assert that the personal social and political values of college faculty members are reflected in their professional work on campus. However, the research methods employed in these studies are not well-suited to make their case. The most significant flaw is the link between the empirical results and their conclusions.[271]

Lee goes on to chide ideologues who have flaunted such flawed studies as factual proof of liberal orthodoxy and hostility to conservatism despite the blatant absence of any concrete evidence:

> It is irresponsible to suggest that the conclusions reached in these reports represent a scientifically derived set of facts. They do not. Passing off personal opinions as facts is not science; it is the antithesis of what serious researchers try to do, regardless of whether they are conservative or liberal.[272]

Regardless of the facts, conservative commentators perpetuate the myth that academia is a breeding ground for radicalism in order to advance a political agenda and introduce draconian measures to combat the liberal-left hegemony that exists solely in their deluded minds. For example, an article written by AEI associates Michael Rubin and Sarah Stern claims that "deep-rooted troubles" in the American academy are a function of radical professors and their curricula. As with other purveyors of patriotic correctness, the authors declare that the professoriate is hostile to traditional American beliefs of freedom and democracy and that it demonstrates contempt for the nation, and "particularly for American exceptionalism."[273] They suggest that students are routinely indoctrinated by their professor's radically perverse anti-Americanism and that students are actively "discouraged from supporting the war effort, thus depriving the country of the contributions of an enormous pool of able young people." Taxpayers, they assert, are unwittingly "underwriting the academic industry" that prevents American students "from properly understanding, let alone contributing to, the War for the Free World."[274] Exactly what Rubin and Stern would consider young people's rightful "contributions" to the war effort remains unclear. However, it seems likely that they would endorse a pedagogical approach that would prepare students to be sent off and killed in whatever foreign frolic the neocons fancy.

To alleviate the problems associated with "the politicized university system," Rubin and Stern make a number of recommendations. Among them—abolishing tenure—at least in publicly funded institutions and revising the hiring process to "prevent academia from becoming a wasteland of 'group think.'" With respect to the latter recommendation, the authors lament the fact that candidates vying for university positions are "evaluated solely by those academics within their particular field and mainly from a single department." Such a process, they maintain "contributes to professors becoming echo chambers of each other's theories." Scholars in the "humanities and social sciences can spend their entire careers" in the academy "without having to subject themselves and their work to rigorous challenge from others who might give a more objective evaluation." The authors insist that "in support of the war effort, it should be mandatory that academic evaluations involve professors from outside the professor's own discipline, with a view to inducing scholars to remain better grounded and well connected to a more realistic macro-picture."[275]

The stunning stupidity and ignorance evident in these recommendations should be apparent to anyone remotely familiar with academe and its attendant protocols. After all, are not departmental faculty members the best arbiters of a candidate's qualifications and the contributions she/he could potentially make in terms of the departments' specific needs? Are not scholars active in, and knowledgeable about, their particular field, its intellectual history and its research methodologies, the most appropriate adjudicators of applicants' scholarship? As for the patently absurd notion of an "echo chamber," two points are worth making. First, as Lazere has perceptively noted, the "political views of faculty members in the humanities and social sciences are, in general, the consequence of their years of independent study, not influenced by outside sponsorship or affiliation" with political party apparatuses.[276] Secondly,

Rubin and Stern assume that the intellectual production of humanities and social sciences professors' is not only homogeneous—which is far from the actual case—but that it also suffers from a lack of "objective" evaluation. Have they not heard about blind peer review—a prerequisite for publication in reputable scholarly journals? Have they not heard of the stringent modus operandi commonly associated with tenure and promotion in which the tenure candidates' work is evaluated by scholars from outside the home institution?

One could reasonably surmise that they are fully aware of the rigors associated with academic life but are blinded by their own narrow-minded ideological commitments—namely, producing students amenable to the dictates and needs of American empire or, in their words, the "macro-picture." The fact that the authors call for mandatory academic evaluations "in support of the war effort" clearly demonstrates that they are less concerned about the intrinsic merits of scholarship and far more concerned with imposing political litmus tests for intellectuals who may be critical of American foreign policy and imperial ambitions. One might also ask Rubin and Stern who should presumably monitor and decide what the politics of a potential new hire or an external assessor (outside a given professor's discipline) should be? The government? David Horowitz? Lynne Cheney? Michael Rubin?

Equally fascinating is another document produced by Kenneth Lee, a contributing writer to *The American Enterprise* and a lawyer with ties to the hard-right Federalist Society. Lee recites the tiresome mantra that universities are dominated by left-wing faculties and administrations that "avoid hiring or tenuring academics with conservative views." He further contends that Republicans and Christian conservatives are a "beleaguered" minority on American campuses. To illustrate his point Lee cites the case of John Lott, author of *More Guns, Less Crime*, "an influential and bestselling book published by the University of Chicago Press." Despite the fact that Lott received his Ph.D. from UCLA at the tender age of 26 and authored over "70 scholarly articles, a number that even the most prolific professors rarely match in their entire careers," Lee bemoans the fact that Lott "has failed to receive a single offer for a tenure-track position from any American university, despite sending his resume to literally hundreds of schools." Lee contends that Lott would not have been "snubbed by the academic world" had his research on guns yielded opposite, "more politically correct" results. Lee reports that, alas, Lott finally found a home "as a resident scholar at the American Enterprise Institute."[277]

A summary of Lott's "research" is in order. In 1998, Lott, an economist who was then working as an instructor at the University of Chicago's Law school, published the aforementioned *More Guns, Less Crime* in which he asserted that arming citizens served as a powerful deterrent to crime and violence. He produced data that purportedly demonstrated that deaths from "multiple-victim shootings dropped 90 percent in states that passed laws permitting concealed weapons."[278] And, he further suggested that "98 percent of the time that people use guns defensively, they merely have to brandish a weapon to break off an attack."[279] Given such "success rates," the book quickly became the bible of the national movement pushing for the enactment of concealed handgun laws that would enable virtually anyone to carry a weapon in public. And, as Wallace-Wells maintains, the book, in effect "tipped the terms of the debate" and handed the gun lobby which "had previously relied on brute politicking to win over lawmakers, a devastatingly effective academic study supporting their side."[280] As a result conservative legislators in several states used his study to establish laws allowing civilians to carry firearms.

But then some disturbing questions began to surface. Originally, Lott had attributed the 98 percent figure to "national surveys" and in a subsequent op-ed that appeared in the *Chicago Tribune*, Lott cited three specific surveys—polls conducted by the *Los Angeles Times*, Gallup, and Peter Hart Research Associates. The problem was that those polls showed no such thing. On other occasions, Lott sourced the 98 percent figure to a study conducted by Florida State University criminologist Gary Kleck. But Kleck's research did not support Lott's assertions. Eventually, Lott claimed that he had derived the 98 percent figure from a "national survey" that he himself had carried out by phone in 1997. When questioned about the data, Lott said that it had been lost in a computer crash. The University of Chicago, where Lott allegedly conducted his study, however, had no record of the research being undertaken. As a result, Lott declared that he had funded the study himself, kept no records, and that he had used students to make the survey calls on his behalf. Remarkably, none of the students who were presumably involved with the national survey were ever identified.

Lott's numerous flip-flops and conflicting explanations about the source of his data and statistics eventually stimulated some skepticism and even a charge of falsifying data by two economists—one from Yale, the other from Stanford. Lott's findings began to be vigorously debated in various venues on the Web and then someone named Mary Rosh, claiming to be a former student of the good professor, began stridently defending Lott's work, his reputation, and his credibility in online forums and debates. A glowing review of his book penned by Rosh even appeared on Amazon.com. Lott ultimately confessed to posing as Mary Rosh to counter his critics—something which he had been doing since 1999. Above and beyond Lott's obvious ethical breaches and his falsification of data, numerous experts—from John Hopkins, Harvard, Stanford, Yale, and even the University of Chicago—have since published peer-reviewed articles exposing flaws in Lott's research and challenging his conclusions.[281]

Given AEI's self-proclaimed commitment to "the highest standards of integrity, intellectual rigor, and excellence"[282] it was rather interesting that amid the swirl of controversy and scandal, the Institute's then-president, Christopher DeMuth, adamantly and repeatedly refused to entertain journalists' questions about the incident. DeMuth even defended Lott, dismissed critiques of his research, and refused to investigate allegations of doctored data. In fact, Lott continued his post at the Institute and, in various papers and editorial pieces, opined on everything from the Florida election fiasco (he claimed that black voters were not discriminated against) to radio talk show host and OxyContin aficionado Rush Limbaugh's firing from ESPN for claiming that black quarterbacks like Donovan McNabb of the Philadelphia Eagles were generally immune from media criticism. Lott even produced a "quick regression analysis" which purportedly demonstrated that the media were "less inclined to criticize black quarterbacks" thereby lending succor to Limbaugh's preposterous allegations.[283] Lott finally left the AEI in 2006 and, since 2008, has been a senior research scientist at the University of Maryland Foundation.

Wallace-Wells maintains that Lott's research misconduct would have likely led to dismissal had he been employed by an academic institution but in a think tank environment that takes a "laissez-faire view of scholastic rigor," it is hardly surprising that Lott got away relatively unscathed. Wallace-Wells captures the significant differences between academia and think tanks:

> ... academia is governed by some basic rules of conduct. Books and papers are peer-reviewed. Up-and-coming scholars know that their work will be scrutinized by tenure committees. Universities have established procedures to investigate accusations of fraud and punish those found guilty of it. Think tanks, by contrast, have few such systems of internal checks. Behavior that would be considered a firing offense in academia is not necessarily considered in the think-tank world, especially when a scholar's work advances the institution's political mission and attracts funding.[284]

Contrary to Lee's contention that Lott was snubbed because of the political incorrectness of his gun research, it is far more likely that legitimate academic institutions would have little use for Lott's type of "expertise." And, contrary to Rubin and Stern's allegations of "group think" and the apparent lack of rigorous "objective evaluation" in the academic setting, it is the think-tank environment in which they themselves are embedded that encourages ethical malfeasance, political conformity, and shoddy scholarship. In such contexts, promoting the conservative movement's agenda—albeit with a scholarly veneer—takes precedence over academic rigor. Whereas the goal of university research is respectable erudition, the goal of think tanks is to develop and promote self-serving narratives.

Intercollegiate Studies Institute and the Collegiate Network

The Intercollegiate Studies Institute (formerly named the Intercollegiate Society of Individualists) was established in 1953 by Frank Chodorov and William F. Buckley served as its first president. Ironically, Chodorov modeled his organization on the Intercollegiate Society of Socialists, the brainchild of Upton Sinclair, which had been established in September 1905 to advance socialist thought on campuses.[285] The ISI, the oldest national college conservative organization in the United States, is currently housed at a 23-acre mansion in Delaware and from 1985 to 2006 it has received grants totaling over $21 million including monies from the Scaife, Olin and Bradley foundations.[286] It has often been characterized as having paleo-conservative tendencies; however, many of its core principles, including beliefs in limited government, personal responsibility, and the free market economy are quite similar to those of neoconservatives.[287] Moreover, many of the authors and lecturers that it supports are easily identified as neoconservatives.

The ISI's main purpose is to promote cultural conservatism and it has long dedicated itself to countering the alleged leftist presence on campus. In a 1990 essay,

ISI president T. Kenneth Cribb, a former advisor to Ronald Reagan, summarized the institute's intent quite succinctly:

> We must ... provide resources and guidance to an elite which can take up anew the task of enculturation. Through its journals, lectures, seminars, books, and fellowships, this is what ISI has done successfully for thirty-six years ... But we should add a major new component to our strategy: the conservative movement is now mature enough to sustain a counteroffensive on that last Leftist redoubt, the college campus ... We are now strong enough to establish a contemporary presence for conservatism on campus, and contest the Left on its own turf. We plan to do this by greatly expanding the ISI field effort, its network of campus-based programming.[288]

And expand they did. Today, the ISI boasts volunteer representatives at over 900 colleges and has more than 65,000 student and faculty members on virtually every campus in the United States. In addition, the ISI conducts more than 300 educational programs on campuses each year—everything from large public lectures to small-group seminars, sponsors various events and speeches, and has dozens of lecturers (including Dinesh D'Souza, Christina Hoff-Sommers, David Horowitz, and Roger Kimball) available for hire listed on its website. It also offers a number of graduate fellowships to students pursuing academic careers including a unique award worth $20,000 for work related to Western civilization studies. It produces three journals, *The Intercollegiate Review*, *Modern Age*, and *The Political Science Reviewer*, distributes an additional four conservative publications and operates ISI books—an imprint of the ISI which claims to publish volumes that "strike at the heart of the prevailing orthodoxies of contemporary scholarship."[289]

The Intercollegiate Review frequently publishes scholarly harangues disparaging multiculturalism, feminism, and other sixties-inspired critical discourses that play to cultural animosities against women, gays, and minorities.[290] In recent years, targeting traitorous intellectuals has become *de rigueur*. In the first issue after 9/11, the journal included an essay by Yale historian Donald Kagan titled "Terrorism and the Intellectuals" in which the author castigated academics who apparently suggested that the "responsibility for September 11" rested with "the United States." He complained about "leftist intellectual orthodoxy" on campuses and the "fashion-able assaults on patriotism" made by privileged yet irresponsible scholars whose despicable behavior should be condemned by those devoted to the nation's special virtues.[291] Kagan echoed the dominant narrative that hatred of the United States stemmed from its commitment to "free, open, democratic," and "tolerant" forms of governance. In so doing, Kagan epitomized the posturing of PC, particularly in terms of the notion of America's exceptionalism.

In Kagan's world, it was unfathomable that reasonable minds could assert that the history of U.S. international policy and actions might have had something to do with the horrors of 9/11. Presumably, rational individuals had no business arguing that a more nuanced understanding of the complexities of international relations, American complicity in arming tyrannical regimes, its flouting of international law, and its dominance of the world economy was needed to fully comprehend acts of terrorism. Contrary to what Kagan contended, however, such a critical stance did not constitute a "blame America" first mentality nor did it represent an assault on patriotism by deluded minds; rather it implied that the events of 9/11 could not be understood without proper attention accorded to the national and international contexts from which they arose. While the portrait painted by Kagan may have been comforting, it was not only at "variance with everything we know;" it also had "all the merits of self-adulation and uncritical support for power."[292] Kagan's attempt, rife with the stench of neo-McCarthyism, to link critical intellectuals with terrorists was predictable given his neoconservative pedigree. He was a signatory to PNAC's 1997 founding statement of principles—an organization that was co-founded by his son Robert. And, his other son Frederick was instrumental in creating the Bush administration's Iraq "surge" strategy.

Another interesting figure associated with the ISI is Marvin Olasky whom the institute lists as one of its "speakers" available for lectures on topics including "Is Compassionate Conservatism an Oxymoron?" and "God, Sex, and Statemanship." Olasky, a professor of journalism at the University of Texas at Austin and the editor of *World*, a national weekly news magazine written from a biblical perspective, coined the phrase "compassionate conservatism" and was one of George W. Bush's most influential intellectual advisers. Like Bush, Olasky is a fundamentalist born-again Christian and their history dates back to 1993, just before Bush was elected governor of Texas. In fact, Olasky's book *Compassionate Conservatism* includes an obsequious introduction written by the former president.

Olasky was also one of the main theorists behind Bush's faith-based initiative—a tax-payer funded mission that essentially allowed religious groups to provide government social programs—including homeless shelters, drug rehabilitation programs, pregnancy counseling, etc.—even if their mission was to preach religion to their clients. Christian nationalist thinkers like Olasky have long dreamt of "replacing welfare with private, church-based charity that would be dispensed at the discretion of the godly."[293] They believe that poverty is not the result of financial lack but, rather, a reflection of poor peoples' moral turpitude. Michelle Goldberg argues that Olasky's ideas

> have helped to shape an ascendant movement that is challenging not just church/state separation, but the whole notion of secular civil society and social services based on empirical research rather than supernatural intervention … Olasky and other supporters of faith-based funding [are] driven by the conviction that the poor and addicted are sinners who need to be redeemed by Jesus Christ … Olasky's work thus serves as a valuable guide to the kind of society that Bush and his Christian nationalist backers are striving to create. His vision is a deeply radical one, heavily influenced by Christian Reconstructionism. He yearns for the days before the New Deal, when sinners could be denied aid until they repented … Olasky identifies two primary enemies as responsible for the country's fall—religious liberalism and 'political socialism,' which he blames for jettisoning a one-on-one, salvation-minded approach to the poor.[294]

Christian Reconstructionism is a doctrine formulated mainly by the late Rousas John Rushdoony and his 1973 book *The Institutes of Biblical Law* is the most "important for the dominionist movement."[295] In that text, Rushdoony drew extensively from the repressive theocratic creed articulated by Calvin in *Institutes of the Christian Religion*, first published in 1536. Echoing Calvin, Rushdoony called for a Christian society that is "harsh, unforgiving and violent" and one that emphasized the inerrant authority of the Bible and the irreconcilability between believers and non-believers. Christian Reconstructionism is deeply antagonistic toward the federal government; in fact, Rushdoony believed that the government should concern itself almost exclusively with national defense while matters pertaining to education and social welfare should be ceded to churches.[296] He called for the dismantling of federal democracy so that it could be replaced with a "network of small sovereign communities run by fundamentalist Christians."[297] Fundamentalists view secular institutions and humanist philosophies as inherently problematic and they believe that the separation of church and state is based on a misinterpretation of the Constitution. They are also quite prominent in seeking to introduce the teaching of "intelligent design" in public institutions at all levels—including colleges and universities in the name of "intellectual diversity." Predictably, Olasky has used his bully pulpit at *World Magazine* to chide "ideologically identical professors" while concomitantly heaping praise on conservative organizations like ACTA and student gestapos committed to battling the scourge of radicalism on college campuses. Apparently Olasky does not think his religious extremism is radical.

The ISI also administers the Collegiate Network (CN)—an association of approximately 120 right-wing student publications from Dartmouth to UCLA that provides its members with annual operating grants, mentoring sessions, training conferences, and paid year-long and summer internships at cooperating national media outlets including *USA Today*, the *Wall Street Journal* and the notoriously right-wing *Weekly Standard*. The campus publications, most of which are disseminated gratis at scores of colleges and universities, have a combined annual distribution of more than two million copies.

The history of the network dates back to 1979 when two University of Chicago students (both students of Allan Bloom) approached the Institute for Educational Affairs (IEA), which had been established by Irving Kristol and William E. Simon with funding from the usual suspects, for financial assistance to counter the "one-sided reporting" that presumably dominated the main student publication on their campus. The students convinced IEA that control of campus publications was firmly entrenched in the hands of leftist radicals who systematically excluded conservative points of view and the IEA eventually provided funding for *Counterpoint*.

The student founders of *Counterpoint* were Tod Lindberg, now a contributing editor to the *Weekly Standard* and a current research fellow at the conservative Hoover Foundation where he also serves as editor of *Policy Review* and John Podhoretz, son of neoconservative royalty and rabid propagandist for all things anti-liberal Norman Podhoretz (another signatory to PNAC) and the aforementioned Midge Decter. John, a former speechwriter for both Reagan and Bush the elder, is a Fox News Channel contributor, a columnist for Rupert Murdoch's tabloid the *New York Post*, editor of *Commentary*, and a contributing editor to *The Weekly Standard* which he helped to launch with Murdoch's backing. Known for writings that are "jokey" recitations of "hoary hand-me-downs from babyhood," Podhoretz was, nonetheless, a dependable ally of the George W. Bush administration.[298] From his various media perches, he reliably provided panglossian support for Bush's military misadventures. And, in 2004 he authored a fawning ode to the Bush presidency, *Bush Country: How Dubya Became a Great President While Driving Liberals Insane*, in which he petulantly cast opponents of the former president's policies as "Bush-haters."

The IEA eventually expanded its grant program and in 1980 the CN was formally established by William Simon and Irving Kristol. In 1990, the Madison Center (which was founded by Allan Bloom and William Bennett in 1988) merged with the IEA to form the now defunct Madison Center for Educational Affairs (MCEA) in order to maintain funding for what was then a consolidated system of 57 conservative student publications. In 1995, the CN moved from Washington, D.C. to Wilmington, Delaware and ISI took over the operations of the network. Since 1995, the CN has received $6,580,000 in funding from the Scaife, Olin and Bradley foundations *alone*.[299] According to its website, the CN's stated mission is "to focus public awareness on the politicization of American college and university classrooms, curricula, student life, and the resulting decline of educational standards" but its real function is to feed and water Ann Coulter wannabes who will then take up their rightful place in what David Brock has called "the Republican noise machine." Indeed, Brock maintains that many young conservatives "choose to train at highly ideological media programs" like those offered by the CN because "they are more interested in politics than in journalism."[300] And it shows.

For the most part, the member newspapers of the CN are staffed by fiery rightists who demonstrate minimal, if any, regard, for the tenets of traditional journalism—including fairness and accuracy. They are, at best, apparatchiks posing as student journalists and they relish in broad siding "liberalism." An October 2004 edition of the *Princeton Tory* typifies this. That particular issue featured a cover photograph—of a young hunter in full camouflage regalia, brandishing a shotgun—accompanied with a declaration that "the state of New Jersey" had declared "open season on the hunting and trapping of all liberal species."[301] Just four years later in October 2008, the *Tory* staff penned an article about the likely election of Barack Obama (which they viewed as an looming travesty) whom they referred to as the first "Muslim-American president" who would take the oath of office "with his hand on the Koran" and who would have difficulty fighting the Wars on Terror and Drugs because he (Obama) is a "former terrorist ally" and a "former druggie." Such is the kind of "journalism" practiced at some of CN's flagship publications.[302]

CN's extremism is also exemplified in the form of James O'Keefe, a founder of the CN-supported *The Centurion* at Rutgers University. In September 2009, O'Keefe and a fellow conservative activist, Hannah Giles, released selectively edited hidden-camera recordings of their interactions with employees of the Association of Community Organizations for Reform Now (ACORN), an organization universally loathed by the right. The videos, in which Giles posed as a prostitute and O'Keefe claimed to be her pimp/boyfriend, were part of a "gotcha journalism" attempt to elicit damaging responses from ACORN employees about how to hide illicit money garnered from prostitution. The footage created a firestorm of controversy and produced howls of protest from conservative politicians and media pundits who praised O'Keefe's antics and called for ACORN's federal funding to be withdrawn. The videos were later found to be heavily doctored and an investigation eventually cleared ACORN employees of any criminal wrongdoing.

Ironically, it was O'Keefe who eventually found himself on the wrong side of the law when he and three other young men were arrested by the FBI for attempting to tamper with telephones in Democratic Senator Mary Landrieu's New Orleans office in January 2010. In addition to O'Keefe, two other men—Stan Dai and Joseph Basel—involved in the plot were associated with right-wing papers supported by the CN. Dai served as the editor-in-chief of George Washington University's *GW Patriot* and Basel had launched *The Counterweight* at the University of Minnesota-Morris. The fourth accomplice was one Robert Flanagan—the son of acting U.S. Attorney for the Western District of Louisiana, William J. Flanagan. All four were charged with entering federal property under false pretenses for the purpose of committing a felony and face up to ten years in prison.

CN's "journalists" are also very enthusiastic about preaching the right-wing gospel on a range of issues—from feminism, multiculturalism, and the "myth" of global warming to the morality of war and the superiority of Milton Friedman's notions of unfettered capitalism. Yet, with respect to the latter they fail to see the fundamental contradictions at the heart of their enterprises. While these free market champions and advocates of "personal responsibility" and "self-reliance" cast them-selves as beleaguered minorities barely surviving on liberal-dominated campuses, the financial muscle behind their publications belies not only such dramatically presented imagery but also their core ideology. In fact, the campus warriors who extol the virtues of free market capitalism write for publications which depend on a form of right-wing welfare provided by foundations and institutes in the form of subsidies. In yet another example of rank conservative hypocrisy, there is a major gap between rhetoric and reality. There really is no comparative counterpart on the liberal left to the CN. Progressive campus papers often struggle with funding issues, lack support from wealthy foundations and alumni groups, and usually depend upon a mix of university funding and advertising dollars for their survival. Since the administrations of universities are often targets of criticism, progressive papers often find themselves in adversarial situations and subject to funding decreases.[303] By contrast, most conservative campus publications are not competing for advertising revenue to sustain their operations; rather the unwavering defenders of free market magic are held up by the concealed but very real hands of their sugar daddies.

What is more disturbing is that so many of the network's newspapers, editors, and writers rely on fanning the flames of nativism, racism, social intolerance and gay-baiting to register their complaints against multiculturalism, affirmative action, various diversity initiatives on campuses and anti-war proponents. The political catechism of the CN network is spiked with rage and bigotry and it is propped up by a stubborn conviction that unsupported opinions presented in a mean-spirited fashion are preferable to complex analysis. Case in point is the former paramour of Ann Coulter and Laura Ingraham, Dinesh D'Souza, whose history warrants a detour here for at last two reasons. First, D'Souza pioneered the noxious "journalism" which has become the hallmark of the CN. His *Letters to a Young Conservative* is chock-full of advice on how to use newspapers and/or magazines as tools to provoke progressives on campuses while concomitantly promoting the conservative agenda.[304] Secondly, he provides a further illustrative example of how rightist organizations gratuitously bestow prestigious sounding designations upon pseudo-intellectuals.

D'Souza was once the Rishwain Scholar at Stanford University's Hoover Institute (another outfit that depends on the milk of the four sisters' teat), yet he has never produced a single peer-reviewed article/essay or publication. In fact, his only academic credential is a BA in English earned from Dartmouth! That someone who has not rightfully earned advanced degrees can be called a scholar is surely a testament to the lack of rigor and standards that are common at corporate-sponsored right-wing think tanks—all that matters are one's political proclivities and a willingness to embrace malevolent mudslinging methods to advance the conservative agenda.

D'Souza founded the *Dartmouth Review*, the first member of the official CN, in 1980 and also served as the publication's editor in the early 1980s. While under his directorship, the paper ran a particularly incendiary piece entitled "Dis Sho' Ain't No Jive, Bro," a parody of African-American students at Dartmouth which featured an "interview" with a member of the Ku Klux Klan, a graphic image of a lynched black man, and some selected words of wisdom from Adolph Hitler himself.[305] The newspaper also commemorated Hitler's birthday and emblazoned the front page with a picture of the Nazi leader. And in yet another piece, written for the Heritage Foundation's *Policy Review*, D'Souza, commenting on gender issues, claimed that: "The question is not whether women should be educated at Dartmouth. The question is whether women should be educated at all."[306]

Evidently, D'Souza's depraved deeds and debauchery endeared him to conservatives and he subsequently served as a domestic policy analyst in the Reagan administration. While his first book, a bromidic biography of bible-thumper Jerry Falwell remains largely unknown and unread, he was catapulted from virtual anonymity to media stardom seven years later after *Illiberal Education*—his jeremiad (funded by rightist foundations and organizations including Olin) against political correctness and affirmative action—was published in 1991. Since then D'Souza, aided and abetted by conservative think tanks, has written, among other tracts, *The End of Racism* and *What's So Great about America*. The former is a 736-page revisionist account of the history of slavery and racism in America which provides a culturalist, rather than a biological, 'explanation' for Black 'inferiority.' In the book, which garnered considerable criticism for its asinine assumptions and preposterous pronouncements, D'Souza attributes the economic disadvantages endured by African-Americans to the 'pathology' of black culture. Allegedly, the real obstacles facing the black community stem from its collective unwillingness to acknowledge its own 'cultural deficiencies.' According to D'Souza, these defects include an excessive reliance on government funding; the normalization of illegitimacy; paranoia about racism; and a resistance to academic achievement which is supposedly perceived among African-Americans as tantamount to 'acting White.'

In addition to arguing that slavery (which he suggests brought blacks into the orbit of modern civilization) and segregation were not as racist as experts and the media have made them out to be, D'Souza makes the outrageous claim that the belief in the persistence of racism is a disturbing and self-serving myth concocted by the black civil rights establishment. In fact, the basic premise of D'Souza's screed is that racism, which he defines as the belief in the innate, natural, biological inferiority of certain racially defined groups, no longer exists. He maintains that those who argue for the relationship between race, intelligence and biology, or what he refers to as the 'old racism' have long been discredited—something which he in turn, interprets as proof that racism no longer exists in American society. Of course, he neither acknowledges nor addresses the "new" cultural racism which is predicated on non-biological notions to explain Black 'inferiority'—a form that he himself applies throughout his work. D'Souza's conclusions were so egregious that they managed to offend even prominent Black conservatives—two of whom, Robert Woodson, Sr. and Glenn Loury, registered their protest by renouncing their affiliation with the AEI which had sponsored D'Souza's tome.[307] The latter, *What's So Great about America*, a miasma of right-wing claptrap, was essentially a post-9/11 exercise in patriotic cheerleading, a defense of American exceptionalism replete with incredulous rationalizations for U.S. unilateralism and the use of naked and brutal force in the service of 'Planet America.'

With one of his latest offerings, *The Enemy at Home: The Cultural Left and its Responsibility for 9/11*, D'Souza has arguably become the Ann Coulter of "research" institutes for his venomous vituperations clearly rival those which the demagogic diva has routinely hurled at liberals and leftists. This treatise, which one reviewer aptly labeled "the worst nonfiction book about terrorism published by a major house since 9/11," seeks to blame the American "cultural left" for the terrorist attacks. According to D'Souza's contorted logic, bin Laden and al-Qaeda were driven to deadly destruction not by American foreign policy or the U.S. government's obstinate support of Israel but rather by the hedonistic, licentious, and secular culture that the U.S. exports to "traditional societies." Forget the fact that al Qaeda attacked the quintessential symbols of American financial and military might—the World Trade Center and the Pentagon; forget complicated geopolitics and American support for assorted tyrannical regimes in the Middle East; never mind that bin Laden himself, in November 2001, cited U.S. aggression as the motivation for his "defensive Jihad." The real culprit is the "left" which has "fostered a decadent American culture that angers and repulses traditional societies" and which has waged "an aggressive global campaign to undermine the traditional patriarchal family and to promote secular values in non-Western cultures."[308]

For D'Souza, then, it is the cultural left and its cronies in government, the media, Hollywood, the non-profit sector, and the universities that are responsible for the "volcano of anger toward America that is erupting" in the Islamic world. Obsessed with lambasting liberalism and naming domestic enemies—among them Hillary Clinton, Michael Moore, Howard Dean, Rosie O'Donnell, Planned Parenthood, the ACLU, and Human Rights Watch—D'Souza encourages "American conservatives" to make common cause with Muslims and others "in condemning the global moral degeneracy that is produced by liberal values."[309] In so doing he not only "endorses much of the jihadist critique of American society" but also gives "a partial moral pass to al-Qaeda and the perpetrators of 9/11."[310] The fact that D'Souza has parlayed the tiresome "blame the left" mantra into a lucrative career likely serves as an inspiration to all those that still toil at right-wing campus rags across the country.

A simple survey of the CN's most prominent publications renders obvious the primary objective of the network's operations—to breed the next generation of what James Wolcott calls "attack poodles," those "alpha males" and "Malibu Barbies" of punditry and "other occult arts" conditioned to pounce at any foe of the radical conservative agenda.[311] The CN enables these lapdogs in training to hone various skills including the juvenile name-calling tactics that are the trademark of Fox News Channel personalities such as Bill O'Reilly, Sean Hannity, and Glenn Beck as well as other right-wing media gasbags who push the boundaries of civility and thrive on calumny and bombast. Consider the post-2004 election remarks of Bernadette Malone (who was known to equate anti-Bush demonstrators with Islamic militants) who cut her "journalistic" teeth at the CN's *Binghamton Review*.[312]

> I am delighted to report that on college campuses on both coasts … [that] there are student-run independent newspapers that are battling the America-hating political scientists, Marxist economics professors, deconstructionist English departments, feminazis, pot-smoking philosophers, Birkenstocked war protestors, and the whole migraine that is the Campus Left. These conservative newspapers … helped to get Bush reelected.[313]

She added, apparently with a straight face, that "Fox News, the *Wall Street Journal*, and other fair and balanced news institutions employ former student editors of conservative newspapers."[314] In this instance, and contrary to the stated lofty goals of raising public awareness about so-called declining educational standards, Malone exposes the genuine aspirations of the CN network—to advance the cause of radical conservatism, provide a forum that turns outrageous (and mainly unsubstantiated) claims about liberal/left shenanigans on campuses into conventional wisdom for large swathes of the public, fuel the knee-jerk anti-intellectualism of the right, and serve as an auxiliary to the Republican Party.

One could reasonably argue that right-wing student scribes who run roughshod over any notion of civility and even the most rudimentary of journalistic principles and who seem to want to immunize themselves to ideas that might challenge or "offend" them are hardly in a position to evaluate the standards of higher education. If anything, these reactionary junior poodles, like their counterparts in the national media, contribute to the wholesale underpinning of journalism for political purposes and to a coarsening of public speech that undermines the very precepts of rationality. Just as the myth of the liberal media has essentially served to weaken journalism's watchdog function and to move media discourse to the right, conservative campus publications that exist, ostensibly, to report on the "dangers" of the liberal/left campus seek to narrow the political spectrum and weaken the very practice of critique and critical thinking. Far from desiring higher standards in education, their purpose is to provide ideological cover for powerful interests and give ballast to the logic of U.S. militarism and rightist ideology. In promoting PC, they want to inoculate the institutions and power arrangements they venerate—corporate America, the military, right-wing Christianity, capitalism, patriarchy, etc.—from any type of serious scrutiny. And, above all, they want to further the spread of what renowned attorney Gerry Spence has fittingly termed the "conservative hate culture."[315]

Heritage Foundation

The creation of the Heritage Foundation, founded in 1973 by the late Paul Weyrich (whom Joe Conason once called the "eminence grise of the religious right in Washington") with financial backing from beer tycoon Joseph Coors, Richard Scaife, and Oklahoma oilman Edward Noble, is typically regarded as one of the single most important events in the development of the national network of right-wing policy-oriented institutions that have been working for decades to transform the American social and political landscape.[316] Heritage boasts sponsorship from more than 275,000 individual and corporate supporters yet it benefits quite handsomely from funding—in the form of grants—that it receives from the four sisters and other conservative foundations. From 1985 to 2006, it received more than $66 million from such sources according to the Media Transparency organization. The foundation's 2009 Annual Report lists total assets of $183,136,434 and its operating revenue/budget for that same year was more than $71 million—one of the largest in its 36-year history.[317] It houses approximately 250 employees including management and professional staff, policy analysts, senior fellows, and communications specialists. It also publishes the journal *Policy Review*. Its board of trustees has included Richard Scaife, Midge Decter, Holland "Holly" Coors and Jeb Bush. Margaret Thatcher, former British Prime Minister and champion of free market fundamentalism, is listed as a patron of the foundation.

Among the various conservative think tanks, the Heritage Foundation is often characterized as the most extreme and has gained some notoriety for its links to Nazi operatives and Reverend Sun Myung Moon's ultra-rightist Unification Church. Moon, of course, is the South Korean theocrat who considers himself the son of God and the new Messiah. Criminally convicted for tax fraud and conspiracy to obstruct justice, Moon has claimed that he will succeed where Christ himself failed in attaining world power. His Unification Church is considered a cult by many and is rumored to practice mass arranged marriages and bizarre sexual practices including Moon's stipulation that his followers place his photograph nearby when they have sex and that spouses wipe their genitalia with something called the "Holy Handkerchief"—which is never supposed to be laundered.[318]

In addition to illegally funding the vicious Nicaraguan Contras during the Iran-Contra affair, Moon's many organizations have been used over the years by the Korean Central Intelligence Agency (KCIA) as propaganda vehicles to maintain high levels of U.S. military and economic aid and the continued presence of American armed forces in South Korea. His far-flung international empire includes *The Washington Times* newspaper, the UPI wire service, television studios in Washington, D.C., a gun factory, and vast real estate holdings.[319] Moon is openly anti-democratic yet he has cultivated a power base among Republican politicians by donating generously to various ultraconservative causes. The Bush family has been one of his major beneficiaries; in fact, Moon has filtered significant funds to the George H.W. Bush presidential library fund.[320] Just before George W. Bush was installed as President, his incoming Attorney General John Ashcroft attended Moon's Inaugural Prayer Luncheon for Unity and Renewal and Bush's Faith Based Initiative provided large amounts of funding to disciples of Moon.

The eccentric Moon aside, Heritage's very founders and financiers have some unsettling historical and contemporary connections. The Coors clan, for example, has long been known for its ties to neo-Nazis and racists. Adolph Coors regularly allowed KKK gatherings and cross-burnings on brewery property in Colorado while William Coors fought vehemently against the passage of the Civil Rights Act. Coors money once bankrolled groups that supported the apartheid government in South Africa and terrorist activity in a number of foreign countries including Nicaragua. The Coors family, which has supported groups working in alliance with Reverend Moon and Christian Reconstructionists, has a reputation for backing far right organizations that have called for the abolition of American democracy and the establishment of a theocratic state. The homophobia of the Coors family is infamous not only because it has financed organizations that view AIDS as God's punishment for homosexuality but also because of the business practices of the Coors Brewing Company. In the 1970s, prospective employees were required to take lie-detector tests and one of the questions asked of them was whether or not they were homosexual.[321] The company is also virulently anti-union and anti-labor and is among the worst of environmental polluters.[322]

In addition to establishing the Heritage Foundation and serving as its president until 1974, Weyrich, who died in December 2008, was often referred to as the New Right's strategic architect, and he had long represented Coors family interests in Washington, D.C. He also helped to start the Moral Majority in 1979 and inspired the formation of the Christian Coalition in 1989. Weyrich also founded—again with help from Joe Coors—the Free Congress Foundation (FCF), a radical organization dedicated to fighting the "Culture War."[323] To that end, the FCF works toward educating "the American people about the real nature of 'Political Correctness' which is actually Marxism translated from economic to cultural terms."[324] The FCF's mission was an extension of Weyrich's "cultural conservatism" project which he began mapping out in the mid-1980s to combat the perceived cultural drift (i.e. the decline of traditional and moral authority) presumably generated by 1960s radicalism and the forces of liberal largesse. Cultural conservatism, largely a populist strategy, was the brainchild of Weyrich who, envisioning the denouement of the Evil Empire's red threat, suggested that rightist leaders embrace social issues as a way to rally conservative ground troops. In 1987, he commissioned a study—*Cultural Conservatism: Toward a New National Agenda*—that outlined the benefits of waging a "culture war" and which found that "antiliberalism" was a far more encompassing theme than was "economic conservatism" for the purposes of advancing a right-wing agenda and capitalist ideology.

Weyrich, often described by his admirers as "the Lenin of social conservatism," was a member of the extreme Catholic right and a self-described enthusiast of pro-Nazi firebrand Father Charles Coughlin.[325] He was known—even among veteran conservatives—as a "fairly unsavory character" and had a history of cavorting with racists that dated back to his involvement with George Wallace's segregationist American Independent Party.[326] Among those who have been associated with the FCF is one Laszlo Pasztor, a former activist in various Hungarian right-wing and Nazi-affiliated groups. During World War II, Pasztor was a leader of the youth group Arrow Cross, the "Hungarian equivalent of the German Nazi Party."[327] He was eventually convicted and served a prison term for being a Nazi collaborator. Pasztor came to the United States in the 1950s and joined the Republican Party's Ethnic Division—in fact, Richard Nixon gave him permission to organize a permanent ethnic arm of the GOP. As a result, Pasztor recruited scores of Central and Eastern Europeans who were Nazi enthusiasts into the American Security Council's Coalition for Peace through Strength which, throughout the Reagan and Bush Sr. administrations, had close ties to the National Security Council and the State Department. The outfit was designed to "network conservatives around hard-line military issues" and its members included, in addition to Nazis, an assortment of white supremacists and anti-Semites.[328] In 1988, Pasztor and several other émigré fascists were named as leaders of George H. W. Bush's presidential campaign's outreach arm, the Coalition of American Nationalities. They were eventually expelled from the campaign only after their exposure as Nazi sympathizers proved embarrassing for the Republican Party.

Another loathsome character who had past dealings with Heritage is Roger Pearson who joined the editorial board of *Policy Review* when Ed Feulner became president of the foundation in 1977. Before he emigrated to the United States in the mid-1960s, the British-born Pearson headed the Northern League—a white supremacist European organization whose members included former Nazi SS officials.[329] Before joining *Policy Review*, Pearson penned four racist tracts during the 1960s including such gems as *Race and Civilization*, based on the writings of Hans Gunther, Hitler's principal racial theoretician, and *Eugenics and Race*— essentially a white nationalist manifesto that championed racial purity.

Despite its sordid past, or perhaps because of it, the Heritage Foundation remains one of the most influential think tanks in the country and it continues to maintain close ties to the Republican Party. Among the speakers it has hosted in recent years are such luminaries as George Allen, the former Senator of Virginia who once aspired to the White House and who was known for displaying a Confederate flag at his home and a noose in his law office.[330] Readers may also recall the controversy which enveloped Allen's 2006 election campaign after he referred to S.R. Sidarth, a Virginia-born American of Indian descent, as "macaca." Sidarth, a senior at the University of Virginia, was documenting Allen's travels and speeches on behalf of James Webb, Allen's Democratic opponent (and eventual victor) in the Senate race. At a Republican event Allen singled out Sidarth, who was the only non-white in attendance, and referred to him as "macaca"—a racial slur against African immigrants that is commonly used in some European cultures. Other featured Republican lecturers included Tom Delay, the former House Majority Leader (and close ally of convicted felon Jack Abramoff) who was indicted by a Texas grand jury on criminal charges for violating campaign finance laws.

Heritage was also well-connected to the Bush II administration. In early 2001 during Bush's transition to the White House, Karl Rove told a gathering of right-wing leaders that Bush "had asked the Heritage Foundation" to review "all the executive orders put in place by President Clinton" and to "recommend which ones should be overturned."[331] Many individuals associated with the think tank eventually served in various positions within the Bush administration. Perhaps the most well-known was George Jr.'s labor secretary, Elaine Chao, once a "distinguished" fellow at Heritage where she no doubt honed the anti-labor posturing that became one of the hallmarks of the Bush presidency. Indeed, workers suffered an especially brutal assault at the hands of the Bush administration which John Sweeney once referred to as the "most anti-worker" in decades.[332] This was made abundantly clear by Bush's repeated refusal to support a significant increase in the minimum wage, his attacks on the rights of various categories of workers to organize, his wholehearted endorsement of outsourcing, and his vigorous backing of corporate-friendly free trade deals that weakened labor power and unions all over the world.[333] Bush's hostility toward labor predated the terrorist attacks but, post-9/11, under the pretext of national security, his anti-union, anti-labor positions were elevated to new heights as he blatantly used the fight against terrorism as an excuse to ban unions and roll back "the rights of workers across the board."[334]

Given that the Heritage Foundation essentially views "New Deal" as "curse words,"[335] it is scarcely surprising that it has been a trailblazer when it comes to conjuring up ways to free corporations from any type of accountability—from providing rationales for the dismantling of worker and consumer protections and union busting to its shameless promotion of deregulation. This is something which dates back to at least the Reagan Administration. In fact, Reagan's first appointment to the National Labor Relations Board (NLRB) was Robert Hunter, a conservative activist, who contributed the chapter on labor that was included in Heritage's hefty 1980 document, *Mandate for Leadership: Policy Management in a Conservative Administration*. In that paper, Hunter advocated increasing the use of NLRB injunctions against unions, gutting the Occupational Safety and Health Administration (OSHA) and radically cutting the Bureau of Labor Statistics.[336] Reagan's agenda was derived almost whole-cloth from Heritage as the 1,077-page *Mandate for Leadership* became the policy bible for his administration. Nearly two-thirds of the publication's two thousand recommendations were adapted by Reagan on everything from taxes and regulation to national defense—including the Star Wars missile defense boondoggle. Between massive tax cuts and channeling trillions of dollars to corporations, particularly those in the defense industry, Reagan's Heritage-inspired policies led to one of the largest national debts in American history.

In the aftermath of the devastating Hurricane Katrina, Heritage shamefully exploited the tragedy to push for a laundry list of conservative proposals—rooted in neoliberal ideology—that would be part of a plan to "rebuild" the Gulf Coast. Included among them were the suspension of environmental regulations, including the Clean Water and Clean Air acts; the suspension of wage labor laws; and the promotion of school choice and vouchers. Berkowitz argued that just as the Iraq war became "a Petri Dish for the neoconservative foreign policy agenda, rebuilding the Gulf Coast in the wake of Hurricane Katrina" was likely to become "the mother of all testing grounds" for the Heritage Foundation's domestic policy initiatives.[337] Shortly after the hurricane struck, several careful observers of Katrina and its aftermath noted that it was neoliberal policies that essentially failed New Orleans in the first place.[338] In a campaign to starve the public sector, Bush cut $71.2 million from the budget of the New Orleans Corps of Engineers, a reduction of 44 percent, which meant that plans to fortify the levees were shelved. The former administration also allowed developers to run roughshod over vast expanses of wetlands—in effect the wetlands were drained and could no longer serve as a natural absorbent and shield between the Crescent City and the storms that threatened it.

Despite evidence of the abject failure of free market fundamentalism in the Gulf Coast pre-Katrina, Heritage and its corporate bedfellows began pushing the government to implement the domestic equivalent of neoliberal structural adjustment programs in the region post-Katrina. As Naomi Klein has aptly noted,

> Katrina was a tragedy, but, as Milton Friedman wrote in his *Wall Street Journal* op-ed, it was "also an opportunity." On September 13, 2005—fourteen days after the levees were breached—the Heritage Foundation hosted a meeting of like-minded ideologues and Republican lawmakers. They came up with a list of "Pro-Free-Market Ideas for Responding to Hurricane Katrina and High Gas Prices"—thirty-two policies in all, each one straight out of the Chicago School playbook, and all of them packaged as "hurricane relief." The first three items were "automatically suspend Davis-Bacon prevailing wage laws in disaster areas," a reference to the law that required federal contractors to pay a living wage; "make the entire affected area a flat-tax free-enterprise zone;" and "make the entire region an economic competitiveness zone (comprehensive tax incentives and waiving of regulations)." Another demand called for giving parents vouchers to use at charter schools. All of these measures were announced by President Bush within a week. He was eventually forced to reinstate the labor standards, though they were largely ignored by contractors ... Within weeks, the Gulf Coast became a domestic laboratory for the same kind of government-run-by-contractors that had been pioneered in Iraq. The companies that snatched up the biggest contracts were the familiar Baghdad gang: Halliburton's KBR unit had a $60 million gig to reconstruct military bases along the coast. Blackwater was hired to protect FEMA employees from looters. Parsons, infamous for its sloppy Iraq work, was brought in for a major bridge construction project in Mississippi. Fluor, Shaw, Bechtel, CH2M—all top contractors in Iraq—were hired by the government to provide mobile homes to evacuees just ten days after the levees broke. Their contracts ended up totaling $3.4 billion, no open bidding required ... As in Iraq, government once again played the role of a cash machine equipped for both withdrawals and deposits. Corporations withdrew funds through massive contracts, then repaid the government not with reliable work but with campaign contributions.[339]

This was merely another example of what Klein has referred to as "disaster capitalism"—a situation where catastrophe is seized upon as an opportunity for profit and where privatization schemes that benefit corporations at the expense of the public interest are introduced when people are still too traumatized by disaster to resist them.[340]

In addition to embracing disaster capitalism, Heritage also expended considerable time and energy providing slavish support for Bush's wars in the form of various "position" papers and by linking young conservative ideologues to the "rebuilding" effort in Iraq. In 2004, eleven individuals who had all posted their resumes at the foundation were contacted by the Pentagon's White House liaison office which informed them that the occupation government in Iraq needed employees to help prepare for an international conference. Many of those contacted, some fresh out of college, needed jobs while others relished the opportunity to explore the world of international relations despite having no foreign service experience. And off to Baghdad they went where six of them, who were nicknamed "the brat pack," eventually ended up overseeing the war-torn country's $13 billion budget and making decisions that affected millions of Iraqis. The problem was that none of them had any pertinent credentials, apart from being Republican supporters of Bush and the war, to undertake such a task. According to one report, "none had ever worked in the Middle East, none spoke Arabic, and few could tell a balance sheet from an accounts receivable statement" but they were nonetheless "put in positions of authority that they had no clue about." In spite of their lack of appropriate training and expertise, the members of the brat pack were paid handsomely—almost all of them ended up earning "the equivalent of six-figure salaries."[341] As they say, nice work if you can get it.

In addition to supplying the Bush White House with advice on how to keep the nation's enemies at bay, Heritage did its best to undercut criticism of the war and the Bush administration by domestic "enemies" like Cindy Ṣheehan. On August 30, 2005 Heritage hosted a forum "The Politics of Peace: What's Behind the Anti-War Movement?" that featured John J. Tierney, a former Visiting Fellow at the foundation, as the main speaker. According to promotional materials circulated by Heritage, Tierney's book, *The Politics of Peace*, was an examination of anti-war protests. What it was in fact was a paranoid neo-McCarthyite diatribe that characterized anti-war activists as anti-American Communists with "ties to North Korea, Cuba and Maoist China."[342] Tierney singled out Sheehan at the event for her "outrageous" behavior (i.e. for having the temerity to keep her famous vigil outside of Bush's Texas ranch) while protesters in general were charged with being leftist ideologues that were part of a "comprehensive, exhaustive, socialistic anti-capitalistic political structure."[343] Tierney should know all about comprehensive political structures since he is part of one. He is currently the Faculty Chairman and Walter Kohler Professor of International Relations at the Institute of World Politics, a Washington, D.C. outfit that describes itself as an "independent" graduate school of statecraft and national security affairs but which is funded by rightist foundations including Bradley and Smith-Richardson.[344] And the publisher of his book, the Capital Research Center is yet another D.C. organization sponsored by Scaife, Bradley, and Olin wealth.

Heritage did not limit itself to sponsoring speakers who condemned "liberal" critics of the war. Dissent, and more specifically any criticism of George W. Bush—even among the ranks of bona fide conservatives—was, for a period of time, apparently taboo within the foundation's hallowed halls as one John Hulsman quickly learned. Hulsman served as the think tank's senior policy analyst and cheerfully did his part—in various *Washington Times* op-eds and on Fox News appearances—to castigate Howard Dean, John Kerry, the French, and other presumed enemies of the Iraq war until he ran afoul of the powers that be at Heritage. As the debacle in Iraq continued to unravel, Hulsman became increasingly critical of the Bush administration's foreign policy and the neoconservative worldview that animated it in essays and in conversations with reporters. On July 7, 2006 Hulsman received a note from his boss, Kim Holmes, wishing him "the very best in his continuing career" and essentially inviting him out the door. While the official line from Heritage was that Hulsman left his $90,000-a-year-position willingly, Hulsman basically admitted that he was fired because he publicly criticized Bush.[345]

Such actions are hardly surprising since Heritage is not known as an intellectually adventurous place. Rather, its "scholar"-employees are expected to toe the ideological line of its financial supporters and to express views and churn out papers that merely back up "an already fixed ideological viewpoint, dictated directly by a tier of Heritage executives who" decide, beforehand, the "organization's position on a given issue, and indirectly by the outside foundations that" hold "Heritage's purse strings."[346] Despite its attempts to paint itself as a non-partisan haven for scholarly ideas and exchange, Heritage is home to "hard-core movement activists" and it essentially serves as a propaganda mill to promote the radical conservative agenda with a scholarly veneer.[347] Like the AEI and other similar institutes, Heritage "loves the lingo of academic life" as evidenced by its array of "endowed chairs, visiting fellows, and distinguished scholars" but it is mainly focused on "selling and promoting its views rather than on developing thoughtful or nuanced ones." As its president Ed Feulner once claimed, the think tank conducts "warfare in the battle of ideas." As a result of this combative mentality, Heritage does not have "very high standards" and for the most part, its "ethical standards are as lax as its intellectual ones."[348] It too bestows scholarly-sounding titles on its cultural warriors despite their lack of academic credentials. For example, reformed right-winger David Brock "assumed the grandiose title of John M. Olin Fellow in Congressional Studies"—a position underwritten by the Olin Foundation—even though he had no advanced degrees.[349] And, despite the fact that its tax-exempt 501(c)(3) designation is supposed to prevent it from lobbying Congress, Heritage "*exists* to aid and hinder legislation before Congress and often boasts about doing so."[350]

In order to disseminate its ideological messages and policy recommendations to as wide an audience as possible, Heritage prides itself on producing reports with concision and speed and in creating easily digestible talking points for both politicians and media personalities. It spends exorbitant amounts of money on marketing its views and relies upon a four-part delivery system consisting of: (i) a public relations division, largely responsible for the media and the general public; (ii) a government relations division, which targets Congress and various government agencies; (iii) an academic relations division, which supplies information to the university community and other research institutes; and (iv) what is referred to as the corporate relations division, through which businesses and corporations are recipients of Heritage propaganda.[351] The foundation also keeps tabs on thousands of journalists who are arranged by specialty in the Heritage computer databases so that when the foundation completes a study on policy or other related matters, it goes out with a synopsis which is then distributed to media outlets. A "Press Room" offers news releases, commentary, easily arranged interviews with its stable of "experts," and an around-the-clock, 24-hour media hotline. Heritage spokespersons and "analysts" regularly appear on television and radio and generate an endless flow of op-ed pieces for newspapers. Borosage argues that Heritage has always "focused more on communications, talking points and rapid-response and attack politics than on ideas" and that its "most significant contribution to Beltway politics" was the "briefcase memo"—a short memo "on an issue of the day, summarizing the right-wing line, a hot fact or two, sound bites and brief refutations of liberal arguments"—all of which are "churned out inside the news cycle, largely by a bullpen of grad students toiling under a good editor."[352] More recently, Heritage has expanded its communications and media apparatus in the form of two state of the art radio studios, located on Capitol Hill, that it provides free of charge to radio hosts (obviously only conservatives need apply) who wish to broadcast their shows from Washington.

In addition to furnishing traditional media enterprises with handy summaries of its reports, Heritage was also one of the first organizations of its kind that attempted to capitalize on new media alternatives. As part of its communications operations, Heritage launched Townhall.com in 1995 as the first conservative web community. In 2005, Townhall.com split from the foundation in order to expand the scope of its mission—the amplification of right-wing voices in America's political debates—and became part of Salem Communications, a for-profit U.S. media company that specializes in evangelical Christian and conservative political talk radio. Among Salem's radio hosts are Mike Gallagher, Michael Medved, and Dennis Prager. Gallagher and Medved were two of five radio hosts who were invited to the White House in the fall of 2006 for a powwow with Bush. The other three were Laura Ingraham, Sean Hannity, and Neal Boortz. In a February 2007 interview with Hannity, Boortz claimed that teachers unions were "much more dangerous than al Qaeda."[353]

In a December 2006 appearance on Fox News which epitomized the fascist predilections of many conservatives, Gallagher suggested that the U.S. government should "round up" actor Matt Damon, *The View* co-host Joy Behar and MSNBC's Keith Olberman (all of whom had been critical of Bush and the Iraq war) and put them in a detention camp until the war's end because of their allegedly traitorous remarks.[354] Medved, known for his often outlandish critiques of "leftist" Hollywood, was once afflicted with a bad case of hysterics over the animated film *Happy Feet*— which he dubbed Crappy Feet—for its supposed anti-religious bias, its endorsement of gay identity, and its propagandistic theme that presumably condemned the human race, celebrated environmentalism and exalted the United Nations—that most despised institution among conservative extremists. Not to be outdone in the hysteria department, Prager became apoplectic after learning that representative Keith Ellison, a Democrat from Minnesota and the first Muslim voted to Congress (in the 2006 mid-term elections) had opted to take his oath of office on the Koran. In a Townhall article, Prager argued that Ellison's choice undermined "American civilization" and suggested that using the Koran was comparable to being sworn in with a copy of Hitler's *Mein Kampf*. He demanded that Ellison use the bible as was 'customary,' at least according to Prager. However, in his rage, Prager apparently forgot to check his facts—swearing-in ceremonies never include the use of a religious book in any kind of "official" capacity.[355] Townhall.com also features eighty columns, both syndicated and exclusive, by writers such as Ann Coulter, Dinesh D'Souza, Jonah Goldberg, and Michelle Malkin.

Given that Heritage is clearly at the center of the radical conservative movement, it predictably joined the chorus lamenting the liberal virus that infects the nation's campuses. This was evident in the form of president Ed Feulner's 2004 essay, "Marketplace of Ideas Would Free Universities from Liberal Tyranny" in which he argued that liberal/left hegemony in the universities had led to "academic stagnation" and that the situation could be rectified if wealthy conservatives financially sponsored courses and programs that would provide students with the opportunity to "expand their education by studying conservative ideas" that would counteract their over-exposure to "liberal ideas." This would apparently benefit students and faculty alike since it would "force liberal professors to rethink some of their long-held convictions" while at the same time enable "conservative professors" to interact "with students without fearing they'd be denied tenure by their liberal colleagues."[356] Typically, Feulner takes as a self-evident truth that conservative faculty are routinely discriminated against in institutions of higher education and presumes that only "liberals" need to rethink their deep-seated assumptions.

But more than this, the language which Feulner employs is quite telling—particularly his usage of the "marketplace of ideas" mantra that is used repeatedly by champions of "ideological diversity."[357] Feulner maintains that students are "certainly consumers of education" and that they would benefit from "competition" if there "was a conservative alternative on every campus." Such a situation, he asserts would help to ensure that students get their "money's worth." Feulner's logic implies that because students are "consumers," they have some right to demand what should be taught in the classroom, as if knowledge were simply a commodity to be purchased according to one's preferences—much like deodorant—and as if popular taste should replace the standards that are typically associated with the professional, scholarly community. In such a scenario, education is reduced to a product that is to be packaged with simplistic labels—conservative or liberal—and geared toward niche markets. Conservatively-inclined students could merely choose to take courses taught by professors who share their ideological predilections so as to avoid feeling "uncomfortable" in the classroom context. Leaving aside the presupposition that knowledge can be neatly categorized and branded with political designations, would this not constitute the kind of "feel-good" culture that the right routinely claims to despise? Shouldn't education be unsettling? Should education not expose students to ideas that may be unfamiliar to them, provoke them to think critically? Contrary to what Feulner argues, students would gain little of "value" if they merely went to university to have their preexisting views confirmed. As Khalidi contends:

If students were coming to be told ideas that they arrived at university with they would be getting nothing of value here. If they were not to be challenged, if they were not to be forced to rethink the things that they come here as 18 year olds ... with, what for heaven's sake would be the point of a university, what would in heaven's name be the point of teaching? We would just arrive with monolithic conventional ideas, and we would leave with monolithic conventional ideas.[358]

And let us return to Feulner's proposal: millionaires and/or billionaires would fund courses that reflect rightist ideology and these courses would, in turn, have to be taught by similarly-minded academics that would have to be hired—presumably through some form of affirmative action for conservatives—by universities to achieve "balance." Such a scenario, in Feulner's opinion, would "improve" the "overall educational environment." Feulner, of course, has little to say about the pedagogical implications of such an approach but it would essentially mean that education would truly be contingent upon ideological considerations, in this case conservative ones, rather than sound scholarship and knowledge of established intellectual traditions. This not only smacks of the indoctrination that right-wingers claim to be combating but it is also illustrative of conservative hypocrisy for the initiative/ proposal goes against the grain of what they have decried for decades: identity politics wrapped in the ideology of victimhood.

Of course, indoctrination is precisely what Heritage values. And cultivating the next generation of right-wing die-hards is central to the foundation's mission as evidenced through its Young Leaders Program, Young President's Club, Heritage Congressional Fellowship, Job Bank, and the Heritage Internship Program—all of which are aimed at college youth. One of the most popular initiatives is the summer internship program, a coveted spot on the young conservative circuit, and one which Heritage spends almost $600,000 a year on. Typically, one in six applicants are accepted and they are subjected to a rigorous screening process to determine if they are sufficiently conservative—all applicants are required to answer a questionnaire "designed to ferret out latent liberalism."[359] The program accepts approximately seventy interns during the summer months, each of whom are paid $7.25 per hour. Some of them are housed in a subsidized dormitory at the foundation's headquarters. During their stay, the students are schooled in rightist principles and ideas, attend regular lectures by Heritage staffers and guest speakers, and often meet members of Washington's conservative inner circle. In keeping with its commitment to family values and core American business principles, among the program's past sponsored speakers was Dennis Hastert, the Illinois Congressman and former Speaker of the US House of Representatives, who once raised funds for Jack Abramoff (a former Chairman of the College Republican National Committee and convicted felon), and who many believe helped to cover up disgraced former Florida Representative Mark Foley's lurid e-mail dalliances with young male pages.

Since the election of President Barack Obama, Heritage has been churning out talking points at a furious pace. On their website, one will find the kinds of fear-mongering sound bites that have become all the rage among hard-core conservatives including presidential wannabe Sarah Palin, the Tea Party crowd, and various Fox

News Channel talking heads.[360] Obama has been chided for allegedly "apologizing for America while bowing before dictators" and "chumming" up with Iran's Ahmadinejad and Venezuela's Chavez. The President is referred to as a socialist who is trying to ram through a radical left agenda including "government-run" health care and his administration has come under fire for exploding the deficit. Conveniently side-stepped is the fact that the primary source of the current deficit was the conservative policies, promoted by Heritage and put into place by the Bush administration—including tax cuts during a time of war and a floundering economy.

Leadership Institute

The Leadership Institute (LI) is one of the three largest conservative campus organizations in the United States and through its various programs it has churned out some of the nation's most famous rightists including Karl Rove, Ralph Reed, and Grover Norquist. The institute is generously funded by Bradley, the DeVos family and the Coors-funded Castle Rock Foundation. And, thanks to grants from another conservative philanthropy—the F.M. Kirby Foundation, whose fortunes were derived from the F.W. Woolworth Company—the LI constructed a large high-tech facility in Arlington, Virginia, aptly named the F.M. Kirby National Training Center, where conservative youth can acquire skills and training in the field of public policy and journalism.[361]

The LI is the brainchild of Morton Blackwell, a lifelong hard-right Republican mover and shaker who also has ties to the FCF. In his youth, Blackwell was a College Republican state chairman and a Young Republican state chairman in Louisiana. He was Barry Goldwater's youngest elected delegate to the 1964 Republican National Convention and a Ronald Reagan delegate at the 1980 convention. He subsequently served as Special Assistant to the President on Reagan's White House staff from 1981 to 1984. In 1979, Blackwell founded the LI in order to prepare conservatives for "success in politics, government and the news media." According to its 2009 financial statements, the LI has assets of $13,960,755 and employs a staff of more than fifty. Over the years, the institute has trained more than 74,000 students who are unwavering in their commitment to "free enterprise, limited government and traditional values" for effective leadership in the "public policy process."[362] The various classes, seminars, and workshops it offers are generally conducted by volunteers recruited from the ranks of the conservative movement's most talented operatives and communicators—this despite the fact that the LI is classified as a 501(c) (3) non-profit, non-partisan "educational" foundation.

In addition to a variety of courses and services including an intern program and an Employment Placement Service, the Institute operates the Broadcast Journalism School which appears to be more of a training ground for right-wing operatives hoping to land media careers than a school of traditional journalism. Indeed, its website advertises the program as a "one-stop," "full-service" intense two-day seminar for conservatives who want a career in journalism. Operating on the liberal media myth, the crash course is designed to "give aspiring journalists the skills necessary to bring balance to the media."[363] For a fee of seventy-five dollars, students receive two days of instruction, two meals a day and all course materials. One of the school's most infamous "graduates" is Jeff Gannon (aka James Guckert) who received White House media credentials and became known for asking George W. softball questions in the midst of contentious news conferences. Despite the fact that Gannon's sole "journalistic" background was derived from his two-day stint at the LI's broadcast school, he referred to himself as the White House correspondent for TalonNews.com and was often called upon by White House Press Secretary Scott McClellan who found "relief" in questions from Gannon after "critical lines of questioning from mainstream news organizations."[364] After Gannon/Guckert launched a particularly pointed attack on Democratic Senate leaders in January 2005, his highly partisan tactics and biased questioning led the watchdog group, *Media Matters for America*, to investigate. The organization quickly discovered two disturbing facts that caused a minor uproar.

First, it was revealed that Talon was operated by Bobby Eberle, a Texas-based Republican Party delegate and activist who also ran GOPUSA.com, a website dedicated to "bringing the conservative message to America." Far from being a legitimate news organization, the now defunct Talon was merely a Republican Party rag. Secondly, *Media Matters* found that Gannon/Guckert used Bush administration and Republican National Committee documents and releases in his Talon "news reports" verbatim and without attribution.[365] As a result, the Bush administration was subjected to some scrutiny for allowing Gannon into press conferences despite his lack of credentials and Gannon was accused of being a "White House tool to soften media coverage of Bush."[366] The real embarrassment for conservatives, however, came after intrepid and relentless bloggers exposed the fact that Gannon/Guckert had been soliciting customers on-line as a gay, military-oriented prostitute.

For most of its 31-year history, the LI focused on grooming students to work in conservative politics and organizations. However, in the last decade or so, Blackwell has increasingly devoted his attention to making the nation's campuses more hospitable to right-wing ideology. In 1997, he established the Campus Leadership Program (CLP), an effort designed to be "the first comprehensive attack by conservative students, campus by campus, against the liberal influences that have overtaken America's colleges and universities."[367] In its first year, Blackwell dispatched one representative armed with posters of Margaret Thatcher and Ronald Reagan to recruit on campuses in the Washington area. The tasks of the field representatives are to identify, enlist, and train student leaders to promote conservative causes and principles via campus publications and organizations.

By 2005, the program had grown to twenty-seven recruiters and 738 groups and in the fall of 2006, it more than doubled its size to sixty recruiters, thanks in large part to a $1 million gift from an anonymous patron and donations from longtime benefactors. The recruiters work for ten weeks during each semester and are furnished with a laptop, a $1,000 food stipend, and $500 for each group or publication they create. The CLP also reimburses them for travel, accommodations, and cell phone expenses. According to tax returns available on its website, the LI spent more than $4.6 million on the CLP in 2008 alone. To date, 1,060 groups and newspapers on 443 campuses have been created.[368]

While the LI works initially to assist students in developing their own organizations, each local campus group is independent of the LI and all other national conservative organizations and directs its own day-to-day operations and decision-making. According to Blackwell and CLP student leaders, this set-up is advantageous because such independence allows the individual groups to engage in activities that "push the envelope"—in other words, activities that might not be sanctioned by chapter-based and more "mainstream" political organizations such as the College Republicans.[369] Recruiters encourage students to view themselves as campus revolutionaries on the front lines in a battle for hearts and minds and to be provocative in their approach.

Race-baiting, in the form of so-called affirmative action bake sales, in which white students pay more for a cookie than students of color in an attempt to demonstrate the "unfairness" of affirmative action programs, is a specialty of the CLP and is not limited to such "events." At the University of Nevada, Reno, the first issue of the *Pack Patriot*, a CLP newspaper whose members use pseudonyms or write anonymously, featured a black and white gradient bar labeled "Race-Based Scholarships Now Available" where the white portion of the bar said "No Scholarship" and the darker portions said "Scholarship!"[370] Other "activist projects" suggested on the CLP website include "National Conservative Coming Out Day" to help "oppressed conservatives" who have been subjected to the teachings of Marxism (which is deemed an "emotional disorder, not a political philosophy") come out of the closet and create "safe zones" on their campuses and "Operation: Merry Christmas" designed to combat the political correctness which has presumably marginalized the celebration at the nation's colleges and universities. Another activist tool kit—with an overview written by none other than Christina Hoff Sommers—urges students to take back St. Valentine's Day from the clutches of feminists who, inspired by Eve Ensler of *The Vagina Monologues*, have used a holiday originally intended to celebrate love and romance, to raise campus awareness (gasp!) about violence against women.[371]

Additional antics that have been promoted by CLP groups and student leaders over the years have included an "Earth Day" carwash in which SUV's were washed for free, an "Animal Rights Barbeque" whose promotional materials included a sign that read "I eat two cows for everyone you don't," an "Illegal Immigrant Tag" event where students received prizes for "catching" other students who dressed in orange prison jumpsuits to represent illegal immigrants, "Operation Red Star" in which students "post red stars on the doors of professors who espouse what the group deems communist principles," and a postering campaign at California State University at San Bernadino that featured fliers warning that "children could be socialized into homosexuality and that homosexual behavior leads to shorter life spans."[372]

The LI is also behind CampusReform.org (CR) which is "designed to provide conservative activists with the resources, networking capabilities, and skills they need to revolutionize the struggle against leftist bias and abuse on college campuses."[373] The mission of CR is to

give conservatives powerful new weapons in their fight for the hearts and minds of the next generation of citizens, politicians, and members of the media. CampusReform.org facilitates the establishment of conservative student networks and supports their development as a powerful voice of activism on their campuses. It makes available new opportunities for groups' interaction with alumni, parents, faculty, and other members of the broader community interested in taking a stand for conservative principles on America's college campuses. Connecting up-to-date communications technologies to a principled stand for limited government, the free market, national defense, and traditional values, CampusReform.org makes possible a new generation of student activism to identify, expose, and combat the radical left now.[374]

In their efforts to "identify, expose, and combat leftist outrages" on campuses, CR's on-line headquarters sponsors a website that encourages students to "report leftist abuse." Conservative victims of such alleged abuse are given four options. Students can review a textbook by reading "scholarly critiques of commonly used" texts and then adding their "own review of biased books" they have been assigned. They can rate faculty members' "personal, grading, discussion, and lecture bias" in order to hold "professors accountable." They can simply share stories of "unfair treatment of campus conservatives" or students can take a survey in order to determine if they have suffered "specific injustices" at the hands of unscrupulous left-wingers and socialists.

Students also have opportunities to attend training sessions in grass-roots youth politics at the LI. At one workshop, conservative apprentices were educated in the fine art of rigging campus elections by Paul Gourley, a veteran mock electioneer from South Dakota and one-time treasurer of the College Republican National Committee. According to Horwitz, one exchange at the training session included the following insights and instructions:

> 'Can anyone tell me,' asks Gourley … 'why you don't want the polling place in the cafeteria?' Stephen, a shy antiabortion activist sitting toward the rear of the class, raises his hand: 'Because you want to suppress the vote?' 'Stephen has the right answer!' Gourley exclaims … [and he] assures them: 'This is not anti-democracy. This is not shady. Just put the polling place somewhere where you might have to put a little bit of effort into voting.' The rest, Gourley explains, is just a matter of turnout.[375]

Horwitz adds that the LI is an apt location to "master the art of mock-election rigging" and that there "is no better master than Morton Blackwell, who invented the trick in 1964 and has been teaching it ever since."[376] Indeed, political dirty tricks and creating "controlled controversy—making your point in a manner so bombastic that your opponents blow their cool—is a Blackwell specialty."[377]

One example of this was on display during the 2004 Republican Convention. Blackwell purchased little pink heart stickers, purple nail polish, and bandages from which he made "Purple Heart Band-Aids" that he then distributed to delegates in Madison Square Garden to ridicule presidential candidate John Kerry's Vietnam Service record. Kerry, a decorated Navy Officer, had been targeted by right-wing groups like the Swift Boat Veterans for Truth which accused him of lying to win combat decorations in Vietnam, including the Bronze Star and the Purple Heart. While the mainstream media reported on the purple heart stunt and credited Black-well for being the mastermind behind it, they failed to explore the connection between Blackwell and Texas businessman Bob J. Perry who gave a whopping $4.5 million to the Swift Boat operation. That connection stems from both men's affiliation with the secretive Council for National Policy (CNP) which deserves further exploration in this context since it has been dubbed "the heart" of the conservative movement by former Secretary of Defense Donald Rumsfeld and the "most influential gathering of conservatives in America" by other prominent Republicans and Christian fundamentalists.[378] One journalist has even called the CNP "the most powerful conservative group you've never heard of."[379]

The CNP was founded in 1981 by Tim LaHaye, the aforementioned right-wing evangelical activist and co-author of the "Left Behind" novels. Among its other founders are Blackwell and Paul Weyrich; conservative fundraising guru Richard Viguerie who, in the 1970s, perfected the direct-mail appeal that provided the "new" right with then-unprecedented cash flows to expound their ideological agenda; and Phyllis Schlafly famously known for leading the opposition to the Equal Rights Amendment. Bob J. Perry was also named in the original CNP incorporation papers. Although the CNP has tried mightily to keep its membership secret, the Institute for First Amendment Studies—a progressive, pro-democracy research group that tracks Christian Right activities—was able to obtain a roster that identified current and formers members. Among them: former Attorney General John Ashcroft, former House Majority Leader Tom DeLay, Holly and Jeffrey Coors, Richard DeVos, Pat Robertson, Bob Jones III (of Bob Jones University), Jerry Falwell, Rev. Moon, and Rev. Rushdoony.[380] Other authors have also cited Senator Trent Lott, Representative Dick Armey, James Dobson (Focus on the Family), Heritage Foundation President Ed Feulner, anti-tax crusader Grover Norquist, ISI president T. Kenneth Cribb, and Federalist Society president Donald Hodel (also a former Reagan cabinet member) as CNP affiliates. Dick Cheney and Donald Rumsfeld have both attended and addressed CNP gatherings and other speakers have included disgraced former Attorney General Alberto Gonzales, and current Supreme Court Justices Scalia and Thomas.[381] George W. Bush gave a speech to the group in 1999 as he was launching his campaign for the presidency. The media were barred from the event and Bush refused to release a public transcript of his address but some of those who wrote about the meeting afterward claimed that Bush promised "to only appoint antiabortion judges if he was elected."[382]

The CNP describes itself as a "counterweight against liberal domination of the American agenda"[383] and was established as the religious right's answer to the Council on Foreign Relations which is regarded as the "fount of the worldwide liberal conspiracy."[384] It meets clandestinely three times a year and brings together "powerful evangelical activists, Republican politicians, and wealthy donors to make plans to pull the country to the right."[385] Although the CNP enjoys tax-exempt status as an "educational foundation," it is shrouded in mystery. As Conason notes:

> It publishes no magazine or journal that is available to the general public. Its Web site is difficult to access and contains little current information. Its three meetings each year are held in lavish hotels and resorts, with the highest possible security. Its members, who pay thousands in annual dues, and its

invited guests are forbidden to discuss what happens at those meetings with the press or the public. But the speeches and discussions are usually taped for distribution to members only.[386]

Why all the secrecy? Could it be, as some have suggested, because the CNP is a theocratic organization that essentially seeks the imposition of fundamentalist Christian ideology in public life? Certainly its membership roster would suggest this, composed as it is of several members of the radical religious right including LaHaye, Dobson, and their ilk. Even Marvin Olasky makes an appearance. The CNP's supposed journal, *Policy Counsel*, which consists mainly of selected speeches from CNP meetings, recently included one by Olasky in which he advocated the overthrow of the National Education Association "regime," an organization "that he described as an 'unelected group that demands allegiance to a central atheistic uniformity.'"[387] If this is the message being espoused by conservative luminaries and veteran activists like Olasky and Blackwell, educators need to equip themselves with knowledge about the groups that are sprouting up like noxious weeds at the nation's institutions of higher education under the bogus banner of balance. Blackwell's student protégés are not seeking balance or equal time, rather they are attempting to transform campuses into breeding grounds for the next generation of what Chris Hedges calls "American fascists."[388]

Young America's Foundation

Along with the ISI and the LI, the Young America's Foundation (YAF) is one of the most dominant and aggressive campus outreach groups in the country. The YAF is an offshoot of Young Americans for Freedom (also known as YAF)—the once powerful, but now much less influential, student group that held its founding meeting at William F. Buckley's Great Elm estate. Despite the similar monikers, the Herndon, Virginia-based foundation discussed here is by far the more prominent of the two groups. The organization's history dates back to 1969 when a group of Vanderbilt University students formed an association called University Information Services (UIS) to combat "the radicals who dominated the campus" and to provide "students with conservative ideas that were missing in their education." By the early 1970s, the UIS became a national association and was renamed the Young America's Foundation. Its stated mission is to ensure that "increasing numbers of young Americans understand and are inspired by the ideas of individual freedom, a strong national defense, free enterprise, and traditional values.[389]

Now housed in the F.M. Kirby Freedom Center, the YAF is run by former Reagan Administration advisor and CNP member Ron Robinson. In addition to presiding over the YAF, Robinson is also a trustee at the Bradley sponsored Phillips Foundation and sits on the board of directors at the American Conservative Union (also funded by the Bradley Foundation), one of nation's oldest lobbying groups on the right. The Phillips Foundation was founded in 1990 to advance constitutional principles and a "vibrant free enterprise system." In 1994, it launched an annual journalism fellowship program that awards grants to working print reporters who produce journalism reflective of American culture and a free society.[390] One of its trustees was the late Robert Novak—the syndicated columnist who essentially helped the Bush administration "out" ex-CIA operative on weapons of mass destruction Valerie Plame, after her husband, former Ambassador Joseph Wilson publicly chastised the Bush administration for lying about intelligence reports that were used to sell the Iraq war to the American public. At the American Conservative Union which was founded by William F. Buckley in 1964, Robinson's fellow members on the board of directors include, among others, Morton Blackwell, Grover Norquist, Tom DeLay, and Wayne LaPierre the chief honcho from the National Rifle Association who once equated gun control and safety advocates with Osama Bin Laden and al Qaeda. LaPierre claimed that such advocates were guilty of "political terrorism"— a "far greater threat" to America's freedom "than any foreign force."[391]

Started with seed money from Scaife, the YAF reported net assets of $33.8 million in 2008—some of which comes from the coffers of the Bradley, Olin and Castle Rock foundations. Boasting that "the conservative movement starts here," YAF provides assistance to college rightists by sponsoring guest lecturers and conferences, providing organizing and training seminars, facilitating networking opportunities, and maintaining a job bank. It also provides what could best be described as a running tribute to the icon of young conservatives—Ronald Reagan.

According to its website, the YAF seized an "extraordinary opportunity" to save a "precious piece of American history"—Reagan's Rancho del Cielo in California— after the organization learned that it "stood in danger of being purchased by people" who apparently had "no regard for its historic value." In 1998, with the blessings of the former president and his wife Nancy, the YAF acquired the 688-acre property that "reflects the endless vistas of freedom and possibility that Reagan considered the fundamental elements of the American experience." Preserving the ranch and "passing on the president's values and ideas" is YAF's way of "thanking Ronald Reagan for all he did" for the "country and the world." According to the organization, the ranch "serves as both a living history lesson and a testament to the true character of Ronald Reagan" and his values which include a "steadfast commitment to freedom, hard work, patriotism, and faith in God." In 2006, with some help from the DeVos family and other right-wing philanthropists, YAF opened the doors of its Reagan Ranch Center, a 22,000 square-foot building that includes classrooms, a theater, meeting rooms and a library of conservative resources, in Santa Barbara, California. Both locations are essentially indoctrination centers used to educate future genera- tions about the wonders of Reagan's legacy[392]

Because so many high school and college students are too young to recall Reagan's actual presidency, they tend to see the former president as his professional image makers and his present-day congressional and media pundit worshippers have tried to present him, namely as a "Norman Rockwellian, mist-shrouded icon of Better Times—an idealized figure of myth."[393] Absent from the YAF's numerous hagio- logical paeans to the "great communicator" who apparently single-handedly brought down the evil empire, is the fact that Reagan's entire political career was bent towards the systematic erosion of equity based initiatives and the curtailing of freedoms both at home and abroad.

From his early days in the hunt for California's governorship when he opposed the 1964 Civil Rights Act and the 1965 Voting Rights Act, to his years in office as president, Reagan served as the strong "mainstream" arm of the ultra-conservative right. In 1980, Reagan kicked off his quest for the presidency (at the invitation of disgraced former Republican Senate Majority Leader Trent Lott) in Philadelphia, Mississippi where sixteen years prior three civil rights activists—James Cheney, Andrew Goodman and Michael Schwerner—who were working for the Mississippi Freedom Summer initiative designed to register black voters in the state, were murdered. With that knowledge in hand and well aware of the fact that in order to garner the Southern White vote, he would have to appeal subtly (and not so subtly) to the virulent racism that was barely containable in some southern white enclaves, Reagan appeared at the Neshoba County Fair, an annual gathering that was famous for diatribes given by segregationist politicians. There, Reagan delivered a rousing speech extolling the racially coded agenda of "states rights." In fact, his speech was sufficiently vitriolic that he was 'rewarded' in turn with an endorsement from the Ku Klux Klan—many of whose members had attended the event.

During his presidency, Reagan demonstrated his skilful public use of coded language—his infamous metaphor "welfare queen" was a thinly veiled critique of black women who presumably rode around in pink Cadillacs while collecting food stamps. In private, he and his staffers were not so subtle. Terrell Bell, Reagan's Education Secretary, noted in his memoir that racial slurs were quite common among the "great communicator's" White House underlings, "including common references to Martin Lucifer Coon." And, as is well known, Reagan was opposed to the establishment of Martin Luther King day.[394] All in all, Reagan helped to perfect the "Southern strategy" and his various attacks on minority populations were perfectly calculated and pitched to the smoldering resentments that characterized the period from 1980 to the early 1990s. Having been a Hollywood actor for many years, Reagan masterfully cultivated an "aw shucks" good natured persona that skillfully masked his racial bigotry and made it seem benign, especially when placed alongside his rabid anti-communism. Despite the fact that Reagan used "race" as a weapon to advance one of the most regressive and vicious social, political, and cultural agendas in American history, his reputation remains largely untarnished as was evident in the week-long media orgy of propagandistic revisionism that ensued in the aftermath of his death.

It is also the case that Reagan unleashed one of the most egregious and relentless "class wars" of the pre-George W. Bush era. His deficit-causing supply-side tax cuts (dubbed voodoo economics by the elder Bush) which were sold with fuzzy math, bogus numbers and sleight-of-hand accounting tricks, essentially benefited the "same people who had financed his rise to politics," particularly "Daddy Warbucks moguls" and "corporate behemoths" and were designed to starve the government to justify draconian spending cuts to social programs intended to help the poor and working classes.[395] As Greider notes:

> Reagan's theory was really "trickle down" economics borrowed from the Republican 1920s (Harding-Coolidge-Hoover) and renamed "supply side." Cut tax rates for the wealthy; everyone else will benefit ... Reagan's great

accomplishment was ideological—propelling the ascendancy of the right—
but the actual governing results always looked more like hoary old interest-
group politics. Wealthy individuals, corporate and financial interests got
extraordinary benefits (tax reductions and deregulation) while the bottom half
got whacked whenever an opportunity arose. His original proposition—cut
taxes regressively, double military spending, shrink government and balance
the federal budget—looked cockeyed from the start. Yet when the logic self-
destructed in practice, conservatives were remarkably content, since they had
delivered the boodle to the right clients. After ... Reagan's economic failure ...
[b]oth parties would spend the next twenty years cleaning up after the
Gipper's big mistake.[396]

Reagan also led the corporate offensive against workers and was openly and actively
hostile to unions, firing PATCO air-traffic controllers en masse after they participated
in a strike for improved pay and working conditions. His was an administration that
diluted workplace safety standards and presided over an S & L scandal that stuck
taxpayers with a bill approaching a trillion dollars. Contrary to the hagiographies
offered up by the YAF, his domestic policies "empowered and enabled some of the
worst elements of public life" in America including "greed, arrogance, neglect and
hypocrisy."[397]

On the foreign policy front, Reagan's record was equally troubling in its cavalier
disregard for democracy and human rights around the globe. While he is often
hailed as the president who brought about democratic reforms in the former Soviet
Union and former Soviet-bloc nations (in and of itself a dubious characterization),
it is important to remember that Reagan "covertly sent arms to the mullahs of Iran"
and courted the murderous regime of Saddam Hussein "even after his use of chemical
weapons; "cuddled up with the fascistic and anti-Semitic junta of Argentina," helped
to fund the brutal death squads in Guatemala and El Salvador that "massacred
civilians;" moved to "normalize relations" with the late Augusto Pinochet—the
Chilean tyrant who admitted to crimes against humanity before his death; and propped
up the heinous tenure of Duvalier in Haiti. Reagan even dispatched his Vice President,
the elder Bush, to the Phillipines where he "toasted dictator Ferdinand Marcos for
fostering 'democracy.'" And, of course, his government supported and trained the
Contra terrorists in Nicaragua.[398] That all of this is a matter of public record does
nothing to dissuade his YAF worshippers who persist in presenting fawning
memorials to the Ronald Reagan "story" where sentimental images and factually-
challenged fables triumph over truth and reality in good patriotically correct fashion.
A simple visit to the YAF website, replete with requisite Reagan-as-handsome-
cowboy imagery, illustrates the epitome of the fictionalization of the Reagan
presidency—dipped as it is in nostalgia and motivated by a kind of historical amnesia
that refuses to acknowledge that a "chilling meanness lurked at the core of Reagan's
political agenda."[399]

In keeping with their adulation for all things Reagan-esque, many of the YAF's
programs and activities are animated by "what can be called the Ronald Reagan
model of campus activism." For students that are "frustrated with the liberal dominance" and "leftist orthodoxy" on campuses, YAF challenges its student foot soldiers

to "adopt a confrontational approach" which the organization likens to Reagan's approach to the Soviet Union:

> Compare how President Ronald Reagan and his predecessors Jimmy Carter, Richard Nixon and others dealt with the former Soviet Union. Reagan's predecessors attempted to appease the Soviets with policies like Détente, but it was Ronald Reagan's confrontational style—calling them an "Evil Empire" and calling for Gorbachev to tear down the Berlin Wall—that led to their collapse. You want to take the same approach when tackling the campus Left and advancing your ideas. The suggestions offered by our advisors are not intended for those who want to take a passive approach to promoting conservatism ... Therefore, expect our advisors to challenge you to aggressively advance your ideas each week! If you choose to follow their strategy, you should expect to be attacked by the Left. Don't let this potential opposition intimidate you. In fact, you should welcome this and view it as another opportunity to expose the Left's intolerance and hyprocrisy.[400]

Of course, the very notion that Reagan was responsible for the fall of the Wall is a part of the mythology upheld not only by YAF but by the neoconservative establishment as well. As Schell notes, far more significant than Reagan's military buildup was the "long policy of containment that preceded it" and even more important still "was the long, slow, scarcely visible but decisive loss of faith in the Soviet empire by the peoples living under its rule" and the "astonishingly creative, non-violent response from Gorbachev" which put the "interests of peace and survival above imperial or ideological interest."[401] Because YAF still clings to the mistaken belief that the Soviet Union was brought to its knees chiefly through American military pressure, it believes that military action can still bring democracy to the Middle East—a fantasy which is still causing untold death and destruction in Iraq. Nonetheless, the YAF promotes such delusional thinking through its various recommended campus activities. While Bush was still in office, one such suggested activity encouraged students to mark the April 9th anniversary of the fall of Saddam Hussein's regime by emphasizing "America's and Iraqi's progress," underscoring the "importance of fighting terrorist {sic} overseas before they attack us at home" and countering the Left which demands "America's retreat." That most of the nation's citizens, and not just the "left," had begun to call for withdrawal from Iraq while George W. Bush was still president seemed to escape the collective consciousness of YAF's war enthusiasts. Moreover, the fact that a whole host of retired generals eventually came out against the ongoing military campaign—something which was unprecedented in American history—is a truth which YAF has conveniently chosen to ignore.[402]

A militaristic theme pervades other YAF programs including its defense of the Reserve Officer's Training Corps (ROTC) and the Junior Reserve Officer's Training Corps (JROTC), two organizations which the YAF claims are routinely "belittled" by "the Left" at "high school and college campuses across the country." In order to defend the rights of students to "associate with the military," help fight "anti-military bias and information" and educate people to the fact that "preserving liberty requires a strong national defense," YAF offers its services and guidance on how to (i) bring pro-military speakers to campus; (ii) challenge schools' administrations to issue public statements of support for military recruiters and ROTC; (iii) permanently memorialize alumni who received a Congressional Medal of Honor; (iv) establish JROTC, ROTC, or regularly host military recruiters on campuses; (v) pay tribute to alumni who were prisoners of war or who are missing in action; and (vi) host fundraisers/donation drives for "boots on ground" soldiers or injured soldiers back home.[403]

With respect to the latter, it became apparent that YAF had no use for the "boots on ground" soldiers who signed a petition asking Congress to withdraw troops from Iraq during the Bush presidency. The "Appeal for Redress," the brainchild of Navy seaman Jonathan Hutto, was worded thusly:

> As a patriotic American proud to serve the nation in uniform, I respectfully urge my political leaders in Congress to support the prompt withdrawal of all American military forces and bases from Iraq. Staying in Iraq will not work and is not worth the price. It is time for U.S. troops to come home.[404]

The fact that the petition, which was first presented to Congress on January 16, 2007, came from an all-volunteer military was "unprecedented." Not since 1969, "when some 1,366 active-duty service members signed a full-page ad in the *New York Times* calling for an end to the Vietnam War," had there been such a dramatic expression of military dissent. The Appeal took anti-Iraq War sentiment that had been "simmering within the ranks" and surfaced it as "a mainstream plea backed by the enormous moral authority of active-duty personnel." It provided "a strong argument that the best way to support the troops" was to recognize their demand to be withdrawn from Iraq."[405] While the Pentagon was powerless to retaliate with official reprisals against those who signed the document, there were certainly subtler risks involved given that the military command exercises enormous power through individual reviews, promotions and assignments. This made the fact that almost 1,800 active duty, reserve, and guard personnel had signed the petition as of April 2007 all the more remarkable. To date, there has been no mention of the Appeal for Redress anywhere on YAF's website. On the contrary, YAF continues to beat the drum for military aggression throughout the Middle East.

While YAF provides visitors to its website with "military facts and talking points," it is certainly selective in what it offers as the example above illustrates. But even more disturbing is the overly romanticized image of the American military that the organization seeks to promulgate in its role as a purveyor of patriotically correct pedagogy. This is a military that advances "freedom" and "democracy"—no mention of imperialism, corporate interests, or torture here. Just a reminder that the military which has been the object of "scorn" and even "hatred" among dreaded leftists is largely misunderstood in part because "good people, have, at times, failed to articulate the role and the purpose" of the nation's armed services but mainly because those "opposed to America's success in advancing freedom, both at home and abroad, have successfully propagated distortions and misinformation about those who serve in the military and how our military operates."[406] In the YAF's alternative universe, there is no Abu Ghraib.

Students who help to organize military-themed events or YAF subsidized campus lectures by such leading lights as Karl Rove, John Ashcroft, David Horowitz,

Ann Coulter, and Mike Wilson, director of *Michael Moore Hates America*, or who recruit others to attend a YAF conference or join Gestapo groups exposing left-wing radicalism can earn points, much like travelers amass frequent flier points, through a program called Club 100. As participants accumulate credits, they are rewarded for their activism with books by authors like Horowitz and Coulter, conservative videos and YAF merchandise. For those eager beavers who tally "100 points each academic year," the reward is an invitation to an "all-expenses paid," "one-of-a-kind" event held each spring at the Reagan ranch retreat that "brings together the nation's leading conservative students with the Movement's top activists and tacticians for a unique weekend of training" and discussions. Bonus points are awarded to those who attend the Reagan Ranch High School Conference, the "only conference in the Conservative Movement designed specifically for high school students," while thirty points are granted to those who partake in YAF sponsored events at the yearly Conservative Political Action Conference (CPAC) which is briefly discussed below.[407]

YAF also supports a number of internships for promising conservative minds. These include summer stints through the Washington, D.C. based Sarah T. Hermann program where students assume responsibility for the planning and execution of the YAF's High School Leadership and National Conservative Student conferences. For their toil and trouble, interns receive a $1,000 monthly stipend and are given free tuition at both YAF summer conferences plus "loads of free books" by conservative writers. Santa Barbara, California based internships require students to help "lead tours of the Reagan ranch as well as host events" at the "historic Presidential site."[408]

In addition to sponsoring and financially subsidizing hundred of speakers a year through its campus lecture series (past speakers have included Coulter, Phyllis Schlafly, Christina Hoff Sommers, D'Souza, Horowitz, Oliver North, Pat and Bay Buchanan, Kenneth Star, and Michael Medved), the YAF also publishes a variety of materials that seek to advance conservative principles. Early books included *American Economics Texts: A Free Market Critique* (1982) and an examination of Christopher Columbus' impact on America entitled *Columbus on Trial* (1992). The foundation also supported the republishing of such classics as Goldwater's *The Conscience of a Conservative*, right-wing publishing guru Henry Regnery's *Memoirs of a Dissident Publisher*, and Burton Folsom's *The Myth of the Robber Barons*. The second edition of an activist text, *Conservative Guide to Campus Activism*, first published in the early 1990s, was re-released in updated form in 2005 and purportedly contained "breakthrough advice on the secrets of activism from leading tacticians of the Conservative Movement including Ann Coulter, David Horowitz, Michelle Malkin, Bay Buchanan and others."[409]

The *2009 Campus Conservative Battleplan* is a thematic, month-by-month guide jammed-packed with activism ideas from September to May—the typical academic year. Activities endorsed in the publication include the "9/11 Never Forget Project" that is intended to thwart the Left's attempts to appropriate the day to "promote its politically correct, multicultural agenda" and to challenge the Obama administration which is purportedly "attempting to sanitize the Anniversary by turning it into another day of 'national service.'"[410] October's roster of suggested events includes an "Advance Intellectual Diversity" day which is designed to "expose the Left's skewed version of diversity" and argue for more "ideological balance" on campuses. Students are encouraged to use "creative fliers" to highlight "left-wing hypocrisy" and work to reveal "professor's voter registration." For convenience sake, the battle plan showcases pictures of sample posters—one of which includes images of Joseph Stalin, University of California professor Angela Davis, and Karl Marx. November's schedule is chockfull of action plans to promote pro-American, pro-capitalist, and pro-military themes. These include a day to commemorate "how Reagan defeated Communism," events that would "challenge your school to teach freedom" as embodied in the writings of free market fundamentalists such as "Milton Friedman," and speeches by pro-military personalities such as Nixon-era thug Gordon G. Liddy whose photograph is prominently displayed in this section of the guide. It was, of course, Liddy (along with E. Howard Hunt) who masterminded the first break-in of the Democratic National Committee headquarters in the Watergate building in 1972. For his role in the burglary, Liddy was incarcerated for more than four years.

In the month of January, students are prodded to review their school's plans to celebrate Martin Luther King day and host a black conservative speaker through YAF who could "provide an alternative viewpoint" to those Black leftists who are routinely summoned to MLK campus celebrations and who use the day to denounce America as a "racist society." February would not be complete without an event to observe Ronald Reagan's birthday while activities for March include "Strong Women Shoot Back"—a "proactive alternative to the feminist program 'Take Back the Night'"—to help "educate and train young women to protect themselves with a firearm." Since March is often recognized as Women's History Month on some campuses, students are also pushed to hold a "Women's Studies Burqa Day Protest" in order to expose women's studies departments' failures to address atrocities towards women in the Middle East and presumably because such programs repeatedly "criticize Christianity" and imply that American women are oppressed. Since, "shockingly, neither Obama nor most women's studies departments seem concerned about the atrocious treatment of women in the Middle East," the protest provides an "opportunity to highlight the true liberal bias present in most women's studies departments." In keeping with the female theme, the guide also proposes "Empowered Conservative Women Week" for the month of March since contemporary "liberal feminists" refuse to recognize the advances made by "leaders" such as "Sarah Palin," "Ann Coulter" and "even Michelle Malkin." As part of a right-wing, week-long jamboree, campus organizers may choose to host a "conservative" woman who could provide "a fresh alternative." Suggested speakers include Coulter, Malkin, and Bay Buchanan. Finally, April calls for April's Liberal Fools Day to highlight the "ongoing hypocrisy practiced by prominent liberals" and "Save the Earth from Environmental Extremism" festivities which should aim to reveal how "environmental extremists use questionable and often inaccurate data to scare Americans into embracing their radical, socialist agenda" and how they repeatedly attempt to convince the government to increase "regulations infringing upon individual freedoms and the free market."

In addition to providing posters that read "I LOVE CAPITALISM" and pictures of the far right's favorite pin-up girl—former Vice-Presidential candidate Sarah Palin—the YAF also compiles the annual 'Dirty Dozen,' a listing of America's top twelve most politically correct college courses that are "supplanting traditional scholarship on Western civilization" and undermining the teaching of "American values, American civics, and American history."[411] And, it has sponsored contests such as the "Intellectual Morons" essay competition that asks students to bash their favorite liberal or leftist scholar. One past winner penned a diatribe against Noam Chomsky, perhaps the most astute critic of American foreign policy alive today.

The National Journalism Center (NJC) was founded by conservative potentate M. Stanton Evans in 1977 and became part of YAF in 2001. The Bradley and Olin-sponsored NJC, referred to as a "unique venture in journalism education," is purportedly devoted to "accuracy, balance, and comprehension of the issues." The program, held three times a year, has trained "scores of students" in the skills of press work and assigned them internships at "cooperating media locations" including ABC, CBS, NBC, CNN, MSNBC, Fox News, the *New York Tiimes*, *Time*, *Newsweek* and *Forbes*. According to the website Sourcewatch, these interns are basically told what to think about policy topics including Social Security, taxation, and environmental regulation in NJC seminars. Over 1,600 students have graduated from NJC's 12-week training session and an estimated 900 of them have gone on to media and media-related positions.[412] Prominent alumni include Ann Coulter, right-wing columnist John Fund of the *Wall Street Journal*, and Maggie Gallagher. Although NJC proclaims its commitment to accuracy, balance, comprehension of issues and rigorous training, like the LI and the CN, its true mission is to churn out journalist-wannabes who will then go on to toe the ideological line and promote conservative ideas in the public sphere. And apparently, NJC's graduates are not above accepting government bribery as the example of Gallagher clearly illustrates.

A graduate of the NJC, Gallagher went on to become a nationally syndicated columnist specializing in anti-feminist, homophobic, and pro-"family values" pontification. In addition to her column, Gallagher has also toiled at the "four sisters" funded Institute for American Values, and written for conservative publications including the *National Review Online*, Townhall.com, the *New York Post*, and *Human Events*. In 2005, it was reported that Gallagher, a prominent advocate for the amendment to ban gay marriage as well as funding for pro-marriage based health and social programs, had accepted a $21,500 contract from the U.S. Department of Health and Human Services to actively prop up President Bush's marriage promotion initiatives. The contract included briefing department officials, ghostwriting articles for them, and penning brochures touting Bush's agenda. Gallagher also received more federal funds—in the form of a $20,000 grant from the Justice Department—to write a report entitled "Can Government Strengthen Marriage?" While on the take, Gallagher regularly wrote, ostensibly as an "independent" journalist, in praise of the Bush administration and its various "pro-family" marriage proposals while castigating critics as nonsensical and anti-family. After she was found to be accepting money to produce what amounted to government propaganda, some newspapers dropped her column but Gallagher was mostly unrepentant and maintained that she had no obligation to reveal that she was on the federal payroll.[413] Thus are the ethical standards taught at the NJC.

The jewel in YAF's crown, however, is its annual National Conservative Student Conference which it has sponsored since 1979. The event, which continues to draw hundreds of young rightists each year, offers an "intensive week of informative seminars and training in campus activism." Conference goers pay a fee of $399.00 ($350.00 for early registrants) which covers tuition, meals, housing, and other materials. The YAF boasts that is able to offer such a "low cost because of the support of our generous supporters."[414] In other words, student attendees benefit from a form of right-wing, corporate-sponsored welfare. In 2006, the roster of distinguished speakers included Ed Feulner of the Heritage Foundation, T. Kenneth Cribb of the ISI, Morton Blackwell of the LI, David Horowitz (vast right-wing campus conspiracy, anyone?), Wayne LaPierre of the NRA, Newt Gingrich, and ABC television personality John Stossel whose deceptive reporting and on-air cheerleading on behalf of free market fundamentalism knows few bounds.[415]

The 2008 event highlighted speakers such as Bay Buchanan, sister of right-wing reactionary Pat Buchanan, LI's Morton Blackwell, neocon kingpin William Kristol, and Michelle Malkin otherwise known as the "Asian pitbull" poster girl of the radical right.[416] Like so many conservative media attack dogs, Malkin sharpened her political spitballing skills at a CN newspaper that was started years ago by her husband Jesse at Oberlin College. After graduating from the ranks of the CN, she began her punditry career at the *Los Angeles Daily News* in 1992, moved to the *Seattle Times*, and eventually became a syndicated columnist who has been routinely criticized for her "oft-unfounded and almost always sensationalist columns."[417] So common and egregious are Malkin's distortions that *Think Progress* maintains a running list of them that is regularly updated.[418] Well known as a fan of racial profiling, particularly in the post-9/11 era, Malkin offered a spirited albeit misinformed defense of the U.S. government's imprisonment of Japanese-Americans in WWII internment camps based on revisionist history in her 2004 book *In Defense of Internment: The Case for 'Racial Profiling' in WWII and the War on Terror*. Malkin also "distinguished" herself on an episode of MSNBC's *Hardball with Chris Matthews* during the 2004 presidential campaign when she suggested that one of John Kerry's Vietnam wounds was self-inflicted.[419] Such are the heroes of the YAF—an organization that claims to respect war veterans. Evidently, that respect only extends to those that share their ideology and who support imperialist military misadventures. In 2009, the annual conference featured right-wing fixture Ann Coulter who preached about why liberals are "wrong about everything." And Michelle Easton, a former official in both the Reagan and Bush Sr. administrations, and founder of the Clare Boothe Luce Policy Institute—another think tank funded by the Scaife, Olin and Bradley foundation—had the crowd cheering when she referred to Sarah Palin as a "gun-toting, moose-hunting, former beauty queen."[420]

Ostensibly, YAF claims to be a steadfast sponsor of "balance in education" and an advocate of the free exchange of ideas but its rhetoric does not necessarily match the reality of its practices. This was clearly revealed at its 2006 student conference. One Roger Custer opened the event with a melodramatic sermon proclaiming that it was a "shame" that the students in attendance had to be there in the first place. But he told the 400 or so conference attendees that their presence was necessary because the liberal campus monopoly left the YAF with no choice but to combat a Left which has "never been for open debate or discussion." The speech was, as Conor Clarke noted, a "paean to the marketplace of ideas—a marketplace that, by Custer's lights, needed to be wrested away from the odious Left and restored to glorious openness." But Clarke observed that it took less than four hours to expose such rhetoric for "what it actually was: bullshit."[421]

Clarke had arrived at the YAF's national student conference intending to cover the event as a reporter for *The Washington Monthly* and to engage conservative ideas for a research project on college organizing that he had already begun. Shortly after Custer's opening salvo, Clarke was confronted by Jason Mattera, YAF's spokesperson. Mattera demanded to know who Clarke was working for and after Clarke informed him of his association with *Washington Monthly*, a paranoid and petulant Mattera asked if Clarke was laboring for any other organization. When Clarke told him that he was also blogging for *Campus Progress*, a liberal student organization, Mattera was ready to escort him, or have one his interns lead him, to the nearest elevator.

Clarke was persistent in calling Mattera on his and the YAF's hypocrisy since Custer had earlier delivered a rousing address on the virtues of openness and exchange. When asked why he was being forcibly removed from an event that preached the free marketplace of ideas gospel, the self-absorbed Mattera responded, "because I said so." Not content with such an intellectually facile retort from a self-proclaimed guardian of "balance" and "openness," Clarke forged ahead asking Mattera if he would have been more welcome had he been a representative from a right-wing publication such as *National Review*. Matttera replied: "You know what? If you were with the *National Review*, I'd get you a seat right up front and have one of my interns give you a massage, and grab you a cup of Sunkist." Not only did Mattera apparently feel comfortable about potentially pimping out his interns for massages and fetching beverages, he evidently saw no contradiction between the lofty tributes to freedom espoused by his organization and his authoritarian behavior. Perhaps this should come as no surprise given Clarke's observations about Mattera as a person who is not an ideas guy but more like a teenager "who lords over his little brother," revels in "power for its own sake," and is "blissfully uninterested in arguments, and completely at ease with force."[422]

Clarke is apparently onto something—not only does Mattera come across as childish, but he also has a mean streak. While an editor at the *Hawk's Right Eye*, a monthly newsletter for college Republicans at Roger Williams University in Rhode Island, Mattera attacked Judy Shepard whose son Matthew was beaten to death in Wyoming merely because he was gay. Shepard had given a talk on campus about her son's ordeal and Mattera used the front page of the September 2003 issue to accuse her of "'preying on students' emotions and naivety [sic] so that she could become 'a mascot for the homosexual agenda.'"[423] The same issue also included an appalling description of the "homosexual rape of a young boy and threw in a joke about 'pedophiles nationwide' who 'condemned the FDA's food pyramid as bigoted and hateful because anus and penis were not listed as separate food groups.'"[424]

YAF also participates in and co-sponsors the Conservative Political Action Conference (CPAC), organized by the American Conservative Union, which meets annually in Washington, D.C. CPAC is a three-day event that brings together the leaders of the American right and their most ardent and rabid foot soldiers. Goldberg argues that the people who attend the event range from very conservative to proto-fascist.[425] Indeed, vendors at the gatherings sell everything from T-shirts sporting images of the World Trade Center aflame with accompanying captions that read "Clinton's Legacy." Bumper stickers proclaiming "No Muslims=No Terrorists," "Proud Member of the Right-Wing Conspiracy," and "End Global Whining," are also popular commodities. One company, Star-Spangled Ice Cream, the right's answer to Ben & Jerry's, distributed samples of "I Hate the French Vanilla" one year. Also available to the purchasing public have been various paraphernalia bearing a "Bring Back the Blacklist" motif.

Thousands flock to the yearly shindig—which, by some accounts, has increasingly become a cesspool for reactionary ideas—to hear the likes of Coulter spew her venom which is most often greeted by the uproarious laughter of the adoring masses. At the 2006 gala, she tarred the citizens of Iran as "ragheads" and warned about violence that would be done to them. She also called for Supreme Court Justices (at least those she considered "liberal") to be murdered. The audience applauded in delight. After Republican presidential hopeful Mitt Romney practically drooled while introducing her at the 2007 conference, Coulter launched into an attack on Democratic presidential candidate John Edwards and called him a "faggot." While her hateful, homophobic remarks surprisingly prompted something of a mild uproar among some discomfited rightists who subsequently urged CPAC organizers not to invite her to future gatherings, her brand of extremism is hardly foreign in such circles. In fact, even conservative writer Andrew Sullivan declared that Coulter "truly represents the heart and soul of contemporary conservative activism; especially among the young."[426] Nor is this type of fanaticism particularly new. In previous speeches delivered at the annual conference, Coulter has suggested that liberals, apparently hell-bent on destroying the country, are animals who support the Taliban and al-Qaeda and she has called for a return to McCarthyism. Although Coulter was not *officially* invited to CPAC in 2008 as a result of her comments about Edwards, she did in fact speak there at an invitation-only event co-sponsored by the YAF. And, she was back in 2009 lambasting liberals, leftists, and the Obama administration.

More ominously, however, was the CPAC launch of a "right-wing youth movement" called "Youth for Western Civilization" (YWC) which held its inaugural reception in February 2009 at the annual event. While CPAC organizers have, in past years, attempted to shield the "reputation" of its "mainstream conservative enterprise by forbidding racist organizations like the Council of Conservative Citizens from participating," the Southern Poverty Law Center (SPLC) has sounded alarm bells about YWC.[427] According to the YWC website, the organization "stands alone in challenging the dogmatic left-wing orthodoxy of American higher education." It is opposed to multiculturalism and affirmative action on college campuses and supports a return to the study of, and pride in, Western culture.[428] The group's logo resembles a fasces—a symbol that was prominent in Benito Mussolini's Fascist Party. YWC was founded by Kevin DeAnna, a graduate student at American University, who worked as a "field representative for LI in fall 2005" and who has worked "for the LI as an organizer for several years as Deputy Field Director for the CLP."[429] DeAnna has posted "several times in recent years to the Spartan Spectator, the website of the Michigan State University chapter of Young Americans for Freedom" which was identified in 2007 as a hate group by the SPLC

> after it organized a 'Catch an Illegal Alien Day' game, sponsored a 'Koran desecration contest,' jokingly threatened to distribute small-pox infected blankets to Native American students, posted 'Gays spread AIDS' fliers, called Latino students and faculty members 'savages,' and invited Nick Griffin, the chairman of the neofascist British National Party, to speak on the MSU campus.[430]

Since its coming out party at the CPAC convention, the YWC has established chapters on ten college campuses and in December 2009, its Vice-President, Devin Saucier, was awarded with a plaque for his contributions as a youth leader at a dinner honoring the legacy of none other than Paul Weyrich.

The YWC, CPAC and YAF all promote a rather brutish brand of reactionary politics rooted in an antediluvian nostalgia for the days when women (unless they are anti-feminist right-wingers) and minorities knew their place and gays were still hidden in the proverbial closet. And like the "Know-Nothings" of the mid-nineteenth century, whose call to arms was a defense of "real" Americans against the invasion of immigrants and riff-raff, CPAC's regularly featured orators and YAF's heroines—from the garish Coulter to the mean-spirited Malkin—rely on similar methods of demonizing and dehumanizing the "other(s)" and exploiting the "natural *fear of difference*," a strategy that Umberto Eco has equated with fascism.[431] And these are precisely the people that the right encourages its young culture warriors to emulate.

National Association of Scholars

The National Association of Scholars (NAS) purports to be an "organization of professors, graduate students, college administrators and trustees, and independent scholars committed to rational discourse as the foundation of academic life in a free and democratic society." Its aim is to "enrich the substance and strengthen the integrity of scholarship and teaching," and promote "an informed understanding of the Western intellectual heritage" which is, according to NAS, necessary to "sustain our civilization's achievements." Concomitantly, the NAS encourages academics who "value reason and an open intellectual life" to challenge perspectives in the "academy that reflexively denigrate the values and institutions of our society" because such tendencies are "often dogmatic in character and indifferent to both logic and evidence."[432] While this sounds quite lofty and dignified, there is, as they say, more to the story.

The origins of the NAS lie in the Campus Coalition for Democracy (CCD) which was founded in 1982 by a small cabal of conservatives including Midge Decter (wife of neo-con Norman Podhoretz and mother of the aforementioned John Podhoretz). The CCD's first president was Stephen Balch who still serves in that capacity at the NAS in addition to sitting on the board of ACTA. The head of the CCD was Herbert I. London, president of the rightist Hudson Institute and former John M. Olin Professor of Humanities at New York University (now professor emeritus at that institution). London, it should be noted, has also been a regular contributing writer for various Sun Myung Moon-owned publications including *The World and I* and the *New York City Tribune* and ran (unsuccessfully) as a Republican candidate for Mayor of New York City in 1989 and for New York State Comptroller in 1994.[433] One of CCD's first conferences featured speakers such as convicted Nicaraguan *contra* supporter Elliott Abrams, *contra* leader Arturo Cruz, and Michael Ledeen who was involved in the transfer of arms to Iran during the Iran-Contra affair. Ledeen, who held the Freedom Scholar chair at the AEI where he worked for more than twenty years, has been called the driving philosophical force behind the neoconservative movement and "the most influential and unabashed warmonger of our time."[434] A former Pentagon, State Department and White House consultant under Reagan, Ledeen was also a top advisor to Karl Rove on international affairs. Ledeen believes "that violence in the service of the spread of democracy is America's manifest destiny" and as such became "the philosophical legitimator of the American occupation of Iraq." In April 2003, just one month into the Iraq war, Ledeen called for regime change in Iran and still continues to advance that idea.[435]

The CCD's earliest conferences spawned a number of hysterical articles that were published in right-wing publications including *Society* and *Commentary*. For example, in the spring of 1986, *Society* featured a series of essays, introduced by Balch, lamenting the "politicization of scholarship" by a rogue band of Marxists and leftists. In October 1986, *Commentary* published a lengthy article by Balch and London entitled "The Tenured Left" which essentially claimed that a motley crew of Marxists, feminists, deconstructionists and other degenerates from the Sixties was well on its way to taking over the academy much to the detriment of Western civilization and American values. Balch and London called for nothing less than a reclamation of the academy by those committed to truth, civilization and "traditional" scholarship (read: pedagogy in the service of American corporate hegemony). Many of the arguments contained in these various articles received a boost with the publication of Allan Bloom's *The Closing of the American Mind* and together they formed the basis of the anti-political correctness campaign of the early 1990s.

By 1987, the CCD was rechristened as the NAS with London as its board chair and Balch as its president and with generous funding from the four sisters and the Coors family among others. Its flagship publication, *Academic Questions*, was also established that year as a vehicle to propagate its views. The first issue, published in the winter of 1987, was a call to arms for conservatives to take back the academy from the clutches of leftist barbarism. In the journal's opening salvo, London dramatically declared that:

Ideological orthodoxy has insinuated itself into the Academy ... The liberal arts disciplines themselves have been infected ... Subjectivity is the reigning deity ... The collaborative search for truth involving faculty members and students has retreated before manipulators shaping the past to serve the present. While the traditional vision of the university promoted the ideals of Western civilization through a broad-minded empiricism and a respect for the world's complexity, the new vision ... relies on dogmatism, conspiracies, relativism, and notions of society that challenge the pillars of liberty and constitutional democracy.[436]

London then went on to state that the purpose of the NAS and its journal was to re-store the "pursuit of truth" to its centrality in academic life and to defend traditional methods and scholarly standards against politicization and ideology. But such noble goals were, and are, unlikely given the NAS's highly partisan agenda, the corporate funding that underwrites it, and its board of directors which has included the aforementioned Donald Kagan, Christina Hoff Sommers, and Irving Kristol who once characterized multiculturalism as a "desperate strategy for coping with the educational deficiencies and associated social pathologies of young blacks."[437]

Far from promoting "rational" intellectual debate, virtually every issue of its journal and its quarterly newsletter targets the same academic fields and discourses—ethnic studies and multiculturalism, feminism and women's studies, environmental studies, Marxism, postmodernism, and deconstruction—through hyperbolic, un-informed and arguably un-scholarly diatribes. While a variety of themes are routinely castigated, the unifying master narrative of NAS's journal is a broad-based attack on the 1960s and leftist scholars. The assaults are generally two-pronged: both intellectual and political. Common to most of the articles is a belief that the radicalism of the 1960s has become ensconced in academia to such an extent that it now constitutes basic, unquestioned elements of campus culture. Also quite prevalent are articles which repeat the tired mantra of liberal bias on campuses and the dangers of the "anti-capitalist aspirations of the Left."[438]

Affirmative action initiatives have also been attacked in the past by such luminaries as Michael Levin, a philosophy professor, and former member of the NAS board of directors, who gained some notoriety in the early 1990s with his public announcements about the genetic inferiority of Blacks and his suggestion that Black students in New York should ride in separate, police-supervised subway cars. (Levin was asked to resign from the board after the controversy surfaced.)[439] NAS was also quite active in supporting the Michigan Civil Rights Initiative—an anti-affirmative action ballot initiative which was passed by Michigan voters in the November 2006 elections—that essentially banned the consideration of race and gender in university admissions.

Given its antipathy toward affirmative action, it is rather peculiar that this 3,500 member-strong organization, with affiliates in forty-six states, has been among the major proponents of the "intellectual diversity" movement which essentially argues in favor of affirmative action for conservative academics. In November 2005, Balch testified in Pennsylvania before the House Select Committee on Academic Freedom and argued that because some faculty members at state-funded universities in Pennsylvania identified with particular political groups (namely the Democratic Party) it was incumbent upon state legislatures to ensure that they did not engage in "advocacy." Advocacy, Balch explained, consisted of any effort to speak or write in support of, and/or to be in favor of, something. (One could probably ask Balch if the NAS campaign in favor of the aforementioned Michigan Civil Rights Initiative constituted a form of advocacy!) Berube aptly noted, the evidentiary standard invoked by Balch was quite telling in that the "preponderance of registered Democrats among the faculty, in and of itself," was taken as grounds for state action.[440]

In his testimony, Balch, who received a National Humanities Medal from George W. Bush in 2007, referred to two studies to bolster his claim about the over-representation of liberals and Democrats on campuses. But as with previously discussed studies, the "findings" of these two reports were also dubious. The first, entitled "Politics and Professional Advancement among College Faculty" was conducted by Stanley Rothman, Robert Lichter and Neil Nevitte. Both Rothman and Lichter are affiliated with organizations funded by Scaife and Olin while this particular research project was sponsored by the Randolph Foundation, another private philanthropy that funds several rightist groups including the aforementioned Independent Women's Forum and Horowitz's Freedom Center. The purpose of the project was to examine the ideological composition of American university faculty in order to determine whether ideological homogeneity had become self-reinforcing. The researchers analyzed a 1999 survey of professors called the North American Academic Study Survey (NAASS) and then compared its results with a 1984 survey of professors by the Carnegie Foundation for the Advancement of Teaching. Based on this comparative analysis, Rothman and his colleagues concluded that the proportion of self-identified liberal professors jumped from 39 percent to 72 percent in the fifteen year span which separated the 1984 and 1999 surveys.

However, the conclusion was very misleading given the fact that the two surveys examined "such dissimilar samples" that one could not "draw valid conclusions about a trend."[441] For example, the NAASS sample included 1,643 faculty members from 183 universities and colleges and the responses were derived from 81 doctoral, 59 comprehensive and 43 liberal arts institutions. The 1984 Carnegie study, on the other hand, contained data obtained from over 5,000 faculty members employed at a variety of institutions including two-year community colleges. Gravois notes that the exclusion of two-year institutions likely skewed the results since, historically, community-college professors are a "relatively conservative bunch."[442] Furthermore, a report from *Media Matters for America* also noted that with respect to the question of ideological orientation, the study's comparison of the 1984 and 1999 surveys violated "a fundamental principle of survey research" for "decades of research" has shown that "altering questions in even subtle ways can produce dramatically different results." Rothman, Lichter, and Nevitte based their conclusion that "a sharp shift to the left" had "taken place among college faculty" on "questions asked in two entirely different ways in the two studies;" one which asked respondents to place themselves "on a ten-point scale," and another that asked them "to select from a list of descriptions."[443]

The second study cited by Balch, "How Politically Diverse Are the Social Sciences and Humanities?" was conducted by Daniel Klein and Charlotta Stern and was "trumpeted by many conservatives as a corrective to the hit-and-miss efforts of previous inquiries by going directly to the source." In order to "improve" upon previous slapdash studies, the researchers sent out 5,486 surveys to professors in six disciplines and set out to tabulate their political orientation based on the respondent's answers to questions about their voting histories and their views on several policy issues. The response was less than overwhelming for as Jacoby argues, "a whopping 70 percent of the recipients did what any normal person would do when receiving an unsolicited fourteen-page survey over the signature of an assistant dean at a small California business school: They tossed it."[444] What's more, after making some additional exclusions, the researchers were left with just 17 percent of their initial pool of potential respondents. And what they found was hardly astounding— more professors in the social sciences voted Democratic than Republican. But beyond that less than shocking revelation, John Lee noted that, in effect, the extremely low response rate to the survey diminished the "usefulness of the findings."[445]

Despite the problematical nature of the studies, Balch contended that the state of Pennsylvania should pursue "intellectual diversity" in hiring in order to remedy the "under-representation of philosophical minorities."[446] Such a move would, of course, likely increase the number of conservative scholars on campuses which is precisely what the NAS would like to see. Balch further added that failure to comply with this policy of right-wing affirmative action should be grounds for withholding funding and governmental intervention in university governance:

> The legislature must expect a full accounting of progress made toward these goals each time the state's universities seek new statutory authority and renewed financial support. If a good-faith effort is being made to overcome these problems, it should leave the remedial specifics to the universities' own decision making. If a good-faith effort isn't made, it should urge governing boards to seek new leadership as a condition of full support. Failing even in that, it might, as a last resort, consider a full-scale organizational overhaul, to design governance systems and institutional arrangements better able to meet the obligations that go with academic freedom.[447]

In his presentation, Balch drew explicitly on the history of affirmative action and employment discrimination law to make his case even though he unequivocally stated that he and his organization were opposed to hiring practices based on racial and gender considerations.

There are a few points worth raising here. Claims such as those made by far-right attorneys like Kenneth Lee, a member of the Federalist Society, who has argued that contemporary civil rights law applies equally to "conservative Republicans" who are discriminated against in American academia (even though no studies have proven that assertion) in ways that are "even starker than previous blackballings by race," are, at the very least, offensive. Affirmative action and other such anti-discrimination initiatives were instituted to ameliorate centuries of oppression and the inability of historically maligned constituencies—such as African-Americans—to have access to education and employment opportunities that had been denied to them. Moreover, such declarations become all the more odious if one reviews the lengthy history of conservative opposition to affirmative action programs in American higher education.[448] But more than this, conservative under-representation at universities is hardly comparable to the forms of institutional repression and racism previously experienced by blacks and other minorities and/or the gender discrimination which had been operative for years. It is also the case, as has been noted by the American Association of University Professors, that most universities have guidelines in place to safeguard against any sort of discrimination, including that of a political nature. Regardless of what Balch and his NAS comrades argue, in using political ideology alone as a criteria in hiring practices race and gender would inadvertently come in through the proverbial back door. After all, it is common knowledge that most conservatives are white males.

Furthermore, the whole issue of "balance," the conservative buzzword used to push the intellectual diversity agenda, must be critically interrogated. Balance, as Fish maintains, is "not a real value;" rather it "is a strategy" that is "political in nature." That is, "balance is not the answer to an intellectual question; it is the attempt to evade or blunt an intellectual question." Contrary to the NAS's stated opposition to the "politicization" of campuses and curricula and Balch's own self-proclaimed dedication to the "search for truth," he is advocating for just that—politicization. On this matter, Fish's observations deserve reproducing here. He argues that one resorts to the rhetoric of "balance"

> not in response to the imperative of determining truth, but in response to pressures that originate more often than not from nonacademic constituencies. This is surely the case with respect to the demand that a college or university faculty should display balance, in its hiring practices or in its tenure decisions or in its course offerings or in the materials assigned by individual instructors. In none of those instances is balance a legitimate educational goal. Take the insistence that faculties be balanced so that there is a proportionate number of conservatives and liberals. That is the least defensible form of balance—called "intellectual diversity" by its proponents, but is really affirmative action for conservatives—because it assumes a relationship and even an exact correlation between one's performance in the ballot box and one's performance in the classroom. There is no such correlation: The politics relevant to academic matters are the politics of academic disciplines, and the fault line of those politics—disputes between quantitative and qualitative social scientists, for example—do not track the fault lines of the national divide between Republicans and Democrats. Thus it is not a coherent argument to say that students will benefit from having conservative as well as liberal professors; for with respect to the different approaches to a topic or a subject, party affiliation is not a predictor of which approach a professor will favor ... The only thing you would get were you to enforce a political balance of persons hired or promoted would be a politicized university.[449]

It should also be noted that calls for government intervention—which is generally eschewed by conservatives—in university affairs is not really about enhancing academic freedom; rather such attempts are aimed to "discredit the university as an independent institution."[450] Writing on the problems associated with the concept of "balance," with respect to the intellectual diversity campaign, Willis makes her observations in a much more pointed fashion than does Fish. She too is worth quoting at considerable length:

> "Balance" is a pernicious concept, implying as it does both that all ideas are equally valid and that they can be unproblematically defined in academe as liberal or conservative—especially by outside observers who have only passing knowledge of what is being said or taught. Some conservatives have expressed outrage that the views of professors are at odds with the views of students, as if ideas were entitled to be represented in proportion to their popularity and students were entitled to professors who share their political or social values. One of the more important functions of college—that it exposes young people to ideas and arguments they have not encountered at home—is redefined as a problem. To a radical right that feels entitled to dominate not only government but all social institutions, the academy is a particular irritant … the academy is inherently a liberal institution, in the sense that it is grounded in the credo of the Enlightenment: the free pursuit and dissemination of knowledge for its own sake. But the right's charge that the professoriate is dominated by liberals requires some, pardon the expression, deconstruction. For the right, "liberal" has become an epithet—roughly equivalent to the "Godless Communist" of an earlier era—that applies to anyone who is not a conservative Republican or a Christian fundamentalist. Most people who are attracted to academic life fit that definition for fairly obvious reasons: We prefer reading, writing, and research to business; care more about job security than the chance to get rich; and are comfortable with (secular) Enlightenment values. The balance-mongers make much of polls purporting to reveal that more professors vote Democratic, but that says less about the liberalism of professors than about the fact that what used to be the right-wing lunatic fringe is now the Republican mainstream. As a practical matter—no matter how much proponents of balance protest that they are merely trying to raise awareness of this issue—redressing the "underrepresentation" of the far right in academe requires coercion: the intimidation of offending liberal professors by students or infiltrators who monitor their classes, and pressure on legislative officials, donors, and trustees to influence faculty hiring decisions and the curriculum.[451]

Two of the major organizations which have employed McCarthy-esque tactics to intimidate liberal and left academics and which have encouraged politicians to intervene in affairs of the academy are David Horowitz's Freedom Center and the American Council of Trustees and Alumni. They are the subject of chapter three.

CAMPUS CONS AND THE NEW MCCARTHYISM

DAVID HOROWITZ'S LONG CRUSADE

At the 2005 College Republican National Convention, David Horowitz, arguably one of the most notorious and caustic pugilists of the culture wars, brought down the proverbial house by asserting that: "Universities are a base of the left. Universities are a base for terrorism." He also informed his obsequious audience that the "future of the free peoples of the world" depended on the "Republican Party" and ultimately on the youthful army of right-wingers in attendance.[452] Such bombast was hardly new terrain for Horowitz who, in late October of 2001, spent three hours speaking to the deleterious Dr. Laura Schlessinger about "campus leftists" who "hate America more than terrorists; this from a man who claims to yearn for 'serious' dialogue.[453]

Of course, long before 9/11, Horowitz had already amassed an impressive fortune (with generous funding from the Scaife, Bradley, Olin, Smith-Richardson/Randolph and other foundations) maligning liberals and leftists who allegedly controlled the media, the entertainment industry, and the levers of power at the nation's institutions of higher learning. At the age of 71, he now controls a sizable empire under the rubric of the David Horowitz Freedom Center (formerly known as the Center for the Study of Popular Culture) dedicated to advancing a far right agenda. Before exploring his corporate-funded kingdom and a few of its various projects and campaigns, it is worth briefly chronicling Horowitz's transformation from a militant leftist to an authoritarian firebrand and Republican strategist.

Horowitz was born in 1939 to a Jewish family in Forest Hills, New York. His parents, Phil and Blanche Horowitz were schoolteachers in Sunnyside Gardens, Queens and they taught (what was then termed) "Negro history" in their spare time. Horowitz recollects growing up in a household filled with prints by William Gropper—the American social realist painter who produced some of the most riveting portraits of social protest and labor unrest and who was actively involved in supporting the organized labor movement throughout his career—and old issues of the Communist Party newspaper *Daily Worker*.[454] In 1952, his father came under intense scrutiny because of his political views and after refusing to answer the question of whether he was a Communist, he was dismissed for "insubordination" despite having served in the school system for twenty-eight years. As a result, his relations with the party became strained and he eventually quit. Nonetheless, the senior Horowitz remained "a fellow traveler, and David grew up in a milieu of red summer camps, Paul Robeson concerts and May Day parades."[455]

After he graduated from Columbia University, Horowitz went to the University of California at Berkeley to begin work on a Master's degree. His arrival there coincided with protests in San Francisco that had been organized to contest the egregious activities of the House Un-American Committee (HUAC). Police used excessive and brutal force to quell the demonstrators and the scenes of such violence were recounted by Horowitz in his 1962 publication entitled *Student: The Political Activities of the Berkeley Students*—one of the first texts of the New Left. That same year, Horowitz moved his young family to Europe, where they would spend six years—most of it in London. In addition to becoming affiliated with the Bertrand Russell Peace Foundation, Horowitz was also greatly influenced by socialist scholar Ralph Miliband and Trotsky biographer Isaac Deutscher. His work during this period consisted of various efforts aimed at reconstructing socialist theory in the aftermath of Stalinist atrocities.

In 1968, Robert Scheer (journalist, professor, and now editor of the online magazine Truthdig) contacted Horowitz about a possible return to California to work at *Ramparts*, which under the editorial leadership of Scheer and Warren Hinckle, had become one of the most vibrant and widely-circulated publications of the New Left. Horowitz obliged his old Berkeley comrade and joined the magazine. Sherman notes, however, that Scheer and Horowitz's camaraderie quickly dissipated. As a result of internecine tensions, Scheer was expelled because he wasn't "left enough for the fiery insurgents."[456] By 1974, Horowitz found himself keeping company with the Bay Area Black Panthers, particularly Huey Newton who Horowitz once referred to as a "political soul mate." Horowitz became Newton's confidant, wrote essays for the Panther's official newspaper publication, and even created a tax-exempt foundation that raised more than $100,000 for the Panther's cause.

In July 1974, Newton was accused of murdering a 17-year-old prostitute, Kathleen Smith. Newton fled to Cuba, failed to make his court appearance, and was consequently placed on the FBI's most-wanted list. After three years in exile, he returned to the United States and was tried twice—based largely on circumstantial evidence— for the offense before being acquitted after both court cases ended in deadlock. The events surrounding Newton's 1974 flight precipitated the departure of many black activists from the party but Horowitz remained. A short time later, Elaine Brown, Newton's successor, asked Horowitz to recommend someone to manage the Panther's finances and he, in turn, suggested Betty Van Patter, a 42-year-old white woman who had been employed at *Ramparts*. Van Patter accepted the position but soon uncovered what appeared to be troubling activities including racketeering, drug operations, and prostitution at a Panther-run bar in Oakland. She apparently reported these practices to Brown who then fired her. On December 13, 1974, Van Patter vanished; her body was found a month later, with a massive head wound, in the San Francisco Bay. Brown denied any Panther involvement in Van Patter's death and, officially, the case remains unsolved. Horowitz, nonetheless, was convinced that the Panthers had somehow been involved. Traumatized and surrounded by "personal darkness," he became clinically depressed. His downward spiral eventually contributed to the collapse of his first marriage after he had a series of extramarital affairs.[457] According to most accounts of Horowitz's life history, this context catalyzed his conversion to the right.

In the early 1980s, Horowitz started hosting "second thoughts" conferences that were essentially revival-like forums where former radicals could purge themselves of leftist ideology, repudiate their pasts, and openly embrace the conservative light. By 1984, he had grown so disillusioned with many of his erstwhile radical compatriots that he cast a vote for Reagan; a fact he later revealed in a highly controversial 1985 *Washington Post* article co-written with fellow turncoat Peter Collier titled "Lefties for Reagan." In 1987, Horowitz made a trip to Managua, Nicaragua, at the request of the State Department, and offered tactical advice to right-wing politicians and journalists on how to defeat the left-wing Sadinista government, which was, at the time, under the murderous assault of the U.S.-backed contra army. Shortly thereafter, Collier and Horowitz documented their ideological trans-formation in *Destructive Generation: Second Thoughts about the Sixties*—essentially an indignant screed against the 1960s that was funded by the Bradley and Olin foundations.[458] The book, beloved by Karl Rove, was one of three that he recomm-ended to George W. Bush in 1993 as Turdblossom began grooming him for his quest for the White House.[459]

In 1988, Horowitz began the Center for the Study of Popular Culture (CSPC), with start-up grants from the Scaife, Olin and Bradley foundations, to "establish a conservative presence in Hollywood and show how popular culture had become a political battleground."[460] An excerpt from the CSPC's original mission state-ment explained that its goal was to "change the leftist, anti-American, elitist culture" that was "dominant in the entertainment industry [and to expose] the idiocies and the viciousness of the radical leftism in universities, the media, main-stream churches, and everywhere else" that the "modern plague" could be found.[461] Throughout the 1990s, he and his fellow culture warriors expended considerable energy battling against the forces of 'political correctness,' affirmative action, and multiculturalism. One of his weapons in that crusade was the tabloid-sized and now-defunct *Heterodoxy*, a monthly publication he had started in 1992 with Collier at about the same time of "the occupation of Washington by the Clintons" which presumably paralleled the "rise to power" of tenured radicals in the universities. According to Collier, the magazine set out, in the famous formula of A.J. Leibling, to "comfort the oppressed" (who in Horowitz and Collier's irrational calculations consisted of downtrodden white conservatives) and "oppress the comfortable."[462]

With the "radical guerillas" of the 1960s ensconced in the ivied towers of academe and dreaded "liberals" running the government, something had to be done.[463] The barbarians had to be put in their place. So for eight years, *Heterodoxy*, which Collier once described as "the cultural equivalent of a drive-by shooting," attacked the "world of PC relentlessly," fingered "its villains" and forced them to do "the perp walk," "named names," "ridiculed the fatuous," and conducted an "intellectual CT-scan on the malignancy that was spreading throughout high culture." When Bill and Hillary left power a "plague" had presumably been lifted. This led Horowitz and Collier to conclude that their "little combat journal" was no longer necessary since a "new generation of culture warriors had wised up" to the scam of liberalism. In other words, mission accomplished. In a symbolic gesture, the magazine ceased publication in 2000 when George W. Bush—that guiding light of honor and integrity—was elected to office.[464] The end of *Heterodoxy* certainly did not spell the end of Horowitz's crusades. If anything, his campaigns of intimidation grew exponentially post-9/11 as we shall see.

In 1998, Horowitz's antics commanded national attention when he helped Michael Savage, the far-right talk show host well known for his inflammatory rhetoric, launch a completely frivolous lawsuit (something which is usually derided among conservatives) against the University of California at Berkeley. Savage, who has a Ph.D. in epidemiology and nutrition science (hardly journalism-related), and who had (at the time) only two years of experience in radio, applied to be the Dean of Berkeley's School of Journalism and was apparently outraged by the fact that he was not granted an interview. Of the numerous conservative voices that have come to dominate the airwaves with churlish rhetoric and ad hominem attacks, Savage is arguably the worst of the bunch. Far from a bona fide journalist, Savage's modus operandi is a malicious blend of narrow mindedness, bigotry, and outrageous and hate-filled remarks. He has repeatedly referred to Third World countries as "turd world nations," has said that the United States is "being taken over by the freaks, the cripples, the perverts and the mental defectives," once referred to former MSNBC reporter Ashleigh Banfield as a "mind slut with a big pair of glasses," called Supreme Court Justice Ruth Bader Ginsburg a "radical left-wing buck-toothed hag," suggested that women "should have been denied the right to vote," claimed that Hispanics "breed like rabbits," and that a "gay and lesbian mafia" wanted to corrupt the nation's children. After a short-lived run on MSNBC television, Savage was fired for telling a caller to "get AIDS and die." After 9/11, he openly called for the reinstatement of the 1918 Sedition Act to deal with anti-war protesters. And, in 2004 even suggested that former presidential candidate John Kerry be "shackled and arrested" for committing sedition after Kerry told a crowd gathered for a campaign speech that Bush was poised to increase the number of National Guard troops (which Bush did) sent into battle (in Iraq) after the 2004 election. Apparently, this amounted to Kerry sharing strategy with Osama Bin Laden. One might conclude that Berkeley made the right decision.[465]

In 1999, Horowitz added race-baiting to his sordid resume with the publication of his book *Hating Whitey and Other Progressive Causes*—a series of previously circulated polemical essays on race, affirmative action, and the left. In this incendiary tract, Horowitz essentially issued ideological fatwas against a number of prominent black leaders and intellectuals including Nobel Prize winner Toni Morrison, Cornel West, Charlie Rangel, and law professor Derrick Bell whom he described (with typical red-scare fervor) as a product of the Communist left. He alleged that anti-white racism was pervasive on the left and within the Black community and the pages brimmed with charges of "black racism" and "reverse discrimination."[466] The text was also replete with outrageous and unsubstantiated claims about black crime and sought to whip up a frenzy about "a multitude of black rapists."[467] In the same year, Horowitz undertook one of his first campus-wide advertising campaigns which consisted of full-page ads headlined "Ten Reasons Why Reparations for Slavery is a Bad Idea" aimed at thwarting what was then becoming a hot-button issue—reparations for African Americans. According to *Time* columnist Jack White, Horowitz's assorted activities and his writings on race make "the anti-black rantings of Dinesh D'Souza seem like models of fair-minded social analysis" in comparison.[468]

Horowitz's racial bigotry is scarcely shocking for his website FrontpageMag.com often includes articles that "flirt dangerously with racism or even praise it outright." One such example was a piece penned by John J. Ray which praised a "very scholarly" book on IQ by Christopher Brand, a devotee of eugenics who believes that blacks are intellectually inferior to whites.[469] Horowitz has also extolled the virtues of Jared Taylor of the Council of Conservative Citizens (CCC), an organization founded in the mid-1990s as an outgrowth of the Citizens Councils of America that were established in the mid-1950s as part of the white segregationist response to federally mandated integration of public facilities. The CCC is closely associated with the American Nationalist Union, a white supremacist organization, and Jared Taylor has been called the "cultivated, cosmopolitan face of white supremacy" by Mark Potok, editor of the Southern Poverty Law Center's magazine *Intelligence Report*.[470]

Horowitz also became a favorite among Republicans as a tactician of party politics. His pamphlet *The Art of Political War*, was published in 1998 after a visit to Austin, Texas, at the invitation of Rove, to discuss strategy and how best to craft the message for a George W. Bush presidential run. In the pamphlet, Horowitz claimed that the Republican Party was suffering from dwindling support because it had failed to engage in politics like war. He then went on to define political war as the "act of purposely misleading the public into believing something other than the truth in order to gain political advancement." And, he encouraged Republicans to make "false statements and gain support unethically if need be."[471] Rove later described the tract as the "perfect guide" to winning on the political battlefield. The Heritage Foundation made sure to distribute 2,300 copies of it to conservative activists prior to the 2000 election and Tom DeLay provided copies to every Republican Congressional officeholder with a cover letter lauding its contents.

Among other things, the booklet channels Lenin's counsel as Horowitz contends that "You cannot cripple an opponent by outwitting him in a political debate ... You can do it only by following Lenin's injunction: 'In political conflicts, the goal is not to refute your opponent's argument, but to wipe him from the face of the earth.'"[472] He also suggests that in political warfare it is the aggressor who usually prevails, that it is imperative to define the issues as well as one's adversaries, that exploiting fear is a form of political art, and that images—symbols and soundbites— are preferable to real arguments and/or proper analyses. In short, Horowitz pro- mulgates a political endgame in which bullying and coercion take precedence over any notions of truth, rational debate and fair play.

Such thuggish tactics were clearly on display during the 2000 election debacle and Horowitz was a ringleader of what Paul Gigot celebrated as a "bourgeois riot." At some point in the Miami circus, a poster to his website sought Horowitz's advice on the Florida recount. In response to a question about what strategy Republicans should employ, Horowitz provided the following nuggets of wisdom:

> This is my answer, courtesy of Al Capone: 'If he comes at you with a fist, you come at him with a bat. If he comes at you with a bat, you come at him with a knife. If he comes at you with a knife, you come at him with a gun.[473]

Horowitz also issued "war room briefings" to Republican operatives on the scene who then intimidated Florida election officials into calling off the recount. Such is the gangster modus operandi favored by Horowitz, whom Jeb Bush once called a "fighter for freedom."[474]

After 9/11, Horowitz took up the task of demonizing any dissent or criticism of the Bush White House. Shortly after the attacks, he berated California Congresswoman Barbara Lee for having the audacity to vote against giving the President a blank check to wage his war on terror. In a September 19, 2001 column, ominously titled "The Enemy Within," Horowitz branded Lee an "anti-American communist" who "supports America's enemies and has actively collaborated with them in their war against America."[475] A week later Horowitz produced another hysterical rant— this time on Salon.com—in which he characterized Noam Chomsky, one of the world's most renowned intellectuals, as a "pathological ayatollah of anti-American hate" and virtually blamed the distinguished M.I.T. professor for the September 11 attacks.[476] Horowitz's organization went so far as to distribute brochures on college campuses emblazoned with the caption "The Ayatollah of Anti-American Hate" that featured a picture of Chomsky with a turban and a beard. While Horowitz's obsession with Chomsky has often bordered on the pathological, he set his sights much more broadly in the post-9/11 milieu.

Beginning in 2001, he embarked on a nation-wide campus witch-hunt accusing apostates who questioned the wisdom of the Bush administration's policies of hating America. While the rubble was still smoldering at Ground Zero, Horowitz used his website to seek support for his "National Campaign to Take Back our Campuses" which would battle the "left's conversion of universities into little more than huge megaphones for anti-American rhetoric."[477] Horowitz utilized a super-patriotic theme—his adversaries were anti-American—that basically constituted a "recycled denunciation" that worked "wonders during the McCarthy period."[478] For Horowitz, it seems, there was little difference between wresting control of universities from the clutches of liberals and leftists and "smoking Al-Qaeda henchmen out of their hillside caves."[479] And, it appears as though assuming the mantle of Joe McCarthy has its financial awards. Horowitz's annual salary exceeds $300,000 and he receives approximately $5,000 for each of the thirty to forty speeches he gives per year.

As noted above, Horowitz's cavalcade of conservative crusades has a lengthy history but, like so many others of his ilk, he sought to gratuitously exploit 9/11 to further a political agenda. The advent of the permanent global war on terror afforded him an opportunity to advance his war against independent, critical thought and the last bastion purportedly controlled by radicals, the academy. This was made clear by none other than Rush Limbaugh. Prashad notes that

in November 2004, the rightwing popular radio host Rush Limbaugh discussed the Horowitz agenda on his nationally syndicated radio programme. The Right had taken care of the 'liberal bias' in the media, he announced, and the new war will be on the academy. The 'culture war' in the 1980s over multi-culturalism had simply gone into abeyance, and it would reopen once more against liberalism and anti-Americanism. For the Right, 9/11 has provided an opportunity to settle all kinds of scores, to quickly tackle the fledgling Left in all its redoubts.[480]

Just as Condoleeza Rice instructed her senior staff at the National Security Council to think seriously about how the U.S. could capitalize on the *opportunities* 9/11 presented to fundamentally change American doctrine and the shape of the world in the wake of the terrorist attacks, provocateurs like Horowitz saw 9/11 as a pretext to reinvigorate the culture wars under the rubric of the "war on terror."

In 2006, the CSPC's board of directors decided to change the name of the organization to the David Horowitz Freedom Center (DHFC). According to Board Chairman Jess Morgan, this decision was based on two primary reasons:

First, when the Center began, just as the Cold War was ending, we thought that the significant issue of our time would be the political radicalization of popular culture. The culture is still a battleground, but after 9/11, it is clear that freedom itself is under assault from the new totalitarianism: Islamic fascism. Secondly, David Horowitz, the Center's founder, has become increasingly identified with issues of freedom at home and abroad. We wanted to honor him and also support the efforts he has undertaken. The name change does this and rededicates us to the mission at hand.[481]

According to the DHFC's 2006 year-end report, authored by Horowitz, the organization is devoted to "defending the freedoms of all Americans and the values and institutions that make them possible." It is a self-described "battle-tank" rather than a "think-tank" whose vanguard mission is to "push the envelope" and "chart the way" for radical conservatism. In his report, Horowitz documents the successes of the Center in "reshaping the battlefield of ideas and institutions" and credits the organization for moving public discourse to the right on a number of related issues. For example, Horowitz claims that he and his foot soldiers are "responsible for the growing willingness of conservatives to identify radicals as 'leftists' and not 'liberals'" thereby invoking the ghosts of McCarthy and anti-communism.

The DHFC is also responsible for introducing a number of new phrases into the daily lexicon, including references to the "fifth column" and the "hate American left" which Horowitz joyfully reported had made their way into the vocabularies of such "mass market conservatives as Bill O'Reilly, Sean Hannity and Tom DeLay." Horowitz and company have also "dared to challenge the educational establishment" by identifying as "political indoctrination" the "curricula of radicalism that tenured leftists are imposing on our students" and by naming as "'dangerous' those professors who use the classroom to propagandize for America's enemies in a time of war." To combat the scourge of academic radicalism, the DHFC has "made the intellectual diversity of our country's universities a national issue" and has sought to "restore the study of Western civilization … to the curricula of higher education."[482]

The report went on to boast about his network's outreach. Among its accomplishments: a combined 32 millions visits to his empire's various websites; an audience that numbered in the tens of millions as a result of the Center's personnel making more than 600 radio and television appearances; press coverage of the Center and its causes in more than 3,000 news stories and articles; distribution and sales of more than 800,000 pamphlets and books; sponsorship of various events which featured such leading right-wing lights as Rush Limbaugh, Ann Coulter, Sean Hannity, former Attorney General John Ashcroft, Newt Gingrich, Dennis Prager, William Kristol, and Jim Gilchrist, the anti-immigration leader of the Minutemen. Additionally, the board of Horowitz's center was, at the time, brimming with well-known conservatives and Republican operatives including David Keene, the chairman of the American Conservative Union—the nation's oldest and largest grassroots lobbying organization, Wayne LaPierre Jr., of the National Rifle Association, and John O'Neill who was a spokesman for the Swift Boat Veterans for Truth.[483]

The DHFC eventually modified its mission statement and now claims that its main purpose is the "defense of free societies." More specifically, the DHFC is committed to combating the efforts of "the radical left and its Islamist allies to destroy American values and disarm" the country as it "attempts to defend itself in a time of terror." Since the "leftist offensive is most obvious" on the "nation's campuses," the "Freedom Center protects students from indoctrination and political harassment."[484]

With a budget of almost $6 million, the DHFC is able to sponsor a number of "ongoing programs" and "campaigns" including Frontpage Magazine (a publication that is so radically right that it embraced Ann Coulter and published her columns after she was fired by *National Review* for making outrageous racist comments about Muslims in 2001), the Wednesday Morning Club, the Individual Rights Foundation, Restoration Weekend, Jihadwatch, the Terrorism Awareness Program, Discover the Networks and, of course, Students for Academic Freedom. For purposes here, I will focus mainly on the latter entity.

Horowista Brownshirts or, Students for Academic Freedom[485]

Horowitz established the disingenuously named Students for Academic Freedom (SAF) in 2003 with the slogan "You can't get a good education if they're only telling you half the story." While it appears as though SAF has lost some proverbial steam since its inception, it played a central role in ginning up hysteria about so-called anti-American academics in the aftermath of 9/11. At the time of its establishment, Horowitz claimed that an organization like SAF was necessary based on the results of two studies of college and university professors' political party affiliations that had "demonstrated" that faculty members were overwhelmingly liberal. Not surprisingly, none other than Horowitz's own CPSC had conducted the "studies."

According to its website, the SAF is a "clearinghouse and communications center for a national coalition of student organizations whose goal is to end the political abuse of the university and to restore integrity to the academic mission as a disinterested pursuit of knowledge." Although it claims to be a "grassroots" social movement advocating students' rights, the SAF is anything but. It is, rather, merely another political franchise of Horowitz's empire that is made possible by the monies that flow from foundation coffers.

Despite its moniker, in its heyday, the SAF was run by three people—none of whom were students—and the major player was Sara Dogan (formerly Sara Russo) who still serves as the organization's national campus director. Before assuming her role at SAF in 2003, Dogan worked for Accuracy in Academia (AIA), an organization that "planted paid informants in the classrooms during the 1980s" in order to identify and intimidate liberal and left-leaning professors.[486] A Washington, D.C.-based right-wing research group, AIA documents and publicizes political "bias" (liberal and left, of course) in education via its monthly newsletter *Campus Report*.[487] Dogan, a Yale graduate, is widely known as an archconservative; a photograph of her in the *Yale Daily News* showed her brandishing a sign that said "Al Gore is the Unabomber." A virulent anti-abortionist, she once maintained a blog "Russo's Republic" wherein she opined on a variety of issues including a woman's right to choose which she, of course, opposes.[488]

These days, Dogan busies herself with overseeing the 150 student chapters of the SAF and running the group's central website. For a while, she also served as Horowitz's mouthpiece, often penning stinging rebukes of those she believed had misrepresented her boss' views and campaigns. For a period of time, SAF's national field director (who, with Dogan, helped students start campus chapters of the organization) and the person in charge of scheduling Horowitz's speaking engagements and meetings with Republican legislators was one Bradley Shipp. Shipp was a former political consultant with a North Carolina-based, Republican media-consulting firm that was once employed by Horowitz and that also ran campaigns for deceased Republican senator Jesse Helms. Helms, who was often heralded as one of the principal figures of the Christian Right was one of the most outspoken critics of de-segregation and an ardent supporter of the late Chilean dictator Augusto Pinochet.

In addition to sponsoring conferences, the SAF also provides an "organizational handbook" designed to assist students in creating "successful and innovative" chapters on their campuses. The handbook is quite comprehensive and spells out every step of the process from registering local SAF chapters with the national organization to conducting recruitment drives. It also provides information on garnering publicity and provides the text of the Student Bill of Rights, sample posters, complaint forms, and other documents that can be customized by student activists. In one breath, Dogan, who authored the handbook, encourages students interested in starting up SAF clubs to emphasize the "non-partisan" nature of the organization. In another, she suggests that local chapters hold social events outside of club meetings including the possibility of contacting political groups such as the Republican Women's Club that has been known to sponsor speeches by assorted rightists, including Horowitz. SAF's claims of disinterestedness and non-partisanship were, and are, disingenuous since its true mission is to serve the interests of Horowitz, his network, his corporate financial backers, and promote PC.

At its apex, the centralized site hosted a "forum on abuses" which made for interesting reading.[489] There students were invited to complete an "academic bias complaint form" to articulate the wrongs which had been perpetrated against them by professors presumably hell-bent on indoctrination. To assist aggrieved students, the form provided a handy directory of professorial and/or institutional "violations" which the SAF deemed inappropriate. They included:

Required readings or texts covering only one side of issues.

Gratuitously singled out political or religious beliefs for ridicule.

Introduced controversial material that has no relation to the subject.

Forced students to express a certain point of view in assignments.

Mocked national political or religious figures.

Conducted political activities in class (e.g. recruiting for demonstrations).

Allowed students' political or religious beliefs to influence grading.

Used university funds to hold one-sided partisan teach-ins of conferences.[490]

After providing details about the "offense" students were also prodded to provide information about what, if any, action they took and what the response of the professor or administration entailed.

Before the forum was removed from SAF's central website (and based on this author's last count), there was a total of 434 complaints documented—hardly a whopping figure given that American higher education is a vast enterprise which consists of more than 1.1 million faculty and 15 million students at 4,000 colleges. Most of the grievances came from students who disagreed with comments or assigned readings that had a liberal/left orientation. Students complained, for instance, about reading lists that included books by noted historian Howard Zinn, Noam Chomsky, and Toni Morrison. Others objected to screenings of Michael Moore's *Fahrenheit 9/11*, Al Gore's *An Inconvenient Truth*, *Outfoxed*, and *Control Room*, a documentary which explored perceptions of the U.S. war in Iraq with an emphasis on Al Jazeera coverage. According to one offended student, the latter was a piece of "pure propaganda" that "demeaned American politics and soldiers." Apparently, the tsunami of propaganda that emanated from the Bush White House was not troublesome to the plaintiff.[491]

Another student whined about a computer science professor who praised the merits of open source software to the detriment of Microsoft (evidence of anti-capitalist sentiment). The inclusion of a reading about "white privilege" irked another undergraduate who felt the topic had *nothing* to do with the plight of Native Americans and which in her/his opinion constituted "anti-white bias." Several others were traumatized by the fact that their instructors made critical remarks about George W. Bush in courses dealing with American politics. One freshman was outraged when her/his professor repeated what the late Jerry Falwell had said after the terrorist attacks— namely that secularists, gays and lesbians, liberals, etc. were largely responsible for 9/11. Apparently, referencing an *actual* statement made by a high-profile religious right leader was tantamount to anti-Christian bias.

For the most part, the examples of victimhood posted by right-wing crybabies to the SAF forum and others similar to it almost never entailed any actual repression of, or institutional reprimand for, the expression of conservative views. Rather, they represented disagreements students had with the utterances made by faculty members and/or other students and material covered in particular classes. Nonetheless, such students (with the encouragement of SAF operatives) deceitfully paraded under the banners of free expression while seeking to render impermissible the expression of political views they deemed "objectionable."

Some of the complaints included in the abuse forum were rather pedestrian in nature, including laments about too many readings, too many assignments, and the like. Ironically, some postings openly mocked the whole premise of the abuse forum as in one suggestion to rename it "Brownshirts for Bush." Others, it appeared, were clearly intended to parody the site. For example, one student who took a course on 20th Century African-American Thought at the University of Washington claimed that her/his professor was "racist" since all of the assigned books were written by African-Americans. In the "action taken" section of the complaint form, the student stated that she/he informed her/his parents that their worst fears had been confirmed—she/he had been exposed to new ideas in college. Someone posing as a student from Bob Jones University (the infamous right-wing institution) bemoaned the "fact" that he was constantly forced to repeat "Darwin is a loon" in all his assignments. Another budding scholar expressed concern that the ideas of Karl Marx were excluded in an introductory economics course.

While such examples introduced a certain degree of levity, there was absolutely nothing humorous about the intent of such forums or Horowitz's various endeavors for they clearly employed a fear-mongering strategy that did have perilous consequences. Consider the case of Oneida J. Meranto, a faculty member at the Metropolitan State College of Denver, who was targeted by conservative students after Horowitz visited her campus in the fall of 2003. After whipping college Republicans into a frenzy about the dangers of anti-American academics in their midst, several of them set out to expose professors they defined as liberal or left-leaning. Meranto became the subject of a hateful campaign by students who demanded she be terminated. For almost a year, she endured numerous hate emails and death threats "generated through Horowitz's emagazine" (FrontPage) and on "conservative radio talk shows." For their efforts, some of the students who initiated the fatwah against Meranto were "rewarded with internships for leading Colorado Republicans."[492]

Just as the Bush administration mastered the art of scaring "the people" into submission, particularly in the run-up to the 2004 presidential election, Horowitz attempted to capitalize on the post-9/11 atmosphere to expand his quasi-fascistic crusade. In such a culture of fear, where anyone who critiqued the government could be accused of "giving comfort" to the enemy or sympathizing with terrorists, the very idea that students were being "abused" and "victimized" appealed to the broader public's sense of constant danger. As McClennen argued, "students and parents" were "easily convinced" that they needed "to fight to protect themselves from the 'imminent threat' of left-leaning professors" who were conspiring to "brain-wash young minds." Essentially, parents and students were "conscripted into a parallel war effort" that allowed them to "imagine" that they were "working to defend the greatness of their nation alongside the soldiers" who were fighting 'over there.'"[493] As with the red baiting that became pervasive during the 1950s, those leading the charge against liberal/left academicians exploited the real fear and anxiety that the public felt about enemies abroad in order to eviscerate legitimate dissent at home.

Moreover, and leaving aside the McCarthyite tenor of SAF's project, what was also pedagogically disturbing about efforts to enlist students to spy and report on their instructors was that such practices, by their very nature, sought to "under-mine the concept of informed authority, teacher expertise, and professional academic standards that provide the basis for what is taught in classrooms." Merely because students may disagree "with an unsettling idea does not mean that they have the authority, expertise, education, or power to dictate for all their classmates what should be stated, discussed, or taught in a classroom."[494] Students, undoubtedly, have the right to express their opinions and one of the central tenets of a critical pedagogical approach is to value the experiences and views that they bring to the classroom. However, that does not negate the fact that faculty are members of the scholarly community whereas students are not. Entry into a learned discourse includes lengthy, extensive and rigorous training. It is premised upon a scholar's acknowledged contributions to their discipline based on a peer-reviewed adjudication process, on arguments rooted in certain forms of reasoning and certain kinds of evidence.[495] Undergraduate students are not trained in the subjects they take but their professors are. Hence, their views with respect to a discipline or subject cannot be equated with those of their instructors.

The majority of complaints recorded by SAF were anecdotal and most of them were not pursued through university grievance protocols. Nonetheless, they were often cited by Horowitz and his sympathizers as "proof" of systemic bias in the academy. It is rather astonishing that Horowitz grew quite comfortable relying on student "snitches" given the views previously expressed in *Heterodoxy*. In the November 1993 issue, a piece entitled "Snitchcraft at Minnesota" openly derided the university for seeking to implement a method by which students could communicate concerns about gender and/or racial insensitivity in the classroom. The magazine ridiculed the very idea of providing students a venue to complain about being "uncomfortable" by remarks made by instructors or fellow students. Yet, that is essentially what Horowitz and his SAF brownshirts were openly advocating with respect to "maligned" conservative students.[496] This is but one example of Horowitz's rampant hypocrisy.

It should also be noted that Horowitz has been known to rely on dubious anecdotes and willfully distort facts in his ideological war. One of the most notorious examples repeated by Horowitz as part of his campaign to promote the "Academic Bill of Rights" (see below) was an incident that took place at the University of Northern Colorado. Horowitz claimed that a criminology professor at that institution had asked students to expound on "why President Bush was a war criminal" for a mid-term essay assignment. It was then alleged that a student was failed (given a grade of "F") when she chose instead to explain why Saddam Hussein was a war criminal. Horowitz maintained that the student testified about her experience (she never did) at a special hearing before the state legislature in December 2003 in a September 13, 2004 article that appeared on FrontPageMag.com and elsewhere. He never provided the names of the student or the professor, nor did he offer any evidence to substantiate his allegations of abuse. Nonetheless, the story was covered and commented upon in other media outlets including *The New York Sun, The Christian Science Monitor*, and on OpinionJournal.com, the website of the *Wall Street Journal*'s editorial page in a piece written by Brian C. Anderson, a senior editor of the conservative Manhattan Institute's quarterly magazine *City Journal*. For the most part, these media parroted Horowitz's uncorroborated claims.

Media Matters for America eventually challenged the veracity of the University of Northern Colorado episode much to the chagrin of Horowitz who accused the watchdog group of slander while vehemently insisting the story was true. The tale of political bias turned out to be completely false according to a report that later appeared on InsideHigherEd.com. In that account, a UNC spokeswoman was quoted as saying that "the test question was not the one described by Horowitz, the grade was not an F, and there were clearly non-political reasons for whatever grade was given."[497] The question on the exam did not ask students to explain why Bush is/was a war criminal; rather, it asked them to discuss the disparity between pre-war proclamations about Iraq's possession of weapons of mass destruction and subsequent revelations that there were no such armaments. In this context, students were asked to explain how the war "might be explained in terms of research on 'deviance'" that had been covered in course reading materials. More specifically, students were to take into account "how the media and various moral entrepreneurs" might have conspired "to create a panic." The question continued, "Where does the social meaning of deviance come from? Argue that the attack on Iraq was deviance based on negotiable statuses. Make the argument that the military action of the U.S. attacking Iraq was criminal."[498]

Additionally, the question was one of two essay questions from which students could choose—in other words, the student was not *required* to answer it in the first place. Nor did the student receive a failing grade due to her political penchants. The course instructor, Robert Dunkley, told InsideHigherEd.com that the student was penalized for failing to meet the page requirement—instead of producing the requisite three pages, she submitted two. Nonetheless, the student received a grade of B in the course overall.[499] Moreover, the UNC spokeswoman stated that all the information the university had about the incident was "inconsistent" with the yarn that Horowitz had spun. Even more fascinating was the fact that the criminology professor savagely attacked by SAF was a registered Republican who was infuriated by Horowitz's mendacious machinations.[500]

A discomfited Horowitz finally conceded that his group's presentation of the case had "several faults," but he remained defiant claiming in a FrontPage headline that while "some of our facts were wrong ... our point was right."[501] What is astonishing but entirely predictable given his fondness for the Big Lie strategy, is that Horowitz has persisted in repeating his distorted version of the Colorado incident both in interviews and on the SAF website which *still* includes an account of the events surrounding the infamous exam. Moreover, in the third chapter of the SAF Handbook, the Colorado episode is *still* cited as an example of what constitutes an abuse of academic freedom.

Another case that bears mention was discussed in the SAF's Second Year Achievement Report that was published in June 2005. The incident involved Ahmad al-Qloushi, a Kuwaiti Muslim student at Foothill College in California who was enrolled in an introductory course on American Government and Politics taught by Professor Joseph Woolcock in 2004. Among other things, SAF claimed that the course "was taught from a consistently anti-American perspective." The report went on to say, however, that the "final straw" for Ahmad "came when the class was instructed to complete a take-home final which asked students to 'Analyze the US constitution (original document), and show how its formulation excluded the majority of the people living in America at that time, and how it was dominated by America's elite interest.'"[502] According to SAF, al-Qloushi instead

> chose to write an essay defending America's Founding Fathers and upholding the Constitution as a progressive document which has contributed to freedom beyond America's borders, but Professor Woolcock refused to grade the essay, claiming that Ahmad needed "regular psychotherapy" and threatened him by stating that he would visit the Dean of International Admissions (who has the power to take away student visas) to make sure he received regular psychological treatment. Students for Academic Freedom helped to make Ahmad's case a national media story, resulting in hundreds of emails sent to Foothill's board of trustees.[503]

SAF was certainly accurate in claiming that it helped to make the case a media story as Fox News was quick to pick up another tale of a crazed anti-American professor victimizing a patriotically correct student as were other media outlets including *The Washington Times* and ABC's *World News Tonight*.[504] Unfortunately, the accuracy ended there as the report conveniently excluded some key information and distorted the facts. To accept SAF's account would involve concluding that the professor suggested that al-Qloushi needed therapy because he had written a pro-American paper. However, in a public response to the student's charges, Woolcock offered a different version of events that is worth quoting at length:

> In mid-November 2004, Ahmad al-Qloushi came to see me at my request to discuss the outline of his Final Research Paper assignment in the course: Introduction to American Government & Politics. He had failed to write the mid-term assignment and had chosen to write his final paper on a topic we both agreed would be a challenge for him. Recognizing that he would have difficulty completing the assignment, I offered him the opportunity to write his paper on a less challenging topic from the mid-term assignment list of topics. We agreed that should he take up the offer, I would not only discount the points he failed to earn at mid-term, but I would also work with him on the outline, and on the review of a draft copy of the paper before he submitted it for grading. Mr. al-Qloushi agreed to do that. However, he turned in his final written assignment without returning for the assistance which we had agreed on earlier. When I read the paper, it became clear to me that it did not respond to the question. In late November, after grading all final papers, I asked Mr. al-Qloushi to come and discuss with me the grade. During this meeting, I sought from him his reasons for reneging on our earlier agreement. In response, he expressed in great detail, concerns and feelings of high anxiety he was having about certain developments which had occurred over ten years ago in his country. Some aspects of his concerns were similar to certain concerns expressed in his paper. Based on the nature of the concerns and the feelings of high anxiety which he expressed, I encouraged him to visit one of the college counselors. I neither forced nor ordered Mr. al-Qloushi

to see a counselor; I have no authority to do so. My suggestion to him was a recommendation he freely chose to accept and which he acknowledged in an e-mail message to me on December 1, 2004. Foothill College counselors are competent and highly respected professionals capable of providing professional services to students and faculty members are always encouraged by the college administration to make such referrals to college counselors as the need may arise. In my conversation with Mr. al-Qloushi, I did not make any reference, explicitly or implicitly, to the Dean of International Students or to any other Dean. In my conversation with Mr. al-Qloushi, I did not make any reference, explicit or implicit, to Mr. al-Qloushi's status as an international student. At the time of our conversation, Mr. al-Qloushi was still enrolled in my class, but after he met with the counselor, he never returned to the class. I deny unequivocally all the allegations Mr. al-Qloushi has attributed to me regarding my suggestion to him that it might be helpful for him to discuss his long-standing concerns with a college counselor, as I have described here. All the other allegations made are false and have no basis whatsoever in fact.[505]

The problem then was not that the student had written a pro-American essay for which he was punished with a poor grade as SAF implied. Rather, the student had not responded adequately to the essay question itself. In fact, after al-Qloushi's essay was posted on the SAF website, a conservative blogger and political science professor, James Joyner, claimed that it was an "incredibly poorly written, error-ridden, pabulum-filled [sic], essay that essentially ignores the question put forth by the instructor" while another politically conservative professor, Steven Taylor, stated that he fully understood why the "essay resulted in a failing grade." In both these cases, SAF twisted facts to represent students as aggrieved parties because of their conservatism while excluding the truth about their academic shortcomings. In this sense, the SAF-sponsored forum for reporting "abuses" provided a scapegoat for students to attribute their poor performance in classes to professors' liberal bias—and this from conservatives who champion 'personal responsibility.'

The Academic Bill of Rights

The *raison d'etre* of SAF is to promote the misnamed Academic Bill of Rights (ABOR) and its cousin, the Student Bill of Rights (SBOR). Both of these bills are ostensibly rooted in the right to free thought for both professors and students. Yet, both seek to impose strict limitations on the views professors can communicate to their students. While the ABOR is intended to be used by legislators and politicians at the state level, the SBOR is crafted so that conservative students can push for its implementation at the nation's colleges and universities. A number of insightful rebuttals to, and critiques of, the ABOR have been put forth by several thoughtful individuals and professional organizations including the American Association of University Professors (AAUP). And, although I rely on some of the previous arguments made by opponents of the ABOR, my intent here is not to regurgitate them. Rather, my aim is to briefly point out some of the obvious contradictions that have marked Horowitz's campaign for "intellectual diversity" and to reveal the hypocrisy that animates his efforts.

First, it is important to state something that many polite academic critics of Horowitz and the ABOR have been reluctant to utter—Horowitz has a serious problem with truth and he shamelessly misrepresents the motives behind his advocacy of the ABOR. For instance, are we to believe Horowitz when he states that the bill would support "all faculty members" including left-leaning ones even though he has characterized leftists as "anti-capitalist," "anti-American" scoundrels who are "intellectually totalitarian" and morally equivalent to "savages?" The former claim came in a 2004 essay Horowitz penned for *The Chronicle of Higher Education*; the latter from a June 2007 interview posted on the SAF website.[506] As David Brodsky has argued, while "consistency is an intellectual and ethical virtue," it is not one of Horowitz's strong suits.[507]

Nonetheless, Horowitz should be credited for his adroit appropriation of various progressive touchstones including the concept of "diversity" which he uses to pursue his conservative platform. His choice of language is obviously deliberate and he has consciously co-opted certain catchphrases commonly associated with the liberal-left (i.e. inclusivity, plurality) to make the ABOR more palatable to a broader audience. In classical Rove-ian fashion, Horowitz has mastered the art of packaging the reactionary agenda of the far right in the progressive language of academia. Horowitz, in fact, essentially admitted to this form of linguistic trickery in his essay, "The Campus Blacklist." Therein, he bragged that he encouraged right-wing students to "use the language that the left has deployed so effectively in behalf of" their own agendas. He prods Horowistas to claim that "radical professors have created 'a hostile learning environment' for conservative students," that there is "a lack of 'intellectual diversity' on college faculties and in classrooms, that the "conservative viewpoint is 'underrepresented' in the curriculum and on its reading lists," and that the "university should be an 'inclusive' and intellectually 'diverse' community."[508] He goes on to say that he has advised students to

> demand that their schools adopt an 'academic bill of rights' that stresses intellectual diversity, that demands balance in their reading lists, that recognizes that political partisanship by professors in the classroom is an abuse of students' academic freedom ... and that a learning environment hostile to conservatives is unacceptable.[509]

Such explicit language—particularly reference to conservative views—is nowhere to be found in the actual text of the ABOR; rather, Horowitz invokes the concept of "intellectual diversity" that is clearly intended to sound innocuous and benevolent. On display in this context are two of the tactics delineated by Horowitz in *The Art of Political War*— "choose the terrain that makes the fight as easy for you as possible" and "define the issues as well as your adversary."[510] In constructing the issue as one of "intellectual diversity," Horowitz makes it difficult for his opponents to mount a successful rebuttal. After all, objections to intellectual diversity could easily be interpreted as endorsements for intellectual homogeneity. And since the concept is based on other kinds of diversity principles (i.e. those based on ethnicity, race, gender, etc.) that have historically been championed by liberals and leftists, Horowitz and his followers can claim that critics of the ABOR are hypocrites.

As is evident from the passage quoted above, Horowitz clearly viewed the ABOR as a vehicle to introduce so-called "balance" (in this case political balance as in more conservative views) in the curriculum and reading lists. Yet, Horowitz has continued to deny that allegation. For instance, at the 2nd annual SAF-sponsored conference on academic freedom which was held in March 2007, Horowitz partici- pated in a panel discussion with Cary Nelson, the president of the AAUP, which was moderated by Scott Smallwood, the senior editor of *The Chronicle of Higher Education*. After Nelson outlined some of the problems associated with attempts to impose "balance," Horowitz stated the following: "In fact, I never use the word 'balance.'" Based on that statement, one can conclude that Horowitz is (1) afflicted with some sort of amnesia that has caused him to forget what he had previously written or that (2) Horowitz lied on the panel. The latter is probably a more accurate explanation given Horowitz's penchant for misrepresentation as a political strategy. As previously noted, *The Art of Political War* is chockfull of advice about how to mislead the public into believing something other than the truth in the name of advancing a political agenda—by any unethical means necessary.

It is certainly true that the word "balance" does not appear within the text of the ABOR (its omission was clearly part of a tactical strategy), but politicians who drafted legislation based on the bill indubitably equated "diversity" with "balance." As Brodksy has noted, in the "practical world of policy formation, 'intellectual diversity' is a euphemism for 'ideological balance' or 'political balance.'"[511] So while Horowitz maintains that the ABOR is politically neutral, politicians have interpreted it quite differently and Horowitz has never sought to discourage them from using the discourse of "balance."

Academic critics of the bill have astutely documented the dangers posed by the imposition of "balance." Would it mean for example, that a course on the Holocaust would have to include readings by anti-Semitic Holocaust deniers? Or, that a course in evolutionary biology would have to give "equal time" to intelligent design (aka creationism) and other crack-pot theories promulgated by the religious right? With respect to the latter, some politicians have argued just that. Rep. Dennis Baxley of Florida is a case in point. A bill he sponsored (H-837) based on ABOR would have given "students who think their beliefs are not being respected legal standing to sue professors and universities."[512] Baxley cited the example of intelligent design as a potential basis for legal action. In other words, a professor who asserted "evolution is a fact" could be sued by a conservative Christian student who was offended by the statement and/or by the fact that creationism was not granted "equal time" in the classroom. Countering critics who lamented the implications of such a bill—i.e. curricula being decided by judges in courtrooms instead of by the professional and scholarly standards of a discipline—Baxley claimed that "freedom is a dangerous thing" since students "might be exposed to things" they "don't want to hear."[513]

In this form, the ABOR-inspired legislation recognizes no authority in the class- room other than an individual who holds a "belief." Professors and students, as bearers of beliefs, are placed on equal footing despite the obvious disparities in academic training while education is reduced to a self-designed laundry list of personal student preferences. If the student-consumer—and in the right's educational discourse, students are invariably conceived of as consumers rather than citizens—is dissatisfied with the product offered, she/he can sue. Three brief points are worth making here.

First, it is important to recall the war on political correctness that reached a fever pitch in the late 1980s and early 1990s. Back then, conservatives were railing against the 1960s and the radical activists of that generation who had presumably taken over the nation's campuses. Authors such as Allan Bloom, Richard Kimball, and Dinesh D'Souza denounced academic disciplines such as women's studies, racial and ethnic studies as illegitimate because they were allegedly rooted in the "feel-good" culture catalyzed by the 1960s. Rightists like Horowitz made careers, particularly in the 1990s, from disparaging the narratives of 'victimology' that presumably provided the scaffolding upon which those disciplines were built. Indeed, the inaugural issue of *Heterodoxy* was crammed with claims about how demands for representation (of women and minorities) were based on *ideological* rather than scholarly considerations. Yet advocates of the ABOR are promoting the same feel-good sensibility with proposed legislation that essentially contends that conservative students are entitled to feel "comfortable" about what they are learning regardless of evidentiary and intellectual standards. And, they vigorously encourage those students to embrace the mantle of victimhood and insist upon inclusion and representation of their views *solely on the basis of ideology*. In a clever move, the right has simply redefined the victim as conservative students are cast as helpless dupes of professorial abuse who need legislative muscle to defend them from the forces of liberal iniquity.

Second, conservatives have long chastised notions of "big government" as paternalistic but in this context they are inviting government to police curriculum on behalf of students who they assume are not intelligent enough to differentiate between political proselytizing and genuine intellectual debate in the classroom. The flip-side of Horowitz's strategy to demonize academics is to infantilize students. If professors are contemptuous dogmatists who transform the classroom into a bully pulpit, who force-feed students left-wing ideology, and terrorize those who disagree, then students are nothing more than unthinking, spineless, empty vessels incapable of formulating their own opinions. In this sense, rightists actually emasculate the purpose of higher education which involves, at the very least, the development of critical thinking through debate, dialogue, and confronting viewpoints that may challenge those held by students. This is paternalistic and patronizing and it is rather counter-intuitive on the part of conservatives who have long preached the gospel of limited government and 'personal responsibility' including, presumably, the responsibility of formulating one's own views.

Finally, one of the rhetorical centerpieces of the conservative movement has concerned itself with "frivolous lawsuits." For years organizations like the Federalist Society, pundits like Ann Coulter and others who seek to make corporations un-accountable to the public, have argued for "tort reform" that would make it difficult for consumers and employees to sue companies for injuries, discrimination, and the like. The standard refrain has been that "trial lawyers" who file "trivial" lawsuits and bamboozle juries into granting outrageous settlements undermine the economy and drive up consumer costs.[514] However, bills similar to H-837 would likely require universities to hire lawyers just to deal with potential lawsuits filed by disgruntled fundamentalist students who did not get their daily dose of creationism in biology class. Such a scenario could lead to increased tuition fees, putting higher education even further out of reach for some working and middle class students. Such contradictions seem to escape the thought capacities of many conservatives. Then again, perhaps the intent *is* to make higher education more financially inaccessible to poorer constituencies and to return to the halcyon days of the academy as a privileged haven of the wealthy.[515]

In the SBOR, Horowitz argues that while "teachers are entitled to freedom in the classroom in discussing their subject," they should be "careful not to introduce into their teaching controversial matter which has no relation to their subject." In short, unless professors are experts in American foreign policy, they have no business discussing, for example, the Iraq war in their classrooms. Of course, Horowitz would likely not apply such standards to himself or his right-wing compatriots. After all, Horowitz's lifeblood is contingent upon his pontificating about subjects—higher education, pedagogy, entire academic disciplines—that he is not professionally qualified to speak about. There is also another provision in both the ABOR and the SBOR that bears mentioning—one that states that "selection of speakers, allocation of funds for speakers programs and other student activities will observe the principles of academic freedom and promote intellectual pluralism." Does Horowitz, mean for example, that right-wing darlings like Rush Limbaugh or Sean Hannity should be paid with university funds to deliver campus orations on American foreign policy, the war on terror, etc., in order to promote "pluralism." If so, one would have to ask what qualifies Hannity or Limbaugh to speak on such topics. Limbaugh, after all, is a former disc jockey and a college drop-out who avoided service in Vietnam because of a pilonidal anal cyst while Hannity, also a college drop-out, is a radio personality with no military expertise or background. As Gabbard and Anijar perceptively note, if the rightists behind the campaign for intellectual diversity have the same low regard for academic standards as they do for the standards of their media and "journalists" (i.e. Fox News, Limbaugh, Hannity, O'Reilly, Gallagher, and Gannon/Guckert), principled academics should not "allow" their tendency to "value difference" get the best of them.[516]

Both the ABOR and the SBOR assert that "curricula and reading lists in the humanities and social sciences should reflect the uncertainty and unsettled character of all human knowledge in these areas by providing students with dissenting sources and viewpoints where appropriate." Here, Horowitz deceptively adopts a kind of epistemological relativism that he spent a good part of the 1990s repudiating. For example, under his editorial leadership, *Heterodoxy* published numerous hysterical rants about the perils of postmodernism, deconstruction, and the like for daring to argue that the history of Western civilization could be interpreted differently than it was by its conservative custodians. Now, however, Horowitz is quite content to wave the banner of relativism because it is politically expedient for him to do so. In an article he penned for *The Chronicle of Higher Education*, Horowitz expressed his incredulity at the AAUP's criticism of his bill since "major schools of thought in the contemporary academy—pragmatism, postmodernism, and deconstruction, to name three—operate on the premise that knowledge is uncertain and, at times, relative."[517]

Here again, Horowitz employs a political sleight of hand by appropriating theoretical concepts associated with the left to disarm his critics. But, Horowitz doesn't really believe in such concepts. After all, one of the stated purposes of the DHFC is, as was noted above, to "restore the study of Western civilization" in the nation's institutions of higher education. If all knowledge is relative, why does Horowitz privilege the canon of 'Western civilization'? Although conservatives have sought, for years, to exalt the 'Western tradition' as a body of knowledge that is transhistorical, pristine, and universal, critical scholars in the humanities and social sciences (some of them postmodernists) have pointed to the legacies of colonialism, imperialism, and oppression which have characterized the enterprise of Western civilization. For this, they have been accused, over the years, of being anti-American and anti-Western by the likes of Horowitz. How then can Horowitz claim in one breath to support intellectual diversity and in another call for the teaching of 'Western civilization'? How can he claim in one breath that the ABOR would protect leftist scholars and then, in another, state that one of the primary purposes of the DHFC is to identify leftist professors who "use the classroom to propagandize for America's enemies in a time of war"? It seems as though Horowitz wants to have it both ways. On one level, he is clearly calling for a sort of academic unity, the teaching of 'Western civilization' because it purportedly embodies pro-American values that are especially important in times of war; on another he invokes the concept of intellectual diversity.

Horowitz has purposely sanitized the language used in the ABOR to mask the proto-fascist agenda that lies beneath the lofty rhetoric. In fact, Brodsky has noted that the text of ABOR is "deliberately deceptive" insofar as it omits "its own public rationale justifying the need for legislation" and "avoids the questions of enforcement and application."[518] But a simple review of Horowitz's websites plainly reveals the rationale for Horowitz's jihad—he wants to purge the academy of critical intellectuals who challenge the dominance of neoconservative militaristic "values," marginalize oppositional thought generally, and create a climate of intimidation. In fact, Horowitz essentially admitted as much when he reminisced about the good old days of the McCarthy era when professors were too frightened to articulate their political views. In an interview that appeared in Temple University's campus newspaper, Horowitz stated that the "goal" of ABOR was to "bring the university back to where Columbia was" when he attended school there. He said: "When I was an undergraduate at Columbia it was the McCarthy era. I entered in 1955, but the atmosphere was there. None of my professors ever uttered a political comment in the classroom ... I would like to see politics taken out of the university classroom."[519]

According to several observers, core features of fascism include the "cult of tradition" and the "disdain and suppression of intellectuals."[520] The cult of tradition ignores that "Western civilization" is itself a social construction and in so doing, obscures its historical constructedness. Instead, it refers to the glorious past as if traditions simply emerged without contradictions and encourages a general historical amnesia and political illiteracy, as well as mystification and mythologization of current world events while advancing a Manichaean worldview. In this sense, one can see how fascism entails a distrust of the intellectual world. For Nazis, universities were "nests of reds" and the "official Fascist intellectuals" were mainly engaged in attacking the "liberal intelligentsia for having betrayed traditional values."[521] These tendencies are evident in the tactics and rhetorical strategies that Horowitz utilizes.

Let me be clear—Horowitz is not an "official" fascist intellectual in the strictest sense; he is not really an intellectual at all. As Blumenthal has pointed out, Horowitz is not a member of the scholarly community. He does not possess a doctorate degree and "unlike the professors he smears, Horowitz's work has never been formally peer-reviewed." He is "taken seriously only with the right's pseudo-intellectual hothouse," and without the "financial feeding tube" provided by his "Scrooge McDuck sugar-daddies," he would likely "wilt into obscurity."[522] Nonetheless, Horowitz has assumed his role as a public pedagogue speaking on behalf of the American Imperium and corporate interests while impugning dissidents for their lack of patriotism. He alleged to be against "orthodoxy" but the targets of his wrath were precisely those that disagreed with his orthodox positions on the "war on terror."

Horowitz is not simply some kind of right-wing crank—he was, and still is, well connected to the radical right's power elite. For years he was quite cozy with Rove and other forces that were associated with the Bush regime. A big part of their efforts to maintain control for eight years rested upon fanning the flames of anti-intellectualism and the advent of the global war on terror provided partisan hacks like Horowitz with a durable rationale for harassing one of the last remaining venues for independent thought. As Beinin argued:

> Since the September 11 terrorist attacks ... supporters of George W. Bush's Manichaean view of the world have mounted a sustained campaign to delegitimise critical thought ... Universities and colleges have been a particular target of policing what may be thought and said ... because they are among the few institutions where intelligent political discourse remains possible in the United States.[523]

Horowitz's contrived indignation about bias and political imbalance in the academy is merely another manifestation of the right's long history of anti-intellectualism which, in addition to circulating falsehoods about "anti-American" scholars, repeatedly paints a portrait of the academy as a sinecure and professors as Machiavellian do-nothings who make hefty salaries for working six to nine hours a week. Moreover, the attacks on higher education were, and are, designed to undermine the very credibility and professional power of academics. In short, if Horowitz, his water-carriers in the right-wing media, and others of their ilk can convince the public at large that the universities are overrun with wild-eyed communists and terrorist sympathizers, they would be in a much better position to immunize themselves and their positions on everything from the war on terror and foreign policy to the environment and global warming from scholarly criticism and scrutiny. That, rather than "balance" is what they really seek. As Giroux notes:

> Horowitz and his allies care little about balance as a principle, whether it be in hiring faculty or promoting open inquiry in the classroom; they seem

far more concerned with intimidating, shaming, and bullying as part of a broader effort to control all social institutions not entirely committed to the values of conservative Republicans, market-driven evangelicals, or Christian fundamentalists. The call for balance by conservatives such as Horowitz [and] the Students for Academic Freedom ... is a red herring whose aim is not to expand critical learning but to shut it down, to mute criticism rather than endorse it as central to any viable notion of politics, education, and citizenship.[524]

Just as the crusades against the so-called "liberal" media were intended to shift public discourse to the right, the well-funded jeremiads against the liberal/left academy are clearly designed to narrow the *political* spectrum of permissible debate. In this regard, it is necessary to acknowledge that the battle Horowitz is fighting is political rather than academic. Horowitz is "not acting as an academic interlocutor;" rather, he is "acting as a politician and looking to win *political* changes *outside* the academy that would radically reshape its internal practices."[525] Throughout the Bush years, Horowitz's ultimate goal was to eviscerate critical thought and progressive initiatives, and undermine universities as democratic public spheres capable of challenging governmental abuses of power, illegal wars, and the manic logic of American imperialism.

He's Got a Little List ...

Part and parcel of Horowitz's campaign to vilify academicians who do not subscribe to his worldview was his book *The Professors: The 101 Most Dangerous Academics in America* published in 2006 by the well-known conservative publishing house, Regnery. With typical hyperbole, the book's inside flap claims that "terrorists, racists, and communists," otherwise known as "professors" are "coming to a campus near you." Today's "radical academics aren't the exception—they're legion" and they spew "violent anti-Americanism, preach anti-Semitism, and cheer the killing of American soldiers and civilians—all the while collecting tax dollars and tuition fees to indoctrinate our children." Moreover, the motley malcontents who "indoctrinate" the nation's children (since when do 'children' attend universities and colleges?) also "promote the views of the Iranian mullahs, support Osama bin Laden, lament the demise of the Soviet Union" and "advocate the killing of ordinary Americans." The above passage clearly demonstrates Horowitz's modus operandi—ideologically mixing age-old anti-communist rhetoric with words like "terrorist" in order to promote blind patriotism. After 9/11, such tactics were employed to disparage criticism of the Bush administration's demonstrably one-sided, pro-Israel foreign policies.

The Professors is yet another example of shoddy scholarship underwritten by right-wing foundations. Moreover, only a very small portion of it was actually penned by Horowitz who relied on his "researchers" to amass the anecdotal "evidence" which is then offered as "proof" of the "enormous damage that several generations of tenured radicals have inflicted on" the American educational system.[526] Michael Apple claims that the book—which is not really a book at all, but rather a "series of very short vignettes of 'the most dangerous' academics in the United States"—is one of the "most noxious books" to be authored in recent years.[527]

A carefully detailed study of Horowitz's screed conducted by the "Free Exchange on Campus" (FEOC) organization found that it was replete with countless "inaccuracies, distortions, and manipulations of fact—including false statements, mischaracterizations of professors' views, broad claims unsupported by facts and selective omissions of information" that did not fit Horowitz's argument.[528] Despite the fact that Horowitz claimed to be concerned with the "professorial task" of teaching, FEOC found the opposite to be true:

> Throughout his book, Mr. Horowitz provides scant evidence of what does go on inside of professors' classrooms, and instead focuses chiefly on the political opinions they express outside of their classrooms. Without sound evidence of what goes on inside professors' classrooms, we believe it is absurd for Mr. Horowitz to charge them with something as serious as indoctrinating their students.[529]

The report went on to state that:

> Overall, the majority of the profiles in Mr. Horowitz's book contain *no* {emphasis added} evidence of professors' in-class conduct whatsoever … Our own count of Mr. Horowitz's footnotes reveals that overall, approximately 80 percent of the evidence he presents relates to things professors have said or written outside of the classroom. To the extent that Mr. Horowitz cites anything at all about what goes in the classrooms of the professors he profiles, his evidence usually amounts to materials that can be found on the internet, such as syllabi or short course descriptions—not accounts from people who have taken courses with the professors, or who have sat in on their lectures, or who have participated in class discussions. In short, eyewitness accounts of any kind are altogether absent from the overwhelming majority of profiles in Mr. Horowitz's book. Furthermore, most of the syllabi, course descriptions and the few other teaching materials that Mr. Horowitz does present tend to show nothing other than that the professors teach what they claim to teach: courses in fields that Mr. Horowitz categorizes as 'ideological,' such as ethnic studies, feminism, or peace studies; viewpoints that represent the perspectives of minority, oppressed, or historically underrepresented groups; or perspectives that are critical of certain policies of the United States government.[530]

In short, perspectives and areas of inquiry that do not reflect a white, conservative, male worldview are targeted for condemnation—so much for Horowitz's commitment to "intellectual diversity."

Naturally, all of the intellectuals included in Horowitz's propagandistic treatise were liberal and/or left-leaning. Among them, Noam Chomsky, Michael Eric Dyson, bell hooks, Robert McChesney, Cornel West, and Howard Zinn—some of the most distinguished scholars in their respective fields. But, Horowitz's ultimate purpose was not simply to castigate specific intellectuals, rather, the major theme that permeated *The Professors* suggested that *any* criticism of the U.S. government (at least when conservative George W. Bush was still in office) was unjustified, "Marxist," and unpatriotic and that any challenges to the practices of the Israeli government were indicative of anti-Semitism.

Given the constant invocation of anti-communist rhetoric, it is hardly surprising that his book corresponds roughly to the McCarthy-esque website "Discover the Network" (DTN) which purports to reveal the labyrinth of "left-wing millionaires and monsters" that are presumably as much of threat to national security as are "terrorists" who seek to do America harm. DTN, which Horowitz characterizes as an online "guide to the political left," presents what he considers extensive connections between prominent liberals and terrorists. The searchable site, staffed by two of Horowitz's apostles, was revealed to the public in February 2005 after approximately two years of preparation, and at a cost of about $500,000 by Horowitz's own estimate. It was met with "scattered applause from the right as an educational tool."[531]

Here one will find the likes of film critic Roger Ebert and songstress Barbra Streisand lumped together with Mohammed Atta and Abu Musab al-Zarqawi. Ebert apparently earned his spot in the pantheon of left-wing ne'er-do-wells for criticizing the "evils of capitalism" and making an unflattering remark about presidential daughter Barbara Bush, whom Ebert allegedly referred to as an "ignorant yob." One wonders if Horowitz was as outraged when right-wing blowhards like Rush Limbaugh engaged in savage attacks against Chelsea Clinton, going so far as to call her a "dog."

Even Supreme Court Justice Ruth Bader Ginsburg is cited as a fellow traveler not only because she did work for the ACLU and has been a champion for "feminist causes" and a woman's right to choose but, most importantly, because she "dissented from the Court's decision that effectively gave President Bush the victory in the 2000 election."[532] In Horowitz's warped mind, even John Kerry, who whole-heartedly supported Bush's invasion, is characterized as a far left freak because of his participation in Veterans Against the War (VVAW) demonstrations against the Vietnam war which had him, presumably, marching "alongside revolutionary communists."[533] Horowitz's venom is not reserved merely for the licentious liberals and leftists among us. Indeed, he has a problem with the dearly departed—including Herbert Marcuse who is labeled the "intellectual godfather of the left" and Herbert Aptheker, the "chief theoretician of the American Communist Party."[534]

Horowitz has been quite busy since the election of President Barack Obama sent him into an apoplectic rage; like other right-wing gasbags he has engaged in routine character assassinations of the President and his administration. For Horowitz and his ilk, Obama is an anti-American socialist who sympathizes with terrorists (see below). Given the amount of excrement that emanates daily from frontpage magazine.com, it is rather remarkable that Horowitz found time to co-author yet another harangue about the "brainwashing" of American students.

Even though his attempt to establish an Academic Bill of Rights and a Student Bill of Rights has limped along with limited success, like a good soldier Horowitz remains steadfast in his commitment to assail the academy. *One-Party Classroom: How Radical Professors at America's Top Colleges Indoctrinate Students and Undermine Democracy*, co-authored with Jacob Laksin, a senior editor at Front Page, closely "resembles the shoddy research and baseless conclusions" of Horowitz's previous book, *The Professors*.[535] According to a report compiled by the FEOC, Horowitz's latest offering "does not meet even minimal standards for sound research methodology" and is brimming with faulty logic, "distorted and inaccurate data" and "highly suspect" assertions.[536] In their detailed analysis of *One-Party*, the authors carefully dissect Horowitz's claims and expose his biased methodological approach that, for the most part, essentially consisted of surfing the web for course syllabi, reading lists, and faculty profiles and then making all sorts of outrageous claims about the state of American higher education.

Horowitz surveyed just 12 institutions out of the more than 4,000 in the United States—approximately one-quarter of one percent of all American universities and colleges—and those twelve institutions (mostly elite schools) were hardly a representative sample of American higher education. Additionally, Horowitz focused on a very narrow range of departments—women's studies, various ethnic studies, sociology, and other related departments in the humanities and social sciences. He did not sample a single course from a business or engineering school and completely omitted any reference to science courses such as biology and chemistry. Moreover, within the departments he did sample, Horowitz directed his attention to only a few select professors.[537] For example, of the twenty-five faculty members in the department of communication studies at the University of Texas, Horowitz singles out Dana Cloud who just happens to be an outspoken critic of Horowitz's neo-McCarthyism.[538]

One-Party Classroom claims to be a list of the 150 "worst courses" in American higher education yet Horowitz admitted that he "had not actually seen a single class in any of the 150 courses he has declared to be the worst in America."[539] Nor did any of the courses profiled include any data "from student evaluations or a similar measure of how most students felt about a course."[540] Instead, Horowitz reviewed on-line syllabi for courses in subjects he already despised (i.e. women's studies, ethnic studies, queer studies, peace studies, etc.) and then makes "an enormous logical leap in asserting that the courses he surveys are examples of anything other than his personal dislikes."[541] In example after example, Horowitz cherry-picks information from "course materials available online, while ignoring other parts of these materials if they are inconvenient to proving his thesis" and in several instances he bases his conclusions and accusations on "blatantly misrepresented data" that "have no basis in fact."[542] In other words, Horowitz follows his own advice as spelled out in the *Art of Political War*—lie, if necessary, to advance and gain support for your cause. Contrary to what Horowitz asserts, *One-Party Classroom* does not reveal a trend toward the politicization of the classroom and the indoctrination of students, rather it demonstrates only "the consistency of Horowitz's biases against higher education."[543]

Jaschik notes that Horowitz's *One Party Classroom* differs from his previous works on academia in at least one way: "women's studies appears to have eclipsed Middle Eastern studies as the greatest threat to American higher education (in Horowitz's view)" and of the 150 worst courses, "59 are in women's studies."[544] Horowitz disagrees with the assumption of many women's studies courses—namely that gender is a fundamental category of analysis. He also claims that women's studies represents the most "egregious example of a discipline that attempts to indoctrinate students" because scholars in the field "explicitly state that they hope to change society."[545] In other words, he castigates women's studies because it addresses gender issues and because some of the courses he surveyed allegedly take up the issue of improving the lot of women's lives. Given his cavalier dismissal of gender as an important area of study and his categorization of figures such as Justice Ruth Bader Ginsberg as anti-American because of her support of feminist causes, it is rather peculiar that Horowitz has attempted to conscript feminism in his hate campaign against what he calls "Islamofascism."

Horowitz's Islamophobia

Under the broader rubric of his center's Terrorism Awareness Project, Horowitz initiated "Islamo-Fascism Awareness Week"(IFAW)—a week-long series of workshops and speeches (hosted by right-wing student groups including the Young Americans for Freedom) which took place on approximately 26 campuses, including elite schools such as Columbia, from October 22–26, 2007. The purpose of the inaugural IFAW was to refute "the two big lies of the political left: that George Bush created the war on terror and that global warming is a greater danger to Americans than the terrorist threat."[546]

Before exploring Horowitz's sudden and convenient concern for women's rights, it is first necessary to briefly examine the very term "Islamofascism" which is, as Pollitt argues, a

> highly emotional propaganda term intended to conflate a variety of groups, from Baathists to Hamas to Al Qaeda to the Taliban, into one big murderball and to move us to war—yesterday Iraq, tomorrow Iran—by evoking the clash of civilizations, religious apocalypse, implacable enemies, the folly of compromise and Hitler.[547]

Republican politicians including George W. Bush and former presidential candidate John McCain often bandied about "Islamofascism" to provide a specious patina of unity to diverse groups and phenomena. The term itself was popularized by Eliot Cohen, scholar of military affairs at Johns Hopkins School of Advanced International Studies and former counselor to Condoleezza Rice, who is regarded by some as the "most influential neocon in academe."[548] It has now become a staple of right-wing commentary designed to whip up and rally foot soldiers—a motley crew of diverse reactionaries and neo-fascists including hard-core racists, anti-immigrant nativists, Christian fundamentalists, right-wing veterans and student groups—to the cause of American imperialism. In many ways, it is a made-up term to justify attacks on any nation in the Middle East and it simultaneously feeds domestic Christian extremism. Hard right evangelicals like Gary Bauer of the Family Research Council routinely deploy the term as has Texas pastor John Hagee who once lobbied members of Congress for "militant support of Israel" and "military action against Iran."[549] References to Islamofascism are also rampant on the Fox News Channel.

IFAW's intent is not to raise awareness at all but rather to couple "Islam" with a powerful epithet (fascism) and play upon people's emotions and ignorance in the interest of promoting a very specific ideological agenda. Part of IFAW's activities included a teach-in on the Oppression of Women in Islam and an attempt to rebuke Women's Studies Departments for "failing" to condemn the repression of women living in Islamic regimes. As previously noted, the scorn that Horowitz heaps on women's studies in *One-Party Classroom*, is based largely on the discipline's activist roots, yet in the context of IFAW, he is challenging women's studies departments to engage in activism! Presumably, it would be acceptable for women's studies programs to criticize *gendered* forms of oppression and perhaps even to demand that changes be made to improve the lives of women—as long as those women live in Islamic nations. Of course, Horowitz and his fellow crusaders are not really concerned with women's rights; rather they exploit the woman question as an easy way to target Muslims.

Remarkably, two of the featured speakers during IFAW were Ann Coulter who has suggested that women in the United States be denied voting privileges and disgraced former Senator Rick Santorum who, in addition to being virulently anti-choice, has also opposed contraception for women. That Horowitz, Coulter, and Santorum claimed to be champions for Muslim women's rights was quite astonishing. And it was certainly amusing to see Coulter and others cut from the same cloth being summoned to oppose theocratic rule in the Muslim world when they support Christian, patriarchal, fundamentalism at home. But, behind the hypocrisy was a very ugly and perilous agenda. Horowitz used the truth about the real oppression of women in nations ruled by fundamentalists in the service of the right's Big Lie—namely that the invasion of Iraq and U.S. aggression in the Middle East in general—were part and parcel of a noble cause to bring "freedom" and more rights to the oppressed.

In the case of Iraq, the oppression of women worsened after the U.S. invasion:

[I]n Iraq … the U.S.-installed puppet government wrote a constitution that established Islam as the official religion, moved marriages and divorces from civil courts to the domain of the clerics, and removed women's rights to child custody after divorces. The U.S. allied with Grand Ayatollah Sayyid Ali Sistani who ordered women to cover themselves, an order that was enforced with be-headings and acid burns. And violence against women generally has skyrocketed under U.S. occupation.[550]

Of course, these were the inconvenient truths that Horowitz deliberately chose to ignore in the interest of buttressing the former Bush administration's warmongering which was, arguably, the real intent of IFAW. Indeed, a large portion of the week's events were given to saber-rattling about Iran and whipping up racist sentiment and anti-Muslim animus to achieve political ends—prolonging the war in Iraq, making a case for an attack on Iran and, of course, castigating the academic left which, according to IFAW's promotional materials has "mobilized to create sympathy for the enemy and to fight anyone who rallies Americans to defend themselves."[551]

Far from trying to raise awareness, those involved with IFAW worked to fortify the facile, Manichaean dichotomy of good versus evil, us versus them. This was exemplified by Horowitz's targeting of Muslim Students Associations which he maintained were creations of the "Islamo-fascist jihad" and his petition drive designed to force students and faculty "to declare their allegiances: either to fighting our terrorist adversaries or failing to take action to stop our enemies."[552] While neo-fascists such as Horowitz like to pose as anti-fascists, it should be noted that when it suits their purposes—as it did in Afghanistan in the 1980s—the "U.S. ruling class which Horowitz fronts for has had no compunction about supporting severely oppressive Islamic movements."[553]

Ironically, IFAW paved the way for the Michigan State chapter of the Young Americans for Freedom—a group so extreme that the Southern Poverty Law Center listed it as a hate group—to invite an *actual* fascist, Nick Griffin, to speak on that campus in 2007. Griffin, the chairman of the far-right British National Party who was convicted in 1998 for incitement of racial hatred related to his Holocaust denials (he has referred to the Holocaust as a "Holohoax"), was brought in to deliver a speech denouncing Islam. Griffin's party opposes black-white marriages, believes that blacks are less intelligent than whites, and has stated that ethnic minorities should be restricted to two to three percent of the British population. While Griffin's speech was not officially part of IFAW events, it took place on the last day and many believed that IFAW-related activities "made it easier for others to attack Islam on campus.[554]

In April 2008, the second IFAW took place on an estimated 100 campuses across America and featured such luminaries as blogger and author Robert Spencer, who despite having no academic background in Islamic Studies, has made a career of Islam-bashing. Spencer is the founder of the notoriously Islamophobic website Jihad Watch and a regular contributor to Horowitz's FrontPage Magazine. Most recently, Spencer expressed his sympathy for Hutaree, an anti-government, Christian militia group based in Lenawee County, Michigan. Members of the organization consider themselves soldiers in a coming battle with the Anti-Christ. In March 2010, nine individuals thought to be Hutaree members were arrested for their alleged involvement in a plot to kill police officers while they attended funeral services for fallen comrades.

Other speakers included Daniel Pipes, director of the Middle East Forum, who established Campus Watch in 2002—a website that "monitors" Middle East Studies on campuses for the field's alleged sins including, among others, its anti-Israel, anti-American bias.[555] Pipes is also well-known for penning a 1990 article in *National Review* entitled "The Muslims Are Coming, the Muslims Are Coming" in which he claimed that "Western European societies are unprepared for the massive immigration of brown-skinned peoples cooking strange foods and maintaining different standards of hygiene." While "all immigrants bring exotic customs and attitudes," "Muslim customs are more troublesome than most."[556] Predictably, he has been an outspoken proponent for the profiling and internment of Muslims in the United States. In addition to his Muslim-bashing shtick, Pipes has added Obama-smearing to his repugnant resume by penning articles for publications such as FrontPage Magazine in which he denounces the President as pro-Arab and anti-Israel. Pipes has also fuelled the right-wing lunatic fringe with his claims that Obama is a closet Muslim.

Tea-Partying and Obama-Bashing 101

Since 2009, Horowitz has become an advocate for, and a darling of, the so-called Tea Party "movement." Here I place the term movement in quotation marks since there are numerous reasons to view the Tea Partyers' claims to be a social movement with a healthy dose of skepticism. Indeed, some have noted that this "movement" is a clear example of "astroturfing" (a PR fronted, fake grassroots "movement") and that it has been funded by corporate special interests and right-wing billionaires, supported by conservative think tanks and heavily promoted by the Fox News network.

The "movement" was initially birthed out of a rant made by former futures trader turned CNBC pundit Rick Santelli. Speaking from the floor of the Chicago Mercantile Exchange on February 19, 2009, Santelli, who has since been dubbed the godfather of the Tea Party movement, launched into an attack on the Obama administration's plan to assist distressed homeowners in danger of foreclosure.[557] Santelli asserted that the plan was "promoting bad behavior" and forcing Americans to "subsidize the losers' mortgages" and proposed a nationwide referendum, via the Internet, on the matter of subsidizing those mortgages.[558] He then called on "capitalists" to join him at a Chicago tea party on the banks of Lake Michigan.

The diatribe went viral generating millions of hits on YouTube and within hours it spawned a website, OfficialChicagoTeaParty.com. By the end of the following week, dozens of rallies and protests against Obama's economic policies began to sprout up across the country. Initially, these were believed to be authentic, spontaneous expressions of grass-roots activism and citizen outrage. It has since been revealed that Santelli's tea party tirade was linked to familiar names in the Republican political machine—from "PR operatives who specialize in imitation-grassroots PR campaigns ('astroturfing') to bigwig politicians and notorious billionaire funders."[559] According to Ames and Levine, the call for a Chicago tea party was the "launch event of a carefully organized and sophisticated PR campaign, one in which Santelli served as a front man, using the CNBC airwaves for publicity" for some of the "craziest and sleaziest rightwing oligarch clans" the "country has ever produced."[560] These include the Koch family, whose deceased scion, Fred Koch, was a co-founder of the extremist John Birch Society. The family fortunes, derived mainly from oil and gas, have helped to support the Koch family foundations which have, in turn, been generous donors to a number of conservative, free-market organizations including the Heritage Foundation which has also been active in promoting the Tea Partyers. Additionally, Tea Partyers have been connected to FreedomWorks, an organization run by Republican former House majority leader Richard (Dick) Armey that has been funded by the Sarah Scaife and Bradley foundations.

Despite its questionable origins, the tea party "movement" has gained momentum and has been given an inordinate amount of attention by the mainstream media. While some have argued that it represents disgruntled working-class people from across the political spectrum who have grown tired of corporate control (i.e. government bailouts of large corporations), the "movement" is "actually quite affluent, suburban, white, male, older, and religious."[561] According to a *CBS* and *New York Times* poll taken in April, 2010, a fifth of Tea Party supporters make more than

$100,000 and a whopping 92% believe that Obama is "moving the country to socialism."[562] The "movement" is essentially a hodge-podge of right-wing Christian evangelicals, militiamen, neo-Birchers, white supremacists, gun nuts, anti-immigration proponents, and "birthers"—those who remain convinced that President Obama is "a Muslim double agent born in Kenya."[563] It is, in short, a "movement" dominated by angry whites who lament "big" government and champion free market fundamentalism. On this point Street and DiMaggio are worth quoting at considerable length:

> Angry though they may be, these right-wing 'populists' hardly come from disadvantaged and working-class sections of the U.S. populace ... 75 percent of them have college educations; 76 percent enjoy household incomes above $50,000 (including a fifth of them making more than $100,000); 78 percent describe their financial situations as 'good' or 'fairly good;' 65 percent of them identify as either middle or middle upper class; 59 percent are men; 75 percent are 45 or older; and 89 percent are white. Consistent with these relatively privileged demographics, 54 percent are open supporters of the Republican Party ... and 72 percent describe themselves as 'conservative.' Fully 57 percent of them (compared to just 27 percent of the U.S. populace as a whole) report having a 'favorable' view of George W. Bush ... and just 6 percent of them (compared to 39 percent of Americans) think that the Bush administration is the primary cause of the current federal budget deficit ... One of their great gripes with Obama, for whom their disapproval is massive (88 percent for Tea Party supporters) ... is that his policies 'favor the poor.' This curious judgment on the corporatist, Wall Street-captive Obama administration is shared by 55 percent of the Tea Party supporters but only 27 percent of the overall populace. Consistent with this revealing 'grievance,' 80 percent of the Tea Party supporters think it is a 'bad idea' to 'raise taxes on households that make more than $250,000 a year ... Nearly three-fourths (73 percent) of the Tea Party crowd thinks that 'providing government benefits to poor people encourages them to remain poor' and does NOT 'help them until they begin to stand on their own' ... Tea Partyers are hardly poor or dispossessed, suffering under the economic collapse and recession, but falsely supporting pro-business, anti-worker policies at their own expense. The 'populist uprising' of the Tea Party crowd over current economic conditions reflects their own comparative affluence and lack of willingness to share the benefits they enjoy with others as well as a related venomous propaganda campaign undertaken by the Republican Party, business, and the right-wing media, designed to manufacture anger among relatively privileged sections of the populace ... The Tea Partyers are symptomatic of a broader egoistic hypocrisy among much of the nation's relatively well-off populace. Their problem is not really with big government and welfare (as long as they benefit); rather they despise government when it is employed to help the poor.[564]

Although Tea Partyers claim to abhor big government and excessive federal spending and express concern about unsustainable debt, they exempt the "$1 trillion-a-year Pentagon system (which accounts for nearly half of the world's military spending and maintains more than 1,000 military bases spread across over 130 nations), global capitalism, and plutocratic tax cuts (for the rich) from their sense of what is undermining the nation's economic prospects."[565] Accordingly, they have had little to say about the role that the Bush administration played in fueling the massive deficit that Obama inherited. Through massive military spending, huge tax cuts for the wealthy few, and a failure to regulate the banking industry, Bush and his conservative brethren were largely responsible for the financial meltdown that crashed the economy before the dreaded Democrats came to power.

Despite strident denials from its members and media supporters such as Rush Limbaugh and Glenn Beck, "racism remains endemic" within the Tea Party "movement."[566] Some have declared that teabaggers are working to promote white Christian ideologies and cultural bigotry—evidence of which was clearly on display in the opening speech of the first Tea Party Nation convention held in Nashville, Tennessee in February 2010 delivered by former Colorado Republican member of the House of Representatives Tom Tancredo. Tancredo, a vehement anti-immigration politician and failed 2008 presidential candidate, lambasted multiculturalism which he suggested had destroyed the social fabric of American society and spoke out against "Islamification." However, his most obvious display of racism came when he stated that Obama was elected because the country did not require "a civics literacy test before people can vote," which was an allusion to the practices of Southern segregationists who would administer difficult qualification tests to blacks to impede their electoral participation. Tancredo's call for a "counter-revolution" based on Judeo-Christian principles was met with resounding applause and a standing ovation.[567] Amid the rabble-rousing and xenophobia, there was another unifying force at the convention— zealous support for former Vice-Presidential candidate Sarah Palin— who was the highly anticipated keynote speaker at the convention. In her address, Palin admonished Obama for his economic policies and for being "weak" on the war on terror. Heavy on the empty rhetoric which she has become known for, Palin's oration was effusive in its praise for the teabaggers whom she claimed represented the future of American politics.[568]

The actions and beliefs of Tea Party supporters have already led some to suggest that the "movement" could easily take on a fascist complexion. For example, Wright notes that while teabaggers "may not be full-blown fascists at this time," they are "definitely leaning in that direction." Wright cites the movement's hyper-patriotism, religious fundamentalism, xenophobia, and hyper-militarism as indicative of its fascistic tendencies and claims that, similar to earlier manifestations of fascism, the Tea Party "movement" thrives on "fear, anger, ignorance and resentment among the people."[569] Perhaps that is why Horowitz has found a friendly home in the Tea Party—it embodies many of the elements of PC.

In April 2010, Horowitz received a standing ovation from a crowd of Tea Party activists who had gathered to hear him speak at an event in Santa Barbara. In his address, Horowitz made the following remarks:

Let me say that I am probably the happiest conservative this year … because I spent 20 years trying to tell conservatives, 'These people are not liberals. They're socialists, they're leftists, and they hate you and they hate this country, and they are very dangerous' ... 'But I'm a happy camper, because for the first time in 20 years, this year people are waking up on the right.'[570]

When the conversation turned to the matter of the Obama presidency, Horowitz expressed his dismay at how "a guy who was brought up Communist" could be elected president and he called Obama a liar.[571]

Horowitz has gone so far as to provide a manual of sorts for Teabaggers. Adapting and revising material from his manifesto, *The Art of Political War*, Horowitz posted a document entitled "The Art of Political War for Tea Parties" on his FrontPage Magazine website. In it he claims that the

> Obama machine is spending trillions of tax-payer dollars to finance their takeover of the American workplace and stifle the independence of the American people. But America is resilient nation {sic} built on the principles of private property and individual freedom, and the resistance to their socialist plans has already begun.[572]

The document goes on to condemn "morally bankrupt" and "clueless" Democrats who position themselves as "champions of the under-represented, neglected and oppressed" in a narrative that resembles a "Marxist Morality Play about the powerful and their victims." Horowitz then mocks the Democratic Party for catering to "America's alleged 'victims'—women, children, minorities and the poor" and claims that conservatives know that "nobody in America is really 'oppressed.'"[573] All of this rhetoric from a man who spent a good part of the last decade whining about how conservative whites have been victimized and oppressed within the academy.

In spring 2010, the DHFC introduced a new campaign, a nationwide *Teach-In to Oppose Barack Obama's Radical Transformation of America* in order to "educate students on the steps Obama has taken to swiftly lead our country down the path to Socialism and Big Brother government." The aim is to "alert America's students to the duplicity of our nation's president." Furthermore, the teach-ins are designed to "expose Obama's radical, anti-American and anti-Israel, power-hungry agenda" which is "threatening the constitutional freedoms, financial security, and physical safety of all Americans."[574] The DHFC pledges to take out "ads in college newspapers around the country educating students on Obama's radical decisions" and to seek "major coverage of these protests from television commentators such as Glenn Beck, Sean Hannity and Bill O'Reilly" as well as the "radio talk show world."[575]

In a student guide that outlines Horowitz's new initiative, the DHFC also promises to work with organizations such as the Young America's Foundation, the Leadership Institute and the Heritage Foundation (all of which were discussed in chapter two) to help bring to campuses

> teams of nationally recognized experts on issues such as the administration's catastrophic health care plan, its assault on the community; its ruinously expensive environmental policies; and its weakness on national security and endless apologies for America and appeasement of foreign dictators.[576]

Accordingly, the guide states that the teach-in panels will be divided into four sections: health care, national security, the economy and the environment. Among potential speakers being promoted by DHFC are the aforementioned Robert Spencer of Jihad Watch, Jonah Goldberg, Chris Horner, Sally Pipes and Donald Lambro.

On March 3, 2010, George Washington University hosted the first in the series of planned teach-ins. The event, which was organized in conjunction with the DHFC and the YAF, took place on the GWU campus in Washington, D.C. and was titled "The Barack Obama Epic Failure Teach-In." The first orator was Donald Lambro, the chief political correspondent for the *Washington Times*, the right-wing newspaper founded in 1982 by Unification Church founder Reverend Sun Myung Moon.[577] Lambro, who received an award from CPAC in 1981 for "outstanding" journalism, has been a featured speaker at seminars sponsored by the National Journalism Center—the Bradley and Olin funded outfit that became part of YAF in 2002. Next on the roster was Chris Horner, the author of *Red Hot Lies: How Global Warming Alarmists Use Threats, Fraud, and Deception to Keep You Misinformed* and *The Politically Incorrect Guide to Global Warming and Environmentalism* both of which were published by the conservative publishing house Regnery. He is a Senior Fellow at the Competitive Enterprise Institute (CEI), yet another think tank that has benefitted from Scaife, Olin, and Bradley foundation largesse, and which receives most of its funding (approximately 40%) from large corporations including ExxonMobil which has given the CEI more than $2 million since 1998.[578] Not surprisingly, the institute is known for generating anti-environmental, corporate-friendly commentary and that is precisely what Horner delivered in his speech on Obama's environmental policy which he claimed was an "excuse to increase government power."[579]

Jonah Goldberg spoke last on national security issues. Goldberg, a current contributor to *National Review* and former employee at the American Enterprise Institute, "has no credentials beyond the right-wing nepotism that has enabled his career as a pundit."[580] His career as a media commentator was literally launched from his mother's coattails and he is certainly no expert on national security. (His mother, Lucianne Goldberg, was at the heart of the Bill Clinton sex scandal after she advised Linda Tripp to secretly tape her conversations with Monica Lewinsky).

In late March 2010, the DHFC and the University of Southern California College Republicans co-hosted another teach-in that featured three speakers—Sally Pipes, David Bahnsen and Victor Davis Hanson. Pipes, a vehement opponent of universal health care, kicked off the event with a sermon opposing the health care reforms proposed by the Obama administration which was predictable given her position as head of the Pacific Research Institute (PRI), a conservative think tank which peddles free market ideology and which is associated with the American Enterprise Institute and the Heritage Foundation.[581] From 1985 to 2005, PRI received $8, 904,800 from a variety of rightist sources including the Lynde and Harry Bradley Foundation and the Sarah Scaife Foundation. Its corporate sponsors include, among others, Chevron, ExxonMobil, and most significantly, the Pharmaceutical Research and Manufacturers of American (PhRMA), one of the largest and most influential lobby organizations in the nation that represents 48 pharmaceutical companies and advocates for industry friendly policies.[582]

David Bahnsen, a former senior VP at Morgan Stanley (a bank that received $10 billion of public money as part of the federal government's bailout of failed financial institutions) and self-proclaimed "disciple of Milton Friedman," "lover of Ronald Reagan" and *"National Review* kind of conservative" spoke about Obama's

"disastrous economic philosophy" and lauded the very kind of free market fundamentalism that precipitated the mid-September 2008 financial crisis which crippled
the global economy and led to one of the biggest recessions since the Great
Depression.[583] Rounding out the panel was Victor David Hanson, a Senior Fellow
at the conservative Hoover Institute and the recipient of a $200,000 prize from the
Lynde and Harry Bradley Foundation in 2008. According to a report about the teach-
in posted on the DHFC website, Hanson spoke about foreign policy in the context
of "moral and cultural relativism practiced by the Democrats in Congress." Hanson's
disdain for relativism is rather amusing since the man who invited him to the event—
none other than David Horowitz—latched onto the concept of relativism while
campaigning for ABOR. In any case, such are the "experts" touted by the DHFC,
most of who are either right-wing Republican gasbags or shills who dance to the tune
of the corporations that pay them.

Despite what Horowitz has claimed over the years, he is merely another far right
ideologue committed not to "truth" and "balance," but to advancing PC in the service
of corporate interests that have supported his various endeavors for decades.

AMERICAN COUNCIL OF TRUSTEES AND ALUMNI (ACTA)
AND THE DEFENSE OF CIVILIZATION

In waging the culture war on academia and specifically liberal/left intellectuals,
Horowitz worked on a parallel track with Lynne Cheney, wife of ex-Vice-President
Dick Cheney, and former head of the National Endowment for the Humanities.
But, while Horowitz has been unabashed in taking the low road in his crusade,
Cheney and her American Council of Trustees and Alumni (ACTA) have *attempted*
(one could argue unsuccessfully) to disguise their brand of McCarthyism in much
more palatable terms.

Founded in 1995 and formerly known as the National Alumni Forum, ACTA
was established by the Intercollegiate Studies Institute (ISI) with seed money from
the Olin and Bradley foundations. It was launched by, among others, Lynne Cheney
and Senator Joe Lieberman. According to its website, ACTA "is a 501(c) (3) tax
exempt, non-partisan, non-profit educational organization committed to academic
freedom, excellence and accountability at America's colleges and universities."[584]
One might, reasonably, question its claim to being non-partisan given its association
with other influential conservative entities including the AEI, NAS, and the Federalist
Society. Its board of directors once included America's self-appointed national
scold William J. Bennett and now boasts NAS president Stephen Balch.

ACTA's president since 2003, Anne Neal, is a lawyer and spouse of Thomas E.
Petri, a Republican representative from Wisconsin. Its former chairman, Jerry L.
Martin—who retired in 2009—held senior positions at the National Endowment of
the Humanities while Lynne Cheney served as NEH chair. In addition, its program
director, Charles Mitchell, has had prior experience working with the Heritage
Foundation, Young Conservatives of Pennsylvania, and the Foundation for Individual
Rights in Education (FIRE), another conservative organization funded by the
Bradley and Scaife foundations. Its board of advisors once included T. Kenneth Cribb,

president of the ISI; Herbert I. London, president of the Hudson Institute, former John M. Olin Professor of Humanities at New York University, and regular contributor to right-wing publications including *National Review* and *American Spectator*, and anti-feminist author Christina Hoff Sommers. It currently counts as "research fellows" two individuals, Erin O'Connor and Maurice Black, who have affiliations with the Moving Picture Institute (MPI). MPI was established by Thor Halvorssen (who was also a founder of FIRE), often referred to as the right's Michael Moore, whose institute makes films that are pro-business, anti-communist, and anti-environmentalist. It too has received funding from foundations including Lynde and Harry Bradley.

While ACTA claims to be an organization committed to, among other things, "academic freedom" and the "free exchange of ideas on campus," the privilege of academic freedom does not apparently extend to those that ACTA (without explanation) defines as barbarians:

> The ideas of academic freedom and free speech are at the core of the American academic tradition. Teachers must be free to teach, students must be free to learn, and freedom in research is essential to the advancement of truth. In the past, systematic threats to academic freedom have been external. Today, however, the threat to academic freedom comes from within. The barbarians are not at the gates; they are inside the walls.[585]

Exactly who are the barbarians? Trotting out the cast of usual suspects, the barbarians are the "politically correct" who are responsible for the "growing political intolerance and abuse of academic freedom on campus."[586] Of course, we have heard this tune before. And, while time and circumstances may have changed, for cultural conservatives, the song as they say has remained the same.

Much of what is labeled political intolerance in such exaggerated statements is actually critique—it is the free speech of students and scholars that the right has no interest in hearing. In fact, cultural conservatives and right-wing crusaders position themselves as champions of free speech only when it suits their purposes. Howard Zinn is instructive on this form of political duplicity:

> The right declares their admiration for such freedom in principle ... But when teachers actually use this freedom, introducing new subjects, new readings, outrageous ideas, challenging authority, criticizing "Western civilization," amending the "canon" of great books as listed by certain educational authorities of the past—then the self-appointed guardians of "higher culture" become enraged.[587]

This hypocrisy is routinely illustrated in ACTA's quarterly publication *Inside Academe* (IA) which, according to the organization's website, goes to over "12,000 readers" including more than "3,500 college and university trustees."[588] The publication regularly features churlish, disingenuous attacks on all things "multicultural" (including women's studies, race and ethnic studies, and gay and lesbian studies). In issue after issue, people who are clearly incapable of reasoned debate childishly ridicule critical scholarly discourses and entire fields of study. This makes a mockery out of ACTA's stated commitment to academic excellence and demonstrates that its alleged admiration for academic freedom and free speech is hollow—if not downright mendacious—in the face of its activities to purge campuses of "different" perspectives and dissent. This became even more pronounced in the aftermath of "9/11" as ACTA sought to apply the Bush Doctrine of "you are either with us or you are with the terrorists" to intellectual life.

The very first page of the fall 2001 edition of IA included a brief section entitled "Defending Civilization" which resuscitated George Will's early 1990's hyperbolic characterization of Lynne Cheney as the "secretary of domestic defense," and which called for a renewed commitment to "Western civilization." In grand, melodramatic fashion, the commentary claimed that:

> It was not only America that was attacked, but civilization. We were attacked not for our vices, but for our virtues—for what we stand for. It is our principles, embodying the ideals of Western civilization and of free societies everywhere, that draw the hatred of those who despise a world based on liberty and the rule of law. A people cannot be expected to defend what they do not understand. As chairman of the National Endowment for the Humanities, Lynne Cheney championed the study of Western civilization and the American past—for which George Will called her "the secretary of domestic defense." Will's point is now more urgent than ever. The bedrock of our ability to sustain ourselves as a civilization is an understanding of those great ideas that animate and inform the human spirit. In response, ACTA has established the Defense of Civilization Fund to press colleges and universities to renew their commitment to the kind of education that sustains a free society and to restore American history and Western civilization requirements. We must defend the homefront.[589]

The hysterical and blatant use of military slang in ACTA's statement echoed Bush's post-9/11 posturing and his tedious claims about the rationale behind the terrorist attacks—a disdain for freedom. In addition to epitomizing the militarization of public discourse, such comments also implied (and not likely inadvertently) that Bush's foreign policy was inherently just, that it should be obediently accepted and never doubted because the "homeland" was in danger of being wounded by irrational evil-doers who hated "our" freedom and democracy. Like Bush, it also cast issues in typical Manichaean fashion. These forms of patriotically correct rhetoric and Manichaeanism were further displayed in a report ACTA issued entitled *Defending Civilization: How Our Universities are Failing America and What Can Be Done About It.*

There is little doubt that *Defending Civilization* was intended to be one of the first salvos in the right's reinvigorated culture war against liberal and left-leaning professors. And, in that quest, the organization shamelessly exploited the tragedy of "9/11" to advance its political agenda. One need only look to the front cover of the report that sported the famous photograph of three New York City firefighters hoisting the American flag amid the rubble of the World Trade Center to confirm that. Lewis Lapham, in fact, likened the document to brazen propaganda:

> For the last four months the curators of the national news media have done their patriotic best to muffle objections to our worldwide crusade against

terrorism ... but I didn't think that we were well on the way to a ministry of state propaganda until I came across "Defending Civilization," a guide to the preferred forms of free speech issued ... by the American Council of Trustees and Alumni. Knowing little else about the organization except what could be inferred from the writings of the conservative and neoconservative ideologues prominently identified as its leading lights ... I took it as a given that the document would read like a sermon preached against the wickedness of the 1960s and the great darkness brought down upon the nation's universities by the werewolves of the intellectual left. It's an old sermon, discredited by the facts but still much beloved by the parties of the right, and I was prepared for the ritual scourgings of Eros, multiculturalism, and modernity. I expected cant; I didn't expect the bringing of what amounted to a charge of sedition against any university or scholar therein failing to pledge allegiance to the sovereign wisdom of President George W. Bush. I've had occasion to read a good deal of fourth-rate agitprop over the last thirty years, but I don't remember an argument as disgraceful as the one advanced by the American Council of Trustees and Alumni under the rubric of 'academic freedom, quality, and accountability.'[590]

The reports' authors, Jerry Martin and Anne Neal, argued that while the vast majority of American citizens (92%) had rallied behind President Bush's decision to go to war (against Afghanistan) after the terrorist attacks, college and university faculty had not been as enthusiastic and hence were the "weak link" in America's response. Such language, in and of itself, parroted that used by the House Un-American Activities Committee (HUAC) in its McCarthy-era witch hunts—in fact, HUAC used exactly "the same label for one of the scientists they pursued."[591] The report essentially depicted the academy as a passivist fifth wheel undermining the re-solve of a nation that responded to the terrorist attacks with "anger, patriotism, and support of military intervention" and scolded some professors for being short on patriotism and long on self-flagellation—an allegation which stemmed from ACTA's perception that some had "pointed accusatory fingers, not at the terrorists, but at America itself."[592]

Echoing the tactics of McCarthy, the original version of the hit list actually named names by citing 117 instances of so-called unpatriotic speech by university professors and administrators—hardly an earth-shattering figure given the vast enterprise of American higher education. After ACTA received some well-deserved criticism in the media (and from Joe Lieberman)[593] for the McCarthyite missive, it issued an edited version of the report without the names. A revised and expanded version published in February 2002 also excluded the names of the offenders but retained much of the inflammatory rhetoric. For example, the report accused professors of ignoring heroism and for failing to condemn the forces of evil:

Rarely did professors publicly mention heroism, rarely did they discuss the difference between good and evil, the nature of Western political order or the virtue of a free society. Indeed, the message of many in academe was clear: BLAME AMERICA FIRST ... The events of September 11 underscored a deep divide between the mainstream public reaction and that of our intellectual elites ... The American public had no difficult calling evil by its rightful name. Why is it so hard for many faculty to do the same?[594]

Such sweeping generalizations mirrored the presidential bombast of George W. Bush who, in many speeches after "9/11," referred to his government as the guardian of goodness and freedom that had to fight evil wherever it lurked. He also added, on numerous occasions, that any nation opposed to his agenda of 'smoking out' the terrorists was a supporter of terrorism. By implication and extension, anyone who dared to criticize or oppose the war on terror was, as former Attorney General John Ashcroft suggested, aiding and abetting the enemy. Hence, those academics who had a difficult time buttressing the simplistic logic of the Bush administration were acquiescent minions of terrorism. Of course, such accusations were ludicrous but any attempts to contextualize the events of "9/11" in relation to American foreign policy or to offer critical perspectives on a militarized policy response were regarded as unpatriotic. The message from ACTA was clear—fall in line behind Bush or else. As Street has argued:

We can note the sheer idiocy of their related idea that to mention factors (including U.S. policies in the Middle East) that caused 9/11 is to justify terrorism ... We can note their false conflation of patriotism with blind loyalty to the current White House's aggressively imperialist and profoundly dangerous foreign policies.[595]

In the revised version of *Defending Civilization*, Martin and Neal included 115 objectionable statements that were part of what they referred to as "campus responses" to "9/11." But, interestingly enough, only 43 (or 37%) were attributed to faculty and this included instructors and lecturers—in other words, part-time workers who can hardly be considered part of an intellectual elite class. The rest of the examples came not from faculty but from students, various speakers at anti-war teach-ins and even protest placards. Others came from third hand sources as many of the quotes in the report were cited from conservative websites and publications including *National Review*, the *Wall Street Journal*, FoxNews.com, and Horowitz's FrontPage Magazine.

Additionally, many of the statements cited in the document were rather innocuous. Consider the following: "Break the cycle of violence" attributed to a Pomona College faculty panel discussing U.S. obligations in the Mideast; "We have to learn to use courage for peace instead of war"—a statement made by a Professor of Religious Studies at Pomona College; and "there is a lot of skepticism about the administration's policy of going to war"—an opinion articulated by a New York University professor of communications. Apparently, the staff at ACTA found such proclamations subversive enough to include them in their litany of "anti-American" comments.

In singling out the "intellectual elite" of the nation for public censure, the document recited the same stale formula that has been a mainstay of what Thomas Frank calls "backlash politics." Central to the jeremiads of backlash politicians and cultural conservatives is an assault on the "liberal elite" that is hopelessly out of touch with salt of the earth Americans. Frank explains that the notion of a liberal elite

> has taken many forms over the years—Spiro Agnew called them 'nattering nabobs of negativism,' the neocons dubbed them 'the new class,' while others simply refer to them as 'intellectuals'—but in its basic outlines the grievance has remained the same. Our culture and our schools and our government, back-lashers insist, are controlled by an overeducated ruling class that is contemptuous of the beliefs and practices of the masses of ordinary people. Those who run America, the theory holds, are despicable ... they are arrogant. They are snobs. They are liberals. The idea of a liberal elite is not intellectually robust. It's never been enunciated with anything approaching scholarly rigor, it has been refuted countless times, and it falls apart under scrutiny. Yet the idea persists.[596]

Of course, the idea of a liberal elite controlling the levers of power in the United States is as baseless as conservative charges of a liberal media controlling the public sphere.[597] Yet, it is has been an effective ideological approach that has enabled conservatives to present themselves as 'on the side' of the little people, the Lilliputians, against the Brobdingnagian forces of the so-called liberal establishment. It also enabled rightists to ideologically position themselves, not only against 'them,' but perhaps more disturbingly as part of an imagined community of 'us.' In this case, the 'us' refers to red-blooded, God-fearing, capitalism-loving, patriotically correct citizens.

As they have been prone to do in the past, cultural conservatives also resort to simplistic formulations that pit the West vs. the Rest, culture/civilization versus barbarism and the primitive contaminating forces of the "other." The sanctimonious indignation that typifies this perspective rests on a defensiveness in which all "others" are seen as intent on ravaging "our" civilization and "way of life." Indeed, this was clearly evident in *Defending Civilization* which attributed the failure of faculty to properly call "evil" by its rightful name to the "moral relativism" which has become a "staple of academic life" and presumably because survey courses in "Western civilization" have been marginalized since the 1960s."[598]

Street observes that much of *Defending Civilization*'s basic thesis echoed William Bennett's holier-than-thou ranting in *Why We Fight: Moral Clarity and the War on Terrorism* which castigated the left-wing takeover of academia and called for a "vast relearning of the American past," an "honest study" of American history "undistorted by the lens of political correctness and pseudosophisticated relativism."[599] Predictably, the cure called for by Bennett was hardly new since it echoed what his friend and co-cultural warrior, Lynne Cheney, had been prescribing in the early 1990s. Although the former Second Lady had no official working role in ACTA when the report was published in 2002, a lengthy quote by her which graced the inside cover, tended to give the document, "the appearance of a quasi-official statement of government policy."[600]

Moreover, while Cheney had no hand in actually writing the report, many of its themes resounded with apodictic familiarity and were hardly distinguishable from the drivel she churned out in the early 1990s—particularly that found in a pamphlet she penned in 1992 with the Pickwickian title *Telling the Truth*. The main arguments of the tract (which then served as the basis for a subsequent book published in 1995) were that (i) the growing politicization on campuses was making it difficult to tell the 'truth;' (ii) liberal and leftist faculty members were guilty of assailing the principles of academic freedom and indoctrinating students in classrooms; (iii) Western civilization courses were being marginalized by an academic "gang of four" (feminists, Marxists, multiculturalists, and postmodern theorists) and; (iv) the very nobility and virtuosity of the 'American way' (which she contended was the high point in world history) were under attack by tenured radicals. Taken together, these dangerous developments were, according to Cheney, responsible for the precipitous decline of academic standards as multicultural mediocrity trumped principles of meritocracy and scholarly excellence.[601] Far from "telling the truth," Cheney's shallow and partisan attack, which was released just six weeks prior to the 1992 election at the height of the anti-political correctness crusade, was devoid of any empirical evidence to substantiate her wild allegations and was rife with anecdotes, innuendos, mistruths, and, in some cases, blatant lies.[602]

Of course, we have learned that telling lies does not faze conservatives as the "they have weapons of mass destruction" Iraq war debacle clearly illustrated. Hence, it came as no shock to see that Cheney's previous lies did nothing to damage her credibility and that her overblown and misleading charges were essentially recycled in *Defending Civilization*. In fact, it was entirely predictable to see Cheney revive the project for cultural conservatism. As Wiener noted in a 2000 article published in the run-up to Bush's presidential campaign, Bill Bennett had told the *Washington Post* that Cheney would be "hard to muzzle" with respect to "culture wars" if she made it to the White House.[603]

There can be little doubt that the subtext of ACTA's report repeated Cheney's long-time assertions that the country and the universities were going to hell in a hand basket because of "academic trends" that valorize "moral relativism" and which "suggest that Western civilization is the primary source of the world's ills."[604] And, of course, the twin bogeymen of Sixties radicalism and political correctness were summoned to explain the moral decay of our institutions of higher learning.

> Until the 1960s, colleges typically required students to take survey courses in Western civilization. Since then, those courses have been supplanted by a smorgasbord of often narrow and trendy classes and incoherent requirements that do not convey the great heritage of human civilization. Accompanying this basic failure is a campus atmosphere increasingly unfriendly to the free exchange of ideas. Students have reported more and more that they are intimidated by professors and fellow students if they question "politically correct" ideas or fail to conform to a particular ideology.[605]

The appeal to a mythical "golden age" in academe is one of the hallmarks of conservative cultural discourse—from the late Allan Bloom to Cheney to ACTA. In fact, at a meeting that ACTA hosted in 2007, one of the speakers blatantly called for a return to the 1950s university, which conjured up a portrait of higher education when "student and faculty populations were far smaller, whiter, wealthier, and more predominately male."[606] So it was hardly novel for the authors of *Defending Civilization* to weave a tale of a lost age of social cohesiveness, a pre-Sixties Shangri-La that was corrupted by the combined forces of political correctness, multiculturalism and critical theory. And, of course, the conservative recipe would not have been complete without a few updated dollops of anti-multiculturalism and pro-Americanism so the authors obliged accordingly:

> ... instead of ensuring that students understand the unique contributions of America and Western civilization—the civilizations under attack—universities are rushing to add courses on Islamic and Asian cultures ... in the rush to add such courses, those institutions reinforced the mindset that it was America—and America's failure to understand Islam—that were to blame.[607]

Martin and Neal then directly quoted none other than Lynne Cheney to further prop up their arguments:

> 'To say that it is more important now [to study Islam] implies that the events of Sept. 11 were our fault, that it was our failure ... that led to so many deaths and so much destruction,' said the American Council of Trustees and Alumni's founding chairman Lynne V. Cheney in a speech on October 5. Instead, said, Cheney, students need to 'know the ideas and ideals on which our nation has been built ... If there were one aspect of schooling from kindergarten through college to which I would give added emphasis today, it would be American history.'[608]

Of course, it would be safe to assume that Cheney's version of American history would likely dispense with some of its disconcerting details—including the prolonged and problematic U.S. intervention in the Middle East. One might also be tempted to ask Ms. Cheney and her ACTA colleagues why it is that their beloved America—presumably the greatest world defender of democracy—has, over the last five decades,

> funded, advised, and sponsored the overthrow of democratically elected reformist governments that attempted to introduce egalitarian redistributive economic programs in countries such as Guatemala, Guyana, the Dominican Republic, Brazil, Chile, Uruaguay, Syria, Indonesia (under Sukarno), Greece, Cyprus, Argentina, Bolivia, Haiti, and the Congo?[609]

Or, for that matter, why America has participated in wars of attrition and attacks on "soft targets" such as "schools, farm cooperatives, health clinics, and whole villages in places such as Cuba, Angola, Mozambique, Ethiopia, Portugal, Nicaragua, Cambodia, East Timor, Western Sahara, Egypt, Lebanon, Peru, Iran, Syria, Jamaica, South Yemen, and the Fiji Islands" or why it has a record of direct military aggression through "invasions and assaults against Vietnam, Laos, the Dominican Republic, North Korea, Cambodia, Lebanon, Grenada, Panama, Libya, Iraq, Somalia, Yugoslavia, and Afghanistan?"[610] It is precisely that legacy which Cheney and ACTA would like to suppress since it represents a serious disconnect between actual historical realities and the myths propagated by PC, including America's alleged commitment to the ideals of 'freedom,' 'democracy' and 'civilization.' Indeed, one might have asked Mrs. Cheney how government-sanctioned torture fit into her version of civilization. After all, she and her husband took to the airwaves to defend the Bush administration's use of torture, including water boarding, as moral and necessary. Such are the "cultural values" they wish to pass on to the next generation.

Domestically, the historical record is equally littered with incongruities between rhetoric and reality:

> Things don't get much more comfortable for ... ACTA's whitewashed notion of the American historical record when we focus on domestic U.S. history, burdened with the shattered dreams and often enough the mangled bodies of slaves, coolies, and industrial workers, and marked by an ongoing conflict between the democratic ideal and the authoritarian power of Big Capital and the corporate plutocracy. [There are] harsh contradictions, both imperial and domestic, between American rhetoric and American reality.[611]

Street adds that

> few parts of the ACTA's argument are more preposterous than the notion that the lessons of closely studying the Founders and their charter documents necessarily inspires patriotic respect for the republic's commitment to "freedom" and "democracy." The Founders included some brilliant individuals, but their brilliance was harnessed largely to the cause of antidemocracy. Drawn from the elite propertied segments of a deeply stratified society ... [t]hey may have diverged on numerous questions but they clearly agreed on one basic principle: the common people, with little or no property, must not have too much power.[612]

Despite their stated objective of wanting students to be more informed about American history, ACTA wants history to be taught *only* in its whitewashed version in keeping with the tenets of patriotically correct pedagogy.

But more than this, while the report as a whole and on its surface, appealed to civility and respect for academic freedom, in an alarming deployment of doublespeak, it condemned the free speech of individuals who dared to challenge the wisdom of the Bush administration's foreign policy and its Machiavellian tendencies. And, as previously noted, it also chastised proposed courses in Islamic studies that may have been beneficial in providing context for the events of 9/11, encouraging critical and reasoned thinking on matters of international policy, and creating greater awareness about other cultures. Therefore, to imply intentionally or unintentionally and, may I add, without providing any concrete evidence that such efforts would automatically reinforce a "blame America" mentality was simply disingenuous. Far from promoting the free exchange of ideas which ACTA states as part of its mission, such posturing demonstrated little respect for difference, dissent, and even democracy itself.

Lynne Cheney and her fellow culture warriors have long fought for greater control over curriculum but they have been far less honest about it than their conservative predecessors like William F. Buckley, Jr. To his credit, the late Buckley was always forthright about his pro-capitalist, pro-Christianity proclivities and his belief that academic freedom should be denied to those who disagreed with those positions. Cheney and ACTA, on the other hand, cowardly resorted to coded phrases like 'Western civilization' and 'free speech' to thinly disguise their agenda and their attempts to maliciously discredit those who refused the brand of PC they were promoting.

This became glaringly obvious towards the end of the report's prefatory remarks that summoned the ghosts of Hitler and Nazism:

> We learn from history what happens when a nation's intellectuals are unwilling to sustain its civilization. In 1933, the Oxford Student Union held a famous debate over whether it was moral for Britons to fight for king and country. After a wide-ranging discussion in which the leading intellectuals could find no distinction between British colonialism and world fascism, the Union resolved that England would 'in no circumstances fight for king and country.' As the *Wall Street Journal* reported: 'Von Ribbentrop went back with the good news to Germany's new chancellor, Hitler: The West will not fight for its own survival.'[613]

The authoritarian fervor epitomized in such comments must be acknowledged for what it was—a blatant effort to equate critique with lending comfort to the "enemy." Substitute Hitler's moniker with that of Osama Bin Laden and the portrait painted by the authors became abundantly clear. This statement, perhaps more than any other, captured the underlying essence of ACTA's report for it was nothing more than a cover for targeting certain forms of intellectual activity, censoring certain political viewpoints, and curtailing the free speech rights of those who protested Bush's policies and the broader war on terror. It also spoke volumes about ACTA's rigid demands for an intellectual culture of unquestioning obedience, one where loyalty to the homeland was demanded at all costs.

It is somewhat ironic that Martin and Neal chose to raise the specter of Hitler in their concluding remarks since it was *their* campaign against dissent in the universities that had a distinctive Nazi ring to it. There are, of course, important differences as there always are when making such historical comparisons. However, it is nonetheless instructive to remind ourselves that Hitler was able to establish policies of intolerance and suppression with robust public support by convincing the populace that such initiatives would result in a stronger, better Germany. His followers proudly proclaimed that a new, patriotic Germany would be born out of pain, fear and danger while concomitantly warning that internal, menacing forces (similar to ACTA's reference to "barbarians") were working to undermine the nation from the inside. Such posturing was part and parcel of the entire process of Nazification and specifically a campaign called "gleichschaltung"—which literally meant "getting everyone in step." ACTA's calls to defend the homefront, their efforts to publicly humiliate dissidents, and other such tactics which brazenly exploited the fear and tragedy associated with "9/11" were eerily reminiscent of "gleichschaltung."

ACTA's Fuzzy Math

While Horowitz pushed for the Academic Bill of Rights, ACTA's attempt to advance PC was presented under the guise of "intellectual diversity." In 2005, the organization published a pamphlet entitled *Intellectual Diversity: Time for Action* that claimed the "most serious challenge for higher education today is the lack of intellectual diversity"—a problem which they argued had been ignored, even denied, for decades by the sentinels of higher education.[614] ACTA defined intellectual diversity, in the simplest terms, as a "multiplicity of ideas" which should be the "foundation of a learning environment that exposes students to a variety of political, ideological, and other perspectives." According to ACTA and, much to its chagrin, in the "world of higher education, diversity has come to mean a preference for a diversity of *backgrounds,* but not a diversity of *views.*" As a result, "when it comes to social, political, religious, and ideological matters, academe has shown a pronounced preference for only one end of the spectrum."[615]

Of course, ACTA contended that it was the liberal/left side of the political spectrum which was overrepresented in academe. To demonstrate this bias, they cited two studies—one by Rothman, Lichter, and Nevitte and the other by Zinsmeister—both of which were previously discussed and both of which were roundly criticized because of their sloppy, politically partisan, pseudo-scholarship. Nonetheless, ACTA approvingly cited the findings as evidence that "faculty imbalance" in conjunction with the idea that "the 'politically correct' point of view has the right to dominate classroom and campus discussions" has led to "fearful consequences for university life." Examples of these fearful consequences included the following:

> Campus panels on current issues are routinely one-sided. This was made abundantly clear by the response to the 9/11 attacks on the United States. A Yale University teach-in on the events of September 11 failed to include a single spokesman in favor of military action. Similarly, Brooklyn College approved a post-9/11 panel without any representatives of the U.S. or Israeli government's point of view.

Additionally,

> When outside speakers who present a different point of view are invited to campus, they are often shouted down, assaulted, or simply disinvited because the universities say they cannot guarantee their safety. Former Secretary of State Henry Kissinger's address at the University of Texas-Austin had to be cancelled because of threats of violent protest. More recently, William Kristol, editor of the *Weekly Standard*, was struck by a pie-wielding student during a speech about U.S foreign policy at Earlham College.

Finally, the document asserted that students were being "pressured to adopt the political views of their professors"—particularly "beliefs and attitudes related to values such as social justice."[616]

Before going any further, it is necessary to briefly consider these introductory statements. First, ACTA's objections to campus teach-ins that did not include advocates of a pro-military action response are almost laughable. For the most part, public and media discourse post-9/11 were overwhelmingly pro-war—from the "liberal" *New York Times* to CNN to the obvious rah-rah militarism of Fox News.[617] Campus teach-ins were, arguably, the only venues where students could potentially be exposed to *different* points of view that were historically informed rather than knee-jerk reactions demanding "revenge" against the forces of "evil." If ACTA were truly dedicated to diversity of opinion, they should have welcomed the fact that alternative perspectives were being articulated on campuses.

Second, ACTA apparently found it unfathomable that students may have planned protests of Henry Kissinger's speech because some actually viewed him as a war criminal based on his involvement in the overthrow of Salvador Allende in Chile, his support of Suharto in East Timor, and the murderous policies he advocated in Vietnam, Cambodia and elsewhere.[618] Moreover, it was peculiar that ACTA seemed to attribute the actions of a pie-throwing *student* to "faculty imbalance." Of course, the suggestion was that students were non-agenic androids who engaged in such activities because they thought they would please their professors by doing so.

Given its alleged concern with faculty "bias" and its impact on students, ACTA undertook a study that attempted to investigate the lack of intellectual diversity as "objectively and systematically as possible."[619] The group commissioned the Center for Survey Research and Analysis (CSRA) at the University of Connecticut to complete a 'scientific' study of undergraduates in the top 50 colleges and universities as listed by U.S. News & World Report. Of course, such a sample was hardly representative of the nation's diverse system of higher education for it did not include any community colleges or regional four-year institutions. Additionally, of all the institutions included, only four were public—the rest were all private. More significantly, the study's findings did not necessarily support ACTA's arguments. In this context, a review of ACTA's assertions and an analysis of the actual survey responses are warranted.

A *total* of 658 students responded to the commissioned study that was conducted in October and November 2004. Students were asked to respond to a series of questions using a five-point scale from "strongly agree" to "strongly disagree," including a "don't know" category. The results of the survey conducted on ACTA's behalf were included in Appendix A of the pamphlet and they were telling insofar as they revealed ACTA's selective interpretation of them.

For starters, ACTA was concerned with "finding out whether in fact professors introduce politics in the classroom." According to ACTA's summary of the findings, the survey found that a "shocking 49 percent of students at the top 50 colleges and universities say that their professors *frequently* injected political comments into their courses, even if they had nothing to do with the subject." The survey then examined the "atmosphere in the college classroom." Did students, for example, "feel free to raise concerns and question assumptions" and "to make up their own minds without feeling pressured to agree with their professors?" ACTA stated that the answers to such queries were "deeply disturbing" since "29 percent of the respondents felt that they had to agree with the professor's political views to get a good grade." The survey also explored "whether students were being exposed to competing arguments on the central issues of the day," whether "book lists" were "balanced and comprehensive" and whether or not students were introduced to "multiple perspectives, rather than just one side of an argument." Again, ACTA claimed a "disheartening response" given that "48 percent reported campus panels and lecture series on political issues that seemed 'totally one-sided'" while "46 percent said professors 'used the classroom to present their personal political views'" and "42 percent faulted reading assignments for presenting only one side of a controversial issue."[620]

Taken together these results, according to ACTA, demonstrated that faculty members were "importing politics in the classroom in a way" that affected "students' ability to learn." Furthermore, "based on social scientific evidence as well as discussions with professors, administrators, trustees, and higher education experts," the group argued that it was clear that:

1) Today's college faculties are overwhelmingly one-sided in their political and ideological views, especially in the value-laden fields of humanities and social sciences; and
2) This lack of intellectual diversity is undermining the education of students as well as the free exchange of ideas central to the mission of the university; and
3) It is urgent that universities effectively address the challenge of intellectual diversity.[621]

A breakdown of the actual responses, however, leads us to different conclusions than those reached by ACTA. First, we must consider the question pertaining to faculty members expressing political views unrelated to the subject material. In the actual survey, the question (number ten in the list of survey questions) was posed thusly: "On my campus, some professors frequently comment on politics in class even though it has nothing to do with the course." According to the results, 14% of respondents strongly agreed with the statement and 35% somewhat agreed. But significantly, 26% somewhat disagreed and 24% strongly disagreed while another 2% either did not know or refused to answer the question. Naturally, the obvious must be stated—while 49% of students agreed that professors "frequently comment on politics in class," 50% disagreed with the statement. But more sinister was ACTA's interpretation of these findings. While the question asked whether *some* professors frequently *comment on politics* even though it has nothing to do with the course, the introduction to the pamphlet stated that "professors *frequently* injected political comments into their courses." In this sense, the latter implied a more deliberate and calculated attempt to "inject" political discussions in the classroom. It was also misleading since the authors did not include the adjective "some" in their summary.

As Lee suggested, the "phrasing in the report" introduced "ambiguity" and implied "that all the professors in the student's experiences" acted this way. It may have been that students had "one or two teachers during their college careers who they felt were biased" but ACTA's phrasing limited "what we know about the extent of the reported bias" and we "certainly cannot assume it to mean all or most teachers."[622] Additionally, there were no indications of what kinds of "comments on politics" were being reported by students. Moreover, given the vagueness of the question, we do not know whether the political comments were of a liberal/left orientation or whether they were conservative in nature.

Second, ACTA referred to the "disturbing" answers about the "atmosphere in the college classroom" insofar as "29 percent of the respondents felt that they had to agree with the professor's political views to get a good grade."[623] Again, such statements need to be contextualized. Question 11 of the survey was worded as follows: "On my campus, there are courses in which students feel they have to agree with the professor's political or social views in order to get a good grade." In response, 7% strongly agreed and 22% somewhat agreed while 22% somewhat disagreed, 46% strongly disagreed, and 3% did not know. In other words, 68% of the students surveyed *disagreed* about being pressured to agree with a faculty member's political views in order to get a good grade—a fact that ACTA conveniently ignored in its summary of the findings.

Third, in an introductory section entitled "The Impact on Students," the report declared that a "disheartening" "48 percent" of students "reported campus panels and lecture series on political issues that seemed 'totally one-sided.'" In response to the question, 48% (15% strongly agreed and 33% somewhat agreed) did indeed suggest that was the case. However, 46% either somewhat or strongly disagreed while 5% did not know. Furthermore, there was no indication of what one-sided referred to! Given that 84% of the students surveyed described their views as radical left (5%), liberal (46%), and moderate (33%), they may have been referring to panels and presentations being skewed to the right. Of course, one would never surmise that by relying solely on how ACTA framed the results to reinforce its faulty claims of overwhelming liberal faculty bias. More importantly, campus panel discussions and presentations have nothing to do with what may transpire in a classroom setting.

Fourth, although ACTA highlighted the 46% of respondents who strongly or somewhat agreed with the statement that "some professors use the classroom to present their personal political views," 53% somewhat or strongly disagreed. Again, the substance of what constitutes "personal political views" was not addressed. We have no way of knowing whether those personal political views were conservative, liberal, left, etc.

Finally, was the assertion that 42% of students agreed that "some courses have readings which present only one side of a controversial issue." However, in response to the question, the majority (54% of respondents) either somewhat disagreed (26%) or strongly disagreed (28%). Moreover, there was no indication of what a "controversial" issue referred to. As John Lee revealed in his analysis of the report, the authors of the study used vague questions and definitions, failed to rule out alternative explanations and generally did not follow the kinds of rigorous standards that guide quality research. The brief examination of the survey contained herein would seem to support Lee's conclusions.

In example after example, ACTA clearly glossed over the results of its commissioned study when they did not jibe with its ideological agenda, misrepresented them, or paradoxically, did not present a "balanced" portrait of the findings. This seriously undermined ACTA's claims about what was "made clear" by their survey. As noted above, ACTA concluded that faculties were "overwhelming one-sided in their political and ideological views" particularly in the "value-laden fields of the humanities and social sciences." And yet, their survey certainly did not "prove" that. Nor did it distinguish—in any of the questions—between courses in the humanities and social sciences and those in other fields including business, natural sciences, and economics. Therefore, to make such an assertion in their summary was at the very least, confusing, if not disingenuous. But even more revealing was that of the students surveyed, only 42% cited their major as a discipline which traditionally falls under the rubric of humanities and social sciences and that percentage includes those in the fine arts—a discipline which is often demarcated from the humanities and social sciences at many institutions. In other words, ACTA's own "evidence" does not support its conclusions. This was, in other words, a "classic example of claiming implications" that went "far beyond the actual data."[624]

Of course, ACTA had no interest in studying the issue of "intellectual diversity" as "objectively and systematically as possible." Rather, they interpreted the data to fit their presuppositions about liberal bias on college campuses and then proceeded to offer "practical suggestions" for dealing with a problem that exists largely in their own minds.

ACTA's real intent is to undermine democratic structures of governance within universities themselves. Fuentes has rightly noted that one of ACTA's goals has been to gain greater control over the boards of trustees at institutions across the country.[625] Indeed, several "conservative Republican governors" have already "appointed trustees who are their political allies rather than independent advocates for the university system."[626] Despite the fact that organizations such as ACTA rhapsodize about freedom and democracy and the free exchange of ideas, their real efforts belie their rhetoric—their aim is elemental control over the academy. As one observer noted in the early 1990s—at the height of the "culture wars" and the controversy over "political correctness"—although attacks on the academy are often waged in the name of defending Western civilization and upholding standards, their real ideological intent is motivated by the need to mold minds that are ignorant of history and incapable of critical reason so that corporate capitalism can be perpetuated generation after generation.[627] This becomes readily apparent if one follows the money that has been poured into organizations such as ACTA by right-wing foundations whose underlying impulse, for more than four decades, has been the promulgation of unfettered free-market ideology—not only at home but the world over. This impetus became even more pronounced after 9/11 as the desire for American-led corporate hegemony intensified among neoconservatives. To 'defend civilization' was, and is, to support neoconservatism and neoliberalism—at home and abroad.

Far from being concerned with the moral fabric of the United States and the teaching of Western civilization, the rightists behind these foundations are pre-occupied with the profits that accrue from corporate rule and American global dominance. Theirs is an attempt to "promote empire abroad and corporate power at home."[628] They recognize, however, that the naked drive for power and dominance does not always play well in Peoria or Thomas Frank's Kansas. So the more palatable patina of "cultural values" is employed to disguise their rapacious ambitions and cultural "anger is marshaled to achieve" what are essentially "economic ends."[629]

As Himmelstein noted two decades ago, the mobilization of big business around a conservative agenda involved an effort to influence politics and policies "in the interest not of specific firms or industries but of capitalists generally" and their class interests.[630] In other words, the right's "culture war" has been, and continues to be, a form of class warfare.

PEDDLING PATRIOTIC CORRECTNESS

Never before has censorship been so perfect. Never before have those who
are still led to believe ... that they remain free citizens, been less entitled to
make their opinions heard, wherever it is matter of choices affecting their real
lives. Never before has it been possible to lie to them so brazenly.[631]

SECRECY, SPIN AND BIG MEDIA: DEMOCRACY UNDER SIEGE

Theorists of democracy generally agree that there are three indispensable functions
that the media serve in a self-governing society. First, the media should act as watchdogs of the powerful and power structures that influence public life; the media
system should also facilitate vigorous public discourse and debate by offering a
wide range of informed views on the most pressing social and political issues of
the day; and it must be capable of exposing deception and corruption. And, while
no one medium may meet all of these criteria, "the media system as a whole must
assure that the whole package is delivered to the whole population."[632] In short, in
a democracy the media should ideally, serve the interests of the people, providing
them with the information needed to participate meaningfully in decision-making. As
Chomsky has noted, where there is even a pretense of democracy, communications
are at its heart.

Regrettably, the American media system, as it is currently configured, fails to
meet these criteria.[633] Control over major media conglomerates is centralized in the
hands of a few dominant corporations whose wealthy owners have a special stake
in maintaining their economic and political power. As a result, mainstream media
coverage tends to be dominated by corporate ideology and the media system itself
is driven by the profit motive at the expense of the public interest.

This unfortunate state of affairs became even more apparent during the Bush era
as three forces converged to undermine the principles of a free press and democratic
communication, and democracy itself in the United States. These included (i) the
government's aversion to transparency and openness; (ii) consolidation of ownership
in media and the tendency for megamedia corporations to operate according to big
business principles rather than civic and democratic values; and, (iii) the entrench-
ment of politically partisan media outlets such as Fox News that essentially function
as propaganda arms of the Republican right. (If there were any doubts about
Fox's political allegiances, they were surely erased after NewsCorp—Fox's parent
company—donated $1 million to the Republican Governors Association in June 2010
in anticipation of the mid-term elections!) Each of these warrants unpacking.[634]

The first undemocratic force is the reluctance of the government to "operate in
the sunshine of disclosure and criticism."[635] While governments have attempted,

historically and under varied circumstances, to squelch journalistic freedom and mislead the press, the Bush administration was arguably one of the most secretive and deceptive in recent history. From the earliest days of his reign, Bush took steps to tighten the government's grasp on information and limit, and in most instances, thwart public scrutiny of his administration's activities. Even prior to 9/11, the administration asserted expansive definitions of executive privilege and restrictive views of the Freedom of Information Act and generally stonewalled congressional requests for information. For example, Bush delayed the release of former President Ronald Reagan's presidential papers, in violation of a post-Watergate law, in order to protect those in his inner circle who were involved in the Iran-Contra scandal when they served Reagan and Bush the father. The White House also insisted on keeping secret members of an energy policy task force chaired by Dick Cheney which, as we now know, was comprised of oil and energy industry executives including the late Kenneth "Kenny Boy" Lay of Enron infamy. Post-9/11, under the guise of the war on terror, the vise on the free flow of information was significantly tightened.

In his book, *Worse Than Watergate: The Secret Presidency of George W. Bush*, John Dean—Richard Nixon's White House counsel during the Watergate scandal— argued that the Bush administration, which he deemed undemocratic and frighteningly dangerous, was far more furtive and authoritarian than Nixon's ever was. Even Larry Klayman, chairman of the conservative group Judicial Watch, called the Bush regime "the most secretive of our lifetime."[636] This was also confirmed by the revelations stemming from the publication of Scott McClellan's book *What Happened: Inside the Bush White House and Washington's Culture of Deception*. McClellan, a former White House press secretary, caused a firestorm of controversy in late May 2008 after suggesting that Bush valued secrecy over transparency and that the administration "lacked real accountability in large part because Bush himself did not embrace openness or government in the sunshine."[637] The level of secrecy in the Bush White House was so egregious that Representative Henry A. Waxman commissioned a study to expose it and entire websites were devoted to revealing the contempt for public disclosure that was the hallmark of the Bush regime.[638]

Bush's penchant for clandestine activities was evident in everything from orders and memoranda justifying extreme and inhumane interrogation methods banned under international laws as forms of torture to the CIA holding prisoners in secret overseas prisons. It was obvious in policies that allowed covert wiretapping of American citizens and vindictive, surreptitiously launched smear campaigns against opponents of the Iraq war such as John Murtha.[639] Repeatedly, the Bush administration flaunted its disdain for the very notion of transparent government, basic civil liberties, and human rights.

In addition to secrecy Bush also engaged in outright deception. Parry contends that "no U.S. political leader in modern history" engaged in "a pattern of lying and distortion more systematically than George W. Bush." He added that "Bush's lies" were not "about petty matters;" rather, his dishonesty was about issues of "war and peace, the patriotism of his opponents, and the founding principles of the American Republic." They were the "kind of lies and distortions more befitting the leader of a totalitarian state whipping up his followers to go after some perceived enemy than [a] President ... seeking an informed debate among the citizenry."[640]

Parry's observations were hardly surprising given that key members of the Bush administration were known to genuflect at the altar of Leo Strauss. According to Lobe not "only did Strauss have few qualms about using deception in politics, he saw it as a necessity.[641] Strauss, a loud proponent of anti-liberalism and a staunch anti-democratic figure, believed that "societies should be hierarchical—divided between the elite which should lead, and the masses that should follow."[642]

More specifically, in *The Concept of the Political*, Strauss defined politics as the struggle of one group to suppress others. Since he believed in the principle of man's 'natural evil,' Strauss maintained that the virtuous few had to rule the majority from above. To aid in this process, the elite few are charged with using "noble lies" to keep the truth from the grubby masses by distracting everyday citizens not only with real or perceived external threats to the homeland but also by developing "nationalist or militantly religious sentiments fanatical enough to ensure their willing-ness to die for the nation."[643]

Joe Conason cites the work of Alan Gilbert, a professor of political science and international studies at the University of Denver (and a former graduate adviser to Condoleezza Rice) who has examined Strauss's relationship with Martin Heidegger and Carl Schmitt, both of whom joined the Nazi Party in the early 1930s. According to Gilbert, Strauss was "mesmerized by Heidegger's and Schmitt's politics," parti-cularly their "anti-cosmopolitanism, their hatred for international peace, their love of militarism and war."[644] While Conason conceded that Strauss's fascist tendencies may not have been fully shared by Bushites, he argued that the neocons "cultish veneration" of Strauss did "place their militarist enthusiasms and imperial ambitions in a context" that contrasted "sharply with their supposed crusade for democracy."[645] Additionally, although the rise to power of the neocons in the Bush era cannot simply be attributed to one academic, it is quite remarkable how many key officials in the administration were influenced by Strauss and sought to enact many of his ideas.[646]

If Strauss and his followers were not necessarily outright fascists, they certainly were anti-democratic. For, in many ways, Strauss' views on the proper management of society parallel those of Walter Lippmann and his notion of the "bewildered herd." While Lippmann flirted briefly with progressive socialist politics during his educational stint at Harvard, his political views eventually underwent a dramatic shift to the right during the course of his life. That shift was exemplified in his well-known works including *Public Opinion* published in 1922 and *The Phantom Public* published three years later. Both of these treatises expressed considerable doubts about the practical feasibility of establishing a true democracy in modern society. Similar to Strauss, Lippmann believed that 'the people' had to be controlled and manipulated by elites, by political insiders, who could shape opinions conducive to maintaining hegemony.

Lippmann was quite attuned to the fact that there was the world "outside" and the "pictures" in people's heads. For Lippmann, it was the responsibility of "insiders" to stage-manage and mold those pictures in order to manage the flow of communication.

In the communication model (often referred to as the dominant paradigm) preferred by Lippmann, a restricted number of "responsible" people have the power and capacity to shape perceptions of what is "good" and "right." Indeed, in a "proper" democracy, according to Lippmann, this small elite would be in a position to take a leading role in society; they would shepherd the public or the "bewildered herd."[647]

If we wish to understand the profoundly undemocratic nature of Lippmann's concept of the bewildered herd, it is imperative to locate the communication model that he exalted within the historical context that birthed the public relations industry. In his magisterial social history of "spin," Stuart Ewen examines the way in which the "fathers" of public opinion and public relations, which includes Lippmann and others like Edward Bernays, unabashedly expressed a hierarchical view of society in which there existed an "intelligent few" who were charged with the responsibility of contemplating and influencing the tide of history. Ewen also situates the emergence of public relations, essentially the science of manufacturing public opinion, in terms of historical power relations and class struggles.

For Ewen, it is necessary to acknowledge that the earliest practitioners and theorists of public opinion and public relations were motivated by a fear of democracy and "the fear of an empowered public."[648] In the eyes of the public relations cadre (who mainly represented the interests of big business), the tradition of progressive muckraking journalism, which had stirred the passions of "the people" and which had been highly critical of the privileged classes and business magnates, had to be quelled lest the masses demand reform. Journalism "that challenged the equity of the business system itself" (i.e. capitalism) had been toying "with the forces of revolt" and was therefore viewed as a palpable threat to the dominant class. It therefore became necessary to "educate the public" about the wonders of American capitalism (and by extension American imperialism and military might), the benevolence of the capitalist class, and to engineer consent to its rule.[649] As Ewen notes, Lippmann's main concern was how to make "rule by elites, in a democratic age, less difficult."[650]

It was easy to see this type of mentality at work during the Bush years. The administration was full of members who were contemptuous of a free press and who took pride in creating their own reality. As previously noted, the Bush White House registered its hostility toward the 'reality' based community of journalists and arrogantly claimed that it could create its own reality in accordance with its political agenda. Such braggadocio and scorn for critical thought is hardly shocking given that one of the leading Straussian disciples in the Bush administration, Deputy Defense Secretary Paul Wolfowitz (one of the major architects of the Iraq war and a prominent member of PNAC), was taught by Strauss' alter ego—the late Allan Bloom—one of the right's most beloved culture warriors.

Frank Rich argued that in the age of George W. Bush, the preference for image and spin over reality, and for deception reached new heights. When Bush came to office, he

> brought his particular zest for public relations. Though he wasn't a practiced actor like Reagan, his cheerleading past had its uses. Bush was more than willing to act out scenarios that could help sell him or whatever product (or policy) he was pushing. In his longtime political guru, Karl Rove, he had a

producer-director-screenwriter who had brought the photo-op techniques pioneered by Reagan's image maven, Michael Deaver, to a whole new level of sophistication and expertise ... Once in office, Bush turned the presidency into an ongoing festival of audiovisual cognitive dissonance. The succession of misleading propaganda ploys had an almost farcical quality.[651]

From its lies about Iraq's weapons of mass destruction to Colin Powell's prop-filled and deceptive presentation to the UN Security Council; from sanitized war coverage and the Pentagon ban on news coverage and photographs of dead soldiers' homecomings to the staged rescue of Jessica Lynch; from the contrived images of the fall of Saddam Hussein's statue in Firdos Square to the President's ridiculous "Mission Accomplished" propaganda stunt, the Bush administration took public relations to levels unimaginable by the best of Reagan's spin doctors. Among the Bushies, as they were called, it was generally held that image was all that mattered and too often a pliant media succumbed to the spin and concealed the truth.

Since Straussians believe in perpetual war and a belligerent foreign policy they did not hesitate to use trickery and deception to first sell the unnecessary war in Iraq and later to paint a rosy picture of "success" in the aftermath of the invasion for the benefit of the American public.[652] A study published in 2008 showed that President Bush and seven of his administration's top officials, including Dick Cheney, Defense Secretary Donald Rumsfeld, and Condoleezza Rice, made "at least 935 false statements in the two years following September 11, 2001 about the national security threat posed by Saddam Hussein's Iraq."[653] The authors of the report contend that

nearly five years after the U.S. invasion of Iraq, an exhaustive examination of the record shows that the statements were part of an orchestrated campaign that effectively galvanized public opinion and, in the process, led the nation to war under decidedly false pretenses ... the Bush administration led the nation to war on the basis of erroneous information that it methodically propagated and that culminated in military action against Iraq on March 19, 2003. Not surprisingly, the officials with the most opportunities to make speeches, grant media interviews, and otherwise frame the public debate also made the most false statements, according to this first-ever analysis of the entire body of prewar rhetoric.[654]

Once the administration got its war on, it was intent on getting an already compliant media in on the spinning. Through the Office of Media Outreach, a taxpayer funded arm of the Department of Defense, Bush-friendly media personalities were invited on government-subsidized trips to Iraq to report the 'good news' which was apparently being underreported in the 'evil,' liberal media. Rampton and Stauber note that the

Office of Media Outreach activities included hosting 'Operation Truth,' a one-week tour of Iraq by right-wing talk-show hosts, organized by Russo Marsh & Rogers, a Republican PR firm based in California that sponsors a conservative advocacy group called Move America Forward. The purpose of the 'Truth Tour' ... was to 'report the good news on Operation Iraqi Freedom you're not hearing from the old line news media ... to get the news straight from our troops serving in Operation Iraqi Freedom, including the positive developments and successes they are achieving. Even before the trip began, however, the radio talkers' take on Iraq was already decided. 'The war is being won, if not already won, I think,' said tour participant Buzz Patterson in a predeparture interview with Fox News.[655]

The Bush gang also saw fit to engage in disinformation campaigns and covert deception abroad. The Pentagon hired a propaganda-making firm to create, in the Iraqi media, an impression of grass-roots support of the American occupation among Iraqi citizens. After Donald Rumsfeld closed the Office of Strategic Influence (that was established shortly after 9/11 amidst White House concerns that the U.S. was losing public support for its war on terror in Iraq and elsewhere in the Arab world) once its controversial existence became public knowledge, he kept it functioning covertly by outsourcing contracts to public relations firms such as the Rendon Group and the Lincoln Group, which won multimillion-dollar Pentagon contracts for media 'analysis' and a media operations center in Baghdad. Eventually, Rendon dropped out of the project and left the Lincoln group in charge. Subsequently, Lincoln hired another Washington-based public relations firm as a subcontractor—BKSH & Associates —an outfit headed by Republican political strategist Charles R. Black. (Black, who worked in conjunction with John McCain's presidential campaign, was forced to apologize after he suggested that another terrorist attack on American soil prior to the November 2008 elections would benefit McCain's presidential aspirations). The PR firms hired to spread disinformation and spin the reality in Iraq were paid "up to $300 million over a five-year period."[656]

On the domestic front, the *New York Times* revealed the existence of the Pentagon military analyst program through which the Pentagon lobbied for war by cultivating a cadre of former military officers who made regular appearances on *Fox News*, *CNN*, and other broadcast networks. The investigation found that the Pentagon program used military analysts in a campaign to generate favorable and flattering news coverage of the Bush administration's wartime performance. More specifically, the effort that "began with the buildup to the Iraq war" sought to "exploit ideological and military allegiances" as well as a "powerful financial dynamic." A majority of the analysts had "ties to military contractors" that were vested in the very war policies these analysts were asked to assess on the air. Those business relationships were hardly, if ever, disclosed to the viewers and in some instances "not even to the networks themselves." A variety of records and interviews demonstrated how the Bush administration used "its control over access and information in an effort to transform the analysts into a kind of media Trojan horse—an instrument intended to shape terrorism coverage from inside the major TV and radio networks." Members of this group essentially "echoed" the Bush administration's talking points, "sometimes even when they suspected the information was false or inflated."[657] In other words, the "Bush administration" brought the same contempt for democratic media practices it exhibited abroad "to the homefront" which was, after all, the most important front in the war on terror.[658]

Although the media essentially toed the White House line, the Bush regime still saw fit to engage in a "war on the press"—a war that undermined "journalists' ability to exercise their First Amendment function to hold power accountable" and to illuminate government operations for the public.[659] The strategies involved in that war included, among other things, "deliberately releasing deceptive information on a regular basis;" producing their own 'news reports' in the form of video news releases" that were distributed gratis to resource-starved media outlets; and "creating and crediting their own political activists as 'journalists' working for partisan operations masquerading as news organizations" as was the case in the Jeff Gannon (aka James Guckert) debacle briefly discussed in Chapter Two. The Bush administration was also known to bribe friendly journalists to promote their ideological agenda. This particular practice became readily apparent when *USA Today* discovered that conservative African-American pundit Armstrong Williams (also a former legislative aide to the late Senator Strom Thurmond) was paid $240,000 to promote Bush's No Child Left Behind (NCLB) policy on his nationally syndicated television show. The Armstrong deal was brokered by the public relations firm Ketchum, a subsidiary of media giant Omnicom, and was approved by the U.S. Department of Education. In addition to the Williams contract, Ketchum was also paid $700,000 to rate media coverage of NCLB and to produce video news releases on the law.[660] Two other "journalists," Maggie Gallagher and Michael McManus, were also paid out of funds derived from the Department of Health and Human Services to support Bush's efforts to promote marriage.

While paying journalists and public relations firms to promote NCLB and other initiatives may pale in comparison to manipulating the public to support a war based on false pretenses, it is clear that purchasing journalistic mercenaries was part of a larger and well-fueled government scheme to blur the line between legitimate news reporting and political propaganda—a sort of PSYOPS operation executed domestically. A 2006 report released by the Government Accountability Office revealed that the Bush administration spent $1.6 billion from "2003 through the second quarter of 2005 on 343 contracts with public relations firms, advertising agencies, media organizations and individuals."[661] Bush and his cronies cunningly and systematically attempted to deceive the nation about most of his major policy proposals. On issues ranging from stem cells to tax cuts to the environment (not to mention the war in Iraq), they "consistently twisted the truth beyond recognition in order to promote" their agenda. Their deceptions were "achieved using some of the most advanced tactics from public relations, and were designed to exploit the failings of the modern media."[662]

Bush's deceptions, however, are interesting not only because they provide some insight into his character, but because they are indicative of a more serious problem in our media environment and our political culture. As the authors of *All the President's Spin* note, Bush was

> simply the highest profile carrier of a virus infecting our political system. Its symptoms are misleading public statements, a disregard for the value of honest discussion, and treating policy debates as little more than marketing challenges—a devastating combination for democracy.[663]

Bush's use of misleading public relations would not have been as effective as it was if it were not for submissive media that were willing participants in promulgating White House propaganda. While one can argue, given the historical record, that the American mainstream media tend to assume an obedient, if not, obsessive patriotic tone during times of international conflict, the coverage of the Bush administration's drive to war in Iraq (as it was in relation to Afghanistan) was particularly disconcerting. For the most part, it was largely devoid of historical context, lacked substantive debate, and most often served to reinforce the simplistic worldview served up by the Commander-in-Chief and the patriotically correct.

The propensity for 'going soft' on Bush, however, dated back to the earliest days of his presidential campaign, the 2000 election debacle, and his subsequent appointment to the White House by the Supreme Court. After the tragic events of September 11th, the mainstream media became even more acquiescent to an administration that had clearly capitalized on the culture of fear created by the terrorist attacks. From color-coded risk alerts and duct tape frenzy to warnings about the "axis of evil" and Iraq's weapons of mass destruction, the Bush administration adroitly manipulated public fear and a press trying to outdo itself in the patriotism game to its advantage. With few exceptions, the mainstream media—particularly in the build-up to and subsequent war in Iraq—were used as propagandistic mouthpieces for Bush's "war on terror" and greatly assisted in generating and maintaining the kind of panic necessary to whip up patriotic fervor and populist support for military aggression. As Schechter maintains, there was "an intimate link between the media, the war, and the Bush administration" and few governments were "as adept at using polling, focus groups, "perception manager," spinners and I.O. or "information operations" specialists to sell slogans to further a "patriotically correct" climate.[664]

In addition, the media were quick to bolster the claims of the White House no matter how outlandish or misleading. Parry aptly noted that "Bush and his advisers" grasped that they faced "few limits" on how far they could push "their political/media advantage." Protected by "an army of media allies," who either shared their conservative ideology or saw the potential financial gain in playing along, Bush learned that he stood "little risk no matter how over-the-top his imagery or assertions."[665]

While some media outlets subsequently admitted, albeit grudgingly, that they failed miserably in fulfilling their watchdog function prior to the onset of the Iraq war and despite a host of revelations exposing government assaults on a free press, far "too many media outlets" continued "to tell the politically and economically powerful, 'Lie to me!'"[666] And, more significantly, the media never questioned the imperialist machinations of the government. Bill Moyers put it thusly:

> Giant, megamedia conglomerates that our Founders could not possibly have envisioned are finding common cause with an imperial state in a betrothal certain to produce, not the sons and daughters of liberty, but the very kind of bastards that issued from the old arranged marriage of church and state ... Never has there been an administration so disciplined in secrecy, so precisely in lockstep in keeping information from the public at large and—in defiance of the Constitution—from their representatives in Congress. Never has so powerful a media oligopoly ... been so unabashed in reaching, like Caesar, for still more

wealth and power. Never have hand and glove fitted together so comfortably to manipulate free political debate, sow contempt for the idea of government itself, and trivialize the people's need to know ... When journalism throws in with power, that's the first news marched by censors to the guillotine. The greatest moments in the history of the press came, not when journalists made common cause with the state, but when they stood fearlessly independent of it.[667]

Of course, the problems in our media environment go well beyond those created by an incompetent press acting as stenographers for the powerful. The true crisis we face today is one due to a highly concentrated profit-driven media system in which the kind of fearless journalism that provides democracy's oxygen is all but impossible. This is the second force to which Moyers refers, namely, the "tendency of media giants, operating on big-business principles, to exalt commercial values at the expense of democratic value." In valorizing profit making, media empires are "squeezing out the journalism that tries to get as close as possible to the verifiable truth" and "isolating serious coverage of public affairs."[668] In such a context, we must ask ourselves how any type of serious, independent journalism can survive at media outlets owned and controlled by enormous, politically active conglomerates.

Today, corporate domination of the media system poses serious challenges to a functioning democracy and a healthy culture. Repeated waves of media mergers have, in essence, made a "handful of multinational corporations the arbiters of public discourse."[669] And, the results have not been pretty. It is obvious that serious discussion of significant issues has given way to shout-fests that have not only coarsened public dialogue but have essentially rendered American political discourse meaningless. Journalism has, for the most part, been replaced with pundit gasbags who pontificate on subjects they often know very little about. Indeed, Alterman states that "few people" have given much thought to "what qualifies someone" to be a pundit and in fact argues that "ignorance is actually an advantage" since it allows one "to ignore the inherent complexity of any given problem with a concise quip."[670] Wolcott adds that a pundit is someone who is "unburdened with too much knowledge, reticence, and modesty" and who is more than willing to "speak" before they think.[671]

It is also the case that an "entertainment" ethos permeates our media culture. On this point, Nichols and McChesney are insightful:

The reality is that the contemporary structures of broadcast media ownership and regulation, as well as recent patterns of consolidation of newspaper ownership and the pressure on all media to turn ever-increasing levels of profit, conspire far more effectively than Karl Rove ... ever could to undermine journalism and, ultimately, to constrain the flow of facts, ideas, and debate that is the lifeblood of democracy. Media today treat Americans as consumers, not citizens. And the theory in the boardroom is that consumers are attracted by entertainment, rather than information. Former Vermont Governor Howard Dean, fresh from the 2004 presidential campaign trail, put it best when he said, "The media is trained to get the entertainment value and screw the facts." In such an environment, Dean's "scream" speech on the night of the Iowa caucuses gets far more attention than Dean's thoughtful critique of U.S. trade policies, even though the scream put no one but a few Dean aides out of work, while the free trade agenda of the Clinton and Bush administrations has shuttered thousands of factories and displaced millions of workers and farmers in the U.S. and abroad. The serious work of covering politics and government is treated as a burden that must be tossed off as quickly as possible in order to get down to the business of celebrity gossip about who is getting Botox injections. The pressure to keep it light has led media companies to deemphasize serious reporting, especially the sort of costly and controversial investigative reporting that gets Washington elites jittery.[672]

As Nichols and McChesney make clear, the media's ability to present different points of view and to produce serious journalism has been all but stifled by media merger mania. Since the corporations that dominate our media system are in the business of making profits—mainly through selling advertising—the very political economy of the institution narrows the scope of debate and lends itself to feel-good stories and images that pose no real threat to what Herman and Chomsky refer to as the "buying mood."[673] The needs of the advertiser are much more important than the needs of citizens and advertisers generally shy away from any association with controversial political or social topics. This may certainly be an ideal media environment for the conglomerates that sell audiences to advertisers and for advertisers who want to maintain and grow their customer base; however, it is hardly good for citizens living in a so-called democratic country.

Television is the primary source of news for Americans—radio, the Internet, news magazines and even daily newspapers—are secondary to television, which dominates the social and political environment in the United States. As such, the public relies chiefly on television for the information that shapes their attitudes, particularly in terms of political issues.[674] Part of the growing uselessness of television "news," which often presents infotainment, derives from economic pressures. As the distinction between informing and entertaining is increasingly blurred, and the demand for large audiences and even larger profit margins dictates, gathering the news has become a matter of getting the best live shots and/or using conventional Hollywood genres to attract viewers. This has become common in reporting on sex scandals, celebrity meltdowns and even in the media coverage of the Iraq war that was replete with its own theme music and video game-like graphics. The late cultural critic, Neil Postman, once remarked that the pervasive influence of the entertainment ethos led to a situation where our politics and our news were transformed into "congenial adjuncts of show business."[675] The problem is not that "television presents us with entertaining subject matter but that all subject matter is presented as entertainment."[676] In the era of media deregulation, news values have essentially given way to the ratings imperatives of entertainment and sensationalistic tabloid fare. In the "Now... This" culture that Postman bemoaned, content providers rather than bona fide journalists deliver the news in fragments, devoid of context, and in a milieu that prefers form over substance, image over reality. As such, our capacity for rational thought and critical engagement with serious issues is diminished. In the course of amusing ourselves to death, democracy is undermined.

Nowhere is this more apparent than in the world of 24-hour cable television news. Once thought to be an "ancillary news provider, the cable news industry is now a major player."[677] And while entities such as *CNN*, *Fox*, and *MSNBC* are called "news channels," a more apt description would be to call them "reality-based entertainment channels" where the "intellectual level" is "one step above pro wrestling."[678] Jeff Cohen's *Cable News Confidential* provides an insider's view of the cable news industry in which he found a "drunken exuberance for sex, crime and celebrity stories, matched by a grim timidity and fear of offending the powers-that-be—especially if the powers-that-be are conservatives." He adds that the biggest fear in cable news is of doing "anything that could get you, or your network, accused of being liberal.[679]

As noted in previous chapters, in order to bludgeon dissent and to shift discourse even further to the right of the political spectrum, conservative think tanks and their corporate-funded spokespersons have long circulated the myth of the liberal media. While far from reflecting reality, that strategy has proven to be quite successful in its effect.[680] Since at least the early 1970s, pro-corporate forces well understood that changing media discourse was a crucial part of "mainstreaming" right-wing ideas and through a well-organized, well-financed campaign, and fervent coterie of activists they essentially succeeded in doing so. Back in the early 1990s, former Republican Party chair Rich Bond even admitted that "conservatives' frequent denunciations of 'liberal bias' in the media were part of 'a strategy.'"[681]

McChesney and Foster contend that the ability of the right-wing campaign to popularize the view that the "news media have a liberal bias has been accomplished to some extent by constant repetition without any significant countervailing position."[682] Additionally, the conservative crusade has meshed "comfortably with the commercial and political aspirations of media corporations."[683] Coupled with policies including the Telecommunications Act of 1996 that allowed for greater concentration of media ownership, such developments have clearly influenced the behavior of the media in recent years and generally contributed to the uber-patriotism exhibited by most media outlets post-9/11.

As I have argued elsewhere, after 9/11, the media generally toed the patriotically correct line of the Bush White House by echoing the "they hate us because we are free" mantra to explain the gruesome tragedy.[684] With a few rare exceptions, the message conveyed by the mainstream media was one of American innocence, vulnerability, and virtue. The media, as we have seen, were also captivated by the vision of an American superpower bestriding the globe and bringing "democracy" to the Middle East—at the barrel of a gun or a drop of a bomb, if necessary. In this sense and in many ways, the media served as the emissaries of empire, willingly promoting PNAC's agenda for *Pax Americana*. Nowhere was this more evident than on the Fox News Channel.

THE FAUX NEWS CHANNEL

When fascism comes to America, it will be wrapped in the flag, carrying a cross.

Pugnacity is a form of courage, but a very bad form.[685]

In addition to the dangers associated with secrecy and the role of private, profit-driven megamedia corporations in undermining democratic imperatives, Moyers named a third force that made a mockery of democratic principles during the reign of Bush. Namely, the "quasi-official partisan press" that was ideologically linked to "an authoritarian administration" that, was in turn, an "ally and agent of the most powerful interests in the world." This convergence dominated the marketplace of political ideas in ways that were unique in American history. As Moyers further noted, one "need not harbor the notion of a vast right-wing conspiracy to think this collusion more than pure coincidence" for conspiracy is "unnecessary when ideology hungers for power and its many adherents swarm of their own accord to the same pot of honey." From the "editorial pages of *The Wall Street Journal* to the faux news of Rupert Murdoch's empire to the nattering nabobs of know-nothing radio to a legion of think tanks paid for and bought by conglomerates—the religious, partisan, and corporate right" raised a "mighty megaphone for sectarian, economic, and political forces" that aimed to "transform the egalitarian and democratic ideals embodied in our founding documents."[686]

Moyers was, of course, alluding to what David Brock has called the "Republican noise machine," a network of media outlets in cable, on talk radio, and in the press which are very pugnacious and "powerful propaganda organs of the Republican Party."[687] The structural changes in the media landscape which have shifted most of our political discourse to the right provides an institutional advantage "for the GOP and conservatism" and is a formidable obstacle to those who oppose not only the right-wing agenda but who care deeply about the democratic principles espoused by Moyers.[688] While the right's well-orchestrated media cacophony stretches from the highly ideological op-eds in the *Wall Street Journal* through to right-wing bloviators who pollute most of our nation's radio airwaves, for my purposes here, I focus mainly on the Fox News Channel which played a key role in advancing PC and attacking the academy.

The Fox News Channel (FNC) was launched in October 1996—just a month prior to the election that saw Bill Clinton trounce his Republican opponent Bob Dole—by right-wing mogul Rupert Murdoch, head of the world's largest media empire, News Corp. Murdoch's media empire began in his native homeland of Australia and expanded to the United Kingdom, Asia, and the United States. He has a network of 175 newspapers worldwide and recently acquired the *Wall Street Journal.* He has extended his reach into other media as well including the Fox broad-cast network, Fox Sports, 20th Century-Fox studios, the HarperCollins publishing house, the Sky and Star satellite systems in Asia and England, and dozens of local American television stations.

Murdoch, who once described himself as a "radical conservative," appointed Roger Ailes as the czar of the FNC and the American media have, arguably, never been the same.[689] In 1996, Ailes claimed that Fox would be "a hard-news network" that would provide "straight, factual information to the American people" so that they would be able to "make up their own minds."[690] However, Cohen noted that Ailes was an "odd choice" to become the news chairman of a media outlet since "he had virtually no background in journalism" but was the "perfect choice to run a partisan propaganda outlet."[691]

Before Ailes became Murdoch's henchman at Fox, he had already earned a reputation as a truculent Republican operative who was more than capable of dirty tricks and smear tactics. A veteran of both Nixon and Reagan's political campaigns, Ailes is perhaps most famous for his role in crafting the media strategy for Bush Sr.'s repugnant 1988 presidential run. With Ailes' assistance, Bush Sr. was able to turn a double-digit deficit in the polls into a resounding victory by "targeting the GOP's base of white male voters in the South and West, using red-meat themes" such as Michael Dukasis' status as a 'card-carrying' ACLU member, and his laissez-faire attitude toward flag-burning and the pledge of allegiance.[692] Then, of course, there was the nasty and stunningly racist advertising campaign that linked Dukakis to rapist Willie Horton. Ailes had also produced Rush Limbaugh's rather short-lived television talk show where he was fond of referring to Bill Clinton as the "hippie president."[693]

Employing the liberal media myth to its advantage, the twenty-four hour news network was intended to provide an alternative to the bleeding heart 'elitists' that presumably controlled the country's mainstream media. In keeping with the right-wing playbook that often casts obscenely wealthy men (mainly white men) as champions of the little guy, Ailes once told *Newsweek* that he abhorred the liberal media elite because they "think they're smarter than the rest of those stupid bastards, and they'll tell you what to think. To a working-class guy, that's bullshit."[694] Presumably, Fox news would speak for, and to, those stupid working-class bastards. As Wolcott puts it, it would tell them "what to think by pretending not to be smarter than them" but rather by "pretending to be one of them, only with more money, a better address, and a nicer wardrobe."[695] Wolcott argues that the FNC cornered the market on "Angry White Males" and cites as evidence the case of Matt Gross, a former editor at Foxnews.com. In a letter to Romenesko's Media News site in 2003, Gross revealed that one of the first directives he received (as leader of his unit) in the early days of the network from a "top suit" at Fox was to "seek out stories that cater to angry, middle-aged white men who listen to talk radio and yell at their television."[696]

We should be reminded that just two years prior to Fox's launch, 62% of white males voted for Newt Gingrich's Republican revolution agenda—a phenomena which represented one of the most potent forms of "identity politics" in recent electoral history. At the time, the economic situation of many white working class males had significantly declined due to changes wrought by trade agreements, loss of manufacturing jobs, and the onset of outsourcing. The jobs that had provided them with a sense of dignity had rapidly dissipated. It was the political right, however, that capitalized on that sense of dislocation and tapped into the deep psychological and emotional ramifications that such dispossession spawned.[697] Talk radio, with its populist imprimatur, had become the forum where disgruntled white males routinely expressed their anger and frustrations. Radio personalities like Rush Limbaugh provided a sense of identity and community for, and forged a sense of symbolic solidarity with, white males suffering from a collective loss of authority. By making women, minorities, and liberals the culprits for the declining material conditions of many white males, rightist ideologues successfully deflected attention away from the real perpetrators of economic decline—the very privileged lords of global capitalism that had profited on the backs of the working and middle classes.

In several respects, the FNC was essentially an extension of right-wing talk radio and the "continuation of the Gingrich Revolution by other means."[698] And, as Wolcott sardonically points out, the network employs a pseudo-populist strategy similar to Limbaugh's:

> Just as Rush turned into the very sort of country-club Republican he professes to scorn (before entering rehab for addiction to Oxycontin, colloquially known as 'hillbilly heroin'), he would enthrall listeners with anecdotes about the celebrity golf tournaments he'd played the previous weekend, the anchors at Fox News are elitists who pretend to be firebrands fighting for you, the average angry white bozo.[699]

Undoubtedly, anti-elitism is an animating theme in Fox's branding strategy. This, however, is hardly surprising since the conservative obsession with the so-called liberal elite has quite a lengthy history dating back to Barry Goldwater's 1964 campaign when none other than Ronald Reagan castigated the "intellectual elite" in his speeches in support of Goldwater's candidacy. Richard Nixon used the charge of elitism as a bludgeon to disparage the role of government and his Vice President, Spiro Agnew, perfected the strategy of casting Democrats as the party of an arrogant, wealthy and pampered, elite and Republicans as spokespersons for the average, overworked and underappreciated Joe. Despite the fact that various election studies over the years have illustrated that the wealthiest Americans (i.e. the economic *elite*) consistently vote for Republicans and despite the fact that conservative policies tend to favor corporations and the rich, the charge of liberal elitism remains a powerful weapon in the conservative arsenal.[700]

Virtually every right-wing campaign includes some repudiation of the "elite" since it allows conservatives to "feel themselves oppressed" even at those times— as was the case during the 2004 election cycle—when they controlled "all the levers of political power in the United States and much of the news media."[701] This strategy was also put to use in the 2008 presidential race that had John McCain's operatives and conservative pundits attempting to paint Democratic nominee, Barack Obama, as an elitist because he liked organic tea and arugula and his wife, Michelle, shopped at Whole Foods. Apparently, food and supermarket choices reflected Obama's elitism but the fact that Cindy McCain, the beer distribution company heiress whose 2006 income was reported to be more than $6 million, had spent $750,000 in one month on credit cards and who jet-setted with her husband back and forth from high end condos and an Arizona ranch did not! In this sense, rightists have been able to redefine elitism as something that is almost exclusively associated with cultural preferences rather than economic realities.

Since its official launch, FNC has become a pivotal hub of the conservative movement's well-oiled media machine and is part of the echo chamber where Republican-friendly news stories are advanced, repeated and amplified, where rhetorical brickbats are regularly tossed at Democrats, and where tales of alleged liberal tomfoolery are exploited for political gain. As Brock contends, the most influential and visible on-air FNC personalities are "political and ideological partisans of a character rarely seen in professional news organizations."[702] A mere sampling of Fox's stable seems to confirm this.

For example, FNC's anchor, David Asman, began his career at the editorial page of the *Wall Street Journal* and was once associated with the conservative Manhattan Institute. He has developed several quasi-documentary reports for the FNC including one that was loaded with energy industry-paid experts denying global warming and several others that celebrated the 'victory' in Iraq. Brit Hume served as Fox's Washington managing editor for twelve years before leaving daily journalism to spend "time with his grandchildren" and "follow his Christian faith."[703] He is currently a senior political analyst for the network and a regular panelist on *Fox News Sunday*. Before joining Fox, Hume was a frequent contributor to the far right *American Spectator* and the Murdoch-owned *Weekly Standard*—a bastion of neoconservatism—currently edited by its founder, William Kristol, and Fred Barnes, an evangelical Christian supply-sider and global warming denier who penned a obsequious biography of George W. Bush entitled *Rebel in Chief* in 2006. In March 2009, at the Media Research Center's annual gala, Hume all but conceded that his network was nothing more than a mouthpiece for the radical right.

In accepting the Media Research Center (MRC) William F. Buckley Award for Media Excellence, Hume thanked Brent Bozell and the MRC for providing him with a "tremendous amount of material" which he put to "tremendous use" for "many years" when he was anchoring *Special Report*.[704] The MRC is a radical conservative media watchdog group run by Bozell, nephew of the late William F. Buckley and son of L. Brent Bozell who assisted Barry Goldwater in writing *Conscience of a Conservative*. Brent Bozell, a member of the ultra-secretive Council for National Policy (see chapter two), was the chief fund-raiser behind Pat Buchanan's un-successful attempt to capture the Republican presidential nomination in 1992. Over the years, the MRC has been funded by, among others, the Bradley, Scaife and Olin foundations for its attempts to "provide intellectual ammunition to conservative activists" in their war against the so-called leftist mainstream media. In the MRC's 2006 Annual Report, Bozell boasted that his organization was a leading source of information for the FNC. This revelation, coupled with Hume's remarks at the gala, seem to suggest that Fox news personalities often serve as stenographers for the right's agenda rather than as journalists who simply "report" so that viewers can "decide."

Then there was the late Tony Snow, a former speechwriter for Bush the elder and a FNC fixture since 1996. Snow often served as a frequent guest host on Rush Limbaugh's radio show and wrote an "unabashedly conservative newspaper column" until Fox brass pressured him to abandon it "to avoid the appearance of bias."[705] He also hosted his own show—the *Tony Snow Show*—on Fox News Radio from 2003 to 2006 where he was often heard criticizing (albeit gently) the Bush presidency from the right. Ironically, he eventually left his perch at Fox to become Bush's third White House Press Secretary, succeeding Scott McClellan and Ari Fleischer. After battling colon cancer, Snow resigned as press secretary, citing his White House salary as inadequate to provide for his family in light of his illness. An agent of right-wing Republicanism, Snow joined the chorus of McCarthy-esque conservatives who labeled academics anti-American. While addressing the Academy of Leadership and Liberty at Oklahoma Christian University in December 2007, Snow lamented the country's second war—the war on God—and also suggested that the average "Iranian is more pro-American than virtually any college faculty in this country."[706]

FNC's former senior vice president was John Moody (currently the CEO of NewsCore, the internal wire service of NewsCorp), a veteran *Time* correspondent, who had been known to disseminate memos to staff instructing them on what topics to cover and how to cover them. A *Media Matters* examination of Moody's memos, some of which were featured in Robert Greenwald's brilliant documentary *Outfoxed: Rupert Murdoch's War on Journalism*, demonstrated a clear pattern of promoting a right-wing agenda and supporting the Bush administration.[707] The *Columbia Journalism Review* noted that several former Fox employees complained of Moody's interference and of management "sticking their fingers in the writing and editing of stories to cook the facts to make a story more palatable to right-of-center tastes." Many of those same former employees added that they had never seen that level of "manipulation" at other news organizations.[708] According to Charles Reina,

> the roots of FNC's [FOX News Channel's] day-to-day on-air bias are actual and direct. They come in the form of an executive memo distributed electronically each morning. Addressing what stories will be covered and, often, suggesting how they should be covered ... The Memo was born with the Bush administration, early in 2001, and, intentionally or not, has ensured that the administration's point of view consistently comes on FNC.[709]

As a network, Fox is committed to the triumph of conservative politics, not a well-informed public. Indeed, its viewers are the "least knowledgeable" when compared with audiences that watch traditional network news and even those who cite cable news networks such as CNN as their primary source of information.[710] From the hosts it hires to the way in which it frames issues, Fox has consistently demonstrated its dedication to advancing the ideological agenda of the right. Despite the blatant partiality of Fox's most prominent personalities, contributors and even guests, FNC network executives scoff at charges of bias and have been careful to cloak its political predilections in slogans such as "Fair and Balanced" and "We Report, You Decide." Yet real reporting—just the facts journalism—is not what FNC is all about. Rather it is a haven for pundits who blur the lines between news and opinion. And it is not reasoned and informed opinion—rather it is shrill, obnoxious, in-your-face opinion. On this issue, Brock's observations merit attention:

> Ailes invented the kind of opinion network first envisioned by Edith Efron in 1971. Efron wanted to supplant news—facts and information—with a "full spectrum of opinion." Because facts and information threatened to undermine its ideology, the right wing long had been hostile to news ... Ailes's project was on a grander scale: He sought to collapse and destroy the distinction between news and opinion. For years, the distinction had been under assault from polemicists like Robert Novak, who insisted he was a "reporter;" from "opinion journalists" at The Wall Street Journal editorial page; from "investigative reporting" in The American Spectator; from "stories" in the Washington Times; from the "correspondents" on The 700 Club; from "internet journalist" Matt Drudge; and, above all, from the braying right-wing radio hosts, who insisted

they were a reliable source of "news." Ailes's contribution was to bring this approach to television, the most powerful and imitative medium of all. Around the clock, FOX News offered opinion, not news.[711]

Despite its contestations to the contrary, FNC is inherently biased but one need not rely on "liberal" critics such as Brock to come to that conclusion. Consider the remarks of a conservative observer writing in *The American Enterprise* online:

> Watch FOX for just a few hours and you encounter a conservative presence unlike anything on TV ... FOX viewers will see Republican politicians and conservative pundits ... Nowhere does FOX differ more radically from the mainstream television and press than in its robustly pro-U.S. coverage of the war on terror. After September 11, the American flag appeared everywhere, from the lapels of the anchormen to the corner of the screen. Ailes himself wrote to President Bush, urging him to strike back hard against al-Qaeda. On-air personalities and reporters freely referred to "our" troops instead of "U.S. forces," and Islamist "terrorists" and "evildoers" instead of "militants" [in] open displays of patriotism.[712]

Anderson goes on to quote Dick Morris praising the FNC's coverage of the Iraq war for providing the audience with a spin-free portrait of what was really going on in Iraq while other news outlets were trucking in bias:

> In the Iraqi war, Dick Morris explains, 'the viewing audience truly saw how incredibly biased the other networks were: ... the plan was flawed, we attacked with too few troops ... the oil wells would go up in flames, there would be street-to-street fighting in Baghdad ... and now we're into this new theme that Iraq is a quagmire and that there aren't any weapons of mass destruction and that Bush lied—and all the while, thanks in part to FOX News, Americans are seeing with their own eyes how much this is crazy spin.[713]

Of course, with respect to Dick Morris—the former Bill Clinton campaign adviser turned Fox News commentator—we need to bear in mind that he has compared the "liberal media" to "Radio Moscow" and accused them of undermining Bush's war on terror.[714] But, what is truly laughable about Anderson and Morris's enthusiasm for the FNC is that it was *their* beloved network that was dealing in spin and patriotic correctness rather than reality and truth.

Indeed, much of Fox's success is derived from the fact that it spends less on genuine newsgathering than any of the other networks. It has a "smaller reporting staff than its competitors but compensates with better bluster" by hiring "on-air talent such as Matt Drudge, Sean Hannity, Oliver North, Bill O'Reilly, and Geraldo Rivera."[715] Rampton and Stauber also note that even "by the time of the Iraq War, Fox News had just 1,250 full-time and freelance employees and 17 news bureaus, only six of them overseas, with operating costs of $250 million." On the other hand, CNN "had 4,000 employees and 42 bureaus, 31 of them overseas, at a cost of about $800 million." And, in the Middle East, "Fox had only 15 correspondents, compared to at least 100 apiece for ABC, CBS, NBC, and BBC." This situation forced Fox to "purchase video footage of Baghdad from Al-Jazeera" as tanks rolled into the city early in the war.[716] Moreover, a study conducted by the University of Maryland's Program on International Policy Attitudes (PIPA) and Knowledge Networks that was released in 2003 clearly and overwhelmingly demonstrated that Fox viewers were significantly more likely to have misperceptions about the Iraq war than consumers of other media sources.[717] The study concluded that people's knowledge of the issues surrounding the Iraq war depended largely upon their primary news source and noted that 80% of Fox viewers held at least one major misperception about the war.

While these findings may have shamed a more reputable network into admitting its failure to inform the public, there was no *mea culpa* from Murdoch or from any of Fox's major personalities. This may lead one to conclude that the FNC was not terribly interested in reporting factual news but much more concerned with selling Bush's wars and right-wing ideology. In fact, Murdoch said as much while speaking at the World Economic Forum in Davos, Switzerland in 2007. In a video clip widely circulated on *YouTube*, Murdoch publicly stated that his media companies, including Fox, had tried to propagandize for the Iraq war and shape public opinion and the war agenda in accordance with Bush administration policy. During the buildup to the 2003 Iraq war *all* of his 175 newspapers editorialized in favor of the invasion. Contrary to its mantra of "we report, you decide," the FNC is nothing more than a calculated mouthpiece for the right despite its attempts to lull its audience into believing that what it is seeing and hearing is unadulterated truth. As Conason argues, "never in the history of American politics or American broadcasting has any media outlet been so closely identified with a president or a party as Fox News" was with George W. Bush and the Republicans. It is "an inappropriate and journalistically illicit relationship" that "crossed whatever normal boundary separates politicians and press organizations." In many ways, while Republicans reigned, Fox News represented "an innovation in the authoritarian mode: a fully dedicated mouthpiece for the state" that was nevertheless unofficial and in the private sector.[718]

Even more disturbing is that Murdoch's media have "done more to cheapen American values and drive the country to fascistic ways of thinking than anything since the McCarthy period in the 1950s."[719] Indeed, as we shall see, Fox's attack poodles took up the cause of a new McCarthyism after 9/11 and they have continued in that vein since Barack Obama was elected to the White House.

FOX'S ATTACK POODLES

In his hilarious account of right-wing media personalities whom he calls "attack poodles," Wolcott identifies some of the major characteristics of this breed: they are "apostles of war"—of both the foreign and domestic variety—and they fight "for an American empire of iron-fisted affluence."[720] Most often, the targets of their wrath are liberals and leftists whom the poodles claim are anti-American, terrorist-sympathizing malcontents. According to these conservative canines, the threats to America are grave and they are both external and internal—external because there are groups that wish to harm the United States; internal because those who dared to question Bush's cowboy foreign policy were cast as a contemptuous fifth column that despised ideals of freedom, democracy, and equality. According to the FNC, the French-loving, latte-drinking liberals were the equivalent of domestic terrorists who undermined national unity and provided ammunition to America's enemies. Fox News defined a "patriotic American as a person who did not question the war nor criticize the Bush administration, its motives, or its decisions." Those that waivered in their support of Bush or the war were designated as being "anti-troops" and thus "anti-American."[721] For years, we were told that if only all Americans would band together, wave the flag, don the sartorial splendor of the red, white and blue, and support George W. Bush, the terrorists would abandon their ways in the face of "our" resolve. So, the pitbulls of partisanship did their utmost to heighten hysteria and prop up PC.

Sean Hannity, RNC Ventriloquist

By all accounts, Sean Hannity is a successful media figure who has parlayed his fanatical anti-liberalism into a very profitable career. He can be seen each night on *The Hannity Show* and he previously co-hosted *Hannity & Colmes* with his wishy-washy "liberal" sidekick Alan Colmes. He is also heard daily on the second most listened-to show in conservative talk radio on the ABC Radio Network. So enamored with Hannity were Fox's head honchos that they gave him a weekly solo show, *Hannity's America*, which kicked off in January 2007. The show was frightening in that it incorporated many of the elements of fascism identified by Laurence Britt including deep-rooted anti-intellectualism, zealous, unthinking patriotism, and the identification of "enemies"—both foreign and domestic—as a unifying cause around which a sense of collective identity could be forged.[722] The identification of enemies/scapegoats as a rallying point is essentially designed to channel frustration and fear—in this case, the fear and frustration of angry white men—in controlled directions. For Hannity, the enemies are always and everywhere, liberals.

In the inaugural broadcast of *Hannity's America*, (which was replaced in January 2009 with a show simply called *Hannity*) the self-righteous host included a segment entitled "Enemy of the State." Academy-Award winning actor Sean Penn was the first recipient of this dubious honor for his candid opposition to the Iraq war and the Bush administration and, apparently, for referring to Hannity as a "whore." After some negative publicity about the Orwellian title, the feature was renamed "Enemy of the Week." The segment, whose visual backdrop (which was highly reminiscent of Horowitz's Discover the Networks website) included pictures of 'anti-Americans' such as Cuba's Fidel Castro, North Korea's Kim Jong-il, Venezuela's Hugo Chavez, Iran's Mahmoud Ahmadinejad alongside those of Penn, Michael Moore, Barbara Streisand, and Alec Baldwin, was a staple of the show along with another that highlighted "A Great American." In Hannity's world, a "great American" is usually someone who blindly embraces the government line—at least when Republicans are in power.

Indeed, he has had no trouble lambasting the government since Obama has been in office and has used his various media platforms to attack the President with the ferociousness of a feral dog. And more recently, he has aggressively promoted the manufactured tea party "movement" (see also chapter three) that has organized anti-government rallies because Obama—whom the lunatic fringe thinks is a socialist—proposed raising the tax rate on the wealthiest of Americans. It should be noted that the proposed tax hike would still be ten percentage points less than it was for most of the Reagan administration, a fact that Hannity and other Fox teabagging advocates have conveniently ignored.[723] Then again, facts do not really matter on the FNC.

Hannity is the best-selling author of harangues such as *Let Freedom Ring: Winning the War of Liberty over Liberalism* and *Deliver Us from Evil: Defeating Terrorism, Despotism, and Liberalism* (both of which were published by the Rupert Murdoch-owned Regan Books) that are best described as little squirts of "lighter fluid on the bonfire of liberal witch-burning."[724] In many ways, Hannity is "the simulacrum of Fox News's ideal viewer: the middle-aged white man with the refillable, flip-top head who's told what to think and repeats what he's been told in a brash voice, convinced that he thunk it up himself."[725] He tends to recite Republican talking points as though they were his own opinions. He was a reliable purveyor of the Bush regime's propaganda and he continues to play the PC card when it suits his partisan political purposes.

Hannity commands up to $50,000 for speaking engagements and travels only in private jets. In July 2008, he signed a co-syndication deal with ABC Radio Networks and Clear Channel's Premiere Radio Networks for $100 million that will keep him on the nation's airwaves for the next five years. Despite his multimillionaire status, he considers himself a "blue-collar guy." This, of course, is in keeping with the FNC's populist façade. In addition to positioning himself as a regular, God-fearing, working stiff, Hannity fashions himself as a moral compass struggling valiantly to lead Americans out of the swampland engendered by the excesses of liberalism. However, beneath the populist, holier-than-thou veneer is a history of unsavory associations with assorted right-wing crazies.

Before he became a fixture on the FNC, Hannity served as host on several confrontational talk radio shows in California, Alabama, and Georgia. One of his first stints came in the late 1980s at the University of California at Santa Barbara's KCSB radio station where he served as a volunteer broadcaster. In 1989, less than a year after his program first aired, KCSB's management canceled his show and charged him with "discriminating against gays and lesbians" after he featured the book *The AIDS Coverup: The Real and Alarming Facts about AIDS* on two shows.[726] Written by homophobic, Christian-right activist and home-schooling advocate, Gene Antonio, the book maintained that the government, the media, and the medical establishment were conspirators in a plot to mislead the public about the spread of AIDS. Among other things, Antonio contended that the disease could be spread by coughing, sneezing, and even mosquito bites but that this was being covered up by those sympathetic to the "homosexual movement." When Antonio was a guest on Hannity's show, both of them engaged in an unseemly slur-fest directed at gay men. According to UCSB's campus newspaper, *The Daily Nexus*, Hannity claimed that "anyone listening to this show that believes homosexuality is a normal lifestyle has been brainwashed" and referred to homosexuality as a lower "form of behavior." Not to be outdone on the homophobic hate meter, Antonio called gay men a "subculture of people engaged in deviant, twisted acts."[727]

With the help of the Santa Barbara chapter of the ACLU, an organization he now routinely maligns, Hannity challenged his dismissal and the decision was reversed. However, he chose not to return to KCSB and instead, employing his trademark modesty, placed a self-promotional advertisement in radio publications declaring himself the most talked about college radio host in America. He was hired by WVNN in Athens, Alabama and later moved to the Atlanta, Georgia radio market to fill a slot on WGST that had been vacated by libertarian ranter and liberal basher, Neil Boortz. But Hannity's big break came when he left Atlanta for New York and was hired by WABC to substitute for their afternoon drive time host during Christmas week. He was eventually hired full-time by WABC after the station cut ties with former host Bob Grant. In his 2002 book, *Let Freedom Ring*, Hannity claimed that he grew up listening to Grant whom he referred to as "one of the most entertaining hosts I'd ever heard."[728] His admiration of Grant speaks volumes.

Grant is widely known as the godfather of the angry talk radio format and a hysterical racist. In 1995, he publicly stated he had no problem with the National Alliance—the largest neo-Nazi group in the United States. His spiel also regularly included references to African Americans as "savages" and the promotion of "The Bob Grant Mandatory Sterilization Program for minorities."[729] A frequent caller to Grant's show was Hal Turner, the northern New Jersey coordinator for Pat Buchanan's 1992 presidential campaign and one of the most vitriolic neo-Nazi public figures in the country. When Grant's show was cancelled by WABC, Turner started calling into Hannity's radio program and was known by his moniker "Hal from North Bergen." On WABC

Hannity inherited Grant's fan base of angry white males … [and] recognized his audience's thirst for red meat, racist rhetoric. However, he knew that if he wanted to avoid Grant's fate, he needed an air of deniability. When 'Hal from North Bergen' began calling his show, Hannity found he could avoid the dangers of direct race-baiting by simply outsourcing it to Turner.[730]

For years, Hannity was more than accommodating to Turner and offered his radio show as a frequent forum for his racist tirades. Turner would call in and bash African-Americans to the delight of Hannity's Neanderthal listeners and the host would remain silent. During a segment in August 1998, Turner reminded Hannity that "if it wasn't for the graciousness of the white man, black people would still be swinging on trees in Africa."[731] Hannity also helped to promote Turner's candidacy for the U.S. House of Representatives that same year and reportedly had a personal relationship with the neo-Nazi, apparently counseling him on his personal life. Turner hosted a webcast, *The Hal Turner Show*, from his home once a week where he often threatened various public officials, particularly federal judges. After the election of Obama, a seething Turner claimed that he would wreak havoc at the presidential inauguration. On June 3, 2009, Turner was arrested in New Jersey for hosting a website that incited residents of Connecticut to "take up arms" against two Connecticut lawmakers and a state ethics official.[732] Three weeks later, he was re-arrested at his New Jersey home for making threats against the United States Court of Appeals in Chicago. The FBI seized a cache of firearms and two hundred rounds of ammunition from his abode. At the time of this writing, Turner is in jail being held without bail.

In 1996, Ailes hired Hannity to host a television program which had the working title, *Hannity and the LTBD*—liberal to be determined—and Hannity himself hand-picked his co-host, Alan Colmes, after auditioning a number of prospects. While the final episode of *Hannity & Colmes* aired on January 9, 2009, Rendall notes that the show figured prominently in Fox's "campaign to market its right leaning programming as "fair and balanced." The show, however, was anything but balanced.[733] In fact, it became the butt of more than a few jokes given that it pitted the pugnacious and ideologically relentless Hannity against the mild-mannered and tepid Colmes. And, when "liberals" other than Colmes appeared to present a so-called counterpoint to Hannity's nightly tirades, they typically proved to be inept sparring partners. In the rare instances when the token liberal was given the opportunity to articulate an actual counter-argument, Hannity swiftly put an end to it by shouting down his opponent, lying, changing the topic, or abruptly ending the "interview." Various studies conducted by *FAIR* and *Media Matters* demonstrated the extreme right-wing bias of the show—not only in terms of the guests who appeared, who were mainly conservatives and/or Republicans, but also in terms of the show's tenor. The title *Hannity & Colmes* was "something of a misnomer" because Colmes acted "essentially as a sacrificial lamb" and was regularly referred to as Hannity's "side-kick."[734] And sadly, Colmes did little to prevent the show he co-hosted from becoming a neo-McCarthyite tool in the right's arsenal.

For most people, McCarthyism is viewed as a stain on the country's history—a bleak era characterized by censorship and paranoia. Not so, for Hannity who was quite open about his desire to see a new age of McCarthyism rise from the ashes of 9/11. Hannity is wildly popular among conservative college groups who herald him as a public intellectual who can speak to a range of issues—from tax policy to terrorism—and they often pay him exorbitant fees to preach to the already converted and rally the right-wing foot soldiers on campuses. What makes Hannity an expert on such matters is difficult to discern since he is a college dropout; however, he was granted an honorary degree in 2005 by the late chancellor of Liberty University, Jerry Falwell. Nonetheless, his popularity among right-wing students is undeniable. Of course, this is hardly shocking since he has routinely provided them with a forum to promote their brand of pitchfork anti-intellectualism.

In November 2005, Hannity used his radio show to invite students to report their left-wing professors to him because, as he put it, "fear is a great motivator." Then, in January 2006, he told one of his callers to secretly tape educators who spoke out against the war and the Bush administration—this after a disgruntled student called to complain that two books being used in a course she was taking were endorsed by—horror of all horrors—Hillary Clinton and Michael Moore. Hannity instructed the caller to stay on the line so he could give her the name of an organization that he praised as battling anti-American, unpatriotic professors. That organization was none other than the *Bruin Alumni Association* (BAA), a group fronted by Hannity wannabe Andrew Jones.

The "idiot winds" of post-9/11 were arguably transmogrified into a tsunami of stupidity in early 2006 when it was reported that Jones, a UCLA alumnus, decided to offer students at his alma mater payment for monitoring so-called radical professors.

Jones had been a *Daily Bruin* columnist from 2000–2003 while studying at UCLA. His polemics routinely targeted political correctness, affirmative action, feminism, and multiculturalism with the racist and sexist zeal common among very angry conservative white males. Jones also founded a paper entitled the *Criterion* and from that perch his puerile pontificating about liberal media bias and a professoriate overrun by wild-eyed revolutionaries earned him a reputation "for being a rather unbalanced chap" even among his fellow right-wingers.[735] Indeed, Jones provided an idea of how he judged the political spectrum by referring to MoveOn.org as "rabid" and suggesting that Fox's Bill O'Reilly was not a "conservative." As leader of the *UCLA Bruin Republicans*, he led the first ever "affirmative action bake sale" in the United States; led counter-protests to "every major anti-war or pro-affirmative action demonstration" and organized pro-war rallies. He was also instrumental in bringing rightists such as William Bennett, Ann Coulter, David Horowitz, Dinesh D'Souza, and L. Paul Bremer to speak on campus.[736]

Eventually, Jones ensconced himself even more firmly in the right's proto-fascist fringe. Borrowing a strategy "right out of the Stalinist playbook," Jones circulated an invitation to UCLA students that asked:

> Do you have a professor who just can't stop talking about President Bush, about the war in Iraq, about the Republican Party, or any other ideological issue that has nothing to do with the class subject matter? It doesn't matter whether this is a past class or your class from this coming winter quarter. If you help expose the professor, we'll pay you for your work.[737]

For their efforts, students could receive $100 for "full, detailed lecture notes, all professor-distributed materials and full tape recordings of every class session;" $50 for "full-detailed lecture notes and all professor-distributed materials," and $10 for an "advisory" that a "class should be examined and professor-distributed materials collected."[738] As Wiener notes, Jones promise of remuneration for ratting out "radical" professors was a tactic that even "Joe McCarthy and HUAC never tried."[739]

Additionally, Jones created an online list of the "Dirty Thirty" at UCLA—a cabal of progressive professors allegedly guilty of poisoning the minds of youth with anti-Americanism, anti-capitalism and other corrupting ideologies. While Jones argued, similar to David Horowitz, that he was concerned with the "politicization" of the classroom, the website profiles of the targeted professors revealed that they were singled out, not for what when on in their classrooms, but rather for positions they took outside the lecture halls, in public forums and, in some cases, at anti-war teach-ins. On the BAA website, Jones claimed that an "unholy alliance" of "anti-war professors, radical Muslim students, and a pliant administration" had made UCLA a major organizing center for opposition to the war on terror. Not surprisingly, all of the educators named in Jones's smear campaign tended to be critics of the Bush administration. UCLA English professor Saree Makdisi, one of the victims of Jones' political profiling, contended that she and her colleagues were being

> targeted for speaking out on the kinds of urgent social matters and universal principles that it has always—in every society and age—been the task of intellectuals to address. The website assumes that any professor who speaks out

in a public forum must at the same time be indulging in ideological abuse of his or her students—proselytizing them, indoctrinating them. And it's actually not just any professor; its only the supposed 'liberal' ones, since 'conservative' faculty are not targeted on the website ... [the] point of the website is not really to produce genuine 'evaluations' of classroom dynamics—a cause that would hardly be well-served by a tiny group of politically motivated zealots accountable to no one and trying to use the cash nexus to break the sacrosanct bond between teacher and students. The point, rather, is to silence voices that go against the zealots' right-wing orthodoxy, and to subject the classroom to outside political surveillance, not simply by vigilante groups like this one, but ultimately by the state itself.[740]

Makdisi further noted that the real impetus behind Jones' crusade was a Senate Bill (SB6) that had been introduced in December 2004 by California's Republican State Senator Bill Morrow. Morrow, a Christian conservative who served on the advisory board of the BAA, introduced a Horowitz-ian "Student Bill of Rights" to "protect" students from "harassment and abuse" by professors. Although the bill never made it out of committee, Jones had explicitly aligned himself with the student academic freedom movement begun by Horowitz and his McCarthyite tactics were clearly designed to garner support for the Senator's initiative.

After the *L.A. Times* reported on Jones' efforts and publicized his "Dirty Thirty" list, several prominent conservatives rushed to distance themselves from the BAA board. Among the defectors were former Congressman Jim Rogan, a UCLA graduate, who served as House manager in the impeachment of President Bill Clinton, KABC radio ranter Al Rantel, and neoconservative historian Stephan Thernstrom. Thernstrom, a senior fellow at the "four sisters" funded Manhattan Institute and former Olin fellowship and Bradley prize recipient, was of course quite prominent in the anti-political correctness hysteria of the early 1990s. He was at the forefront of those lamenting that academic freedom and the right to free speech were being circumscribed by politically correct fanatics intent on destroying the First Amendment privilege in the name of protecting the rights of "groups" (read: "minority" groups) and that professors were being subjected to censorship tactics by students.

Indeed, an incident involving Thernstrom was one of the most frequently circulated examples of politically correct, left-wing repression during the 'culture wars' after he was allegedly accused of being a "racist" by some students who had been enrolled in his "Peopling of America" course. These charges came after Thernstrom had made some objectionable comments, including some that suggested that Jim Crow laws were beneficial; that affirmative action amounted to government-enforced preferential treatment of minorities; and that the cultural practices of Blacks were the cause of poverty in African-American communities. Upon hearing of the student complaints, Thernstrom accused Black students of participating in "McCarthyism of the Left" and claimed that being called a racist in the 1990s was akin to being called a Communist in the 1950s. In an article written for the NAS journal *Academic Questions*, Thernstrom whined that he had been a target of the "ludicrous," "pathetic," and "outrageous" efforts of a few students who showed little respect for the concept of academic freedom.[741]

However, the students in question had not charged the professor with being a racist, but merely suggested that some of his comments had been questionable, somewhat insensitive, and that his perspective on Black life was somewhat simplistic and not reflective of the range of Black experience. For example, in a letter to the *Harvard Crimson,* one student claimed that she had not accused Thernstrom of racism, but rather had questioned his sensitivity when "affirmative action" was "incompletely defined" and when he stated that because of "feelings of inadequacy," black men "beat their wives and take off."[742] Remarkably, Thernstrom took this to be an example of 'left-wing McCarthyism.' Yet upon examining the student's statement, it is apparent that she was merely asking that the professor engage in some critical self-reflection and recognize that some of his statements could reasonably be interpreted as stereotypical. Ironically, Thernstrom, who was never listed on a public website as a racist and who claimed to be the victim of thought control back in the early 1990s, did not have a problem signing on to Jones' McCarthyite campaign and his attacks on academic freedom—at least not until Jones' tactics received widespread condemnation in both the domestic and international press. However, hypocritical conservatives like Thernstrom did not necessarily object to Jones' little list but rather to his attempts to pay students for spying on their professors.

Such was also the case with David Horowitz. After a week of outraged reaction against the BAA (whose advisory board also included Shawn Steel, a co-founder of the California campaign to recall Democratic governor Gray Davis; George W. Bush's one-time nominee for Labor Secretary Linda Chavez; and the AEI's John Lott), Horowitz distanced himself from Jones for "baiting people." Horowitz condemned Jones, who had previously worked for him at the former Center for the Study of Popular Culture, for not properly running an academic freedom campaign and for playing into the hands of its detractors. In other words, Horowitz chided Jones for using tactics that were too crude when compared to his own attempts to silence dissent in the name of 'academic freedom.' Whatever Horowitz's motivation for publicly scolding Jones, they shared the same reactionary mission—the BAA was merely a more blatant manifestation of Horowitz's campus campaign. What's more, such a reprimand from Horowitz was, in many ways, a "bit like being lectured on boxing etiquette by Mike Tyson."[743]

Despite Horowitz's reaction and the fact that several conservatives decried Jones, Hannity was only too happy to provide Jones' with a forum not only on his radio program but on *Hannity & Colmes* just three days prior to the fifth anniversary of "9/11." With the notorious Oliver North sitting in for Hannity, the FNC deliberately "gave a PR boost to right-wing McCarthyism on college campuses" when the show hosted Jones "without a balancing guest and without mentioning" that he had initiated a pay-to-spy scheme. Instead, Jones was portrayed as an "independent expert" and the head of the BAA. There was no mention of his McCarthy-esque agenda and Alan Colmes' critical questioning was given short shift when compared to North's "sympathetic portion." Moreover, no one was on hand from UCLA to offer an alternative perspective and Jones was left alone to make "incendiary and unsubstantiated claims such as "White (UCLA) students are denigrated on a daily basis."[744]

167

In 2006, *Hannity & Colmes* showcased David Horowitz's book about the "101 most dangerous" professors in the country. Beginning on Monday, February 13, Horowitz appeared nightly and was given free reign to spew bilious anti-intellectual claptrap with very little in the way of rebuttal from the resident liberal Colmes. Among those targeted by Horowitz and Hannity was Ward Churchill (see below) whose saga and eventual firing from the University of Colorado at Boulder is all too familiar in academic circles.[745] Churchill had long been the FNC's poster-child for academic bad behavior, having been tarred and feathered by virtually all FNC personalities. So intense and bizarre was the network's obsession with Churchill that one was left wondering if the professor was related to the Clintons.

Another academic who was maliciously attacked during Hannity and Horowitz's week-long orgy of hate was University of Illinois professor Bill Ayers whom Horowitz accused of being a follower of Charles Manson. Of course, Ayers, a former member of the Weather Underground during the 1960s, eventually became a FNC fixation during the 2008 presidential campaign as the network, in good red-baiting fashion, attempted to paint Barack Obama as a leftist extremist because he and Ayers were both involved in an education reform group, the Chicago Annenberg Challenge. During the quest for the White House, a centerpiece in the effort to depict Obama as a treacherous enemy of the people was Hannity's hour-long special entitled "Obama & Friends: History of Radicalism" which "drew on a series of marginal and shadowy writers and researchers to offer up a series of allegations and half-truths" about Obama's supposed ties to Louis Farrakhan, Muslim fundamentalists, and of course Ayers.[746] In one

> especially lunatic segment, Andy Martin, a writer with a history of making anti-Semitic statements, claimed that Obama, in deciding to work as a community organizer in Chicago after college, had "probably" been recruited for the job by Ayers, who was seeking to test his suitability for joining his radical political movement, the aim of which was to bring about in America a "socialist revolution." Martin offered not a shred of evidence to back up this charge. Nonetheless, the image of Obama-as-Ayers-front-man became a staple on talk radio and in the blogosphere.[747]

Even though Obama's connection to Ayers was weak, smear merchants such as Hannity employed contemptible guilt-by-association tactics that harkened back to the McCarthy era. And, the election of Obama has not diminished Hannity's propensity for such tactics—he continues to rant and rave about Obama's ties to Ayers and his so-called radical socialist agenda.

Bill O'Reilly, Father Christmas

Fox's formula is rather simple and consistent—it's all about attitude. Its "anthem is all percussion, all the time."[748] Loud, raucous, and in-your-face. Arguably, the embodiment of that formula is Bill O'Reilly. Bill, the eldest of two children born to William, an oil company accountant, and Angela O'Reilly in New York City, grew up in Westbury on Long Island where he attended parochial school. After graduating from a private Catholic all-boys high school in nearby Mineola, he went to Marist College, another private institution in Poughkeepise, New York where he earned a B.A. in history in 1971. He eventually obtained a Master of Science in Broadcast Journalism from Boston University in 1976.

After a series of various reporting and anchoring positions, O'Reilly joined *Inside Edition*, a syndicated "infotainment" program that was arguably a direct precursor to the high-pitched, tabloid-inspired FNC, in 1989. In his sixth year at *Inside Edition*, which was experiencing dwindling ratings, O'Reilly grew restless with the show and decided to enroll in the Kennedy School of Government at Harvard University.[749] At Harvard, O'Reilly was approached by Ailes, who was then recruiting talent for the FNC that was scheduled to launch a year later. Ailes hired O'Reilly to anchor *The O'Reilly Report* and the show debuted in the 6:00 p.m. slot with the inauguration of the FNC in October 1996. For the first year and a half, the show suffered from weak ratings but then, in 1998, the Monica Lewinsky scandal erupted. Shortly thereafter, Ailes moved *The O'Reilly Report* into primetime and renamed it *The O'Reilly Factor*. The shift to the 8:00 p.m. slot coupled with O'Reilly's unrelenting drubbing of all things Clinton proved to be a winning formula for both the network and O'Reilly as the ratings began to soar. The 2000 election eventually catapulted O'Reilly past all his cable competition—a feat that only exacerbated his already inflated ego. Despite losing millions of viewers over the last few years, the *Factor* still captures among the highest ratings of prime-time shows on 24-hour cable news channels (a fact that the self-congratulatory host constantly reminds his audience of) and the high-decibel host is paid $10,000,000 in salary. O'Reilly's dominance, however, is not limited to cable news; he has written five top-selling non-fiction books and another one entitled, *Pinheads and Patriots: Where You Stand in the Age of Obama*, is due out in September 2010. He also pens a column that is carried in hundreds of newspapers and many websites repurpose his content for online users. His *Radio Factor* was among the top-10 rated programs heard on more than 400 radio stations as well as satellite operator Sirius XM until he cancelled the show in early 2009.

The O'Reilly Factor bills itself as a "No Spin Zone" and the host has repeatedly proclaimed that the intent of the program is to present audience members with straight facts so that they can then make up their own minds on any given issue. O'Reilly has also stated that his show is fair to all points of view. However, as Peters has demonstrated in his study of the *Factor*, O'Reilly's style is "doused with hyperbole, intolerance, arrogance, and dismissal of alternative voices."[750] Moreover, the "fear and prejudice" that O'Reilly's words and graphics invoke, his over-the-top blind patriotism, his use of repetition and simplistic slogans and sound bites, bear a "striking similarity with techniques used to convey propaganda" and is evocative of "Soviet agitprop."[751]

Unlike obvious GOP apparatchiks such as Hannity, O'Reilly claims to be an independent thinker, beholden to no party—this despite the fact that he was registered as a Republican in Nassau County, New York. After a reporter at the *New York Daily News* uncovered that information, O'Reilly maintained that it was a clerical error and that there was no box to register his Independent status. However, contrary to O'Reilly's assertions, the voter registration form did provide an "I do not wish to enroll in party" box—O'Reilly checked off Republican.[752] Regardless of his past official political party affiliation and his assertions of ideological independence, O'Reilly undoubtedly espouses positions aligned with the right. As *SourceWatch* has aptly noted, the *Factor* "plays a fundamental ideological and propagandistic role" and its primary "purpose is to uncritically propagate" the positions of "right-wing ideologues" and to "disparage critics" of right-wing policy and ideology, the latter of which often involves "character assassination" and the repeated use of denigrating comments.[753]

In spite of his relatively privileged upbringing and his contemporary status as a multimillionaire, O'Reilly claims a working-class heritage and fashions himself a watchdog for the "little guy." As he put it in his 2006 book, *Culture Warrior* the "*Factor* concept is very simple: Watch all of those in power ... so they don't injure or exploit the folks, everyday Americans."[754] Over the years, he has cultivated an image as a populist who single-handedly fights for the interests of the "common folk" against oily politicians, weak-kneed jurists, elitist journalists, and, of course, radical professors. His *raison d'être* is bashing liberals or what he sometimes calls secular progressives (S-Ps). According to O'Reilly, there is an ongoing culture war between his fellow "traditionalists" and the evil S-Ps.

In *Culture Warrior*, O'Reilly sizes up the battlefield (literally following PC to a tee): on one side are those who believe in America as a force of good in the world, the free enterprise system, family, faith (specifically Christianity), and traditional values and, on the other, are those who favor European-style internationalism, expunging the public sphere of all references to God, moral relativism, and the "communist" freeloader mentality of taxing the rich to provide social services such as housing, health care, and early childhood education to the less fortunate. O'Reilly denounces the so-called erosion of societal discipline flowing from the S-P "movement" that is presumably led by wealthy financier George Soros, whom O'Reilly describes as "public enemy number one," and University of California-Berkeley professor George Lakoff, who O'Reilly claims is a favorite of Fidel Castro.[755] In attempting to mobilize the righteous among us against the sinister forces of S-P, O'Reilly offers a "code" that he encourages traditionalists to embrace. He cautions his fellow warriors to take the high ground in the battle and not to indulge in the kinds of unethical tactics apparently employed by the S-Ps, including personal attacks, cheap shots, and invective. Then O'Reilly provides over 200 pages of cheap shots and vindictiveness aimed at various "liberal" media personalities, Hollywood celebrities, and the ACLU.

O'Reilly's hypocrisy is interminable—he chides S-Ps for engaging in character assassinations, name-calling, smear campaigns, and vilification and yet that is *his* stock and trade. A research study published in 2007 demonstrated that O'Reilly called a person or a group a derogatory name once every 6.8 seconds on average or nearly nine times every minute during the editorial commentaries that open his program each night.[756] The study used "seven devices" (name calling, glittering generalities, transfer, testimonial, plain folks, card stacking, and bandwagon) derived from the Institute of Propaganda Analysis (IPA) that was founded in 1937, to analyze O'Reilly's *Talking Points Memo*—the opening segment of his nightly show. The researchers found that O'Reilly "used all seven of the propaganda devices in his commentaries, but name calling" was "the backbone of his communication strategy."[757]

The findings led the authors of the research report to conclude that O'Reilly shared "several common traits" with Father Charles Coughlin—the firebrand Catholic priest who hosted one of the most popular radio programs in the 1930s.[758] Coughlin, a vehement critic of the New Deal, whose radio show was once referred to as a "variation of the fascist agenda applied to American culture" was also an ardent anti-Semite who became one of the "few apologists for Adolf Hitler and the reign of terror brought about by the Nazi Party in Germany."[759] Coughlin's mix of religion and politics delivered with an authoritative broadcasting style also earned him the dubious distinction as the "father of hate radio."[760]

Similar to Coughlin, O'Reilly often mixes politics and religion—something that is quite apparent in his yearly campaign disparaging various entities for presumably waging a "War on Christmas." While it was his FNC colleague John Gibson who actually wrote a best-selling polemic, *The War on Christmas: How the Liberal Plot to Ban the Sacred Christian Holiday is Worse Than You Thought* on the topic in 2005, O'Reilly, joining the John Birch Society, has become the media face of the battle against secular culture's "demonization" of the Christian celebration. Beginning in December 2004, O'Reilly and Hannity began reporting on various isolated hullabaloos involving the public display, or lack thereof, of symbols associated with Christmas. That same year, O'Reilly began a recurring segment called "Christmas Under Siege." Since then O'Reilly's annual conniption fits have become *de rigueur* on the *Factor*.

In both *Culture Warrior* and from his FNC roost, O'Reilly has argued that the purported "war" on Christmas is part of the "secular progressive agenda" designed to "get Christianity and spirituality and Judaism out of the public sphere."[761] For O'Reilly, this is a two-front war with assaults coming from both the government that has been bullied by politically correct groups and ACLU types into expunging any trace of Christmas from the public square and from the private sector in the form of infidel retailers who have replaced the traditional "Merry Christmas" with secularist greetings such as "Happy Holidays." Such gestures, according to O'Reilly and his fellow comrades in the Fox-hole, represent a form of persecution aimed at Christians, something that is both ironic and disturbing: ironic, given the hegemony of Christianity in the United States and disturbing since the suggestion that Christians are threatened each time a cashier says "Happy Holidays" makes a mockery of those around the world who are truly experiencing genuine religious oppression. Allegedly, the war on Christmas is an element of the broader culture war being waged by those covertly engaged in a mission to turn America into a secular state.[762] For as O'Reilly reminds us, if "you can get religion out, then you can pass secular progressive programs, like legalization of narcotics, euthanasia, abortion at will, [and] gay marriage" since "the objection to those things is religious-based, usually."[763]

Of course, O'Reilly's defense of Christmas is part of a patriotically correct narrative that bolsters beliefs of America as a white, Christian nation and it is imperative to acknowledge that white nationalist sentiment has animated the campaign to defend Christmas—long before O'Reilly assumed his role as the culture-warrior-in-chief.

The "war on Christmas" dates back to the heyday of the culture wars of the 1990s and to unsavory characters such as Peter Brimelow. The 63-year-old Brimelow, who is married to a former Heritage Foundation intern, has been the editor of, and/or associated with, several publications including *Fortune, Forbes Magazine* and *National Review*. He has authored books such as *The Worm in the Apple: How the Teachers Unions are Destroying American Education* and appeared on *The O'Reilly Factor* in 2003 to discuss how teachers unions were undermining education. In that interview, Brimelow informed O'Reilly that teachers' unions were "infested" with "left-wing loonies," likened teachers to "inmates" who were "running the asylum" and suggested that unionized educators were to blame for a failing education system because "management has no control."[764] Brimelow also argued in favor of privatizing education, advocated for school vouchers, and claimed that the collective bargaining powers legally granted to teachers' unions had to be rescinded.

Brimelow also wrote *Alien Nation: Common Sense About America's Immigration Disaster,* published in 1995, in which he argued that the influx of "'weird aliens with dubious habits' from developing nations was eroding America's white Christian 'ethnic core,' and in turn, sullying its cultural underpinnings. The War on Christmas was, in his view, a particularly pernicious iteration of the multicultural 'struggle to abolish America.'"[765] Brimelow has also stated that "Third World immigration has "changed the character of America," claimed that a historically white-dominated America should remain that way, and expressed concern that his blond-haired, blue-eyed son would grow up in a country in which whites had lost their majority status.[766]

After some establishment conservatives shunned him because of his "unabashed racial resentment" Brimelow founded what has since become the internet's "leading anti-immigration web journal, VDARE.com." The website encourages reduced immigration—not just illegal immigration—into the United States and guest contributors have included white supremacists such as Jared Taylor who also oversees the magazine *American Renaissance*.[767] The site also carries archives of columns penned by racists such as Sam Francis, who edits the newspaper of the white supremacist Council of Conservative Citizens, a group that has described blacks as a "retrograde species of humanity."[768] Additionally, VDARE has become the "staging ground for the War on the War on Christmas" and a forum for anti-Semitism as Brimelow's writers have "dared to name the true anti-Christian Grinch: Jews."[769] For example:

> The winner of Brimelow's 2001 War on Christmas competition, a 'paleo-conservative' writer named Tom Piatak, insisted that those behind the assault on Christmas 'evidently prefer' Hanukkah, which he called the 'Jewish Kwanzaa,' a 'faux-holiday.' 'Teaching children about Hanukkah, rather than the beliefs that actually sustained Jews on their sometimes tragic and tumultuous historical journey,' Piatak fumed, 'inculcates negative lessons about Christiantity, not positive ones about Judaism.' VDare's 2005 War on Christmas winner, Steve Sailer, a Eugenics enthusiast and author of the new biography of Barack Obama, *America's Half-Blood Prince,* picked up where Piatak left off. 'American Jews,' Sailer wrote, 'those exemplars of successful assimilation now seem to be de-assimilating emotionally, becoming increasingly resentful, at this late

date, of their fellow Americans for celebrating Christmas.' Sailer went on to quote at length from a column by the purportedly Jewish writer, Bert Prelutsky, called 'The Jewish Grinch Who Stole Christmas.'[770]

VDARE has become a "meeting place for many on the radical right" and has been classified as a hate group by the Southern Poverty Law Center.[771]

More recently, Brimelow argued that the most important issues in the 2008 presidential election were not the war in Iraq or the economic crisis but rather immigration and race. In a keynote address, he told an audience at the first meeting of the H.L. Mencken Club (a relatively new organization intended to provide an environment for the "intellectual right" and whose leaders include Jared Taylor and other "academic racists"), that John McCain had lost because of those issues and because McCain failed to portray Obama as "the affirmative-action candidate." The receptive audience agreed with Brimelow's claim that the way to win future elections is "to get white votes" for whites are the true Americans.[772]

While O'Reilly is a little less blatant than Brimelow in espousing nativist rhetoric, he has been known to express frequent concern for the decline of white, Christian male dominance, especially in the context of discussions about immigration policy. Neiwart contends that he has been one of the "major media figures responsible" for fueling the "ugly racism," "hysterical fearmongering" and "bigotry" that has characterized recent debates about the issue.[773] A simple "google" search of the terms "Bill O'Reilly" and "white, Christian male power structure" will locate a video of the *Factor* host sounding off in an exchange with John McCain. In the video, O'Reilly states:

> But do you understand what the New York Times wants, and the far-left want? They want to break down the white, Christian, male power structure, which you're a part, and so am I, and they want to bring in millions of foreign nationals to basically break down the structure that we have. In that regard, Pat Buchanan is right. So I say you've got to cap with a number.[774]

More importantly, O'Reilly's outburst was not an aberration. In April 2006, he told his radio audience that he had uncovered the "hidden agenda" of those in favor of immigrant rights—namely that there was a "movement" in the country whose aim was to "overthrow" the "white privileged Christian nation" and to institute an "open border" so as to encourage "the browning of America."[775] On the May 16, 2006 edition of the *Factor*, in a discussion about opposition to the idea of deploying the National Guard to secure the border, O'Reilly claimed that entities such as *The New York Times* and "many far-left thinkers believe the white power structure that controls America is bad, so a drastic change is needed." He went on to say that "according to lefty zealots, the white Christians who hold power must be swept out by a new multicultural tide, a rainbow coalition, if you will."[776]

O'Reilly's contempt for multiculturalism is not limited to debates about immigration policy. He has targeted "anti-American," "left-wing" teachers and college professors for allegedly teaching "diversity" and "tolerance" rather than teaching "history" and preaching "about the nobility of America." As a result, "lots of American kids know little or nothing about their country, including what they owe their country."[777] While O'Reilly has not precisely articulated the kind of history curriculum that students should be taught, it is quite likely that it would resemble a version of American history such as that advocated by Lynne Cheney and ACTA. The so-called anti-Americanism of educators became an obsession for O'Reilly post-9/11 in his almost nightly tirades about the Ward Churchill affair. As previously noted, Churchill became the Fox News Channel's whipping boy but, arguably, no one cracked the whip more relentlessly than O'Reilly.

Approximately twelve hours after the attacks of September 11, 2001, Churchill composed and posted on-line what was, undoubtedly, a polemical essay entitled "Some People Push Back." Citing numerous historical and contemporary examples of American imperialism, genocide and hypocrisy, the former University of Colorado professor argued that the United States need look no further than its own foreign policy back yard to explain the events. Churchill began his essay assuming, like so many others did in the immediate aftermath of 9/11, that Iraqis were responsible for the attacks. Early in the essay, Churchill discusses the first Gulf War and makes references to the "Highway of Death," a six-lane road between Kuwait and Iraq, where thousands of retreating Iraqi military personnel were "slaughtered in a single day."[778] He also claimed that the attacks were a predictable response to the devastating effects of the economic embargo that had been imposed on Iraq throughout the 1990s. But what would eventually send the media into an apoplectic frenzy was a reference to those who perished in the Twin Towers as "little Eichmanns" who, although not directly responsible for the deplorable conditions in the Middle East, nonetheless "formed a technocratic corps at the very heart of America's global financial empire."[779]

Even after the culprits of the terrorist attacks were identified as members of Al-Queda, in the months and years that followed Churchill repeated many of the essay's more general themes, focusing on the lengthy history of injustices perpetrated by the U.S. government and military, in a number of public presentations after 9/11 and in a subsequent book, *On the Justice of Roosting Chickens: Reflections on the Consequences of U.S. Imperial Arrogance and Criminality* that was published in 2003. However, his remarks did not garner any significant national attention until he was invited to deliver a lecture at Hamilton College in upstate New York about American Indians and the prison system. In mid-December, 2004, Professor Nancy Rabinowitz's Kirkland Project for the Study of Gender, Society and Culture dis-seminated its schedule of upcoming spring lectures which included Churchill. The Kirkland Project (KP) had been a lightning rod for the right even before the invitation had been extended to Churchill, having been subjected to criticism for the progressive bent of its speakers and for welcoming controversial figures to participate in its activities.[780] In fact, the KP was even targeted for "elimination by a small circle of reactionary faculty members working in concert with off-campus organizations" such as ACTA and David Horowitz's then-named Center for the Study of Popular Culture.[781]

One of the most vocal critics was Theodore Eismeier, a professor of government at Hamilton College who had been known for regularly investigating the speakers invited by the KP. After hearing about Churchill's upcoming lecture, Eismeier apparently did some research, came across the essay and was horrified by Churchill's description of the World Trade Center victims as "little Eichmanns." Eismeier then approached members of the administration and threatened them with a public relations scandal. Subsequently, the college president approached Rabinowitz for her opinion on the matter. After she suggested that the college should stand firm for freedom of speech, a decision was made to have Churchill appear on a larger panel that would include conservative speakers. However, that option did not sit well with Eismeier who denounced the idea of the panel as being "akin to inviting a representative of the KKK to speak and then asking a member of the NAACP to respond."[782]

Shortly thereafter, public attacks began to circulate in the local media. The story first appeared in the Hamilton College student newspaper on January 21, 2005 and was picked up five days later by the *Syracuse Post-Standard*. Eventually news about the Churchill affair spread to the right-wing blogosphere and was the topic of an editorial in the *Wall Street Journal* on January 28, 2005. Then the blustering bully of the FNC latched onto the controversy. That same evening, O'Reilly opened his "Top Story" segment by condemning Churchill as a "vile human being" for comparing the 9/11 "victims to a Nazi" and chastised Hamilton College for even inviting him to participate in a public forum. O'Reilly called for the firing of the college's Chancellor and claimed that "alumni should not give a nickel to the school."[783] For three consecutive nights, O'Reilly provided his viewers with Hamilton president Joan Hinde Stewart's e-mail address and encouraged his faithful followers to contact her and "let her know" how they felt about Churchill's scheduled appearance.[784]

A spokeswoman for the college later claimed that Hamilton had been inundated with phone calls and that it had received more than 8,000 emails urging the school to cancel Churchill's speaking engagement. And, within days of O'Reilly's harangue on the *Factor*, Churchill had received over one hundred violent threats. Former New York Governor George Pataki subsequently joined the fray in late January by publicly denouncing Hamilton and, on February 1, 2005, Stewart announced that Churchill would not be speaking because of threats of physical violence. That same evening, the jubilant O'Reilly offered his own spin on the situation in this "talking points" segment. Questioning Stewart's explanation for the cancellation based on safety reasons, O'Reilly opined that Stewart had probably realized that "donations to the college would plummet" and that her own "job security" would be threatened. He also claimed that Hamilton was "home to radical professors" and that it was a "troubled college."[785] He then proceeded to trot out none other than David Horowitz who alleged that Hamilton's funders were outraged because the college was lacking in "intellectual diversity" and because it was a "bastion of radicalism."[786]

King argues that the hundreds of messages sent to Hamilton constituted a "popular panic prompted by various conservative media outlets, particularly Fox News" and other members of the right-wing chattering class. After examining five hundred electronic comments submitted to the college, King concluded that, taken together, they accomplished three things. First, they demonized Churchill as "inhuman and un-American," constructed him "as a monster: an abject Other beyond the bounds of civilization" and therefore undeserving of the "constitutional guarantee of free

speech." Second, they condemned "Hamilton College for its incivility and association with evil." The mere extension of an invitation to Churchill was "tantamount
to supporting terrorism" and given the college's "proximity to New York City"
scheduling the lecture presumably "demonstrated the institution's lack of humanity
and empathy for the victims of 9/11." Finally, the comments advanced and erased
"the very freedoms said to define American greatness."[787]

But more than this, O'Reilly contributed to a phenomenon that is becoming all
too common in the right-wing media—the creation of moral panics. In the classic
definition of the phrase, Cohen describes the moral panic thusly:

> Societies appear to be subject, every now and then, to periods of moral panic.
> A condition, episode, person or group of persons emerges to become defined
> as a threat to societal values and interests ... [and] is presented in a stylized and
> stereotypical fashion by the mass media; the moral barricades are manned by
> editors, bishops, politicians and other right-thinking people; socially accredited
> experts pronounce their diagnoses and solutions ... Sometimes the panic is
> passed over and is forgotten ... at other times it has more serious and long-
> lasting repercussions and might produce such changes as those in legal and
> social policy or even the way society conceives itself.[788]

A moral panic is therefore a product of imaginative intensity, a heightened sense of
a collapse of boundaries between what is acceptable and what is not. As O'Reilly
himself put it when speaking of Churchill: "We're a tolerant society here, but some
things cannot be tolerated."[789]

Whatever one may think of Churchill's opinions is quite beside the point for as
Palczewski et al. remind us, "Churchill's *comments* were not attacked on the basis
of their inaccuracy; *Churchill* was attacked."[790] For the most part, little attention was
accorded to the actual content of the essay; rather Churchill himself was "quickly
rendered into a caricature of academia" and when it finally did receive widespread
attention, "it did so against a backdrop of official public memory that rendered his
argument outrageous and unacceptable."[791] Indeed, given that the official post-9/11
narrative was so deeply rooted in notions of American innocence and patriotic
correctness, Churchill's essay—which might have encouraged some critical reflection
about American foreign policy among its readers—was instead greeted with a
"backlash of monumental proportions."[792] The backlash quickly evolved into a moral
panic about the academy itself as repeated references were made—particularly on
the FNC—to unpatriotic, left-wing professors whose hatred of the United States
was demoralizing the troops and undermining the 'war on terror.' O'Reilly made
dozens of references to the Churchill controversy on both his television and radio
shows, including one during this "Talking Points Memo" on March 3, 2005 in which
he called Churchill a "traitor" and a man deserving of scorn and reprimanded the
University of Colorado for enabling him.[793] But as Schulz and Reyes note,

> the repetitions of the critique served not as moments for debate or dialogue
> about Churchill's larger argument, but functioned instead as a ready referent
> for O'Reilly's "talking points" monologue in which he regularly denounced
> parts of the academy as patently anti-American.[794]

In this regard, Churchill proved to be a convenient scapegoat and began to function as an example of the "kind of irrational, liberal logic" that was said to be "infecting college campuses across the nation."[795]

Another one of O'Reilly's targets was M. Shahid Alam, an economics professor at Northeastern University, who was the topic of the February 2, 2005 episode of *Factor*. Alam had written a piece entitled "America and Islam: Seeking Parallels," that was published in *Counterpunch* in late December, 2004. In the essay, Alam made two central points—first, that the 9/11 attacks represented an Islamist insurgency and that the attackers believed that they were fighting, as Americans did in the 1770s, for "their freedom and dignity against a foreign occupation/control of their lands." Secondly, he asserted that the attacks were the "result of a massive political failure of Muslims to resist their tyrannies locally."[796] A day later, he began receiving menacing emails in a campaign orchestrated by the conservative website "Little Green Footballs." Shortly thereafter, other rightist websites including David Horowitz's frontpagemag.com and Daniel Pipes campuswatch.org began posting excerpts from the essay prompting an outpouring of more hate mail and even death threats directed at Alam. A few days later, in early January 2005, *Counterpunch* published another of his essays, "Testing Free Speech in America" in which Alam elaborated on some of the points made in the previous article. Afterwards, both he and Northeastern University were flooded with nasty and threatening communications from right-wingers who were appalled by the analogy that Alam had drawn between the insurgents and American revolutionaries.

On February 1, 2005, Alam received a call from *Fox* asking him for an interview because they were producing a program about him. On the advice of the ACLU and others, Alam declined the invitation. He contacted *Fox* and said that while he could not do the interview, he would be willing to answer any questions. The network did not take Alam up on his offer. Instead O'Reilly, who referred to Alam as "another nutty professor" who "thinks the 9/11 killers are like America's founding fathers," invited Horowitz's fellow neo-McCarthyite, Daniel Pipes, to pontificate about Alam. After O'Reilly provided yet another "update" on Churchill, he introduced Pipes who described Alam as a "combination of a Marxist and a radical Muslim." According to Pipes, Alam "sees the Western colonial enterprise as the source of all the problems of the non-Western world" and harbors "a venom towards the United States." The fact that Alam is an immigrant to America was particularly troublesome to Pipes who seemed to imply that, as a result, Alam had no right to criticize U.S. policy in the Middle East. Pipes then proceeded to quote from something the professor had written about the U.S. role in pushing globalization to the detriment of many economies and citizens in the Third World. The banter continued as Pipes and O'Reilly attempted to discern whether or not Alam was "rooting for the terrorists to win the war on terror" and then the conversation simply shifted to a more broad-based attack on the left and the website *Counterpunch* which was labeled as "vicious" and "anti-American."[797]

Pipes is a regular guest on the FNC and in introducing Pipes to his show, O'Reilly simply referred to him as the director of the Middle East Forum and campuswatch.org without, of course, providing any background about these organizations. The Middle

East Forum (MEF), a right-wing think tank that has received funding from the Bradley Foundation, was established in 1990 by Pipes who, for a time, held teaching positions at the University of Chicago, Harvard, and the Naval War College but failed to land a tenure-track position—a situation that was likely due to his inability to produce "original scholarship" and his preference for instead "churning out" essays that were published in right-wing magazines such as *Commentary*.[798] The MEF's journal *Middle East Quarterly*, which was not peer-reviewed until 2009 and whose senior editors include Michael Rubin of the AEI, has been described by Sourcewatch.org as hard-line Zionist and has published such informative gems as "Western Feminists: At the Service of Radical Islam." Vehement in his support of the Israeli far right, Pipes has been called an "anti-Arab propagandist" and has been known to refer to Muslims as "barbarians" and "potential killers," prompting James Zogby to suggest that "Pipes is to Muslims what David Duke is to African-Americans."[799]

Pipes is a vociferous advocate for violent military intervention in the Middle East and opposes any peace negotiations between Palestinians and Israelis. Given his militaristic stance and disdain for diplomacy many were outraged when, in 2003, George W. Bush, nominated Pipes to the board of the United States Institute of Peace, a federally funded body that is dedicated to "peacebuilding" and whose members must be confirmed by the Senate. After howls of protest from Democrats and many Arab and Muslim groups, Bush bypassed Congress and temporarily appointed Pipes to the board in 2004.[800] Upon hearing of the nomination, even Christopher Hitchens, who shared Pipes exuberance for the war in Iraq and is a fellow critic of Islam, argued that the Senate should disqualify Pipes because of his "uninformed" positions. Hitchens even went so far as to call Pipes "a person who confuses scholarship with propaganda and who pursues petty vendettas with scant regard for objectivity."[801] And he added, that "Pipes spits and curses at anything short of his own highly emotional agenda."[802]

Pipes had used the MEF to smear Middle East scholars (his utter contempt for the late Edward Said is quite well known) for years but amidst the post-9/11 xenophobia and nativist sentiment that gripped large swathes of the population, his star began to rise. Within a year of the terrorist attacks, Pipes appeared on "110 television and 450 radio shows;" his op-eds graced the pages of the *Wall Street Journal* and the *Los Angeles Times* and the *Philadelphia Inquirer* even "described him as 'smoking hot.'"[803] His various screeds have also found their way to David Horowitz's FrontPageMagazine and numerous other rightist websites. Pipes is obsessed with what he sees as radical Muslim penetration of American institutions and has stated on various occasions that Muslims should be considered among the enemies within. Not surprisingly, Pipes' comments have been featured on the afore-mentioned VDARE.com website and have been cited by white nationalists such as James Fulford.[804]

Press has noted, however, that Pipe's major impact has not come from "analyzing foreign affairs" but rather from "pointing a finger at a purported fifth column lurking in a place conservatives have long suspected of harboring one: academia."[805] Accordingly, in 2002, Pipes took it upon himself to police the discipline of Middle

Eastern studies and launched what could only be called a modern day blacklisting website, *Campus Watch* (CW), a special project of the MEF. Similar to David Horowitz and ACTA's post-9/11 activities, both of which were explored in the previous chapter, CW's first act was "to post McCarthy-style 'dossiers' on the Internet singling out eight professors critical of American and Israeli policies."[806] Subsequently, the professors were attacked by spammers who flooded their email accounts with large numbers of huge files. Juan Cole, a University of Michigan professor, reported that his email was disabled by thousands of hate messages just a day after his name appeared on CW. In protest, more than one hundred scholars contacted CW and asked that they too be added to Pipes hit list as a gesture of solidarity. Pipes gladly obliged and labeled them "apologists for suicide bombings and militant Islam."[807]

When Stanley Kurtz of the *National Review* began a campaign to pressure politicians to pass legislation (HR 3077) that would establish an advisory board of government appointees to study, monitor, appraise, and evaluate area studies programs in universities—specifically those responsible for educating students about the Middle East—Pipes was an enthusiastic sponsor of the bill. Apparently, he shared Kurtz's view that Middle Eastern studies "purvey extreme and one-sided criticism of American foreign policy."[808]

Similar to O'Reilly, Pipes has no interest in legitimate, rationale debate with the scholars he criticizes. Rather, he

> impugns their motives, tossing out labels like "self-hating" and "anti-American," and lifting quotes out of context to portray his targets as closet sympathizers with Osama bin Laden and Saddam Hussein.[809]

Moreover, Pipes' greatest achievement was to "capitalize on the fears generated by 9/11 in order to cast doubt on the motives and agenda of an entire profession—while keeping his own ideological agenda largely obscured from view."[810] And *The O'Reilly Factor* was just one of many FNC venues that enabled Pipes to spout his vitriolic anti-Arab, anti-Muslim tirades and garner support for his McCarthyesque crusade against the academy.

Glenn Beck, Crybaby Conservative

Glenn Beck is a recent edition to the FNC, having joined the network in 2009 but he has quickly earned a reputation for his incendiary rants and his militant anti-liberalism. Each day, on both his nationally syndicated talk-radio show aired by Premiere Radio Networks, a subsidiary of Clear Channel Communications, and on his nightly television program on *Fox*, Beck channels one of this heroes—Joseph McCarthy—and delivers "some of the worst" McCarthyite oratory to millions of his faithful listeners and viewers.[811] Beck's particular brand of McCarthyism is rooted in unfounded malevolent defamation and unscrupulous fear-mongering. He repeatedly vilifies those who disagree with his far right views by accusing them of being unpatriotic and disloyal to their country, calling them terrorists and Islamofascists, or worst of all—socialists. Indeed, his demagoguery is especially appealing to those radical right-wingers who are "most susceptible to conspiracy theories and prone to latch on to eccentric distortions of fact in the name of opposing 'socialism.'"[812] Among the FNC's kennel of knaves, Beck stands out as "the most unhinged and extremist of all" and his over-the-top antics even prompted *Time Magazine* to ask whether "mad man" Beck was "bad for America."[813] A brief recounting of his rather peculiar personal history is necessary in order to contextualize Beck's ascendance to the dizzying heights of right-wing paranoia.

According to Alexander Zaitchik, the author of *Common Nonsense: Glenn Beck and the Triumph of Ignorance*, "Beck has constructed a persona anchored in a biography of struggle and redemption." Beck's story is a tale of "resurrection," one of a "born-again patriot rescued from nihilism" who now fancies himself as a savior—destined to rescue America from the evils of liberalism. He is known for his "bipolar unpredictability and maudlin dramatics."[814] Years before he became a FNC mainstay, he was an unpopular child obsessed with radio and magic tricks. According to Beck, he knew early on that radio was his destiny. His mother, an alcoholic who eventually committed suicide, sparked his "initial fascination with the medium" when she presented him with a "double-record collection of comedic and dramatic radio productions from the Depression and war years" entitled "The Golden Years of Radio" on his 8th birthday. Beck has said that he was mesmerized by the "magic" of radio and how it could create pictures in his head; listening to the collection allegedly had an "immediate and lasting impact" on him.[815]

His quest to create his own pictures, or "theatre of the mind" began at the age of 13 when he landed his first radio gig in 1977 at a Mount Vernon, Washington local AM station, KBRC, after winning a contest held by the station manager to serve as a guest DJ. At the age of 15, while a high-school junior, he was hired at KUBE 93 in Seattle based on an "audition tape that station managers thought was the polished work of an older man." After working various jobs at radio stations in Seattle, Provo, Washington, D.C., and Corpus Christi, Beck landed at WRKA in Louisville where he became known for doing "black guy impersonations" which Zaitchik contends were just "one sign of the young Beck's racial hang-ups."[816]

His real "broadcasting innovation" in Kentucky, however, came "in the realm of vicious personal attacks on fellow radio hosts," particularly those directed at Liz Curtis, an overweight host of an afternoon advice show on another AM news-talk station "whom Beck had never met and with whom he did not compete for ratings." For at least two years, Curtis was used as fodder for Beck's "drive-time fat jokes" and he would often employ "Godzilla sound effects to simulate Curtis walking across the city or crushing a rocking chair." Curtis never responded to Beck's constant goading which only infuriated Beck and fuelled his "hunger for a response." As his attacks on Curtis "escalated and grew more unhinged" a colleague of Curtis,' Terry Meiners, decided to intervene. Meiners apparently told Beck to "lay off Curtis" and suggested that he should instead attack morning DJs like himself, who "could return fire." Beck scoffed at the idea and continued with the "fat jokes, which were exceedingly cruel, pointless, and aimed at one of the nicest people in radio." Meiners later claimed that "Glenn Beck was over-the-top childish from Day One, a punk who tried to make a name for himself by being disruptive and vengeful."[817]

Louisville was also where Beck began "experimenting with another streak that would become more pronounced in later years: militaristic patriotism and calls for the bombing of Muslims." Zaitchik notes that the "birth of Glenn Beck as Radio Super Patriot" can be traced back to April 15, 1986, the morning after Reagan ordered U.S. warplanes to bomb the Tripoli palace of Moammar Gadhafi in retaliation to a bombing that had taken place at a Berlin nightclub that was frequented by American servicemen. After opening his show with a prayer and Lee Greenwood's "God Bless the USA," Beck played patriotic music all morning. There was one song he played repeatedly, a "New Wave-ish spoof titled 'Qaddafi Sucks,'" which became a huge hit with his listeners, many of whom called Beck to inform him of how "inspired they were by his patriotism" and to applaud him for "standing up for America." When one caller argued that Reagan should have dropped even more bombs, Beck agreed and stated that "we should've went over there and bombed the hell out of 'em.'"[818] Although the combination of fat jokes, racial impersonations and Gadhafi songs made waves for awhile, Beck failed to produce numbers. While he was at the helm of the morning drive show, WRKA fell to third place in the market and Beck was fired.

He later landed in Pheonix at KOY FM where he became known as the "king of dirty tricks" and for having an "outsize and mischievous ego." He was also apparently very skilled at being "a grandstanding, pompous idiot and shaking the brushes for attention." After another gig in Houston turned sour, Beck was once again fired for not garnering enough audience share to justify his large salary. Word began to spread that Beck was difficult to work with and "prone to wild behavioural swings" and at the age of 26 he was known in the radio industry as "damaged goods."[819] Beck eventually went to Baltimore, partnered with Pat Gray and together they hosted a morning show at the city's leading Top 40 station, WSBS—also known as B104. While there, Beck was becoming "increasingly unraveled when not working." He was drinking heavily, taking medication for his "mental" and "psychological ills," and many of his colleagues regarded him as a sadist for the way in which he treated his co-workers (Beck once fired an assistant for bringing him a pen he did not like to sign an autograph).[820] Eventually, he was given the pink slip yet again for failing to command audience ratings.

In 1992, Beck and Gray joined KC101 in New Haven, Connecticut where Beck continued his downward spiral. He was mixing illegal narcotics with prescription drugs and allegedly washing them down with alcohol. Not surprisingly, he earned a reputation for being a temperamental and volatile braggadocio who would not tolerate anyone questioning his authority. By 1994, Beck's marriage to his first wife Claire was crumbling amid his struggle with alcohol and drug abuse; his partner Pat Gray was tiring of his drama queen antics and Beck became suicidal. That same year, however, Beck pulled back from the precipice, attended his first Alcoholics Anonymous meeting, and apparently achieved sobriety in 1995. After emerging from his pattern of destructive behavior, he began to imagine a future outside of the Top 40 radio format. In this regard, it is important to note that shortly after Beck had moved to KC1O1 in 1992, the station was purchased by Clear Channel. While it was not "immediately obvious," this development would prove to be "momentous" in Beck's career.[821] At the time, Clear Channel was a bit player in the radio world,

with ownership of just 16 stations nationally. However, after Congress relaxed ownership rules regulating the industry, Clear Channel's empire began to grow rapidly.[822]
At the same time Clear Channel purchased KC101, it also picked up WELI, which
was then New Haven's foremost news and talk station. This would eventually be
quite significant in the trajectory of Beck's rise to stardom since having "this sister
station would prove crucial to Beck's early start in talk radio."[823] Before the end of
the decade, a melding of the two stations' content would also create what the
country would come to know as The Glenn Beck Program.

The Glenn Beck Program debuted in January 2000 on WFLA in Tampa Bay,
Florida and was then officially launched on 47 stations nationwide in January 2002.
Currently, the three hour radio show is heard daily on over 300 stations and on the
satellite radio service XM. It is the third highest-rated national radio talk show
among adults 25–54.[824] For almost two years, Beck also hosted a primetime nightly
news commentary show on CNN's *Headline News* but in October 2008 he was lured
to the FNC, where his nightly television show first aired in January 2009. One of
his inaugural guests was Tea Party darling Sarah Palin who, in April 2010, referred
to Beck as "America's professor of common sense." Palin added that Beck's intent
is to educate "an audience hungry for truth" and cited his "desire to teach Americans
about the history of the progressive movement" which is a "damaged brand."[825]

Similar to O'Reilly, Beck routinely denounces "progressivism." Here it is important
to recall that in the most basic sense, the progressive movements of the early
twentieth century called for government regulation and oversight of corporate
power and malfeasance. They also stressed workers' rights and encouraged an active,
informed citizenry to participate in local and national politics. In Beck's campaign
against progressivism, "these strands are woven into a thread that ties together
socialism, Communism, fascism and the supposedly far-left politics of the Obama
administration."[826] According to Beck, the progressive movement is the enemy
of the Constitution and even America itself. And, in typical Manichaean
fashion, he weaves a storyline of the nation as a battlefield between God-fearing,
patriotic defenders of liberty and freedom (and especially free markets!) and evil, big
government, liberal conspirators. However, the mode in which Beck presents his
views is reminiscent of what historian Richard Hofstadter once called the paranoid
style in American politics. This paranoid style is rooted in

> the belief that 'the old American virtues have already been eaten away by cosmo-
> politans and intellectuals; the old competitive capitalism has been gradually
> undermined by socialistic and communistic schemers; the old national security
> and independence have been destroyed by treasonous plots, having as their
> most powerful agents not merely outsiders and foreigners as of old but major
> statesmen who are at the very centers of American power.'[827]

While some factions on the right have long subscribed to this approach to politics,
it is still rather shocking to "actually see a television personality in the year 2010
lumbering around a silent, empty set, mugging for the camera, and scrawling
on a chalkboard in full-on 'paranoid style' mode."[828] Indeed, what the FNC is
programming "on a daily (unhinged) basis is unprecedented in the history of American
television, especially in the form of Beck's program."[829]

Beck sees conspiracies everywhere and his monologues often invoke the ghosts of McCarthy when he whines about domestic enemies who are stealthily trying to transform America into a socialist nation. He has often been aided and abetted by David Horowitz who has become a regular guest on Beck's program. Together they have condemned both the academy and the public education system as breeding grounds for communism which Beck often claims is disguised by liberals as "progressivism." In Beck's paranoid mind, educators have become a stand-in for the evil empire—they are the enemies within seeking to inculcate in youth a socialistic mindset that is destabilizing traditional American values. Beck has claimed that "universities teach garbage" and has even suggested that sending one's children to public schools is unpatriotic.[830] In April 2010, he advocated homeschooling as the duty of every God-fearing, right-thinking American parent. And, on his June 22, 2010 radio program he went so far as to call for the abolition of the public school system which he believes is part of a vast conspiracy to indoctrinate children and turn them into pinko-loving zombies.

Given his disdain for public education and American universities, Beck's announcement in summer 2010 that he was starting his own "university" was perhaps predictable, if not highly unusual for a college dropout. Glenn Beck University (GBU) is actually an unaccredited online website and is available to anyone willing to subscribe to Beck's paranoid, conspiratorial worldview and dole out $9.95 per month. GBU even has its own Ivy League-esque crest that features a feather, a buffalo, the disembodied head of George Washington, and a Latin motto, "Tyrannis Seditio. Obsequium Deo" which, roughly translated, means "Revolution against tyrants, submission to God." According to the description on his website, GBU is a "unique academic experience bringing together experts in their fields of religion, American history and economics. Through captivating lectures and interactive online discussions, these experts will explore the concepts of Faith, Hope and Charity and show you how they influence America's past, her present and most importantly her future."[831]

In reality, there are only three "professors" who currently offer on-line lectures, the most controversial of whom is David Barton, a graduate of Oral Roberts University (ORU) and a former math teacher, who is the founder and president of WallBuilders, a "Texas-based organization devoted to remaking America as a Christian nation."[832] Barton's national, "pro-family" organization is dedicated to "America's forgotten history and heroes," with an emphasis on the "moral, religious and constitutional foundation on which America was built."[833] WallBuilders believes that this foundation has been "seriously attacked and undermined" and therefore seeks to exert "influence" within the government, education, and the family by teaching about the "Godly foundation of America," providing "information" to government officials so that they can develop public policies in accordance with "Biblical values" and encouraging Christians to get involved in civic life.[834] The organization has been characterized as far-right for its promotion of Christian theocracy in the United States and because of its affiliation with racist white identity groups which maintain that Anglo-Saxons are "the true children of Israel, while blacks are 'mud people' and Jews are the spawn of Satan."[835]

Since the late 1980s, Barton—a self-proclaimed historian who merely holds a BA from ORU—has made a career out of writing books and producing videos that argue that "the separation of church and state is a myth fostered by God-hating secularists," that most of the founding fathers shared the beliefs of the contemporary religious right and that "they intended Christianity to be central to American government."[836] Although this runs counter to most available evidence and mainstream history, Barton, like other Christian nationalists, has sought to establish a revisionist view of American history—something which has invited the derision of some Republicans including Senator Arlen Specter, who writing in the Harvard Journal of Law and Public Policy in 1995, claimed that Barton's arguments ranged from "the technical to the absurd" and "proceed from flawed and highly selective readings of both texts and history."[837]

In addition to being an evangelical minister, Barton is also a GOP political activist. In 1997, he was elected vice chairman of the Texas Republican party and quickly became an important link between Beltway Republicans and the Christian nationalist grass roots. In 2002, pastors from around the country received an invitation to a policy briefing at the Bush White House that was printed on WallBuilders stationery. The letter did not provide any indication about what the briefing was about, only that it would feature a "number of administration officials" as well Congressmen Tom Delay, Dick Armey and others. It concluded with the following passage: "In prayer that our government will once again rest upon *His* shoulders, and that we will again become one nation *under* God." It was signed by Barton. While Bush was campaigning for reelection in 2004, Barton was hired by the Republican National Committee to give a series of "get-out-the-vote speeches to groups of clergy around the country."[838] Beck's embrace of David Barton is hardly surprising since the Christian Nationalist movement has its roots in the anti-Communist John Birch society—the conspiracy-minded group founded in 1958—that has also influenced Beck's brand of Mormonism which is discussed below.

While bashing the academy and liberalism is a common trope on the FNC, what makes Beck's bromides stand out is the way in which they are delivered. Beck once called himself a "rodeo clown," an apt self-description for a man who is more an entertainer than a credible political commentator.[839] For Beck, patriotic correctness is a form of performance art—something that becomes quite evident to any critical observer of his daily buffoonery. Beck models himself as "an old-time preacher, delineating heaven and hell to a chorus of Amens. He likes to weep on camera and gesticulate wildly." From his "crisp business suits" to his "light tan studio makeup and obsessively groomed silver-grey hair," Beck packages himself to look like a "mega-church televangelist."[840]

Sobbing, sometimes uncontrollably, is part of Beck's repertoire—something that he often uses to simultaneously express his love of country and his fear of the 'progressive movement.' Beck's theatrical weeping has led some observers to label him as the "Crying Conservative." Beck is alone

among cable news and talk-radio personalities, he frequently chokes up, his lips quiver, he wipes his eye, and he holds tortured misty pauses until he can hold them no more. For more than a decade, Beck has been crying on the radio, on television, on stage, in interviews, and even in scripted commercials. Sometimes the tears are implied; at other times, such as during a 2009 stage performance, he gets into a fetal position on the floor and bawls. But whatever the gradation, he owns the scale. It defines him like nothing else. This is not an accident. As they were always intended to do, Beck's tears have become a distinctive corporate-brand handle. They mark him clearly from everyone else in the broadcasting industry ... He began practicing the act during his transition from Top 40 to talk radio in the late 1990s ... [and] he was known for being ... able and willing to fake cry on cue ... The role of Crying Conservative is well suited to Beck's dramatic personality and emotional needs. But that alignment doesn't make his execution of the character any less cynical. Sometimes Beck's use of tears is so patently faked that it's funny; at other times, it's just nauseating.[841]

When Beck launched his career as a conservative commentator, the airwaves were full of bombastic, tough-guy know-it-alls—from the boorish O'Reilly to the "cigar-chomping bloviator Rush Limbaugh."[842] And while the "macho Sean Hannity captured the cocky vibe of the early Bush years," Beck now "channels the mood of many on the right."[843]

Undoubtedly, Beck has become the voice of a misplaced right-wing populist anger and his ersatz vulnerability, feigned tears, and over-the-top fear mongering are clearly directed to the "only people who matter to his business: conservatives who hate liberals."[844] From his various media posts and in such literary gems as *Arguing with Idiots: How to Stop Small Minds and Big Government*, a paean to the free market and a harangue against health care, unions and the American education system to his ode to Thomas Paine, *Glenn Beck's Common Sense: The Case Against an Out-of-Control Government*, which has been called a "grotesque distortion of American history" and Paine's views, Beck has consciously appealed to the radical right with his garden variety red-baiting.[845] His histrionic, McCarthy-esque, and anti-intellectual persona has undoubtedly been shaped by his Mormonism, a religion he adopted not long after he got sober.

Among the practices that differentiate Mormonism from other forms of Christianity is a "highly stylized social ritual known as bearing testimony." Once a month, Mormons gather to speak about "what they know to be true" in a format that is a cross "between an open-mic poetry slam and an Alcoholics Anonymous meeting."[846] Whether or not what one believes to be true is actually rooted in fact is quite beside the point since these emotional events are ritualistic declarations in which "pure feeling trumps" rational argument. In fact, bearing testimony is considered to be "the Mormon equivalent of speaking in tongues."[847] Beck's daily diatribes are most often nonsensical and have no basis in reality such as the time when he wondered aloud about whether the Federal Emergency Management Agency (FEMA) was setting up concentration camps to round up pious Christians who were under attack in an Obama America that was plunging into the abyss of godless communism. Yet his tearful deliveries are apparently convincing among the right-wing faithful:

The way Beck has built his movement and his audience is a microcosm of the method by which the Mormon Church grew into a worldwide religion. Like an earnest young missionary spreading the good word through emotional speeches to confused Latin America villagers, Beck has brought his gut self-revelations to the angry, not-so educated audiences of Fox News and AM talk-radio, employing emotional intensity ... to conquer doubts of his sincerity and prove his access to powerful truths.[848]

And, among those who study Mormon rituals, Beck's public ability to cry on cue is considered to be a combination of "Mormon culture and the practiced delivery of media professional."[849] Moreover, Mormonism has "not only made an art of fake crying, it has institutionalized Beck's favorite mode of speech, the sentimental monologue." This mode of address encourages a sense of religiously inspired certainty that lies outside of "argument, fact, or logic."[850]

For Beck, liberalism is the new communism and just as McCarthy sought to purge the nation of traitorous reds, Beck believes his mission in life is to deliver Americans from the evils of special interest groups, unions, and organizations such as the ACLU. Beck's politics have undeniably been influenced by the teachings of the late W. Cleon Skousen, a fellow Mormon widely regarded as a crackpot even among bona fide conservatives. During his lifetime Skousen, an anti-communist historian who died in 2006 at the age of 92, produced dozens of books and pamphlets on such topics as the red menace, new world order conspiracies, Christian child rearing practices, and Mormon end-times prophecy.

In the late 1950s and early 1960s, rightists began peddling accounts about the dangers of the red menace and groups such as the Church League of America and the John Birch Society, which Skousen was an ardent supporter of, organized to "channel, feed and satisfy Cold War paranoia."[851] Skousen was at the heart of this movement, became a celebrity on the "far-right speakers circuit" and worked for "both the Bircher-operated American Opinion Speakers Bureau" and the "Christian Anti-Communism Crusade" that had been founded by Fred Schwarz and which is still in existence to this very day.[852] Eventually, Skousen's outlandish witch-hunts began to attract the attention of J. Edgar Hoover's FBI which amassed a 2,000 page dossier on his activities. It is quite telling that Hoover, himself a zealous anti-communist, believed that Skousen was a threat to the republic. In fact, by 1963, Skousen's rantings were considered so extreme that conservative organizations began to distance themselves from him, believing that he had "gone off the deep end." In 1969, Carol Quigley, a Georgetown University historian, claimed that "Skousen's personal position" was "perilously close to the 'exclusive uniformity'" of "Nazism" and by the end of the 1970s, even the Mormon Church began to disavow his work.[853] Yet, Skousen subsequently "found rehabilitation on the intellectual margins of Reagan's Washington" and in 1980 he was appointed to the Council for National Policy—the furtive organization previously discussed in chapter two.[854] While at the CNP, Skousen became one of the earliest proponents of privatized Social Security and he also formed "relationships with other evangelical church leaders" and aligned the Church of Latter Day Saints with "an increasingly religious" Republican Party.[855]

Skousen's writings were relatively unknown to most Americans until Beck resurrected them from the dustbin of history in 2007. Particularly fascinating to Beck is Skousen's book, *The 5,000 Year Leap*, first published in 1981. The book is a heavily illustrated and factually challenged attempt to explain American history through an unspoken lens of Mormon theology. As such, it is an early entry in the ongoing attempt by the religious right to rewrite history. Fundamentalists want to define the United States as a Christian nation rather than a secular republic, and recast the Founding Fathers as devout Christians guided by the Bible rather than deists inspired by French and English philosophers. 'Leap' argues that the U.S. Constitution is a godly document above all else, based on natural law, and owes more to the Old and New Testaments than to the secular and radical spirit of the Enlightenment.[856]

A new edition of the book, complete with an obsequious foreword by Beck, was recently published and he has vigorously promoted it to his audience as a necessary read for understanding "American free enterprise."[857] The text has also become the bible of the "9/12" project which was officially launched by Beck on the March 13, 2009 episode of his FNC show. In what some have called a shameful and opportunistic example of exploiting 9/11, the project calls for a return to the sensibilities that apparently were on display the day after the terrorist attacks. Yet, Neiwert contends, rightfully in my opinion, that Beck's 9/12 project is better described as one of the "most fascistic" things to "appear on the American political horizon."[858] Although Beck's plea is ostensibly for a unified America—beyond red and blue states and the kind of rancorous political partisanship that he himself promotes—a simple review of some of the core tenets of the 9/12 project illustrate its theocratic Christian bent and its dedication to greed capitalism.

9/12ers, as they are sometimes called, adhere to a set of principles that include the idea that 'America is good.' This, of course, is in keeping with one of the central tenets of PC— "American greatness"—which, though largely a secular idea, is linked in this context to the "symbol systems" of the "Christian Right" that "promote American 'manifest destiny.'"[859] 9/12ers also cite a profound belief in "God" as the center of one's life, and the sanctity of the traditional family as the ultimate source of authority as opposed to the government. The 9/12 manifesto also exalts the right to life, liberty and the pursuit of happiness with the caveat that "there is no guarantee of equal results" and asserts that the government cannot force any individual to be charitable—the fruits of one's labor are to be shared as the individual sees fit.[860]

Beck's particular take on religiosity demonizes any reference to the very Christian concept of social justice. In fact, in March 2010, Beck created a national controversy that drew a harsh rebuke from many Christian leaders when he urged members of his audience to abandon their churches if they made any mention of social justice which, Beck asserted, was essentially a code word for Nazism and communism. Using two pictures, one of a swastika and another of a hammer and sickle as props, Beck claimed that advocates for social justice share philosophical ground with Nazis and communists and he warned his viewers not to be fooled by them since their true intent is to force the redistribution of wealth on an unsuspecting populace. It appears as though Beck wants to ensure that his own massive wealth is kept safe from the unwashed hands of the undeserving poor. After all, Beck's fans who champion him as a protector of the "little guy," have made him a very rich man. According to *Forbes* magazine, he made $32 million from his empire Glenn Beck,

Inc., in 2009 largely because he has mastered the art of monetizing "virtually everything that comes out of his mouth."[861] In that year, his radio and television shows earned him $12 million while speaking events, a digital newsletter, and Beck-themed merchandise added another $7 million to his pocketbook. Most profitable was print—books and the magazine *Fusion* brought in $13 million.[862]

The 9/12 project also insists that it is not "un-American" to "disagree with authority" and that no one should have to answer to the government, rather the government is accountable to the people. This principle is rather preposterous and is also indicative of the historical amnesia that afflicts so many on the contemporary right. While George W. Bush was in office, Beck often insinuated that the President's critics were traitors and terrorist sympathizers. Questioning the government's motives and actions was tantamount to treason. And to this day, Beck continues to defend the former administration—including its use of torture. In an appearance on *Fox and Friends* in 2009 Beck actually quoted Jack Bauer, the fictional character from the television show *24*, to "prove" the righteousness of torture. On another occasion, he went so far as to state that it was "far from clear" as to whether water boarding qualified as torture under the "law."[863] Like most right-wing charlatans, Beck has demonstrated that it is only patriotically correct to criticize the government when Democrats are in power.

Beck's hypocrisy is even more apparent when one considers some of the twelve values espoused by the 9/12 project. Included in that list are such unobjectionable things as hope, honesty and sincerity—noble ideals that Beck undercuts at virtually every turn. Contrary to what Sarah Palin has said about Beck's desire to "teach" the "truth," he engages in outright mendacity that is designed to both frighten and flatter his audience by wedding the "operatic impulses of the demagogue to the grim mutterings of the conspiracy theorist."[864] This has made him a darling of the Tea Party crowd. As Romano maintains,

> Tea partiers are driven by the belief that the America that elected Barack Obama isn't their America, and Beck comforts them by telling them they're right: that the America they love, the America they now feel so distant from, the America of faith and the Founders and some sort of idyllic *Leave it to Beaver* past, is still there, waiting to be awakened from Obama's evil spell. And he flatters them by saying that the coastal elites are too stupid or too lazy to figure out what's really going on; only his loyal viewers are perceptive enough to see the truth, and ultimately, to save the nation.[865]

Along with Tea Partyers and David Horowitz, Beck has been a major purveyor of the "Take Back America" theme that has dominated right-wing discourse since the election of Barack Obama. He has used his bully pulpit to promote events such as the Tax Payer March on Washington which his 9/12 project helped to organize along with other groups including Freedom Works which is chaired by former Republican House Majority Leader Dick Armey and funded, in part, by the Scaife and Bradley Foundations. Freedom Works' website even features an exclusive link called "Partner with Beck" that prompts the Beck faithful to take advantage of a "special offer"—a "Take America Back" action kit which includes a DVD that lays out Freedom Works' "master plan to mobilize freedom-loving Americans to save our great country."[866]

Many of those so-called "freedom-loving" folk converged on the nation's capital on September 12, 2009 to take part in the aforementioned march which one observer dubbed as the "right's fringe festival."[867] The crowd consisted mainly of "insane birthers and Glenn Beck-worshipping tea-partiers, proud racists and gun-toting anti-government loons" who were all united by their hatred of the Obama administration and liberals in general.[868] Amidst Confederate flag-waving and shouts of "White Power," individuals carried placards that read "McCarthy Was Right!" and "This Time We Come Peacefully and Unarmed."[869] Unfortunately, others have indeed taken up arms and the result has, in some cases, been deadly.

DANGEROUS DEMAGOGUERY AND LETHAL ANTI-LIBERALISM

Arguably, one of the traits shared by the FNC's stable of leading television personalities is a deeply rooted hatred for liberals and organizations that are perceived to esteem liberal values. Whether the odium is directed at celebrities such as Sean Penn or film maker Michael Moore or targeted at gun-control lobbyists or the ACLU, trafficking in anti-liberal rhetoric has been a hallmark of Murdoch's propaganda apparatus. Any forward-looking optimism that makes social justice and/or cultural diversity central to its vision is considered subversive or, at the very least, a threat to the 'American way of life.' Central to Fox's particular brand of mean-spirited anti-liberalism is a profound mistrust of government—at least, as previously noted, when so-called liberals occupy the White House. But it is important to acknowledge that this anti-government stance, promoted by self-proclaimed conservative Christians such as Beck, Hannity and other FNC figures who also happen to genuflect at the altar of the free market, provides ideological cover for corporate power and capitalist interests while at the same time opening the door for right-wing populist "movements" such as the Tea Party. By equating all that is good and patriotic with capitalism, the free market fundamentalism that actually led to, for example, the recent global economic meltdown is spared from any serious scrutiny. On this topic, McChesney provides some valuable insights:

> With the economic system off-limits to criticism (even invisible in its main power dimensions), attention necessarily gravitates to government as the root of all evil. The state must therefore be the *source* of the people's problems; and indeed, it seems very seldom to operate in their real interests. It is the state after all, that imposes taxes that seem to provide ordinary people few benefits; runs deficits, the burden of which falls disproportionately on those who gain the least; and controls the military and the police. In today's Tea Party ideology, engineered principally by the right, capital is deemed natural, while the state is unnatural—imposed from without on those who would otherwise be free. The social crisis is then seen as a crisis of too much government, too much interference by state interests in the natural order of things. Capitalism is treated as an elemental force, like the wind and tides, or a mere by product

of human nature. The reality of power in today's society is hidden behind the mist generated by this false 'naturalism.'[870]

Aside from its transparent anti-liberalism, its fulminations against Democrats, its panegyric support of the Republican Party, and more recently its populist pandering to the radical right, the most insidious role of the FNC has been to naturalize unfettered capitalism and to bolster corporate rule. As I noted in a previous chapter, when the conservative movement was in its infancy, one of its stated goals was to garner media support for the free market system by any and all means necessary. In the FNC, that movement has found an enthusiastic partner to achieve its aims. While the FNC and its leading lights often claim to value tradition, the Constitution, and institutions inherited from a mythical America past, their dedication to a particular economic philosophy—that which emerged from the teachings of Milton Friedman— has always been paramount. Just as many other conservative organizations have used hot-button cultural issues to disguise what is, at heart, an economic agenda, so too has Rupert Murdoch's Fox empire. By using buzzwords, images, and sound bites, the FNC has proven its mastery at exploiting simmering resentments and scapegoating women, minorities and the poor in the realm of cultural politics. This, however, is hardly shocking given the network's commitment to manipulating white populist anger and fueling hostility toward government.

Since its very inception, the FNC was designed to capitalize on the angry white male syndrome that had cast a pall over the political landscape in the early-to-mid 1990s. It began by offering a script through which suburban country club conservatives, the religious right, servants of American oligarchy (white, middle-class rightists), and even "average Joes" could define themselves as under attack from an assortment of domestic enemies including sixties radicals, feminists, "special interest" groups (i.e. racial and ethnic minorities) or from the growing threat of an increasingly intrusive federal government. It is important to recall that when the FNC was launched one of Murdoch and Ailes' first objectives was to channel that intense anger toward the government of then-President Bill Clinton who, despite being a fiscal conservative and a champion of the free market, was perceived by those on the right as a "Big Government" liberal. Not surprisingly, many of the same deranged, irrational claims made about the Clinton White House by far-right demagogues and militia types back then have been repackaged for the Obama era.

This is evident if one considers just one line from *The Clinton Chronicles*, a 1994 "documentary" film made by Pat Matrisciana for Citizens for Honest Government (CFHG), an organization which Political Research Associates noted was a prime example of the "practical linkage among the Republican Party, the conservative Christian Right, Christian-Right theocrats and hard-right conspiracism."[871] Between 1994 and 1996, CFHG covertly paid more than $200,000 to a variety of individuals who made false but damaging allegations about Clinton as part of a sustained and well-orchestrated political propaganda campaign to turn public opinion against the President. The discredited film, which was rife with outlandish declarations about the Clintons' involvement in mysterious deaths including the infamous case of Vince Foster, was promoted and distributed by none other than Reverend Jerry Falwell via television infomercials. And, ironically enough, the filmmaker, Matrisciana, who had ties to a reporter who worked at one of Richard Scaife's newspapers, spoke at a "Take America Back" event in Washington in 1997 which quickly turned into a pro-impeachment rally (Randall Terry, the founder of the radical anti-abortion group Operation Rescue also addressed that same gathering).

The film's introduction claimed that "the hijacking of America was underway" and ominously warned that "its impact on future generations would be incalculable."[872] As Boehlert rightly notes, such a statement would sound quite familiar to "any casual viewer" of the FNC "since Obama's inauguration."[873] Today, the FNC is not only exploiting simmering resentments—it is helping to create them. The network is essentially espousing the same kind of detestable rhetoric and lunatic conspiratorial chatter that thrived during the 1990s and is "legitimizing accusatory hate speech in a way no other television outlet in America ever has before."[874] And, the intensity of the hate-mongering has only escalated since Obama assumed the presidency. As a result, even conservative stalwarts such as David Frum have taken umbrage with the network's recent excesses. Amidst the health care reform debacle that had paranoid right-wingers believing they would be imprisoned if they did not buy health insurance—a fantasy promulgated by the likes of Beck and O'Reilly—Frum criticized the FNC for peddling in half-truths and was promptly forced out of his fellowship at the American Enterprise Institute for daring to stray from the GOP party line. Even Senator Tom Coburn, a staunch conservative from Oklahoma and a major opponent of health care reform, scolded Fox for inciting the kind of hysteria that was good for ratings but universally awful when it came to accurately informing the public about the legislation.[875]

Beyond health care hysteria, the FNC has recklessly stoked the fires of paranoid right-wing victimization. Fox viewers have repeatedly been told that the 'liberals' now in power are out to get them, their guns, and their freedoms. In addition to claiming that the Second Amendment is under attack, Beck has ventured into the realm of delusion by stating that the "Big Brother" government will soon be able to dictate to citizens what they can eat, drive, and how they set the temperature controls in their homes. In this regard, he and other FNC commentators have been actively trying to mainstream the most outrageous beliefs held by those on the far right fringe. As Boehlert observes, "Fox News has signed on as a TV partner and has agreed to embrace—and air to a national audience—militia-like allegations" about the Obama administration. The network has descended into the "right-wing conspiracist subculture in order to portray the new president as the worst kind of villain imaginable"— as somebody who is plotting to "take away guns" and who is, apparently, "not above employing fascism to obtain his goals."[876] And, we should also be reminded that FNC personalities such as Beck have also sought to stir up the seething racial bigotry which is barely containable in many right-wing circles with his assertions that Obama is a "racist" who "has a deep-seated hatred for white people" and "the white culture."[877]

In April 2009, an internal report by the Department of Homeland Security (DHS) warned that the American political climate was beginning to resemble that which existed in the early 1990s, a period that was marked by a dramatic upsurge of right-wing Christian extremism and the growth of militia groups. The report merely identified signs of extremism based on historical precedent and contemporary conditions including a prolonged economic downturn, the demonization of immigrants, fears about the Second Amendment right to bear arms, the banking crisis which precipitated age-old paranoia about Jewish cabals that allegedly control financial institutions and the election of the first black president.[878] However, when the DHS memorandum was made public, conservatives were outraged by what they claimed was a politically motivated assessment of the threat and what they deemed an anti-Republican report. Blowhards such as Rush Limbaugh lashed out at DHS Secretary Janet Napolitano and Republican National Committee Chairman, Michael Steele, told the FNC that the report epitomized "the height of insult." Steele denounced the report as an attempt to target conservatives who had a different philosophy from that of the administration and to cast them as terrorists. The indignation, however, began to ring hollow when the study proved to be prescient.

On April 4, 2009, a recently unemployed man by the name of Richard Andrew Poplawski got into an argument with his mother, with whom he shared a Pittsburgh apartment, about a dog urinating in the dwelling. He was apparently drunk and became belligerent at which point his mother called the police to have him removed from the premises. Poplawski then donned a bulletproof vest, armed himself with three guns, including a semi-automatic AK-47 style rifle, and lied in wait for the police to respond to the domestic disturbance call. When the officers arrived at the scene, Poplawski opened fire. After a standoff that lasted several hours, three officers were dead and another two were seriously injured. According to several different accounts, Poplawski, a registered Republican and member of Stormfront, a white supremacist website where he was a regular visitor and frequent poster, was convinced that the Obama administration was hell-bent on confiscating the guns of American citizens.

Poplawski was an avid fan of radical talk show host and conspiracy theorist Alex Jones who even some conservative bloggers have labeled an anti-government "freak" who is popular with the "tin foil hat crowd."[879] Jones, who has been hyping the menace of a totalitarian world government for years, made an appearance on "Freedom Watch," a "proudly paranoid" web show on Fox.com hosted by retired New Jersey judge and conservative activist, Andrew Napolitano, whose webcasts regularly explore what Obama is doing to endanger the liberty and property of Americans. (Remarkably, the FNC and its bloviators did not seem concerned with Americans' civil liberties when they were being decimated by Bush; nor did they seem riled by the massive transfer of wealth from the working classes to the rich that remains one of the enduring legacies of the Bush era.)

Once Napolitano introduced him as "the one, the only, the great Alex Jones," Jones—echoing much of the same rhetoric as Beck—launched into a tirade about how the Second Amendment was under fire.[880] Then, with unbridled enthusiasm, Jones began to praise Glenn Beck who had begun warning about the "looming New World Order" just as he himself had been doing for years. Napolitano thanked Jones for his insights, claiming the interview had been a "pleasure."[881] Whether or not Poplawski saw his hero, Alex Jones, on Napolitano's webcast remains unknown.

However, just weeks before he went on his murderous spree, Poplawski uploaded a video clip of Beck referring to the aforementioned FEMA concentration camps.

On May 31, 2009, Dr. George Tiller, was shot through the eye at close range during services at the Reformation Lutheran Church in Wichita, Kansas while serving as an usher and distributing church bulletins. For over four years, Bill O'Reilly harassed Tiller through both his incendiary rhetoric and by sending some of his producers to ambush the doctor and his lawyer. Tiller, who was one of the few medical practitioners in the United States who performed late-term abortions, first appeared on O'Reilly's radar during the February 25, 2005 broadcast of the *Factor.* O'Reilly and his guests subsequently discussed Tiller on another 28 episodes before his death. O'Reilly referred to Tiller as a "baby killer," called his clinic a "death mill," accused him of "executing babies," compared him to a Nazi, and warned of "judgment day." Although O'Reilly never directly encouraged vigilante "justice" for Tiller, he nonetheless put him squarely in the public eye and helped to make him a focus of the anti-abortion movement which has a lengthy history of violence. As Winant has argued, O'Reilly bore much of the responsibility for the "characterization of Tiller as a savage on the loose, killing babies willy-nilly thanks to the collusion of would-be sophisticated cultural elites ... and scofflaw secular journalists."[882] Tiller's killer, Scott Roeder, a Republican anti-abortion militant was also a member of the anti-government Montana Freemen. He was found guilty of first degree murder and sentenced to life without parole for 50 years in April, 2010.

The Tiller murder was followed by another shooting on June 10, 2009, when James W. von Brunn, a long-time foe of the federal government, opened fire at the United States Holocaust Museum in Washington, D.C. A security guard was shot and the gunfire sent museum visitors scrambling for cover—the guard consequently died of his injuries. von Brunn, who was 88 at the time of the shootings, was a long-time White supremacist and anti-Semite and subscribed to conspiracy theories about Jews, blacks and other minorities. He was a member of the now defunct American Friends of the British National Party which was addressed by fascist Nick Griffin on at least two occasions. A number of news organizations noted that Obama's visit to, and speech at, the Buchenwald concentration camp on June 5 may have sparked von Brunn's murderous rampage.[883]

In late March 2010, nine people believed to be members of Hutaree, a Michigan militia that is part of the larger Patriot movement, were arrested for plotting to murder law enforcement officers. The plan was to kill a number of officers and then attack police vehicles that would have been transporting other police officers attending funeral services for their dead colleagues with improvised explosive devices (IEDs). Members of Hutaree–which, according to their website, means Christian warrior–believed that such attacks would demoralize law enforcement. Once that happened, they believed they could wage war on the federal government—their real target.

Prior to these incidents, some prominent FNC personalities were identified as favored authors of Jim Adkisson. On July 27, 2008 Adkisson shot dead two parishioners and wounded another seven at the Tennessee Valley Unitarian

Universalist Church in Knoxville. According to its website, the church had worked for desegregation, racial harmony, women's and gay rights since the 1950s.[884] The church's social liberalism made it the target of Adkisson's wrath. In a sworn affidavit and in his manifesto, Adkisson stated that he was motivated by a hatred of Democrats, liberals, African Americans and homosexuals and targeted the church because of its liberal (Beck might say social justice) teachings. He also believed that all liberals should be killed because they, along with major media outlets, were ruining the country, its institutions and because they were allegedly undermining the "war on terror."

Like so many victims of the Bush economy, Adkisson was also apparently frustrated by his inability to find employment and the fact that his food stamps were scheduled to be cut. Yet, he was angry at what he called the "liberal movement" and he, undoubtedly, embodied the archetypal angry white male that the FNC has deliberately courted through the years. In a subsequent search of his abode, police found copies of Hannity's *Let Freedom Ring: Winning the War of Liberty over Liberalism*, Bill O'Reilly's *The O'Reilly Factor: The Good, the Bad, and the Completely Ridiculous in American Life*, and frequent Fox guest Michael Savage's *Liberalism is a Mental Disorder*. Of course, the presence of such books in the home of an obviously disturbed, socially alienated individual does not make their authors accessories to Adkisson's killing spree. Yet it is difficult to ignore the pernicious role played by the hateful political ideology that has become a staple of the FNC in motivating such horrific acts.

For years, the vitriol spewed against liberals and humanists such as those who attended the Tennessee Church has been a dominant feature of the network's over-arching narrative. The sort of bigotry and anti-government sentiment that evidently consumed some of these felons has been tolerated and sanctioned by many on the right—not just Fox personalities—but several of the FNC's favorite regulars including the Ann Coulters of the world. Certainly, one cannot draw a causal link between the rantings of Hannity, O'Reilly, and Beck and the actions taken by individuals such as Adkisson, Poplawski, von Brunn and the plots hatched by the Hutaree militia. However, there is little doubt that Fox bears some responsibility in spreading the kind of paranoid insurrection rhetoric that is fueling the recent documented rise in hate groups and militia-type organizations.

In Spring 2010, the Southern Poverty Law Center (SPLC) released a report that showed that the number of extremist groups in the United States "exploded in 2009" as militias and other groups that subscribe to wild, anti-government conspiracy theories exploited the populist anger that has gripped large swathes of the population. Anti-government "Patriot" groups—militias and other radical right organizations that view the federal government as the enemy came "roaring back to life" after more "than a decade out of the limelight." *Rage on the Right: The Year in Hate and Extremism* documented a 244% increase in the number of active Patriot groups in 2009. Militias, the paramilitary arm of the Patriot movement, were a major part of the increase—they grew from 42 militias in 2008 to 127 in 2009. The report mentioned that the Patriot movement's central ideas are being promoted by people with large audiences and specifically named Glenn Beck as one of them.

Despite the perilous nature of Fox's lurch to the radical right, it is doubtful that Murdoch or Ailes will fire the likes of Beck and other FNC "commentators" who are, arguably, helping to usher in an area of proto-fascism. For as Karlin has astutely argued, such personalities are profitable to Murdoch's empire. More significantly, they are key players on a team designed to "protect corporate rule" by playing the "Pied Piper and leading the misinformed off the cliffs" while the forces of capital continue to pick their pockets.[885]

CONCLUSION

For more than four decades, the corporate, secular, and religious branches of the right have poured hundreds of millions of dollars into constructing an ideological infrastructure that has conducted "research," published studies, sponsored conferences, and developed media outlets with one primary aim—to extol the 'virtues' of the free market. Sometimes, these virtues are blatantly championed but most often they are shrouded in moralistic sermons about liberty, values, and 'Western civilization' that equate capitalism with 'democracy' and 'freedom.' In other instances, theocratic rhetoric about America as a 'righteous empire' is used to sanction U.S.-led global capitalism as a gift from the Almighty. Regardless of the vocabulary that is used and the 'culture war' narrative in which it is often couched, each of the foundations, think tanks, policy institutes, and campus organizations explored in this work share that ultimate goal; it is their *raison d'être*. It was this infrastructure that spawned the alliance of neoconservatives and religious fundamentalists that cynically manipulated the events of 9/11 to advance PC in an attempt to garner 'mainstream' support for a radical right agenda—specifically a unilateralist foreign policy designed to harness the full force of the military in the service of a corporate agenda and the domestic rollback of decades of democratic advances that have been made not only on campuses but in civil society at large.

In the paranoid and persecuting environment of post-9/11 America, this consortium enjoyed considerable success in labelling as subversive, ideas that, in a saner polity would have not been accorded demonic qualities and deemed traitorous. Capitalizing on a climate of fear, the failure of the national media to fulfill their role as watchdogs of the powerful, and the pusillanimous inertia of Congress, proponents of PC were literally given a free hand to resurrect the witch hunts of the McCarthy era and to deem as un-American those who dared to exercise the civic courage to dissent, to question the authoritarian and imperial conduct of the Bush administration that had little regard for democratic principles and which, more often than not, expressed its outright scorn for them. Wrapped in the flag and brandishing the cross of righteousness, the patriotically correct undertook a ruthless campaign of intimidation whereby anything short of a messianic embrace of the Market, God and Empire was reviled as seditious.

The damage already wrought by this coalition cannot be underestimated; the effects still resonate to this very day, not only on campuses but in the larger body politic. Liberal values such as openness, equality, justice, respect and tolerance for difference—principles that formed the institutional and philosophical basis of the nation—are still under siege as the right and its crusading army of Norman Rockwell proto-types vilify such values as antithetical to the splendor and safety of America. And we must remember that conservatives have no intention of abandoning their anti-democratic project for as history has clearly demonstrated, they are committed to a protracted struggle to "remake" America and indeed the world in their image.

It is vital to recognize that much of the campaign for PC, framed by the right as a challenge to the enforced liberal/left orthodoxy that prevails in the ivied towers of

197

academe is, in fact, part of a much broader offensive against progressive thought. The real target of PC is the progressivism that has historically animated various struggles for workers' and civil rights, environmental protections, access to decent education, and other public goods. Progressivism is also rooted in the idea that governments have a role to play in restraining the excesses of big business, providing a safety net for the less fortunate among us, and promoting the public interest rather than narrow corporate interests. It is precisely these ideas, even in their most watered-down versions, which rightists have sought to disembowel decade after decade and they have been passionate and persistent in this pursuit.

Opposition to the liberal/left academy has never been a mere passing fancy for the conservative movement; it has been a centerpiece of its agenda for many years. Rightists wish to "take back" the university because it remains one of the principal locations in advanced capitalist society for the articulation of radically oppositional views. Despite the fact that the academy is circumscribed by its socio-economic context and that it often contributes to the manufacturing of an 'intelligentsia' which produces knowledge conducive to the maintenance of the status quo, it is viewed as an obstacle to the complete triumph of conservative hegemony. In a cultural milieu dominated by a profit-oriented media system that functions largely as a guard dog of capitalist ideology and in a context in which both political parties are as beholden to corporate interests as to render them virtually undistinguishable, the academy is one of the few realms in which progressive ideas still have some degree of currency.

Much to the chagrin of right-wingers, universities have long been incubators for dissident thought and movements for social change; the mass mobilizations against imperial wars, racial, gender and sexual oppression, and other forms of social injustice have often been nurtured on campuses by faculty and students who had the temerity to speak truth to power. But perhaps much more threatening to the corporate interests that have funded the crusade for PC is that campuses *have*, on occasion, been breeding grounds for active resistance to the destructive dynamics of their beloved Friedmanite turbocapitalism. For example, in the mid-1990s, groups such as "Students Against Sweatshops" initiated campaigns that revealed the sweatshop labor that was producing campus apparel; they forged common ground with other activists, trade unionists, social justice advocates and independent media producers to reveal the sordid underbelly of capitalist globalization. After years of identity politics and single-issue organizing, the WTO protests signalled a turning point in the "history of movements of recent decades" for it was free market capitalism itself that was being named as the "enemy;" much of the opposition to this system was cultivated at the nation's colleges and universities.[886] For those who fancy a return to the robber baron era, the academy is indeed a dangerous place; they fear the power of critical discourse that interrogates the legitimacy of corporate rule and feeble justifications for elite control and social inequality.

This is all the more reason for the struggle for academic freedom to be taken seriously by progressive educators and all those who desire a more egalitarian society. The battle about what is taught, how knowledge is produced and for what purpose, is both—at the symbolic and practical levels—a battle for the hegemony of society at large. This is something that conservatives and corporatists have long understood and it is why they have attempted, through various means, to diminish the role of the university as a democratizing force in our society.

The university, as a space for critical intervention, must therefore be engaged, head-on, urgently and unrelentingly. This is no part-time task; it will require the dedication of intellectual activists who are willing to commit themselves to the fight for a more robust democracy. These activists must foster the civic courage to ask disturbing questions that may irritate dominant powers. As the moneyed manacles of conservatism seek to further the rightward drift of our political discourse, progressive pedagogues must be diligent in protecting the academy as a space where the 'ruthless criticism' of all that exists is possible. To cede this space by virtue of indifference would be perilous.

But even as we recognize the importance of academic settings for nurturing critical thought, we cannot behave as though such spaces are the only relevant sites for informed discussion and the production of oppositional knowledge. Activist scholars must work from within the academy and at the edges—the borders—and connect with extra-academic organizations and groups to develop a language of analysis and critique that can help us to discern the complexities of the current social fabric and the political-economic context in which it is embedded.

In order to confront the fundamentalist nationalism and fascistic tendencies enveloping the U.S. at the current historical juncture, radical educators must interrogate the symbolically over-determined ideologies of right-wing Christians including their science fiction rapture theology and the pride they exhibit in taking anti-intellectual positions on just about anything related to the public good. We must beat back the stampeding armies of the right that are shepherded by cynical leaders and dyspeptic demagogues who are only too willing to accord blame for the real problems that exist in our society on scapegoats including racial minorities, immigrants, feminists, gays and lesbians, and of course, liberals and leftists. We must challenge those who willingly bathe in the effulgence of talk-radio and media personalities who routinely use their potent propaganda platforms to engage in a mean-spirited and primitive patriotism that condemns political dissent as anti-American.

We must demonstrate, in very practical and actionable ways, how the quality of our lives can be improved; how struggles for social justice can be advanced through careful analysis and oppositional work. But we must also move beyond half-hearted calls for social justice that are antiseptically cleaved from demands for economic justice and the project of combating capitalist globalization. Powerful right-wing forces are determined and united in promoting free market fundamentalism; progressives must be equally united and resolute in contesting an ideology that praises greed, individualistic accumulation and selfishness over sharing, compassion and the collective good. David Harvey reminds us that neoliberalism is "profoundly suspicious of democracy;" it is therefore imperative to resist the routine conflation of capitalism with democracy and democracy with the "free market" for as McChesney cautions, "neoliberalism is the immediate and foremost enemy of genuine participatory democracy, not just in the United States but across the planet."[887] We must recognize that within the discourse of the free market, the very notion of the public good is constantly devalued and, in some cases, even "eliminated as part of a wider rationale for a handful of private interests to control as much of social life as possible in order to maximize their personal profit."[888] Any discussion of, and any hope for, a reinvigorated democracy in our time must confront the neoliberal agenda, expose its antidemocratic tendencies and vigorously oppose the exploitative and unsustainable relations of capitalism.

Progressive intellectuals need to be fearless in confronting the myths propagated by the patriotically correct, myths of a benevolent American empire—those make-believe constructions that dull critical sensibilities and promote a perpetual state of historical amnesia. This is not anti-American; it is part and parcel of a truthful pedagogy that exposes the predatory role played by U.S. imperialism in advancing the neoliberal agenda. The globalization of capitalism has not in any sense been held accountable to democratic interests despite the best efforts of its cheerleaders to hide its diabolical nature behind the non-sequitur claim that the free market promotes "democracy." The establishment view is all too quick to ignore the death and destruction wrought by the 'empire of barbarism' that is aided and abetted by the largest military arsenal ever assembled to benefit the elite few over the labouring masses.

We must take seriously the impassioned pleas of Arundhati Roy who implores us to remember that the battle to reclaim democracy must begin in America. She writes:

> [T]he only institution more powerful than the U.S. government is American civil society. The rest of us are subjects of slave nations. We are by no means powerless, but you have the power of proximity ... Empire's conquests are being carried out in your name, and you have the right to refuse.[889]

We must refuse empire's march from within the belly of the beast if we believe that democracy should be something more than the "Free World's whore," something more than a "euphemism for neo-liberal capitalism."[890] We can no longer afford to remain indifferent to the horror and savagery unleashed by capital's barbaric machinations; nor can we ignore the role played by U.S. militarism in enforcing a free market agenda that wreaks havoc with any semblance of democracy both at home and abroad.

But more than this, progressives must also advance an alternative social vision of what the world might look like if freed from the mind-numbing ideologies of the corporate-military-media complex; one that rescues the principle of hope from the abyss of cynicism and complacency and applies it to imagining something different, something beyond the social universe of capital. Above all, we must safeguard the embers of hope smoldering amid the rubble of war and the wreckage of capitalism's wake and fuel the fires of hope for a more humane world wherever they may burn. We must listen to the voices which cry out for genuine freedom rather than free markets, peace rather than plunder.

NOTES

1 Ann Coulter, cited in Willis, 2004, p. 21.

2 Cheney, cited in Ostroy, 2009.

3 Cited in Willis, 2004, p. 134.

4 McLaren, 2005, p. 226.

5 Beck's views are explored in Chapter Four.

6 BuffaloBest.com, cited in Willis, 2004, p. 39.

7 My use of the term "the right" is not intended to suggest that such an entity exists as a homogeneous monolith. Indeed, there are differences and factions within the broader right but there are at least two camps that coalesce in their attacks on higher education and the so-called liberal academy: cultural and religious conservatives (Christian nationalists) who valorize "traditional" values and who seek to have religious doctrines and perspectives taught in public schools (i.e. intelligent design) and neo-conservatives who are keen on promoting corporate rule and education in the service of American empire.

8 See Alterman, 2005.

9 Cited in Dionne Jr., 2005.

10 See the editorial entitled "The Captive Mind" in *The Nation*, April 2005, pp. 3–4.

11 Schrecker, 1988; Zinn, 1991.

12 Piereson, 2005.

13 Cited in Blumenthal, 2005, p. 2.

14 Giroux, 2006, p. 8.

15 Doumani, 2006, p. 23.

16 Schrecker, 2006.

17 Parenti, 2004, p. 2.

18 Taylor, 2005, p. 39.

19 McClennen (2006, p. 44) explains how Loyalty Day was established in an effort to draw attention away from the communist and socialist inspired celebration of workers' rights associated with Mayday (May 1). She adds that Loyalty Day was set aside as a day to symbolize "the reaffirmation of loyalty to the United States and for the recognition of the heritage of American freedom."

20 See http://www.whitehouse.gov/news/releases/2003/04/200330430-26.html

21 McMurtry, 2002, pp. xii–xiii.

22 James, 2003, p. 74.

23 Schulz and Reyes, 2008, p. 636.

24 Sturken, 2007, p. 25.

25 Ibid, p. 7.

26 Ibid, p. 4.

27 Ibid, p. 16.

28 Hal Foster, cited in Sturken, 2007, p. 24.

29 Faludi, 2007, p. 8.

30 Noonan, 2001, p. 1.

31 Ibid, p. 3.

32 Ibid.

33 Cited in Wilkinson, 2006, p. 32.

34 *People Weekly*, 2002.

35 See Scatamburlo-D'Annibale, Suoranta and McLaren, 2007.

36 Of course, Bush's jet flight was totally unnecessary. While the White House first claimed that the dramatic jet landing was needed because the ship would be hundreds of miles out to sea and therefore unreachable by helicopter, the *USS Abraham Lincoln* was within helicopter range but that didn't offer the exciting visuals of a theatrical landing and Bush in a flight suit. For more on this

example of the Bush administration's propaganda tactics and others, see Scatamburlo-D'Annibale, 2005.

[37] Liddy, cited in Ducat, 2004, p. 244.

[38] Ducat, 2004, p. 244.

[39] Ducat, 2004, p. 229.

[40] Ibid, p. 230.

[41] Taylor, 2005.

[42] Juhasz, 2006, p. 17.

[43] Galeano, 2003.

[44] McMurtry, 2002, p. 88.

[45] Ibid, pp. 88–89.

[46] Quoted in Rich, 2006, p. 3.

[47] Alterman, 2003, p. 3.

[48] Croteau, 1998. See also David Brock's discussion of various studies in chapter three of *The Republican Noise Machine: Right-Wing Media and How it Corrupts Democracy.*

[49] This statement was made by Louis Boccardi, former chief executive of the Associated Press in 2003, and cited in Brock, 2004, p. 90.

[50] Alterman, 2003, p. 11.

[51] Brock, 2004, p. 8–9.

[52] Kristol claimed that "the liberal media were never that powerful, and the whole thing was used as an excuse by conservatives for conservative failures" as cited in Alterman, 2003, p. 2.

[53] Brock, 2004, p. 97.

[54] Ibid, p. 109.

[55] See Hayes, 2007.

[56] Jacoby, 2005, p. 14.

[57] Parenti, 2000, p. 85.

[58] Doumani, 2006, p. 38.

[59] This quote is derived from an unnamed Bush official cited in Scarborough, 2004, p. iii.

[60] Debord, 1988, p. 24.

[61] Moyers, 2001.

[62] I am using the term Friedmanite here to refer to the economic philosophy of Milton Friedman. See Dreyfuss, 2001 for a discussion of Norquist's ideological and political agenda.

[63] Bugliosi, 2001.

[64] Frank, 2008, p. 4.

[65] Friedman, cited in Klein, 2007, p. 11.

[66] Aaron, 2004.

[67] The Heritage Foundation is discussed in Chapter Two.

[68] See Democratic Policy Committee, 2003 and CNN.com "New Executive Orders Outrage Organized Labor," February, 2001.

[69] Mosher, 2001; DeYoung, 2001.

[70] See Planned Parenthood's "George W. Bush's War on Women: A Chronology" at http://www.heart land.org.

[71] McGarvey, 2005.

[72] Lynn, 2003.

[73] See for example Milbank, 2001.

[74] Woodward, 2002, pp. 31–32.

[75] Cited in Dixon, 2004.

[76] Hughes, 2004, pp. 267–268.

[77] Roy, 2004, p. 11.

[78] Doumani, 2006, pp. 15–16.

[79] Doumani, 2006, p. 16.

[80] Coulter, 2001.

[81] The exchange took place in the context of Robertson's "The 700 Club" show.

[82] Cockburn, 1991, p. 691.

[83] Moyers, 2005, p. 29.

[84] Taylor, 2005.

[85] Phillips, 2006, p. 22.

[86] Diamond, 1995.

[87] Gabbard and Atkinson, 2007. These authors convincingly argue that while neoliberalism and neoconservatism are often presented as inherently conflicting ideologies, they actually complement one another in practice.

[88] Bush, 2001[a].

[89] Bush, 2001 [b].

[90] See Palast 2003, 2006 and Kellner, 2001.

[91] Roy, 2003, p. 2.

[92] Roy, 2003, p. 2.

[93] Cited in Parenti, 2002, p. 42.

[94] For an historical summary of American intervention in the Middle East, see "Timeline of Empire: U.S. Intervention in the Middle East," at http://revcom.us/a/v23/1120-29/1125/timeline.htm.

[95] Gowans, 2003.

[96] See http://www.newamericancentury.org

[97] Duss, 2010, p. 14.

[98] Ibid.

[99] It is also important to note that several original members of PNAC, including Vice President Dick Cheney, have intimate ties with the oil industry.

[100] Shorris, 2004.

[101] Conason, 2007, p. 43.

[102] Kristol et al., 2001.

[103] Editorial Board of the *World Socialist Web Site*, 2003.

[104] Klein, 2007, p. 328.

[105] Ibid.

[106] Juhasz, 2006, p. 4.

[107] Ibid, pp. 4–5.

[108] Juhasz, 2006, p. 3–4.

[109] Ibid, p. 18.

[110] Juhasz, 2006, p. 19.

[111] Friedman, 1999, p. 4.

[112] Ibid, p. 13, 15.

[113] Galeano, 2000, p. 33.

[114] Ibid, p. 6.

[115] Katsiaficas, 2003.

[116] Klein, 2007, p. 297.

[117] Ibid.

[118] Harris and Milibank, cited in Klein, 2007, p. 297.

[119] Cypher, 2007, p. 6.

[120] Ibid.

[121] Ibid, p. 7.

[122] Klein, 2007, p. 298–299.

[123] Klein, 2007, p. 12.

[124] Greider, 2003.

[125] Sammon, 2002, pp. 382–383.

[126] Conason, 2003, p. 183.

[127] Ibid.

[128] Ibid, p. 184.

[129] See Bleifuss, 2005.

[130] Moyers, 2004.

[131] Giroux, 2005.

[132] See Franklin Delano Roosevelt's Second Inaugural Address of January 20, 1937 at http://www.presidency.ucsb.edu/ws/index.php?pid=15349.

[133] Blumenthal, 1988; Landay, 2002; Krehely, House & Kernan, 2004.

[134] Tucker, 2002.

[135] Nock, 1935, pp. 12–17, 44–45.

[136] Tucker, 2002.

[137] Tucker, 2002.

[138] Ibid.

[139] Jacoby, 2005, p. 11.

[140] Ibid.

[141] Buckley was also greatly influenced by the 1953 publication of Russell Kirk's *The Conservative Mind.*

[142] Blumenthal, 1988, p. 26.

[143] Diamond, 1995, p. 29.

[144] Blumenthal, 1988, p. 30.

[145] Ibid.

[146] These were extracted from "The Magazine's Credenda," *National Review,* Nov. 19, 1955, p. 6.

[147] In the early 1950s, Chodorov, who held an editorial position at the aforementioned magazine *Human Events,* outlined a fifty-year project to reform the American academy in favour of "freedom." The ISI is subsequently discussed in further detail.

[148] See http://www.isi.org

[149] Diamond, 1995, p. 21.

[150] Evans, 1961, p. 71.

[151] The full text of the Sharon Statement can be found at http://www.yaf.com

[152] See http://www.yaf.com

[153] See, for example, Phillips, 2006.

[154] By the early 1980s, however, Goldwater had become disillusioned with the Republican Party and annoyed by the profound influence of the Christian Right whose views conflicted with his libertarian streak. His granddaughter, CC Goldwater, has suggested that Goldwater would likely have been appalled by the George W. Bush administration and its Christian fundamentalist base. See Goldwater, 2006.

[155] Covington, 1997; Rich, 2005.

[156] Covington, 1997.

[157] Landay (2002) claims that Powell's communiqué was "less a memo" and more of a "militant manifesto of political action."

[158] Krehely, J., House, M., & Kernan, E., 2004, p. 9.

[159] The full text of Powell's memo is available at http://reclaimdemocracy.org/corporate_accountability/powell_memo_lewis.html

[160] Cited in "Introduction" to "The Powell Memo" at http://reclaimdemocracy.org/corporate_accountability/powell_memo_lewis.html

[161] In a section of the memo discussing the "tone of the attack," Powell cites two leading figures within the neoliberal movement—Arthur Shenfield who had worked closely with conservative darling Friedrich von Hayek and Milton Friedman, often referred to as the godfather of neoliberal economic theory. See Gabbard and Atkinson, 2007.

[162] Himmelstein, 1990, p. 137.

[163] Levitas, 1986.

[164] Gramsci, 1971.

[165] Frank, 2004, pp. 5–6.

[166] Willis, 2006, p. 14. Willis's essay is, in fact, an insightful critique of Frank's marginalization of cultural issues but she nonetheless concedes that Republican administrations' have exploited the religious right to further economic ends and corporate agendas.

[167] Frank, 2008, p. 30.

[168] Behan, 2003.

[169] Lapham, 2004, p. 3.

[170] Howell (1995) contends that the foundations are referred to as the "four sisters" because they tend to act in concert.

[171] Rob Stein, cited in Lapham, 2004, p. 3.

[172] See for example, Brock, 2003; Kaiser, 1999; Kaiser and Chinoy, 1999; Rothmyer, 1981, 1998.

[173] Time magazine once dubbed Scaife "the ultimate patron" of the Clinton haters. See Lacayo, 1998.

[174] Broder and Conason, 1998.

[175] Kaiser and Chinoy, 1999; Franken, 2003. In addition to the Arkansas project, Scaife funded (to the tune of $4 million) the Landmark Legal Foundation and Judicial Watch—two law firms that relentlessly pursued Clinton and his administration.

[176] Berlet and Lyons, 2000, p. 313.

[177] Kaiser and Chinoy, 1999.

[178] Blumenthal, 2006.

[179] Ibid.

[180] Horowitz's empire is explored in Chapter Three.

[181] Kaiser, 1999.

[182] Sarah Mellon's father, Thomas, began amassing wealth during the latter part of the nineteenth century through shrewd real estate investments and a lending business that eventually became known as the Mellon Bank. In time, the Mellon empire included (in addition to the bank) significant blocks of stock in Gulf Oil and Alcoa. See Rothmyer, 1981.

[183] According to Cordelia Scaife May, Richard's sister, their mother was a "gutter drunk." Richard, who was also an alcoholic for most of his life, eventually got on the wagon after a stint at the Betty Ford Clinic. See Kaiser, 1999.

[184] Kaiser, 1999; Hersh, 1978.

[185] Kaiser and Chinoy, 1999.

[186] Judis, 2001.

[187] Cited in Kaiser and Chinoy, 1999.

[188] Alterman, 2004.

[189] These figures are derived from a review of the various Scaife foundations 2005, 2006, 2007, and 2008 annual reports which are available at www.scaife.com.

[190] Muwakkil, 2003.

[191] Lewis's essay, entitled "The Roots of Muslim Rage," appeared in volume 266, no. 3 of *Atlantic Monthly*. See Beinin, 2006.

[192] See http://www.publiceye.org/tooclose/jbs.html

[193] See http://www.mediatransparency.org

[194] See http://www.jbs.org and Berlet and Lyons, 2000, p. 176, 178.

[195] Cited in Goldberg, 2006, p. 161.

[196] See http://www.mediatransparency.org

[197] Cited in Berkowitz, 2006.

[198] The Institute for Educational Affairs was created in 1978 by William Simon and Irving Kristol with grants of $100,000 each from the Olin Foundation, the JM Foundation, the Scaife Family Trusts, and the Smith-Richardson Foundation. Dedicated to funding right-wing students and scholars, the IEA merged with the Madison Center (founded by Allan Bloom and William Bennett) in 1990. The hybrid organization known as the Madison Center for Educational Affairs is now defunct.

[199] Brock, 2003, p. 49.

[200] Each time he was sworn into office, Ashcroft asked to be anointed with cooking oil in the manner of King David. This ritual earned him the nickname of the Crisco kid. See McLaren, 2005, p. 214.

[201] See http://www.mediatransparency.org

[202] Krehely, House and Kernan, 2004, p. 61.

[203] Wilayto, 2001.

204 See http://www.mediatransparency.org

205 Wilayto, 2001.

206 Cited in Krehely, House and Kernan, 2004, p. 61.

207 Goldberg, 2006, p. 121.

208 Information about grants awarded by the Bradley Foundation can be found at http://www.bradleyfdn.org

209 This figure is derived from the Bradley Foundation's annual reports that are available at http://www.bradleyfdn.org

210 Maguire, 2006, p. 111.

211 Cited in Maguire, 2006, p. 111.

212 These figures are derived from the 2004, 2005, 2006, 2007, 2008, and 2009 lists of Bradley Foundation grants awarded. It should be noted that the same institutes often receive funding under different 'programs.' For example, an organization may receive monies through "intellectual infra-structure" grants and "donor intent" grants.

213 See http://rightweb.irc-online.org/profile/653

214 Miller, 2005.

215 See Miller, 2005 and http://www.olin.com/about/history.asp

216 DeParle, 2005.

217 Simon, 1978, pp. 229–230.

218 Ibid, pp. 230–232.

219 Simon served as the Olin Foundation's president until his death in 2000. Michael Joyce then assumed the helm before he left to join the Bradley Foundation. The last executive director was James Piereson who oversaw affairs until the foundation closed in 2005.

220 Krehely, House and Kernan, 2004, p. 14.

221 See http://newcriterion.com

222 See Kimball 2005 for his "battle plan" to take back the university from the clutches of left-wing scholars presumably corrupted by the "values of Woodstock."

223 Journalist Jason DeParle (2005) has, in fact, argued that the Federalist Society would not even exist if not for the Olin Foundation.

224 Greene, 2005, p. 2.

225 Ingraham once posed for a *New York Times Magazine* cover in a skimpy leopard-print miniskirt. See Alterman, 1997.

226 See Brock, 2003.

227 For his part, Hayek firmly believed that history had proven the family, the church, and the free market to be the three most enduring institutions of human civilization. He received the U.S. Presidential Medal of Freedom in 1991 from George H.W. Bush.

228 See Diamond, 1995[b], p. 26.

229 Lenkowsy's resume includes a stint at the American Enterprise Institute.

230 Richardson, 1984.

231 The annual reports are available at http://www.srf.org/databank/documents

232 See mediatransparency.org

233 Bolton resigned in December 2006 after Senate confirmation of his reappointment seemed unlikely given the Democratic Party victories in the 2006 mid-term elections.

234 Barbara Olson was associated with the Federalist Society and authored a damning book about Hillary Clinton. She perished while aboard American Airlines Flight 77 which was flown into the Pentagon on September 11, 2001.

235 See http://www.iwf.org

236 O'Beirne was also a former regular panelist on CNN's *The Capital Gang*.

237 The book was published in 2003 by Regan Books, the right-wing imprint of book publisher Harper Collins which is owned by archconservative and media mogul Rupert Murdoch.

238 Spindel, 2003, p. 109.

[239] For critical reviews of Sommers' aforementioned texts, see Flanders, 1994; Houppert, 2002; Rotundo, 2000; and Wilson, 1994.

[240] Hoff Sommers, 2006.

[241] Similar efforts to "take back the campus" from the presumed grip of liberals are subsequently elaborated on.

[242] Saloma, 1984.

[243] See "AEI's Diamond Jubilee, 1943–2003" at www.aei.org.

[244] Blumental, 1988, p. 32. See also Scatamburlo, 1998.

[245] Wallace-Wells, 2003.

[246] Toler, 1999.

[247] Blumenthal, 1988; Himmelstein, 1990; Peschek, 1987.

[248] This, according to the International Relations Center. See http://rightweb.irc-online.org/profile/1431.

[249] Cited in the AEI's 2009 Annual Report, p. 16. The report is available at http://www.aei.org

[250] Wallace-Wells, 2003.

[251] Messer-Davidow, 1993, p. 54.

[252] A former White House official once claimed that "without AEI, Reagan never would have been elected." See Easterbrook, 1986.

[253] In late 2001, Frum was contacted by chief presidential speechwriter Mike Gerson. Frum's task was simple: he was to provide a justification for a war on Iraq. Thus was born the "axis of evil" cited in George W. Bush's January 29, 2002 State of the Union address. See Scatamburlo-D'Annibale, 2005.

[254] Holmes, 2006, p. 31.

[255] Yoo also had a hand in providing legal rationale for former President Bush to conduct unauthorized surveillance of telephone and email communications between the United States and overseas. See Holmes, 2006.

[256] Leopold, 2009, p. 4.

[257] Wallace-Wells, 2003.

[258] Berkowitz, 2003.

[259] Mark and Louise Zwick cited in Berkowitz, 2003.

[260] Allen, Jr., 2003.

[261] Zinsmeister, 2002.

[262] Cited in Plissner, 2002.

[263] Wall Street Journal, August 30, 2002.

[264] Plissner, 2002.

[265] Jacoby, 2005, p. 13.

[266] Ibid.

[267] Searls-Giroux, 2005, p. 322.

[268] Kurdziel and Bidikov, 2006.

[269] Zipp and Fenwick, 2006, p. 311.

[270] Ibid, p. 320.

[271] Lee, 2006, p. 28.

[272] Ibid, p. 29.

[273] Rubin and Stern, 2005.

[274] Ibid.

[275] Ibid.

[276] Lazare, 2005, p. 2.

[277] Lee, 2002.

[278] Wallace-Wells, 2003.

[279] Cited in Noah, 2003.

[280] Wallace-Wells, 2003.

[281] In addition to Noah (2003) and Wallace-Wells (2003), see the website of the Brady Campaign for handgun control (http://www.bradycampaign.org) for more on the Lott saga.

[282] See http://www.aei.org/about

NOTES

[283] Wallace-Wells, 2003.

[284] Wallace-Wells, 2003, p. 4.

[285] Sinclair drafted a call for the formation of the Intercollegiate Socialist Society in 1904 which he then circulated among leading socialist intellectuals (including Jack London who served as its first president) for endorsement. The ISS was formally launched on September 12, 1905 at a restaurant in downtown New York and it existed until 1921. See http://www.marxisthistory.org/subject/usa/eam/ iss.html for more information on the organization's history.

[286] This figure is derived from the website of Media Transparency.

[287] In the late 1980s, particularly after the 1988 election of George H.W. Bush, a sharp divide between neoconservatives and paleoconservatives began to manifest itself. Bush's identification with multi-national elites alienated the Christian Right from mainstream Republicanism despite the fact that Dan Quayle (a staunch religious rightist) served as his Vice-President. Whereas neoconservatives emphasized U.S. global dominance and foreign policy, paleoconservatives embraced a strict Christian morality, Eurocentric monoculturalism, and an isolationist form of nationalism. See Berlet & Lyons, 2000.

[288] Cribb, 1990, p. 29.

[289] See http://www.isi.org

[290] See the archives of the journal on the institute's website for numerous examples.

[291] Kagan, 2002, p. 3, 5, 7.

[292] Chomsky, 2001, p. 31.

[293] Goldberg, 2006, p. 109.

[294] Ibid, p. 109, 110, 112.

[295] Hedges, 2006, p. 12.

[296] Ibid, p. 13.

[297] Ibid, p. 158.

[298] This characterization of John Podhertz's is derived from Wolcott, 2004, p. 51.

[299] See http://mediamattersnetwork.org/factcheck/201001270004

[300] Brock, 2004, p. 68.

[301] See the archives at http://www.princetontory.com

[302] See the October 2008 issue of the *Princeton Tory* at http://www.princeton.edu/~/tory/issues/2008-10.pdf.

[303] For a discussion on this issue, see for example Ruby-Sachs and Waligore, 2003.

[304] See especially chapters four and five of D'Souza's *Letters to a Young Conservative*.

[305] See "Know Your Right-Wing Speakers: Dinesh D'Souza" at http://www.campusprogress.org/tools/ 118'know-your-right-wing-speakers-dinesh-dsouza

[306] Cited in Henson, 1991, p. 6.

[307] For a lengthier critique of *The End of Racism*, see Scatamburlo, 1998.

[308] Cited in Bass, 2007.

[309] Cited in Pollitt, 2007, p. 9.

[310] Bass, 2007.

[311] Wolcott, 2004, p. 17.

[312] Malone, long since graduated from SUNY-Binghamton, has worked in various right-wing media venues. Her conflation of anti-Bush sentiment with Islamic radicalism is cited in Follman, 2004.

[313] Cited in Berkowitz, 2004.

[314] Ibid.

[315] Spence, 2006.

[316] Weyrich died in December, 2008.

[317] See www.heritage.org

[318] McLaren and Jamarillo, 2007, p. 166.

[319] The *Washington Times* was put up for sale in May 2010 after intra-family warring among Moon's children led to the paper's $35 million subsidy being cut off.

[320] For more on Moon's organizations and activities, see Boettcher and Freeman, 1980; Gorenfeld, 2003; and Parry, 2006.

[321] Spence, 2006, p. 64.

[322] See Bellant, 1988[a.]

[323] The FCF evolved from the Committee for the Survival of a Free Congress and the Free Congress Research and Education Foundation.

[324] See http://www.freecongress.org

[325] Lapham, 2004, p. 6.

[326] Conason, 2001, p. 2.

[327] Bellant, 1988[b], p. 5.

[328] Bellant, 1988[a], p. 49.

[329] Bellant, 1988[b], p. 60.

[330] Younge, 2005, p. 11.

[331] Cited in Berkowitz, 2001.

[332] Cited in Swanson, 2004.

[333] See Rasmus, 2005.

[334] Bacon, 2003, p. 19.

[335] Krugman, 2003.

[336] See http://www.mediatransparency.org for its profile on the Heritage Foundation.

[337] Berkowitz, 2005, p. 1.

[338] See Parenti, 2005 and Reed, Jr., 2006.

[339] Klein, 2007, p. 410–412.

[340] See also Klein 2005 and 2006.

[341] See Cha, 2004.

[342] Cited in Berkowitz, 2005[b].

[343] Tierney cited in Milbank and Cooperman, 2005, p. A5.

[344] The Institute of World Politics received grants totaling $4,091,097 from 1993 to 2005 according to www.mediatransparency.org.

[345] For a more detailed account of Hulsman's fall from Heritage grace, see Ackerman, 2006.

[346] Brock, 2003, p. 79.

[347] Brock, 2003, p. 77.

[348] Weisberg, 1998.

[349] Brock, 2003, p. 77.

[350] Weisberg, 1998.

[351] Messer-Davidow, 1993, p. 52.

[352] Borosage, 2003.

[353] See http://thinkprogress.org/2007/02/20/boortz-teachers-terrorists for a link to the video clip of the interview.

[354] See http://www.newshounds.us/2006/12/19 for a transcript that includes Gallagher's remarks.

[355] See "Right-Wing Radio Host Fabricates Controversy To Attack First Muslim Congressman" at http://thinkprogress.org/2006/11/30/koran-bible-prager-ellison

[356] All quotes are from Feulner, 2004.

[357] The conservative campaign for intellectual and ideological diversity is explored in the next chapter.

[358] Khalidi cited in Goodman, 2005.

[359] DeParle, 2005.

[360] The tea party "movement" is briefly discussed in Chapter Three.

[361] Costa and Maloy, 2005; Krehely, House, and Kernan, 2004.

[362] See http://www.leadershipinstitute.org

[363] Ibid.

[364] Savage and Wirzbicki, 2005.

[365] See http://mediamatters.org/items/200501280001

[366] Savage and Wirzbicki, 2005.

[367] Blackwell, cited in Goode, 1999.

[368] See Field, 2007 and the CLP website at http://www.campusleadership.org/about-us.cfm

[369] Horwitz, 2005.

[370] Panhorst, 2005.

[371] See the "resources" heading at http://www.campusleadership.org for a variety of tool kits that include sample press releases, posters, and suggestions for campus activities.

[372] Cited in Field, 2007.

[373] See http://www.campusreform.org/about

[374] Ibid.

[375] Horwitz, 2005, pps. 1–2.

[376] Horwitz, 2005, p. 2.

[377] Ibid.

[378] Posner, 2005.

[379] Ambinder, 2002.

[380] See http://www.sourcewatch.org/index.php?/title=Council_for_National_Policy

[381] See Brock, 2003; Conason, 2007; Goldberg, 2006, and Hedges, 2006.

[382] Hedges, 2006, p. 136.

[383] Ambinder, 2002, p. 2.

[384] Conason, 2007, p. 147.

[385] Goldberg, 2006, p. 11–12.

[386] Conason, 2007, p. 149.

[387] Cited in Posner, 2005, p. 4.

[388] Hedges, 2006.

[389] See the YAF's official website at http://www.yaf.org

[390] Five years later, in 1999, the Phillips Foundation established its College Leader Program which provides renewable cash awards to undergraduates who demonstrate leadership on behalf of freedom and American values. See http://www.thephillipsfoundation.org for more information.

[391] LaPierre cited in Noah, 2002.

[392] See both http://www.yaf.org/mission/index.cfm and http://reaganranch.yaf.org/ranch/index.cfm

[393] Colapinto, 2003.

[394] Wise, 2004.

[395] Greider, 2004, p. 5.

[396] Ibid.

[397] *The Nation*, 2004, p. 3–5.

[398] See Scatamburlo-D'Annibale & McLaren, 2010 and *The Nation*'s editorial of June 28, 2004, p. 3.

[399] Greider, 2004, p. 5.

[400] See Activism 411, Activism Made Easy on the YAF website.

[401] Schell, 2004, p. 6.

[402] For more detailed account of the "revolt" of the generals, see Whalen, 2006.

[403] See http://students.yaf.org/activists/rotc/index.cfm

[404] See http://www.appealforredress.org

[405] Cooper, 2007, p. 11.

[406] See http://students.yaf.org/activists/rotc/index.cfm

[407] See http://www.yaf.org and http://students/yaf.org/conferences/highschool/index.cfm

[408] See http://students/yaf.org/conferences/index.cfm

[409] See http://www.yaf.org

[410] All quotes from this publication that are cited below are extracted from the 2009 YAF Battle Plan which is available on-line at http://www.yaf.org

[411] Cited in Brown, 2007.

[412] See http://www.yaf.org/mission/index.cfm; http://njc.yaf.org/about/index.cfm; and http://www.source watch.org/index.php?title=National_Journalism_Center

[413] See http://www.sourcewatch.org/index.php?title=Maggie_Gallagher

[414] See http://students.yaf.org/conferences/college/index.cfm

[415] For a critique of Stossel's "reporting"—particularly a recent paean to education privatization—see Hart & Jackson, 2006.

[416] This characterization of Malkin can be found in Nahm (n.d.).

[417] See Campus Progress's "Know Your Right-Wing Speakers" series at http://www.campusprogress.org

[418] A lengthy list of Malkin's misrepresentations and falsehoods, catalogued and debunked, can be found at http://thinkprogress.org

[419] For a copy of the transcript of the August 19, 2004 episode of *Hardball*, see http://www.msnbc.msn.com/id/5765243/

[420] Some videos of the conference's speakers are available on the YAF website.

[421] Clarke, 2006.

[422] All quotes from Clarke, 2006.

[423] Cited in Rampton and Stauber, 2004, p. 79.

[424] Ibid.

[425] Goldberg, 2005.

[426] Sullivan, 2007.

[427] Holthouse, 2009.

[428] See http://www.westernyouth.org

[429] Holthouse, 2009.

[430] Ibid.

[431] Eco, 1995, p. 58.

[432] See http://www.nas.org/nas.html

[433] Siano, 1996.

[434] Huberman, 2006, p. 5.

[435] Beeman, 2003.

[436] London, 1987/1988, p. 3–4.

[437] Cited in Campbell, 2001.

[438] Campbell, 2001.

[439] See Weisberg, 1992 and Miller, 1995.

[440] Berube, 2006.

[441] See *Media Matters for America*, 2005.

[442] Gravois, 2007, p. 2.

[443] *Media Matters for America*, 2005.

[444] Jacoby, 2005, p. 13.

[445] Lee, cited in Gravois, 2007, p. 3.

[446] Balch, 2005, p. 12.

[447] Balch, 2005, p. 32–33.

[448] Berube, 2006.

[449] Fish, 2005, p. 2–3.

[450] Willis, 2005, p. 1.

[451] Ibid.

[452] Cited in Blumenthal, 2005.

[453] Cited in Berkowitz, 2004.

[454] See http://www.gropper.com and http://www.marxists.org/subject/art/visual_arts/satire/gropper/index.htm

[455] Sherman, 2000, p. 13. Sherman's account of Horowitz's personal and political journey is one of the most comprehensive I've encountered. I therefore rely on it heavily in what follows.

[456] Ibid, p. 14.

[457] Ibid, p. 15.

[458] Collier and Horowitz express their appreciation to both foundations in the acknowledgements section of their book.

[459] See Rampton and Stauber, 2004, p. 4.

[460] See http://www.horowitzfreedomcenter.org

461 Cited in Brodsky, 2005, p. 4.

462 See Collier, 2005.

463 See the premier issue of *Heterodoxy* at http://www.frontpagemag.com (another Horowitz outfit) which began re-publication of all eight years of *Heterodoxy* in 2005. All issues of the magazine will eventually be archived in the Issues section of Horowitz's www.discoverthenetworks.org.

464 Collier, 2005.

465 For various discussions on Savage's "illustrious" career, see Berkowitz, 2003; Fritz, 2003; Fost, 2003; and MediaMatters.org

466 Horowitz, 1999.

467 Sherman, 2000, p. 16.

468 White, cited in Sherman, 2000, p. 12.

469 Wise, 2002, p. 3.

470 Potok quoted in Roddy, 2005. See also Wise, 2002. For an examination of the CCC, see Diamond, 1995.

471 Horowitz, cited in Meranto, 2005, p. 229.

472 Horowitz, 2000, p. 24. It should be noted that Horowitz's original 1998 pamphlet was slightly expanded and published under the title, *The Art of Political War and Other Radical Pursuits*, in 2000.

473 Cited in Powell, 2001, p. C01.

474 Cited in Berkowitz, 2005.

475 Horowitz, 2001[b].

476 Horowitz, 2001[a].

477 Cited in Durham, 2004, p. 18.

478 Brodsky, 2005, p. 4.

479 Blumenthal, 2006.

480 Prashad, 2005, n.d.

481 Cited in Berkowitz, 2006.

482 All quotes are derived from the DHFC's 2006 year-end report which is available at http://www.horowitzfreedomcenter.org

483 Jacobson, 2005.

484 See http://www.horowitzfreedomcenter.org/about

485 I am appropriating the term "Horowista" from Bill Berkowitz's article entitled "Horowitz's Campus Jihads." The term designates the "hearty and growing band of followers of right wing provocateur David Horowitz and his Students for Academic Freedom."

486 Meranto, 2005, p. 227.

487 The AIA, is of course, the little sister of Accuracy in Media (AIM) which was started in the 1960s to identify "liberal bias" in the mainstream media.

488 For more on Sara Russo/Dogan, see Williams, n.d.

489 It now appears as though some of the individual chapters of the SAF run their own complaint forums and the "forum of abuses" section no longer appears on the central SAF website.

490 The original complaint form was once available on http://www.studentsforacademicfreedom.org but as of April 2009 it has disappeared from the website.

491 See Scatamburlo-D'Annibale, 2005 for an examination of the Bush administration's propaganda campaign and mainstream media coverage during the run-up to the Iraq war.

492 Meranto, 2005, p. 216.

493 McClennen, 2006, p. 50.

494 Giroux, 2006, p. 24.

495 Hollinger, 2005.

496 See *Heterodoxy*, vol.2, no. 3.

497 See *MediaMattersforAmerica*, specifically, http://mediamatters.org/items/200503080001 and http://mediamatters.org/items/200503160001

498 Riordan, 2005.

499 Ibid.

[500] See the aforementioned items at *MediaMattersforAmerica* and Riordan, 2005.

[501] See Horowitz's *Front Page Magazine* commentary which appeared on March 15, 2005.

[502] See the Students for Academic Freedom Second Year Achievement Report available at http://www.studentsforacademicfreedom.org

[503] Ibid.

[504] On February 17, 2005, al-Qloushi appeared on *Hannity & Colmes* and claimed that Woolcock that "threatened [him] into seeking regular psychological treatment … by threatening [his] visa status." Not surprisingly, Woolcock's response to al-Qloushi's version of events was completely ignored on the show. See "*Hannity & Colmes*, Horowitz ignored facts undermining GOP student's claim that professor failed him for 'pro-American' paper" at http://mediamatters.org.

[505] Woolcock, 2005.

[506] See Horowitz's "In Defense of Intellectual Diversity" and "Indoctrination U: Interview with David Horowitz" which was posted at http://cms.studentsforacademicfreedom.org/index.php?option=com.content&task=view&id=2474&Itemid=67 on June 11, 2007.

[507] Brodsky, 2005, p. 8.

[508] Horowitz, 2003[a].

[509] Horowitz, 2003[a].

[510] Horowitz, 2003 [b], p. 350, 351.

[511] Brodsky, 2005, p. 13.

[512] Vanlandingham, 2005, p. 1.

[513] Ibid, p. 2.

[514] See Spence, 2006, particularly chapter ten, "Kill All the Lawyers."

[515] While the Florida bill did not pass, similar bills have been developed and passed in other states.

[516] Gabbard and Anijar, 2006.

[517] Horowitz, 2004, p. 2.

[518] Brodsky, 2005, p. 13.

[519] Siriwardane, 2006 cited in Wilson, 2008, p. 5.

[520] See Eco, 1995 and Britt, 2003.

[521] Eco, 1995, p. 58.

[522] Blumenthal, 2006, p. 1.

[523] Beinin, 2004, pp. 101–102.

[524] Giroux, 2006, p. 28–29.

[525] Farrell, 2007.

[526] Horowitz, 2006, p. xlviii.

[527] Apple, 2006, p. 1.

[528] Free Exchange on Campus, 2006, p. i.

[529] Ibid, p. iii.

[530] Ibid, p. iv–v.

[531] Gorenfeld, 2005, p. 2.

[532] See http://www.discoverthenetworks.org

[533] Ibid.

[534] Ibid.

[535] See *Facts Still Count: An Analysis of David Horowitz's 'One-Party Classroom'*, p. 1. The document is available on-line at freeexchangeoncampus.org

[536] Ibid, p. 3.

[537] Ibid.

[538] See Cloud, 2009.

[539] Jaschik, 2009, p. 1.

[540] *Facts Still Count*, p. 5.

[541] Ibid, p. 4.

[542] Ibid, p. 6.

[543] Ibid, p. 2.

[544] Jaschik, 2009, p. 1.

[545] Ibid, p. 2.

[546] See http://www.terrorismawareness.org/islamo-fascism-awareness-week

[547] Pollitt, 2007, p. 1.

[548] See Leupp, 2007 and for a profile on Cohen, see http://rightweb.irc-online.org/profile/1100.html

[549] Kaplan, 2007, p. 2.

[550] Taylor, 2007.

[551] See http://www.terrorismawareness.org

[552] Akhavi, 2007; Doster, 2007, p. 47.

[553] Dylan, 2007.

[554] Jaschik, 2007. See also MacDonald and Rendall, 2008.

[555] Pipes and his organizations are discussed in more detail in Chapter Four.

[556] Pipes, 1990.

[557] It should be noted that Santelli subsequently tried to distance himself from the Tea Partyers and released a public statement stating that he hoped President Obama's stimulus plan would be successful. See Ames and Levine, 2009.

[558] See Ames and Levine, 2009 and McGrath, 2010 on the rise of tea party activism.

[559] Ames and Levine, 2009.

[560] Ibid.

[561] Street and DiMaggio, 2010.

[562] Cited in Street and DiMaggio, 2010.

[563] McGrath, 2010.

[564] Street and DiMaggio, 2010.

[565] Ibid.

[566] Ibid.

[567] Pilkington, 2010.

[568] Zenike, 2010.

[569] Wright, 2010.

[570] McFadden, 2010.

[571] Ibid.

[572] Horowitz, 2009.

[573] Ibid.

[574] The student guide is available on-line at http://freedomcenterstudents.org

[575] The Fox News Channel's embrace of the radical right is a subject taken up in chapter four.

[576] See the "Student Guide: Teach-In to Oppose Barack Obama's Radical Transformation of America."

[577] See chapter two for a brief discussion of Reverend Moon.

[578] See sourcewatch.org

[579] See the report on the first teach-in at GWU at http://freedomcenterstudents.org

[580] Neiwert, 2008.

[581] Of course, the Obama administration's health care reforms were eventually passed and, unfortunately, they were quite industry-friendly.

[582] See sourcewatch.org

[583] Bahsen's claims about being a Friedman disciple, lover of Reagan, and National Review kind of conservative are derived from his website www.davidbahnsem.com. See also the story about, and video of, the USC teach-in at http://freedomcenterstudents.org

[584] See www.goacta.org

[585] See www.goacta.org/issues/academic_freedom.html

[586] Ibid.

[587] Zinn, 1991, p. 148.

[589] See goacta.org

[589] Inside Academe, Fall 2001, vol. vi, no. 4.

[590] Lapham, 2002, p. 6.

[591] Chihara, 2001.

[592] Martin and Neal, 2002, p. 1.

[593] After the release of the 2001 ACTA report, Lieberman wrote a letter to ACTA to express his disapproval of the report which he considered to be unfair and inconsistent for an organization allegedly devoted to promoting academic freedom. He also requested that his name be removed from any ACTA correspondence suggesting that he was a co-founder of the group. (Smith, 2007)

[594] Martin and Neal, 2002, pp. 3–5.

[595] Street, 2003, pp. 284, 285.

[596] Frank, 2004, pp. 114–115.

[597] See for example, Alterman, 2003; Parry, 2003.

[598] Martin and Neal, 2002, p. 5.

[599] Bennett, cited in Street, 2003, p. 282.

[600] Beinin, 2004, p. 102.

[601] In fact, while head of the National Endowment of the Humanities (NEH) Cheney, in her efforts to pack the advisory board with right-wingers, nominated Carol Iannone. Iannone, whose nomination was eventually killed by the Senate, had gained fame (some might say notoriety) for penning a *Commentary* article in which she claimed that giving National Book Awards and Pulitzer Prizes to African-American female authors such as Toni Morrison and Alice Walker sacrificed "the demands of excellence to the democratic dictatorship of mediocrity" (Iannone, cited in Wiener, 2000, p. 14).

[602] See for example, Wilson, 1995; Alterman, 2001.

[603] Wiener, 2000, p. 13.

[604] Martin and Neal, 2002, p. 5.

[605] Ibid.

[606] Gravois, 2007, p. A11.

[607] Martin and Neal, 2002, pp. 6–7.

[608] Ibid, p. 7.

[609] McLaren, 2005, p. 197.

[610] Ibid, p. 198.

[611] Street, 2003, p. 284.

[612] Ibid, p. 286.

[613] Martin and Neal, 2002, p. 7.

[614] See ACTA, 2005, p. 1. This particular pamphlet is not attributed to any author(s), therefore it is cited here as ACTA 2005. All quotes below—unless otherwise specified—are derived from this pamphlet.

[615] ACTA, 2005, p. 1.

[616] ACTA, 2005, pp. 3–4.

[617] See Scatamburlo-D'Annibale, 2005.

[618] On Kissinger's war crimes, see Gee, 2002; Herman, 1997; and Hitchens, 2001.

[619] ACTA, 2005, p. 5.

[620] Ibid, p. 6.

[621] Ibid, p. 7.

[622] Lee, 2006, p. 12.

[623] ACTA, 2005, p. 6.

[624] Lee, 2006, p. 13.

[625] Fuentes, 1998.

[626] Berkowitz, 2001.

[627] Cockburn, 1991.

[628] Wolin, 2003, p. 13.

[629] Frank, 2004, p. 5.

[630] Himmelstein, 1990, p. 9.

[631] Debord, 1988, p. 22.

[632] Nichols and McChesney, 2005, p. 12.

[633] Chomsky, 1997.

[634] Moyers, 2005.

[635] Moyers, 2005, p. viii.

[636] Klayman, cited in Elsner, 2002, p. 1.

[637] McClellan cited in Loven, 2008.

[638] Waxman's report can be obtained at http://oversight.house.gov/features/secrecy_report/pdf/pdf_secrecy_report.pdf. See also Public Citizen's website http://www.bushsecrecy.org.

[639] According to a January 12, 2006 report in the HuffingtonPost.com, the Bush administration called upon high-ranking military leaders to denounce Congressman John Murtha of Pennsylvania who was an outspoken critic of the war in Iraq and who had called for the withdrawal of U.S. troops at the time.

[640] Parry, 2006, p. 1.

[641] Lobe, 2003, p. 2.

[642] Ibid.

[643] McLaren and Jaramillo, 2007, p. 125.

[644] Gilbert, cited in Conason, 2007, p. 44.

[645] Conason, 2007, p. 45.

[646] For a more in depth discussion of Strauss' aversion to modern liberal democracy, see Taylor 2005. And, for a more extensive treatment of Strauss's political thought, see Drury, 1988.

[647] For an elaboration on Lippmann's concept of the bewildered herd, see Scatamburlo-D'Annibale, Suoranto, Jaramillo, and McLaren, 2006.

[648] Ewen, 1996, p. 13.

[649] Ibid, p. 63.

[650] Ibid, p. 157.

[651] Rich, 2006, p. 17, 19.

[652] For a more detailed account of the spin and propaganda employed by the Bush administration and media coverage of it in the build-up to the Iraq war, see Scatamburlo-D'Annibale, 2005.

[653] Lewis and Reading-Smith, 2008, p. 1.

[654] Ibid. The study and a fully searchable data base of the materials analyzed is available at http://www.publicintegrity.org

[655] Rampton and Stauber, 2006, pp. 28–29.

[656] Ibid, p. 31.

[657] Barstow, 2008.

[658] Nichols and McChesney, 2005, p. 54–55.

[659] Alterman, 2005, p. 1.

[660] Raphael, 2005.

[661] Lee, 2006, p. 1.

[662] Fritz et al., 2004, p. 2.

[663] Ibid.

[664] Schechter, 2003, p. 1.

[665] Parry, 2003, p. 3.

[666] McChesney and Nichols, 2008, p. 12.

[667] Moyers, 2005, p. ix.

[668] Ibid, p. viii.

[669] Nichols and McChesney, 2005, p. 4.

[670] Alterman, 2003, p. 31–32.

[671] Wolcott, 2004, p. 73.

[672] Nichols and McChesney, 2005, pp. 7–8.

[673] Herman and Chomsky, 1988.

[674] See, for example, Bennett, 2005 and Morris, 2005.

[675] Postman, 1985, p. 3.

[676] Ibid, p. 87.

[677] Morris, 2005, p. 57.

[678] Cohen, 2006, p. 2. It should be noted, however, that as the disastrous consequences of the Bush administration's policies were coming to light, *MSNBC* became much more critical, largely due to the presence of Keith Olbermann.

[679] Cohen, 2006, p. 2.

[680] See for example, Alterman, 2003; Croteau, 1998; Husseini and Solomon, 1998; McChesney and Foster, 2003; McChesney, 2004; Scatamburlo, 1998.

[681] Ackerman, 2001, p. 1.

[682] McChesney and Foster, 2003, pp. 12–13.

[683] Ibid, pp. 14–15.

[684] See Scatamburlo-D'Annibale, 2005; Scatamburlo-D'Annibale, Suoranta and McLaren, 2007.

[685] Both quotes are from Sinclair Lewis. See http://www.brainyquote.com

[686] Moyers, 2005, pp. ix–x.

[687] Brock, 2004, p. 2.

[688] Ibid, p. 3.

[689] Cited in Cohen, 2006, p. 56.

[690] Auletta, 2003, p. 58.

[691] Cohen, 2006, p. 53.

[692] Ackerman, 2001, p. 2.

[693] See Ackerman, 2001 and Wolcott, 2004.

[694] Cited in Wolcott, 2004, p. 167.

[695] Ibid, p. 168.

[696] Ibid, pp. 168–169.

[697] See Gitlin, 1995 and Scatamburlo, 1998.

[698] Wolcott, 2004, p. 170.

[699] Ibid, p. 171.

[700] See Ehrenreich, 2004 and Frank, 2004.

[701] Alterman, 2008, p. 14.

[702] Brock, 2004, p. 317.

[703] Gough, 2008.

[704] See "Brit Hume confesses to Fox News right-wing bias" at http://www.newscorpse.com/ncWP/?pd226.

[705] Ackerman, 2001, p. 5.

[706] Snow, cited in Shakir, 2007. In April 2008, Snow joined CNN as a conservative commentator. He died in July 2008.

[707] See http://www.mediamatters.org

[708] Ackerman, 2001, p. 8.

[709] Cited in Brock, 2004, p. 319.

[710] Morris, 2005, p. 68. Morris also found that Fox News offers more "soft news" than other cable networks such as CNN; that it does the best job of attracting audiences that are more close-minded, less knowledgeable and engaged as a whole and that Fox viewers prefer news that shares their own point of view on politics and issues.

[711] Brock, 2004, p. 316.

[712] Anderson, 2003, pp. 1–2.

[713] Morris, cited in Anderson, 2003, p. 3.

[714] Rampton and Stauber, 2004, p. 182.

[715] Rampton and Stauber, 2004, p. 69.

[716] Ibid, pp. 69–70.

[717] Kull, et al., 2003.

[718] Conason, 2007, pp. 126–127.

[719] Cole, 2007.

[720] Wolcott, 2004, p. 9, 11.

[721] Proffitt, 2007, p. 78.

[722] Britt, 2003.

[723] Krugman, 2009.

[724] Wolcott, 2004, p. 187.

[725] Ibid, p. 187–188.

[726] Rendall, 2003, p. 4.

[727] Cited in Rendall, 2003, p. 5.

[728] Hannity cited in Blumenthal, 2005, p. 2.

[729] Blumenthal, 2005, p. 1.

[730] Ibid, p. 2.

[731] Blumenthal cited in Karlin, 2008, p. 3.

[732] See Neiwart, 2009.

[733] Rendall, 2003, p. 1.

[734] Ibid, pp. 1–2.

[735] Cooper, 2006, p. 1.

[736] See the profile of Andrew Jones on www.bruinalumni.com/andrew.html

[737] Cited in Makdisi, 2006, p. 1.

[738] Jaschik, 2006, p. 2.

[739] Wiener, 2006, p. 6.

[740] Makdisi, 2006, p. 1.

[741] Thernstrom, 1990, p. 14.

[742] Cited in D'Souza, 1991, p. 195.

[743] Alam, 2006, p. 2.

[744] See "FOX News Does Its Part For Right-Wing McCarthyism On Campus" at http://www.news hounds.us/2006/09/10/fox_news_does_its_part_for_rightwing_mccarthyism

[745] In April 2009, a jury in Denver found that Churchill was improperly fired by the University of Colorado but the verdict was vacated in July 2009 by Judge Larry Naves. Naves' high school guidance counselor and the man credited for helping him get into the University of Denver was John Rice, the father of former Secretary of State Condoleezza Rice.

[746] Massing, 2009.

[747] Ibid.

[748] Gitlin, 2003, p. 2.

[749] O'Reilly received his Master's in Public Administration in 1996.

[750] Peters, 2010, p. 15.

[751] Ibid, p. 13.

[752] Franken, 2003, p. 75.

[753] See Sourcewatch.org for a profile on O'Reilly.

[754] O'Reilly, 2006, p. 3.

[755] Ibid, p. 41, 31.

[756] See Conway, Grabe and Grieves, 2007.

[757] Ibid, p. 205.

[758] Ibid. p. 200.

[759] Ibid, p. 199.

[760] See, for example, Warren, 1996.

[761] Media Matters for America, 2005.

[762] In a chapter entitled, "Armies of the Night" from *Culture Warrior*, O'Reilly discusses the nefarious nature of the secular progressive "movement."

[763] O'Reilly cited in Media Matters for America, 2005.

[764] *The O'Reilly Factor*, 2003.

[765] Blumenthal, 2008.

[766] Beirich and Potok, 2003.

[767] Blumenthal, 2008.

[768] Beirich and Potok, 2003.

[769] Blumenthal, 2008.

[770] Ibid.

[771] Beirich and Potok, 2003.

[772] Southern Law Poverty Center, Intelligence Report, Spring 2009.

[773] Neiwart, 2009.

[774] O'Reilly cited in Neiwart, 2009.

[775] *Media Matters*, April 14, 2006.

[776] O'Reilly cited in Neiwart, 2009.

[777] *Media Matters*, October 25, 2007.

[778] Churchill, 2001. There has been some controversy over the number of dead as a result of the attack on the "Highway of Death," which is officially known as Highway 80. Estimates have ranged from a few thousand to 100,000.

[779] Ibid.

[780] In 2004, Rabinowitz's Kirkland Project invited Susan Rosenberg, a former political prisoner who was incarcerated for supporting the activities of the Weather Underground, to teach a one-month seminar on writing memoirs. After howls of indignation from rightists, Rosenberg backed out. See Proyect, 2005.

[781] Churchill, 2007, p. 18.

[782] Cited in *Revolutionary Worker*, 2005. No individual author is listed for this publication.

[783] O'Reilly, 2005.

[784] Churchill, 2007, p. 19.

[785] Ibid, p. 20.

[786] Ibid.

[787] King, 2009, pp. 35–36.

[788] Cohen, 1972, p. 28.

[789] Cited in *Revolutionary Worker*, 2005.

[790] Palczewski, C.H. et al., 2006, p. 352.

[791] Schulz and Reyes, 2008, p. 633.

[792] Ibid, p. 632.

[793] O'Reilly, 2005.

[794] Schulz and Reyes, 2008, p. 640.

[795] Ibid, p. 641.

[796] Alam, 2005.

[797] See transcript of *The O'Reilly Factor*, February 2, 2005.

[798] Press, 2004.

[799] See McNeil 2002 and Zogby cited in Spencer, 2003.

[800] Saturen, 2008.

[801] Hitchens, 2003.

[802] Ibid.

[803] Press, 2004.

[804] Berlet, Rastegar and Chamberlain, 2002.

[805] Press, 2004.

[806] Ibid.

[807] Press, 2004. See also Saturen, 2008.

[808] Saturen, 2008.

[809] Press, 2004.

[810] Ibid.

[811] Beck has expressed his admiration for McCarthy on numerous occasions—one of the most recent being on June 4, 2010 when he told his audience that while McCarthy may have used bad tactics, he was "absolutely right."

[812] Zaitchik, 2009[b].

[813] See Lendmen, 2009 and Von Drehle, 2009.

[814] Zaitchik, 2009.

[815] Ibid.

[816] Ibid.

[817] All quotes above are derived from Zaitchik, 2009.

[818] Zaitchik, 2009.

[819] Ibid.

[820] Ibid.

[821] Ibid.

[822] Clear Channel is now a behemoth in the radio industry and owns over 1200 stations in the United States.

[823] Zaitchik, 2009.

[824] See http://www.premiereradio.com

[825] Palin, 2010.

[826] Hart, 2010.

[827] Romano, 2010.

[828] Ibid.

[829] Boehlert, 2009.

[830] Beck made these comments on the April 22, 2010 edition of the *Glenn Beck Program*.

[831] See http://www.glennbeck.com

[832] Goldberg, 2006, p. 44.

[833] See http://www.wallbuilders.com. It should also be noted that WallBuilders "pro-family" agenda is propped up by a virulent form of homophobia and that Barton helped to make the Texas Republican Party one of the most anti-gay in the country. In its 2004 party platform, the Texas GOP asserted that the "practice of sodomy tears at the fabric of society, contributes to the breakdown of the family unit, and leads to the spread of dangerous, communicable diseases. Homosexual behavior is contrary to the fundamental, unchanging truths that have been ordained by God, recognized by our country's founders, and shared by the majority of Texans" (cited in Goldberg, 2006, p. 71).

[834] See http://www.wallbuilders.com

[835] Goldberg, 2006, p. 45.

[836] Ibid, p. 44.

[837] Cited in Montopoli, 2010. Of course, Arlen Specter switched to the Democratic Party in 2009 claiming that he found himself increasingly at odds with contemporary Republican philosophy.

[838] Goldberg, 2006, p. 46.

[839] Beck cited in Stelter and Carter, 2009.

[840] Laurence, 2009.

[841] Zaitchik, 2010.

[842] Ibid.

[843] Von Drehle, 2009.

[844] Zaitchik, 2010.

[845] Corcoran, 2009.

[846] Zaitchik, 2010.

[847] Ibid.

[848] Ibid.

[849] Ibid.

[850] Ibid.

[851] Zaitchik, 2009[b].

[852] Ibid.

[853] Quigley, cited in Zaitchik, 2009[b].

[854] Zaitchik. 2009[b].

[855] Ibid.

[856] Zaitchik, 2009[b].

[857] Ibid.

[858] Neiwert, 2009.

[859] Taylor, 2005, p. 84.

[860] See http://www.the912project.com

[861] Rose, 2010, p. 56.

[862] Ibid.

[863] Beck, 2009.

[864] Almond, 2009.

[865] Romano, 2010.

[866] See http://www.freedomworks.org

[867] Jones, 2009.

[868] Sullivan, 2010.

[869] See for example, Jones, 2009 and Sullivan, 2010.

[870] McChesney, 2010, pp. 13–14.

[871] See "Profile: Citizens for Honest Government—Pat Matrisciana" (n.d.) at http://www.publiceye.org/conspire/clinton/Clintonculwar8-13.html

[872] Cited in Boehlert, 2009, April 16.

[873] Boehlert, 2009, April 16.

[874] Ibid.

[875] Montopoli, 2010.

[876] Ibid.

[877] Beck, cited in Lendman, 2009.

[878] See for example, Walsh 2009 for a brief summary of the nine-page DHS report.

[879] Boehlert, 2009, April 7.

[880] Ibid.

[881] Ibid.

[882] Winant, 2009.

[883] While awaiting his trial, von Brunn died in January 2010.

[884] Carson, 2008.

[885] Karlin, 2009.

[886] See for example Starr, 2001 and Zinn, 2000.

[887] Harvey, 2005, p. 66; McChesney, 1999, p. 11.

[888] Giroux, 2004, p. 46.

[889] Roy, 2004, p. 67.

[890] Ibid, p. 54, 56.

REFERENCES

Aaron, C. (2004). Mission accomplished? Lowlights of the Bush administration. *Dissent*. Retrieved May 16, 2009, from http://www.dissentmagazine.org/article/?article=333

Ackerman, S. (2006, August 7). The growing ranks of the conservative purged. *The New Republic*. Retrieved February 23, 2007, from http://www.tnr.com/doc.mhtml?i=w060807&s=ackerman080706

Ackerman, S. (2001, July/August). The most biased name in news. *Extra!* Retrieved May 30, 2008, from http://www.fair/org

Akhavi, K. (2007, October 27). Welcome to 'Islamo-Fascism Awareness Week'. Retrieved December 4, 2007, from http://www.antiwar.com/ips/akhavi.php?articleid=11824

Alam, M. J. (2006, January 30). A snapshot of the right wing tactics. *Alternet*. Retrieved March 5, 2006, from http://www.alternet.org/wiretap/31536

Alam, M. S. (2005, February 2). O'Reilly's fatwah on "un-American" professors: Fox News puts me in its crosshairs. *Counterpunch*. Retrieved February 7, 2008, from http://www.counterpunch.org/shahid 02022005.html

Allen, J., Jr. (2003, February 14). American Catholic leaders protest Novak visit to Vatican. *National Catholic Reporter*. Retrieved September 16, 2006 from http://www.natcath.org/NCR_Online/archives/ 021403/021403d.htm

Almond, S. (2009, September 12). Glenn Beck is the future of literary fiction. Retrieved June 23, 2010, from http://www.salon.com/books/feature/2009/09/12/rightwing_bestsellers

Alterman, E. (2008, April 14). Who are they calling elitist? *The Nation, 286*(14), 14, 16–18.

Alterman, E. (2005, April 21). Bush's war on the press. *The Nation*. Retrieved June 5, 2008, from http:// www.thenation.com/doc/20050509/alterman

Alterman, E. (2004, October 14). Think again: 'Ideas have consequences: So does money'. *Center for American Progress*. Retrieved October 25, 2006, from http://www.americanprogress.org/issues/2004/ 10/b222111.html

Alterman, E. (2003). *What liberal media: The truth about bias and the news*. New York: Basic Books.

Alterman, E. (2001, November 29). A growing campaign for patriotic correctness on campus. *Consortium News*. Retrieved July 3, 2005, from http://www.msnbc.com/news/663403.asp

Alterman, E. (1997, October 21). How to succeed in media by being a clueless right-wing babe in a leopard skin miniskirt. *Salon*. Retrieved November 14, 2006, from www.salon.com/media/1997/10/21 ingraham.html

Ambinder, M. (2002). Vast, right-wing cabal? Meet the most powerful conservative group you've never heard of ABCNews.com. Retrieved May 23, 2003, from http://abcnews.go.com/sections/politics/ DailyNews/council_020501.html

American Council of Trustees and Alumni (2005). *Intellectual diversity: Time for action*. Washington, D.C.: ACTA Publications. Retrieved April 15, 2006, from https://www.goacta.org/publications/ downloads/IntellectualDiversityFinal.pdf

Ames, M., & Levine, Y. (2010, March 3). The Rick Santelli 'Tea Party' controversy: Article kicks up a media dust storm. eXiled Online. Retrieved April 30, 2010, from http://www.alternet.org/story/129656

Anderson, B. (2003, n.d.). Why FOX news beat the mainstream media. Retrieved June 30, 2008, from http://www.taemag.com/issues/articleid.17888/article_detail.asp

Apple, M. (2006, April 27). A review of The Professors: The 101 most dangerous academics in America. *Teachers College Record*. Retrieved May 13, 2007, from http://www.tcrecord.org

Auletta, K. (2003, May 26). Vox Fox: How Roger Ailes and Fox News are changing cable news. *The New Yorker*. Retrieved April 6, 2010, from http://www.kenauletta.com/voxfox.html

Bacon, D. (2003). Screened out: How 'fighting terrorism' became a bludgeon in Bush's assault on labor. *The Nation, 276*(18), 19–20, 22.

Balch, S. (2005, November 9). *Report to the select committee of the Pennsylvania House of Representatives*. Retrieved April 16, 2007, from http://www.nas.org/reports/Balch_PA_Reps/pa_legisl_statmt.pdf

REFERENCES

Barstow, D. (2008, April 20). Behind TV analysts, pentagon's hidden hand. *The New York Times.* Retrieved September 7, 2009, from http://www.nytimes.com.2008/04/20/us/20generals.html

Bass, W. (2007, January 14). Incendiary. [Review of The enemy at home: The cultural left and its responsibility for 9/11]. *The Washington Post.* Retrieved February 14, 2007, from http://www. washingtonpost.com

Beeman, W. (2003, May 8). Who is Michael Ledeen? *Alternet.* Retrieved April 11, 2007, from http://www. alternet.org/story/15860

Behan, R. (2003, June 4). The free-market Al-Qaeda: Neoliberal think tanks and the harm they do. *The Baltimore Chronicle.* Retrieved November 15, 2006, from http://www.baltimorechronicle.com/ jun03_behan.html

Beinin, J. (2006). The new McCarthyism: Policing thought about the Middle East. In B. Doumani (Ed.), *Academic freedom after 9/11* (pp. 237–266). New York: Zone Books.

Beinin, J. (2004). The new McCartyhism: Policing thought about the Middle East. *Race & Class, 46*(1), 101–115.

Beirich, H., & Potok, M. (2003). Keeping America White. *Southern Poverty Law Center Intelligence Report,* Issue # 112. Retrieved May 27, 2010, from http://www.splcenter.org

Bellant, R. (1988a). *The Coors connection: How Coors family philanthropy undermines democratic pluralism.* Boston: South End Press.

Bellant. R. (1988b). *Old Nazis, the new right, and the Republican party.* Boston: South End Press.

Bennett, L. (2005). *News: The politics of illusion* (6th ed.). New York: Longman.

Berkowitz, B. (2006, March 3). Michael Joyce (1942–2006). *Media Transparency.* Retrieved November 3, 2006, from http://www.mediatransparency.org

Berkowitz, B. (2005a, September 15). Heritage foundation capitalizes on Katrina. *Media Transparency.* Retrieved February 22, 2007, from http://www.mediatransparency.org/story.php?storyID=85

Berkowitz, B. (2005b, August 26). The politics of slander. *Media Transparency.* Retrieved January 10, 2007, from http://www.mediatransparency.org/story.php?storyID=82

Berkowitz, B. (2005c, July 14). David Horowitz's battlefield academia. *WorkingForChange.* Retrieved April 23, 2007, from http://www.commondreams.org/views05/0714-23.htm

Berkowitz, B. (2004, November 30). The kids are all Right: Collegiate network turns 25. *Media Transparency.* Retrieved October 24, 2006, from http://www.mediatransparency.org.recipientprofile. php?recipientID=74

Berkowitz, B. (2004, October 8). Horowitz's campus jihads. *WorkingForChange.* Retrieved October 9, 2004, from http://www.workingforchange.com/itemid=17838

Berkowitz, B. (2003, March 7). Ousting a rightwing Savage. *Alternet.* Retrieved May 30, 2007, from http://www.alternet.org/story/15333

Berkowitz, B. (2003, February 21). Michael Novak's divine mission. *WorkingForChange.* Retrieved October 24, 2006, from http://www.workingforchange.comprintitem.cfm?itemid=14538

Berkowitz, B. (2001, June). The Heritage foundation soars. *Z Magazine.* Retrieved January 14, 2007, from http://www.zmag.org/ZMag/articles/june01berkowitz.htm

Berlet, C., Rastegar, M., & Chamberlain, P. (2002). *Nativism.* Retrieved June 5, 2010, from http://www. publiceye.org/ark/immigrans/Nativism.html

Berlet, C., & Lyons, M. (2000). *Right-wing populism in America: Too close for comfort.* New York: The Guilford Press.

Berube, M. (2006). What does "academic freedom" mean? *Academe.* Retrieved April 12, 2007, from http://www.aaup.org/AAUP/pubsres/academe/2006/ND/Feat/beru.htm

Blumenthal, M. (2008, December 9). Who started the war on Christmas? *The Daily Beast.* Retrieved April 22, 2010, from http://www.thedailybeast.com/blogs-and-stories/2008-12-09/who-strated-the-war-on-christmas

Blumenthal, M. (2006, April 26). The demons of David Horowitz. Retrieved May 10, 2007, from http://maxblumenthal.blogspot.com/2006/04/demons-of-david-horowitz-since-david.html

Blumenthal, M. (2006, September 11). ABC 9/11 docudrama's right wing roots. *The Nation.* Retrieved November 22, 2006, from http://www.thenation.com/doc/20060925/path_to_911

Blumenthal, M. (2005, June 28). Generation chickenhawk. *The Nation.* Retrieved July 22, 2005, from http://www.thenation.com/doc.mhtml?1=20050711&s=blumenthal

Blumenthal, M. (2005, June 3). Hannity's soul mate of hate. *The Nation.* Retrieved April 4, 2007, from http://www.thenation.com/doc/20050620/blumenthal

Blumenthal, S. (1988). *The rise of the counter-establishment: From conservative ideology to political power.* New York: Harper and Row.

Bleifuss, J. (2005, January 31). R.I.P FDR? *In These Times.* Retrieved November 15, 2006, from http://www.inthesetimes.com/site/main/article/1905

Boehlert, E. (2010, April 6). Post-Hutaree: How Glenn Beck and Fox News spread the militia message. Retrieved June 18, 2010, from http://mediamatters.org

Boehlert, E. (2009, April 16). Fox News' militia media: mainstreaming the fringe. Retrieved June 29, 2010, from http://mediamatters.org

Boehlert, E. (2009, April 7). Glenn Beck and the rise of Fox News's militia media. Retrieved February 11, 2010, from http://www.truthout.org

Boettcher, R., & Freeman, G. (1980). *Gifts of deceit: Sun Myung Moon, Tongson Park and the Korean scandal.* New York: Holt, Rinehart & Winston.

Borosage, R. (2003, February 13). Questionable heritage: Thirty years of a right-wing think tank. Retrieved February 22, 2007, from http://www.tompaine.com/Archive/scontent/7269.html

Britt, L. (2003). Fascism anyone? *Free Inquiry Magazine, 23*(2). Retrieved April 4, 2005, from http://www.secularhumanism.org/index.php?section=library&page=britt_23_2

Brock, D. (2004). *The Republican noise machine: Right-wing media and how it corrupts democracy.* New York: Crown Publishers.

Brock, D. (2003). *Blinded by the right: The conscience of an ex-conservative.* New York: Three Rivers Press.

Broder, J., & Conason, J. (1998, June 8). The American Spectator's funny money. *Salon Newsreal.* Retrieved September 7, 2006, from http://www.salon.com.news/1998/06/cov_08news.html

Brodsky, D. (2005, November). "Academic Bill of Rights" wrongs academic freedom, privileges right-wing power in higher education. *The Faculty Advocate, 6*(1&2). Retrieved June 11, 2007, from http://cas.umkc.edu/aaup/abor.htm

Brown, J. (2007). Conservative group lists annual Dirty Dozen, most PC college courses. Retrieved November 4, 2008, from http://www.culturallegacy.org

Buckley, W. F. (1986[orig. 1951]). *God and man at Yale: The superstitions of 'academic freedom.'* Illinois: Regnery Gateway.

Buckley, W.F. (1955, November 19). The magazine's credenda. *National Review.* Retrieved January 7, 2007 from http://www.nationalreview.com/articles/223549/our-mission-statement/william-f-buckley-jr

Buckley, W.F., & Bozell, B. (1954). *McCarthy and his enemies: The record and its meaning.* Chicago: Henry Regnery Co.

Bugliosi, V. (2001). *The betrayal of America: How the Supreme Court undermined the constitution and chose our president.* New York: Nation Books.

Bush, G. W. (2003, May 1). *Loyalty day, 2003: A proclamation.* Retrieved July 20, 2006, from http://www.whitehouse.gov/news/releases/2003/04/20030430-26.html

Bush, G. W. (2001a, September 11). *Statement by the President in his address to the nation.* Retrieved October 8, 2006, from http://www.whitehouse.gov/news/releases/2001/09/20010911-16.html

Bush, G. W. (2001b, September 20). *Address to a joint session of Congress and the American people.* Retrieved October 8, 2006, from http://www.whitehouse.gov/news/releases/2001/09/20010920-8.html

Campbell, B. (2001, May 24). State education commission coming under fire. *Colorado Springs Independent.* Retrieved April 16, 2007, from http://www.csindy.com/2001-05-24/news2.html

Carson, B. (2008, July 29). Jim Adkisson read books by Savage, O'Reilly, and Hannity. *NowPublic.* Retrieved June 14, 2009, from http://www.nowpublic.com/culture/jim-adkisson-read-books-savage-oreilly-and-hannity

REFERENCES

Cha, A. E. (2004, May 23). In Iraq, the job opportunity of a lifetime: Managing a $13 billion budget with no experience. *Washington Post*. Retrieved January 23, 2007, from http://www.washington post.com

Chihara, M. (2001, December 26). The silence on terrorism. *AlterNet*. Retrieved March 17, 2004, from http://www.alternet.org/story.html?StoryID=12145

Chomsky, N. (2001). *9/11*. New York: Seven Stories Press.

Chomsky, N. (1997). *Media control: The spectacular achievements of propaganda*. New York: Seven Stories Press.

Churchill, W. (2007). The myth of academic freedom: Personal experiences of a liberal principle in the neoconservative era (fragments of work in progress). *Social Text, 25*(1), 17–39.

Churchill, W. (2001, September 12). Some people push back: On the justice of roosting chickens. Retrieved October 7, 2006, from http://www.ratical.org/ratville/CAH/WC091201.html

Clarke, C. (2006, August 1). My open exchange with a conservative spokesman ... before he threw me out of his conference. *Think Progress*. Retrieved March 30, 2007, from http://thinkprogress.org/2006/08/01/yaf-ejection

Cloud, D. (2009, April 29). The McCarthyism that Horowitz built: The cases of Margo Ramlal Nankoe, William Robinson, Nagesh Rao, and Loretta Capeheart. *MRzine*. Retrieved May 21, 2009, from http://www.monthlyreview.org/mrzine/cloud290409p.html

CNN.com. (2001, February 18). *New executive orders outrage organized labor*. Retrieved March 12, 2008, from http://transcripts.cnn.com/TRANSCRIPTS/0102/18/sm14.html

Cockburn, A. (1991, May 27). Bush and P.C.—A conspiracy so immense. *The Nation, 685*, 690–691, 704.

Cohen, J. (2006). *Cable news confidential: My misadventures in corporate media*. Sausalito, CA: PoliPoint Press.

Cohen, S. (1972). *Folk devils and moral panics: The creation of the mods and rockers*. Londong: MacGibbon and Kee.

Colapinto, J. (2003, May 25). Armies of the right: The young hipublicans. *New York Times Magazine*. Retrieved November 11, 2006, from http://www.bucknellconservatives.org/press/NYT.shtml

Cole, J. (2007, February 4). *Informed comment*. Retrieved July 20, 2008, from www.juancole.com/2007/02/sunni_arab_guerillas_massacre-155html

Collier, P. (2005, August 26). Heterodoxy lives. *Front Page Magazine*. Retrieved April 25, 2007, from http://www.frontpagemag.com/Articles/ReadArticle.asp?ID=19271

Conason, J. (2007). *It can happen here: Authoritarian peril in the age of Bush*. New York: St. Martin's Press.

Conason, J. (2003). *Big lies: The right-wing propaganda machine and how it distorts the truth*. New York: St. Martin's Press.

Conason, J. (2001, April 24). Blinded by the right. *Salon*. Retrieved December 3, 2006, from http://archive.salon.com/news/col/cona/2001/04/24/weyrich.html

Conway, M., Grabe, M. E., & Grieves, K. (2007). Villians, victims and the virtuous in Bill O'Reilly's 'No Spin Zone'. *Journalism Studies, 8*(2), 197–223.

Cooper, M. (2007, January 8/15). About face: The growing antiwar movement in the military. *The Nation, 284*(2), 11–14, 16.

Corcoran, M. (2009, August 3). Trying to make 'Sense' of Glenn Beck: The conservative icon's latest book blends Beck's typical hyperbole with a gross misrepresentation of Thomas Paine's political views. Retrieved May 2, 2010, from http://www.campusprogress.org

Costa, N., & Maloy, S. (2005, February 11). Jeff Gannon's alma mater: The Leadership Institute. *Media Matters for America*. Retrieved March 9, 2007, from http://mediamatters.org

Coulter, A. (2001). This is war. *National Review*. Retrieved November 7, 2001 from http://old.National review.com/coulter/coulter.shtml

Covington, S. (1997). How conservative philanthropies and think tanks transform US policy. *Covert Action Quarterly, 63*. Retrieved March 1, 2001, from http://mediafilter.org/CAQ/caq63/caq63think tank.html

Cribb, T.K. (1990). Conservatism and the American academy: Prospects for the 1990s. *The Intercollegiate Review, 25*(2), 23–30. Retrieved May 17, 2008, from http://www.mmisi.org/ir/25_02/crib.pdf

Croteau, D. (1998, July/August). Challenging the "liberal media" claim. *Extra!, 4–9.*

Cypher, J. M. (2007, June). From military Keynesianism to global-neoliberal militarism. *Monthly Review.* Retrieved June 7, 2009, from http://monthlyreview.org/0607jmc.htm

Debord, G. (1988). *Comments on the society of the Spectacle.* London and New York: Verso.

Decter, M. (2003). *Rumsfeld: A personal portrait.* New York: Regan Books.

Democratic Policy Committee. (2003, November 4). The Bush administration's anti-labor record is bad for working families. Retrieved May 14, 2008, from http://democrats.senate.gov/dpc/dpc-newcfm?doc_name=sr-108-1-385

DeParle, J. (2005, June 14). Next generation of conservatives (by the dormful). *The New York Times.* Retrieved January 6, 2007, from http://www.nytimes.com/2005/06/14/politics/14heritage.html

DeParle, J. (2005, May 29). Goals reached, donor on right closes up shop. *The New York Times.* Retrieved July 12, 2005, from http://www.nytimes.com/2005/05/29/politics/29olin.html

DeYoung, M. (2001, January 24). U.S. taxpayers still foot bill for abortions abroad. Retrieved May 17, 2009, from http://www.all.org/world/wo010124.htm

Diamond, S. (1995a). The *Christian right seeks dominion: On the road to political power and theocracy.* Retrieved March, 2008, from http://www.publiceye.org/eyes/sd-theo.html

Diamond, S. (1995). *Roads to dominion: Right-wing movements and political power in the United States.* New York: Guilford Press.

Dionne, E. J. (2005, June 28). The new McCarthyism. *The Washington Post.* Retrieved June 30, 2007, from http://www.washingtonpost.com

Dixon, N. (2004, May 5). How the Bush gang seized the 'opportunity' of 9/11. Retrieved June 24, 2009, from http://links.org.au/node/402

Doster, A. (2007, December). Wingnut awareness week: Neocons beat the war drum on college campuses. *In These Times, 31*(12), 47–48.

Doumani, B. (Ed.). (2006). Between coercion and privatization: Academic freedom in the twenty-first century. *In Academic freedom after September 11.* (pp. 11–57). New York: Zone Books.

Dreyfuss, R. (2001, May 14). Grover Norquist: 'Field marshal' of the Bush plan. *The Nation.* Retrieved November 15, 2006, from http://www.thenation.com/doc/20010514/dreyfuss

Drury, S. (1988). *The political ideas of Leo Strauss.* New York: St. Martin's Press.

D'Souza, D. (2002). *Letters to a young conservative.* New York: Basic Books.

D'Souza, D. (1995). *The end of racism: Principles for a multicultural society.* New York: The Free Press.

D'Souza, D. (1991). *Illiberal education: The politics of race and sex on campus.* New York: Free Press.

Ducat, S. (2004). *The wimp factor: Gender gaps, holy wars and the politics of anxious masculinity.* Boston: Beacon Press.

Durham, M. (2004). The American right and the framing of 9/11. *The Political Quarterly, 75*(1), 17–25.

Duss, M. (2010, April 5). Attack of the Cheneys. *The Nation, 290*(13), 11–12, 14, 17.

Dylan, R. (2007). David Horowitz's reactionary road show must be confronted and exposed: You can't defeat fascism by ignoring it. *Revolution*, 103. Retrieved June 2, 2009, from http://revcom.us/a/103/islamo-fascism-awareness-week-en.html

Easterbrook, G. (1986). Ideas move nations: How conservative think tanks have helped to transform the terms of political debate. *The Atlantic Monthly, 257*(7), 66–80. Retrieved June 27, 2005, from http://www.theatlantic.com/politics/polibig/eastidea.htm

Ehrenreich, B. (2004, July 1). Dude, where's that elite? *New York Times.* Retrieved July 22, 2008, from http://www.commondreams.org

Eco, U. (1995, November/December). Eternal fascism. *UTNE Reader, 72*, 57–59.

Editorial Board. (2003, June 21). Weapons of mass destruction in Iraq: Bush's 'big lie' and the crisis of American imperialism. *World Socialist Web Site.* Retrieved September 14, 2006, from http://www.wsws.org/articles/2003/jun2003/wmd-j21.shtml

Elsner, A. (2002, September 3). Bush expands government secrecy, arouses critics. Retrieved June 5, 2008, from http://www.fas.org/sgp/news/2002/09re090302.html

REFERENCES

Evans, M. S. (1961). *Revolt on the campus*. Chicago: Henry Regnery Co.

Ewen, S. (1996). *PR! A social history of spin*. New York: Basic Books.

Faludi, S. (2007). *The terror dream: Myth and misogyny in an insecure America*. New York: Picador.

Farrell, H. (2007, June 11). Why we shouldn't play nice with David Horowitz: A response to What's Liberal about the Liberal Arts. Retrieved July 2, 2007, from http://crookedtimber.org/2007/06/11/why-we-shouldn't-play-nice-with-david-horowitz-a-response-to-what's-liberal-about-the-liberal-arts

Feulner, E. (2004, November 2). Marketplace of ideas would free universities from liberal tyranny. Retrieved February 9, 2007, from http://www.heritage.org/Press/Commentary/ed110204a

Field, K. (2007, January 12). Recruiting for the right. *The Chronicle of Higher Education, 53*(19), A33. Retrieved March 15, 2007, from http://chronicle.com/weekly/v53/i19/19a03301.htm

Fish, S. (2005, April 1). On balance. *The Chronicle of Higher Education*. Retrieved January 2007, from http://chronicle.com/article/On-Balance/44890/

Flanders, L. (1994, September 1). The "stolen feminism" hoax. *FAIR/Extra*. Retrieved October 4, 2006, from http://www.fair.org/index.php?page=1246

Follman, M. (2004, August 25). Right-hook. *Salon*. Retrieved January 19, 2007, from http://www.salon.com/story/opinion/right_hook/2004/08/25/mc.protest/index.html

Fost, D. (2003, July 9). Savage says he's sorry—but stays fired. *San Francisco Chronicle*. Retrieved May 30, 2007, from http://www.sfgate.com/cgi-bin/article.cgi?file=/c/a/2003/07/09/MN158024.DTL

Fox News: The O'Reilly Factor (2005, February 2). Professor [Shahid Alam] compared terrorists to founding fathers. Retrieved June 1, 2010, from http://www.danielpipes.org/2394/professor-shadid-alam-compared-terrorists-to-founding

Frank, T. (2008). *The wrecking crew: How conservatives rule*. New York: Metropolitan Books.

Frank, T. (2004). *What's the matter with Kansas? How conservatives won the heart of America*. New York: Henry Holt and Company.

Franken, A. (2003). *Lies and the lying liars who tell them: A fair and balanced look at the right*. New York: Dutton.

Freedom Center Students (2010). Student guide: Teach-in to oppose Barack Obama's radical transformation of America. Retrieved June 3, 2010 from http://freedomcenterstudents.org/wp-content/uploads/2010/02/Student-Guide-for-Obama-Teach-in.pdf

Free Exchange on Campus (2006, May). Facts count: An analysis of David Horowitz's The Professors: The 101 Most Dangerous Academics in America. Retrieved April 17, 2009, from http://www.freeexchangeoncampus.org

Free Exchange on Campus (2009, April 13). Facts still count: An analysis of David Horowitz's One Party Classroom. Retrieved July 22, 20009 from http://www.freeexchangeoncampus.org

Friedman, T. L. (1999, March 28). A manifesto for the fast world. *New York Times*. Retrieved June 27, 2006, from http://www.globalpolicy.org/nations/fried99.htm

Fritz, B., Keefer, B., & Nyhan, B. (2004). Excerpt: All the President's Spin. Retrieved June 12, 2008, from http:// www.mediabistro.com/articles/cache/a2124.asp?pntvs+1&

Fritz, B. (2003, February 19). Savage with the truth. Salon.com. Reprinted in C. Willis (Ed.), *The I hate Ann Coulter, Bill O'Reilly, Rush Limbaugh, Michael Savage, Sean Hannity reader*. New York: Thunder Mouth Press, 2004, 319–324.

Gabbard, D., & Atkinson, T. (2007). Stossel in America: A case study of the neoliberal/neoconservative assault on public schools and teachers. *Teacher Education Quarterly* (pp. 85–109). Retrieved June 4, 2010, from http://www.teqjournal.org

Gabbard, D. & Anijar, K. (2006). Think-tank fascism & the jihad against liberal professors. *Public Resistance*, 2(1). http://web.mac.com/publicresistance/iWeb/publicresistance/Public Resistance.html

Galeano, E. (2003, February). Terror in disguise. *The Progressive*, 18–19.

Galeano, E. (2000). *Upside down: A primer for the looking-glass world*. New York: Henry Holt.

Gasper, P. (2007). Bush's other failing war. *International Socialist Review, 51*, 28–29.

Gee, M. (2002, June 11). Is Henry Kissinger a war criminal? *Toronto Globe & Mail*. Retrieved April 4, 2009, from http://www.commondreams.org/views02/0611-03.htm

Giroux, H. (2006). Academic freedom under fire: The case for critical pedagogy. *College Literature*, *33*(4), 1–42.

Giroux, H. (2005). Cultural studies in dark times: Public pedagogy and the challenge of neoliberalism. *Fast Capitalism*. Retrieved November 15, 2006, from http://www.henryagiroux.com/online_articles/DarkTimes.htm

Giroux, H. (2004). *The terror of neoliberalism: Authoritarianism and the eclipse of democracy*. Boulder, CO: Paradigm Publishers.

Gitlin, T. (2003, February 1). We disport, we deride. *The American Prospect*. Retrieved May 3, 2009, from http://www.prospect.org/cs/articles?article=we_disport_we_deride

Goldberg, M. (2006). *Kingdom coming: The rise of Christian nationalism*. New York: W.W. Norton & Company.

Goldberg, M. (2005, February 19). Among the believers. Salon.com. Retrieved April 11, 2007, from http://dir.salon.com/story/news/feature/2005/02/19/cpac/index.html

Goldwater, C. C. (2006, September 16). Goldwater today: CC Goldwater on what her grandfather would make of today's GOP. *Newsweek*. Retrieved October 30, 2006, from http://www.msnbc.msn.com/id/14863898/site/newsweek

Goldstein, R. (2003, March 24). Neo-macho man. *The Nation*.

Goode, S. (1999, February 1). A new offensive in the campus culture war—Morton C. Blackwell; Campus Leadership Program—interview. *Insight on the News*. Retrieved March 15, 2007, from http://www.findarticles.com

Goodman, A. (2005, April 6). Columbia U. Prof Rashid Khalidi: *Freedom of speech and academic freedom are necessary for unpopular and difficult ideas*. Retrieved April 14, 2005, from http://www.democracynow.org/2005/4/6/columbia-u-prof-rashid-khalidi-freedom

Gorenfeld, J. (2005, April 12). Roger Ebert and Mohammed Atta, partners in crime. *Salon*. Retrieved May 16, 2008, from http://www.salon.com/news/feature/2005/04/12/horowitz_database

Gorenfeld, J. (2003, September 24). Bad Moon on the rise. *Salon*. Retrieved October 8, 2004, from http://www.salon.com/news/feature/2003/09/24/moon/print.html

Gough, P. (2008, November 5). Fox News' Brit Hume leaving for family, religion. *Reuters*. Retrieved December 12, 2008, from http://www.reuters.com

Gowans, S. (2003, January 8). Ex-Bush speechwriter: I was to provide a justification for war. *What's Left*. Retrieved May 18, 2005, from http://www.globalpolicy.org/security/issues/iraq/attack/2003/0108speechwriter.htm

Gramsci, A. (1971). *Selections from the prison notebooks* (Q. Hoare & G. N. Smith, Ed. and Trans.). New York: International Publishers.

Gravois, J. (2007, October 19). *Chronicle of Higher Education*, *54*(8), p. A11.

Greene, A. (2005, December 2). Funding father: John Olin, the money man behind the vast right-wing conspiracy. *Campus Progress*. Retrieved October 25, 2006, from http://www.campusprogress.org/soundvision/671/funding-father

Greenslade, R. (2003, February 17). Their master's voice. *The Guardian*. Retrieved June 17, 2008, from http://www.guardian.co.uk/media/2003/feb/17/mondaymediasectioniraq

Greider, W. (2004, June 28). The Gipper's economy. *The Nation*, *278*(25), 5–6.

Greider, W. (2003, May 12). Rolling back the 20th century. *The Nation*. Retrieved November 9, 2006, from http://www.thenation.com/doc/20030512/greider

Hart, P. (2010, April). Glenn Beck gets progressively more paranoid. *Extra!* Retrieved June 23, 2010, from http://www.fair.org/index.php?page=4052

Hart, P. & Jackson, J. (2006, May/June). Stossel's "stupid" schools: A beginner's course in deceptive reporting. *Extra!* Retrieved April 11, 2007, from http://www.fair.org/index.php?page=2894

Harvey, D. (2005). *A brief history of neoliberalism*. Oxford and New York: Oxford University Press.

Hayes, C. (2007, June 11). Hip heterodoxy: Neoclassical economics still reigns, but its critics are gathering steam. *The Nation*, *284*(23), 18, 20–24.

Hedges, C. (2006). *American fascists: The Christian right and the war on America*. New York: Free Press.

Henson, S. (1991, September 20). The education of Dinesh D'Souza. *The Texas Observer*, 6–7, 9.

REFERENCES

Herman, E. (1997). Pol Pot and Kissinger: On war criminality and impunity. *Third World Traveler*. Retrieved March 7, 2009, from http://www.thirdworldtraveler.com/Kissinger/PolPotKissinger-Herman.html

Herman, E., & Chomsky, N. (1988). *Manufacturing consent: The political economy of the mass media*. New York: Pantheon Books.

Hersh, B. (1978). *The Mellon family: A fortune in history*. New York: William Morrow.

Himmelstein, J. L. (1990). *To the right: The transformation of American conservatism*. Berkeley, CA: University of California Press.

Hitchens, C. (2003, August 11). Pipes the propagandist: Bush's nominee doesn't belong at the U.S. Institute for Peace. *Slate*. Retrieved April 4, 2007, from http://slate.msn.com

Hitchens, C. (2001, March). The case against Henry Kissinger, Part One: The making of a war criminal. *Harper's Magazine*. Retrieved March 7, 2009, from http://www.thirdworldtraveler.com/Kissinger/CaseAgainst1-Hitchens.html

Hollinger, D. (2005, February 28). What does it mean to be 'balanced' in academia? *History News Network*. Retrieved April 14, 2008, from http://hnn.us/articles/10194.html

Holmes, S. (2006, May 1). John Yoo's tortured logic [Review of The powers of war and peace: The constitution and foreign affairs after 9/11]. *The Nation, 282*(17), 31–32, 34, 36–39.

Holthouse, D. (2009, February 26). 'Right-Wing Youth' group debuts at CPAC. *Southern Poverty Law Center: Hatewatch*. Retrieved May 18, 2010, from http://www.splcenter.org

Horowitz, D. (2009). The art of political war for tea parties. *FrontPage Magazine*. Retrieved June 6, 2010, from http://frontpagemag.com/2009/12/01/the-art-of-political-war-for-tea-parties-by-david-horowitz

Horowitz, D. (2006). *The professors: The 101 most dangerous academics in America*. Washington: Regnery Publishing.

Horowitz, D. (2004, February 13). In defense of intellectual diversity. *The Chronicle of Higher Education*. Retrieved March 4, 2007, from http://chronicle.com/article/In-Defense-of-Intellectual/10135

Horowitz, D. (2003a, April 18). The campus blacklist. *Front Page Magazine*. Retrieved June 11, 2007, from http://www.frontpagemag.com/Articles/ID=7357

Horowitz, D. (2003b). *The art of political war*. Dallas, TX: Spence.

Horowitz, D. (2001b, September 26). The sick mind of Noam Chomsky. Salon.com. Retrieved November 14, 2006, from http://archive.salon.com/news/col/horo/2001/09/26/treason/index_np.html

Horowitz, D. (2001a, September 19). The enemy within. FrontPageMagazine.com. Retrieved April 22, 2007, from http://www.frontpagemag.com/Articles/ReadArticle.asp?ID=4520

Horowitz, D. (1999). *Hating whitey and other progressive causes*. Dallas, TX: Spence

Horwitz, J. (2005, May 25). My right-wing degree. Salon. Retrieved March 1, 2007, from http://dir.salon.com/story/news/feature/2005/05/25/blackwell/index.html

Houppert, K. (2002, November 25). Wanted: A few good girls. Retrieved October 4, 2006, from http://www.thenation.com/doc/20021125/houppert

Howell, L. (1995, July 19). Funding the war of ideas—conservative foundations. *Christian Century*. Retrieved November 1, 2006, from http://www.findarticles.com/p/articles/mi_m1058/is_n22_v112/ai_17099791

Huberman, J. (2006, June 23). Who's really screwing America. *The Nation*. Retrieved April 16, 2007, from http://www.thenation.com/doc/20060710/huberman/5

Hughes, K. (2004). *Ten minutes from normal*. New York: Viking.

Husseini, S., & Solomon, N. (1998, July/August). The right-leaning rolodex. *Extra!* 13.

Independent Women's Forum. (2004, April 5). Top then things professors do to skew you. Retrieved January 8, 2007, from http://www.iwf.org/issues/issues_detail.asp?ArticleID=559

Jacobson, J. (2005, May 6). What makes David run: David Horowitz demands attention for the idea that conservatives deserve a place in academe. *Chronicle of Higher Education, 51*(35), A9.

Jacoby, R. (2005, April 4). The new pc: Crybaby conservatives. *The Nation, 280*(13), *11*, 13–16.

James, J. (2003). Imprisoned intellectuals: War, dissent, and social justice. *Radical History Review, 85*, 74–81.

Jaschik, S. (2007, October 29). Furor over anti-Islam speaker. *Inside Higher Ed*. Retrieved April 29, 2010, from http://www.insidehighered.com/news/2007/10/29/islam

Jaschik, S. (2006, January 18). The new class monitors. *Inside Higher Ed*. Retrieved June 3, 2007, from http://www.insidehighered.com/news/2006/01/18/ucla

Jensen, R. (2001, March 24). Horowitz and the myth of the radical university. *Common Dreams News Center*. Retrieved November 18, 2006, from http://www.commondreams.org

Jones, S. (2009, September 16). The right's fringe festival. *The Nation*. Retrieved April 26, 2010, from http://www.thenation.com

Judis, J. B. (2001). *The paradox of American democracy*. New York: Routledge.

Juhasz, A. (2006). *The Bush agenda: Invading the world, one economy at a time*. New York: Regan Books.

Kagan, D. (2002). Terrorism and the intellectuals. *The Intercollegiate Review*.

Kaiser, R. G. (1999, May 3). Money, family name shaped Scaife. *Washington Post*, p. A1. Retrieved September 11, 2006, from http://www.washingtonpost.com/wp-srv/politics/special/Clinton/stories/scaifemain050399

Kaiser, R. G., & Chinoy, I. (1999, May 2). Scaife: Funding father of the right. *Washington Post*, p. A1. Retrieved September 11, 2006, from http://www.washingtonpost.com/wp-srv/politics/special/Clinton/stories/scaifemain050299

Kaplan, E. (2007, October 26). The culture war descends on Columbia. *The Nation*. Retrieved December 4, 2007, from http://www.thenation.com/doc/20071112/kaplan

Karlin, M. (2009, August 27). FOX won't fire Glenn Beck: Here's why. Retrieved February 11, 2010, from http://blog.buzzflash.com

Karlin, M. (2008, April 1). Max Blumenthal probes Hannity's history with talk radio's 'angry white men'—and fanning the flames of racial politics. *A Buzzflash Interview*. Retrieved June 4, 2008, from http://blogbuzzflash.com/interviews/102

Katsiaficas, G. (2003). Conclusion: The real axis of evil. In C. Boggs (Ed.), *Masters of war: Militarism and blowback in the era of American empire* (pp. 343–355). New York: Routledge.

Kellner, D. (2001). *Grand theft 2000: Media spectacle and a stolen election*. Lanham, MD: Rowman & Littlefield.

Kimball, R. (2005, May). Rethinking the university: a battle plan. *New Criterion, 23*. Retrieved November 8, 2006, from http://www.newcriterion.com/archive/23/may05/universe.htm

Kimball, R. (1990). *Tenured radicals*. New York: Harper and Row.

King, C. R. (2009). Some academics try to push back: Ward Churchill, the war on truth, and the improbabilities of interruption. *Cultural Studies/Critical Methodologies, 9*(1), 31–40.

Kirkpatrick, J. (1984, August 20). *Address to the Republican national convention*. Retrieved December 29, 2006, from http://www.cnn.com/ALLPOLITICS/1996/conventions/san.diego/facts/GOP.speeches.past/84.kirkpatrick.shtml

Klein, N. (2007). *The shock doctrine: The rise of disaster capitalism*. New York: Metropolitan Books.

Klein, N. (2006, August 30). Disaster capitalism: How to make money out of misery. *Guardian Unlimited*. Retrieved February 28, 2007, from http://www.guardian.co.uk/comment/story/01860675,00.html

Klein, N. (2005, May 2). The rise of disaster capitalism. *The Nation*. Retrieved February 23, 2007, from http://www.thenation.com/doc/20050502/klein

Krehely, J., House, M., & Kernan, E. (2004). *Axis of ideology: Conservative foundations and public policy*. Washington, DC: National Committee for Responsive Philanthropy.

Kristol, W., et al. (2001, September 20). Letter to President Bush on the war on terrorism. *Project for the New American Century*. Retrieved March 4, 2003, from http://www.newmaericancentury.org/Bushletter.htm

Krugman, P. (2009, June 12). The big hate. *The New York Times*. Retrieved February 11, 2010, from http://www.nytimes.com/2009/06/12/opinion/12krugman.html

Krugman, P. (2009, April 12). Tea parties forever. *The New York Times*. Retrieved June 4, 2009, from http://www.nytimes.com/2009/04/13/opinion/13krugman.html

Krugman, P. (2003, September 11). *A Buzzflash interview*. Retrieved February 22, 2007, from http://www.buzzflash.com/interviews/03/09/11.krugman.html

Kull, et al. (2003, October 2). Misperceptions, the media and the Iraq war. Retrieved May 22, 2008, from www.worldopinion.org/pipa/articles/international-security-bt/102/php?lb=brusc&pnt=102&nid=&id

Kurdziel, D., & Bidikov, L. (2006). Liberal faculty: A debate. *Campus Magazine Online*. Retrieved January 10, 2007, from http://www.campusmagazine.org

REFERENCES

Lacayo, R. (1998, April 13). Hale storm rising. *Time Magazine*. Retrieved September 12, 2006, from http://www.time.com/time/magazine/article10,9171,988120,00.html

Landay, J. (2002, August 20). The Powell manifesto: How a prominent lawyer's attack memo changed America. *Media Transparency*. Retrieved October 25, 2006, from http://www.mediatransparency.org

Lapham, L. (2004). Tentacles of rage: The Republican propaganda mill, a brief history. *Harper's Magazine*, *309*(1852). Retrieved February 6, 2007, from http://www.mindfully.org/Reform/2004/Republican-Propaganda1sep04.htm

Lapham, L. (2002). Mythography. *Harper's Magazine*, *304*(1821), 6–9.

Laurence, C. (2009, April 6). Glenn Beck: The latest blowhard on Fox News. *The First Post*. Retrieved February 11, 2010, from http://www.thefirstpost.co.uk

Lazare, D. (2005, July 20). Money and motives. *Inside Higher Ed*. Retrieved Ocotber 25, 2006, from http://www.campus-watch.org/pf.php?id=2113

Lee, C. (2006, February 14). Bush administration spent $1.6 billion to spin the news. *The Washington Post*. Retrieved June 12, 2008, from http://www.truthout.org/article/bush-administration-spen-16-billion-spin-news

Lee, K. (2002, September). Time to fight back. *Diversity*. Retrieved January 8, 2007, from http://www.taemag.com/issues/articleid16857/article_detail.asp

Lendman, S. (2009, September 18). Glenn Beck's demagoguery, right wing entremism, and racism. *Dissident Voice*, Retrieved June 14, 2010, from http://dissidentvoice.org/2009/09/glenn-becks-demagoguery-right-wing-extremism-and-racism

Leopold, J. (2009, March 20). Torture memo author John Yoo blames ruined reputation on "hippies, protesters and left-wing activists". *Alternet*. Retrieved April 16, 2009, from http://www.alternet.org

Leupp, G. (2007, October 10). Horowitz's latest hate campaign heads for campus: Spreading awareness or smearing a religion? *Counterpunch*. Retrieved December 4, 2007, from http://www.counterpunch.org/leupp10102007.html

Levitas, R. (1986). *The ideology of the new right*. Cambridge: Polity Press.

Lewis, C., & Reading-Smith, M. (2008). False pretenses. *The Center for Public Integrity*. Retrieved June 2, 2010, from http://projects.publicintegrity.org/WarCard.

Lobe, J. (2003, May 19). Leo Strauss' philosophy of deception. *Alternet*. Retrieved March 31, 2005, from http://www.alternet.org/story/15935

London, H. (1987/88). A call to the academy. *Academic Questions*, *1*(1), 189–190.

Loven, J. (2008, May 30). McClellan details culture of secrecy in Bush White House. Retrieved June 5, 2008, from http://www.wtopnews.com/?nid-116&sid-1227475

Lynn, B. (2001, January 29). Bush launches unprecedented assault on church-state separation, says watchdog group—giving tax dollars to churches violates Constitution and will lead to lawsuits, says Americans United. *Americans United for Separation of Church and State Press Release*. Retrieved June 4, 2006, from http://www.au.org/press/pr12901.htm

MacDonald, I., & Rendall, S. (2008, October 14). Islamofascism awareness week: Anti-Muslim smear-casting on campus. *CommonDreams.org*. Retrieved April 22, 2010, from http://www.commondreams.org/view/2008/10/14–12

Maguire, J. (2006). *Brainless: The lies and lunacy of Ann Coulter*. New York: Harper Collins.

Makdisi, S. (2006, January 22). Witch hunt at UCLA. *Los Angeles Times*. Retrieved July 8, 2008, from http://articles.latimes.com/2006/jan/22/opinion/op-makdisi22

Martin, J. L., & Neal, A.D. (2002). *Defending civilization: How our universities are failing America and what can be done about it*. Washington, D.C.: American Council of Trustees and Alumni.

Massing, M. (2009). Un-American: Have you listened to the right-wing media lately? *The Columbia Journalism Review*. Retrieved May 17, 2010, from http://www.cjr.org/essay/unamerican_1.php

McChesney, R. (2010). Capitalism, the absurd system. *Monthly Review*, *62*(2), 1–16.

McChesney, R. (2004). *The problem of the media: U.S. communication politics in the 21st century*. New York: Monthly Review Press.

McChesney, R. (1999). *Rich media, poor democracy: Communication politics in dubious times*. Urbana, IL: University of Illinois Press.

McChesney, R., & Foster, J. B. (2003). The 'left-wing' media? *Monthly Review, 55*(2):1–16.

McChesney, R., & Nichols, J. (2008, June 16). Who'll unplug big media? Stay tuned. *The Nation, 286*(23), 11–12, 14.

McClennen, S. A. (2006). The geopolitical war on U.S. higher education. *College Literature, 33*(4), 43–75.

McFadden, K. (2010, April 16). Political activist David Horowitz talks candidly at tea party event. Retrieved May 12, 2010, from http://www.noozhawk.com

McGarth, B. (2010). The movement: The rise of Tea Party activism. *The New Yorker*. Retrieved April 30, 2010, from http://www.newyorker.com/reporting/2010/02/01

McGarvey, A. (2005, May 30). Dr. Hager's family values. *The Nation*. Retrieved June 16, 2007, from http://www.thenation.com/issue/may-30-2005

McLaren, P. (2005). *Capitalists & conquerors: A critical pedagogy against empire*. Lanham, MD: Rowman & Littlefield.

McLaren, P., & Jaramillo, N. (2007). *Pedagogy and praxis in the age of empire: Towards a new humanism*. Rotterdam and Taipei: Sense Publishers.

McMurtry, J. (2002). *Value wars: The global market versus the life economy*. London: Pluto Press.

McNeil, K. (2003, November 11). The war on academic freedom. *The Nation*. Retrieved May 4, 2007, from http://www.thenation.com

Media Matters for America. (2009, April 22). Beck: "Whether or not you're morally in favor of water-boarding or not, it is a far cry from torture." Retrieved March 12, 2010, from http://mediamatters.org/mmtv/200904220035

Media Matters for America. (2007, October 25). O'Reilly: "[S]tudies indicate ... most teachers ... bring in a {sic} anti-American viewpoint to the sense that they don't preach about the nobility of America." Retrieved June 3, 2010, from http://mediamatters.org/research/200710250002

Media Matters for America. (2006, April 14). O'Reilly claimed to have exposed the "hidden agenda" behind the immigrant rights movement: "the browning of America." Retrieved June 3, 2010, from http://mediamatters.org/research/200604140009

Media Matters for America. (2005, November 21). O'Reilly: "War" on Christmas part of "secular progressive agenda" that includes "legalization of narcotics, euthanasia, abortion at will, gay marriage." Retrieved May 28, 2010, from http://mediamatters.org/items/200511210003

Media Matters for America. (2004, September 22). Savage: Kerry has "committed sedition; "should be immediately shackled and arrested." Retrieved May 30, 2007, from http://mediamatters.org/items/200409220001

Meranto, O. J. (2005). The third wave of McCarthyism: Co-opting the language of inclusivity. *New Political Science, 27*(2), 215–232.

Messer-Davidow, E. (1993). Manufacturing the attack on liberalized higher education. *Social Text, 33*(4), 40–80.

Milbank, D., & Cooperman, A. (2005, August 31, A5). Conservative author is seeing red in America: Cindy Sheehan: anti-American communist? *Washington Post*. Retrieved February 23, 2007, from http://www.washingtonpost.com/wp-dyn/content/artille/2005/08/30/AR2005083001862

Milbank, D. (2001, July 26). Bush lacks the ability to force action on the hill. *Washington Post*, p. A01.

Miller, A. (1995). Professors of hate. In R. Jacoby & N. Glauberman. (Eds.), *The Bell Curve debate: History, documents, opinions* (pp. 162–178). New York: Times Books.

Miller, J. (2005). *A gift of freedom: How the John M. Olin foundation changed America*. New York: Encounter Books.

Montopoli, B. (2010, July 2). Glenn Beck University? Yes, Glenn Beck University. Retrieved July 26, 2010, from http://www.cbsnews.com/8301-5035440162-20009560-503544.html

Morris, J. (2005). The Fox News factor. *The Harvard International Journal of Press/Politics,* 10(3), 56–79.

Mosher, S. (2001, January 2). Bush could use executive orders to save lives. Retrieved June 10, 2009, from http://www.heartland.org

Moyers, B. (2005). Foreword. In R. McChesney, R. Newman, & B. Scott. (Eds.), *The future of media: Resistance and reform in the 21st century* (pp. vii–xxiii). New York: Seven Stories Press.

REFERENCES

Moyers B. (2004). This is your story—the progressive story of America. Pass it on. Retrieved July 26, 2004, from http://www.utoronto.ca/csus/pm/moyers.htm

Moyers, B. (2001, November 19). Which America will we be now? *The Nation*. Retrieved June 20, 2005, from http://www.thenation.com/doc/20011119/moyers

Muwakkil, S. (2003, June 6). Neocon convergences. *In These Times*. Retrieved November 1, 2006, from http://www.inthesetimes.com/comments.php?id=216_0_3_0_C

Nahm, H. Y. (n.d.) Michelle Malkin: The radical right's Asian pitbull. *Goldsea Asian American*. Retrieved June 2, 2009 from http://www.goldsea.com/Personalities/Malkin/malkin.html

Neiwart, D. (2009). Projection much? Glenn Beck warns: 'Fascism is on the rise.' *CrooksandLiars*. Retrieved April 6, 2010, from http://crooksandliars.com/david-neiwart/projection-much-glenn-beck-warns-fas

Neiwart, D. (2009, June 4). Hannity's old buddy Hal Turner arrested for threatening Connecticut officials. *CrooksandLiars*. Retrieved July 13, 2009, from http://crooksandliars.com/david-neiwart/hannity's-old-buddy-hal-turner-arrest

Neiwart, D. (2009, February 3). O'Reilly declares war on New York Times after it calls him out on immigration. *CrooksandLiars*. Retrieved June 3, 2010, from http://crooksandliars.com

Neiwart, D. (2008, January 8). Jonah Goldberg's bizarre history. *The American Prospect*. Retrieved May 4, 2010, from http://www.prospect.org

Newscorpse.com. (2009, March 21). Brit Hume confesses to fox news right-wing bias. Retrieved June 2, 2009, from http://www.newscorpse.com/ncWP/?pd226

Nichols, J., & McChesney, R. (2005). *Tragedy & farce: How the American media sell wars, spin elections and destroy democracy*. New York: The New Press.

Noah, T. (2003, February 3). The Bellesiles of the right? *Slate Magazine*. Retrieved December 6, 2006, from http://www.slate.com/id/2078084

Noah, T. (2002, May 2). The NRA's moral equivalence. *Slate Magazine*. Retrieved March 28, 2007, from http://slate.msn.com/?id=206227

Nock, A. J. (1935). *Our enemy, the state*. New York: Arno Press.

Nock, A. J. (1936). Isaiah's job. *Atlantic Monthly*. Retrieved September 18, 2006, from http://www.lewrockwell.com/orig3/nock3b.html

Noonan, P. (2001, October 12). Welcome back, Duke. *OpinionJournal*. Retrieved April 14, 2009, from http://www.opinionjournal.com/columnists/pnoonan/?id=95001309

O'Beirne, K. (2005). *Women who make the world worse: and how their radical feminist assault is ruining our schools, families, military, and sports*. New York: Sentinel.

O'Reilly, B. (2006). *Culture warrior*. New York: Broadway Books.

O'Reilly, B. (2005, January 28). Top Story: Ward Churchill at Hamilton College. Retrieved May 25, 2006, from http://billoreilly.com

O'Reilly, B. (2005, March 3). Professor Ward Churchill is a traitor. Retrieved June 3, 2010, from http://www.foxnews.com

Ostroy, A. (2009, May 25). Dick Cheney is America's #1 terrorist. Retrieved April 7, 2010, from http://www.huffingtonpost.com/andy-ostroy/dick-cheney-is-americas.1-b-207432.html

Palast, G. (2006). *Armed madhouse*. New York: Dutton.

Palast, G. (2003). *The best democracy money can buy: The truth about corporate cons, globalization and high-finance fraudsters*. New York: Penguin Books.

Palczewski, C. H., et al. (2006). Ripe for controversy: Churchill's 9/11 essay. In P. Riley (Ed.), *Engaging argument: Selected papers from the 2005 NCA/AFA summer conference on argumentation* (pp. 348–358). Annandale, VA: Speech Communication Association.

Palin, S. (2010, April 29). Glenn Beck. *Time Magazine*. Retrieved June 22, 2010, from http://www.time.com

Panhorst, J. (2005, March 16). New conservative newspaper stirs controversy. *Zephyr*. Retrieved March 15, 2007, from http://zephyr.unr.edu/zephyr/spring05/story3/packpatroit.html

Parenti, M. (2005, September 3). How the free market killed New Orleans. *ZNet*. Retrieved February 22, 2007, from http://www.zmag.org

Parenti, M. (2004). *Superpatriotism*. San Francisco: City Lights Books.

Parenti, M. (2002). *The terrorism trap: September 11 and beyond*. San Franciso: City Lights Books.

Parenti, M. (2000). The myth of the liberal campus. In G. D. White (Ed.), *Campus, Inc.: Corporate power in the ivory tower* (pp. 85–92). Amherst, NY: Prometheus Books.

Parry, R. (2006, June 14). The Moon-Bush cash conduit. *Consortiumnews.com*. Retrieved June 27, 2006, from http://www.consortiumnews.com

Parry, R. (2006, October 30). *All the President's lies*. Consortiumnews.com. Retrieved October 30, 2006, from http://www.consortiumnews.com

Parry, R. (2003, June 2). America's Matrix. *Consortiumnews.com*. Retrieved July 6, 2003, from http://www.consortiumnews.com

People Weekly. (2002, December 2). Retrieved March 5, 2005, from http://www.people.com/people/archive.

Peschek, J. G. (1987). *Policy planning organizations: Elite agendas and America's rightward turn*. Philadelphia: Temple University Press.

Peters, C. (2010). No-Spin zones. *Journalism Studies*, 1–20.

Phillips, K. (2006). *American theocracy: The peril and politics of radical religion, oil, and borrowed money in the 21st century*. New York: Viking Penguin.

Piereson, J. (2005, October 3). The left university. *Weekly Standard*. Retrieved November 4, 2006, from http://www.weeklystandard.com/Content/Public/Articles/000/000/006/120xbklj.asp

Pilkington, E. (2010, February 6). Prejudice and principle brew at tea party meet. *The Guardian*. Retrieved April 30, 2010 from http://www.guardian.co.uk/world/2010/feb/05/tea-party-united-states

Pipes, D. (1990, November 19). The Muslims are coming! The Muslims are coming! *National Review*. Retrieved May 16, 2010, from http://www.danielpipes.org/198/the-muslims-are-coming-the-muslims-are-coming

Plissner, M. (2002, December 30). Flunking statistics: The right's disinformation about faculty bias. *The American Prospect*. Retrieved October 25, 2006, from http://www.prospect.orgprint-friendly/print/V13/23/plissner-m.html

Pollitt, K. (2007, February 5). Ayatollah D'Souza. *The Nation, 284*(5), 9.

Pollitt, K. (2007, November 19). David Horowitz, Feminist? *The Nation*. Retrieved December 4, 2007, from http://www.thenation.com/doc/20071119/pollitt

Posner, S. (2005, February 21). Secret society: Just who is the Council for National Policy, and why aren't they paying taxes? *The Gadflyer*. Retrieved March 14, 2007, from http://gadflyer.com/articles/print.php?ArticleID=260

Postman, N. (1985). *Amusing ourselves to death: Public discourse in the age of show business*. New York: Penguin Books.

Powell, M. (2001, March 28). A radical transformation: Former 60's agitator David Horowitz has changed his politics, but not his tone. *Washington Post*, p. C01. Retrieved May 22, 2007, from http://www.tysknews.com/Articles/radical_transformation.htm

Prashad, V. (2005, January 2). An academic front of the right. *Frontline* 22, 15–28. Retrieved February 6, 2008, from http://www.frontlineonnet.com/fl2202/stories/20050128000606400.htm

Press, E. (2004, April 22). Neocon man. *The Nation*. Retrieved June 8, 2010, from http://www.thenation.com

Proffitt, J. M. (2007). Challenges to democratic discourse: Media concentration and the marginalization of dissent. *The Review of Education, Pedagogy, and Cultural Studies*, (29), 65–84.

Proyect, L. (2005, May 9). *The persecution of Ward Churchill*. Retrieved June 4, 2009, from https://louisproyect.wordpress.com.2005/05/09/the-persecution-of-ward-churchill

Rampton, S., & Stauber, J. (2006). *The best war ever: Lies, damned lies, and the mess in Iraq*. New York: Penguin Books.

Rampton, S., & Stauber, J. (2004). *Banana Republicans: How the right-wing is turning American into a one-party state*. New York: Tarcher/Penguin.

Raphael, C. (2005, February 10). Spinning media for government. *CorpWatch*. Retrieved June 12, 2008, from http://www.corpwatch.org/article.php?id=11836

REFERENCES

Rasmus, J. (2005). *The war at home: The corporate offensive from Ronald Reagan to George W. Bush.* San Ramon, CA: Kyklos Productions.

Reed, A., Jr. (2006, September 18). Undone by neoliberalism. *The Nation.* Retrieved February 22, 2007, from http://www.thenation.com/doc/20060918/reed

Rendall, S. (2003). An aggressive conservative vs. a 'liberal to be determined': The false balance of *Hannity & Colmes. Extra!* (November/December). Retrieved March 27, 2006, from http://www.fair.org/index.php?page=1158

Revolutionary Worker #1268. (2005, February 20). The witch hunt against Ward Churchill. Retrieved May 2, 2009, from http://www.kersplebedeb.com

Rich, A. (2005). War of ideas: Why mainstream and liberal foundations and think tanks they support are losing in the war of ideas in American politics. *Stanford Social Innovation Review.* Retrieved November 1, 2006, from http://www.ssireview.org/pdf/2005SP_feature_rich.pdf

Rich, F. (2006). *The greatest story ever sold: The decline and fall of truth from 9/11 to Katrina.* New York: Penguin Books.

Richardson, R. (1984, December 20). The report on the universities. *Inter-Department Memo.*

Riordan, M. (2005). Academic freedom takes a step to the right. *PR Watch.* Retrieved January 15, 2007, from http://www.prwatch.org/prwissues/2005Q3/saf.html

Roddy, D. (2005, January 23). Jared Taylor, a racist in the guise of 'expert.' *Pittsburgh Post-Gazette.* Retrieved May 22, 2007, from http://www.commondreams.org/views05/0123-02.htm

Romano, A. (2010, April 13). Unified theory of Glenn Beck. *Newsweek.* Retrieved June 18, 2010, from http://www.newsweek.com/2010/04/12/unified-theory-of-glenn-beck

Rose, L. (2010, April 26). Crying all the way to the bank. *Forbes.* 185(7), 56–60.

Rothmyer, K. (1998, April 7). The man behind the mask. *Salon Newsreal.* Retrieved September 14, 2006, from http://www.salon.com.news/1998/04/07news.html

Rothmyer, K. (1981, July/August). Citizen Scaife. *Columbia Journalism Review.* Retrieved August 16, 2006, from http://archives.cjr.org/year81/4/scaife.asp

Rotundo, A. (2000, July 2). Untitled [Review of The war against boys: How misguided feminism is harming our young men]. *The Washington Post.* Retrieved September 23, 2006, from http://www.washingtonpost.com/wp-srv/style/books/reviews/waragainstboys0703.htm

Roy, A. (2004, February 9). The new American century. *The Nation, 278*(5), 11–14.

Roy, A. (2004). *An ordinary person's guide to empire.* Cambridge, MA: South End Press.

Roy, A. (2003, August 24). The loneliness of Noam Chomsky. Retrieved June 15, 2008, from http://www.chomsky.info/onchomsky/20030824.htm

Rubin, M., & Stern, S. (2005, November 30). Recruit academia. Retrieved October 25, 2006, from http://www.aei.org/publications/pubID.23501/pub_detail.asp

Ruby-Sachs, E., & Waligore, T. (2003, February 17). Alternative voices on campus. *The Nation.* Retrieved February 22, 2007, from http://www.thenation.com

Saloma, J. (1984). *Ominous politics: The new conservative labyrinth.* New York: Hill & Wang.

Sammon, B. (2002). *Fighting back: The war on terrorism—from inside the Bush White House.* Washington, DC: Regnery Publishing, Inc.

Saturen, V. (2008, February 27). Daniel Pipes tracks our nation's traitorous professors so you don't have to. Retrieved June 7, 2010, from http://www.campusprogress.org/rws/2589/the-21st-centurys-joseph-mccarthy

Savage, C., & Wirzbicki, A. (2005, February 2). White House-friendly reporter under scrutiny. *The Boston Globe.* Retrieved March 15, 2007, from http://www.boston.com/news/nation/washington/articles/2005/02/02/white_house_friendly

Scarborough, R. (2004). *Rumsfeld's war: The untold story of America's anti-terrorist commander.* Washington, DC: Regnery Publishing Inc.

Scatamburlo-D'Annibale, V., & McLaren, P. (2010). Class-ifying race: The compassionate racism of the right and why class still matters. In Z. Leonardo (Ed.), *Handbook of cultural politics and education* (pp. 113–140). Rotterdam/Boston/Taipei: Sense Publishers.

Scatamburlo-D'Annibale, V. & McLaren, P. (2009). The reign of capital: A pedagogy and praxis of class struggle. In M. Apple, W. Au & L. Gandin (Eds.), *The Routledge international handbook of critical education* (pp. 96–109). New York: Routledge.

Scatamburlo-D'Annibale, V., Suoranta, J., & McLaren, P. (2007). Excavating hope among the ruins: Confronting creeping fascism in our midst. In D. Carlson & C. Gause (Eds.), *Keeping the Promise: Essays in Leadership, Democracy and Education* (pp. 79–116). New York: Peter Lang.

Scatamburlo-D'Annibale, V., Suoranta, J., Jaramillo, N., & McLaren, P. (2006). Farewell to the 'Bewildered Herd': Paulo Freire's Revolutionary Dialogical Communication in the Age of Corporate Globalization. *Journal for Critical Education Policy Studies, 4*(2), 30. http://www.jceps.com/index.php?pageID= article&articleID=65

Scatamburlo-D'Annibale, V. (2006). The new 'P.C.?': Patriotic correctness and the suppression of dissent on American campuses. In J. Klaehn (Ed.), *Bound by power: Intended consequences* (pp. 12–45). Montreal: Black Rose Books.

Scatamburlo-D'Annibale, V. (2005). In 'sync': Bush's war propaganda machine and the American mainstream media. In J. Klaehn (Ed.), *Filtering the news: Essays on Herman and Chomsky's propaganda model* (pp. 21–62). Montreal: Black Rose Books.

Scatamburlo, V. (1998). *Soldiers of misfortune: The new right's culture war and the politics of political correctness.* New York: Peter Lang.

Schell, J. (2004, June 28). Cold war to Star Wars. *The Nation, 278*(25), 6–7.

Schecter, D. (2003, May 1). The link between the media, the war, and our right to know. *Mediachannel.org.* Retrieved June 14, 2003, from http://www.mediachannel.org/views/dissector/moveon.shtml

Schrecker, E. (2006, February 10). Worse than McCarthy. *The Chronicle of Higher Education.* Retrieved December 21, 2006, from http://chronicle.com/weekly/v52/i23/23b02001.htm

Schrecker, E. (1988). *No ivory tower: McCarthyism and the universities.* New York: Oxford Press.

Schulz, D. P., & Reyes, G. M. (2008). Ward Churchill and the politics of public memory. *Rhetoric & Public Affairs, 11*(4), 631–658.

Searls-Giroux, S. (2005). From the 'culture wars' to the conservative campaign for campus diversity: or, how inclusion became the new exclusion. *Policy Futures in Education, 3*(4), 314–326.

Shakir, F. (2007, December 17). Tony Snow: 'The second war in this country is 'the war on God'. *Think Progress.* Retrieved July 13, 2009, from http://www.thinkprogress.org/2007/12/17/tony-snow-war-on-god

Sherman, S. (2000, July 3). David Horowitz's long march. *The Nation, 271*(1), 11–16, 18–19.

Shorris, E. (2004). Ignoble liars: Leo Strauss, George Bush, and the philosophy of mass deception. *Harper's Magazine, 308*(1849), 65–71.

Siano, B. (1996). The great political correctness panic, or: How I learned to stop worrying and love the thought police. *The Brian Siano Website.* Retrieved April 6, 2007, from http://www.briansiano.com/The%20Great%20Political%20Correctness%20Panic.htm

Simon, W. E. (1978). *A time for truth.* New York: Reader's Digest Press.

Smith, C. (2007, March 27). The American Council of Trustees and Alumni's "Intellectual Diversity" agenda. Retrieved May 4, 2007, from http://www.campusprogress.org

Sommers, C. H. (2006, October 16). Bias rules UNM law school. *American Enterprise Institute.* Retrieved October 24, 2006, from http://www.aei.org/publications/pubID.25014,filter.all/pub_detail.asp

Sommers, C. H. (2000). *The war against boys: How misguided feminism is harming our young men.* New York: Simon and Schuster.

Sommers, C. H. (1994). *Who stole feminism? How women have betrayed women.* New York: Simon and Schuster.

Southern Law Poverty Center. (2009). *Intelligence Report,* Issue #133. Retrieved May 27, 2010, from http://www.splcenter.org

Spence, G. (2006). *Bloodthirsty bitches and pious pimps of power: The rise and risks of the new conservative hate culture.* New York: St. Martin's Press.

Spencer, R. (2003, April 22). Dr. Daniel Pipes and his critics. *FrontPageMagazine*. Retrieved June 4, 2010, from http://www.frontpagemag.org

Spindel, B. (2003). Conservatism as the 'sensible middle': The Independent Women's Forum, politics, and the media. *Social Text, 21*(4), 99–125.

Starr, A. (2001). *Naming the enemy: Anti-corporate social movements confront globalization.* London: Zed Books.

Stelter, B., & Carter, B. (2009, March 30). Fox News's mad, apocalyptic, tearful rising star. *The New York Times*. Retrieved June 23, 2010, from http://www.nytimes.com

Street, P. (2003). By all means, study the founders: Notes from the democratic left. *The Review of Education, Pedagogy, and Cultural Studies*, (25), 281–301.

Street, P., & DiMaggio, A. (2010, April 10). What populist uprising? Part I: Facts and reflections on race, class, and the tea party 'movement'. *MRzine*. Retrieved April 30, 2010, from http://mrzine.monthly review.org/2010/sd210410p.html

Sturken, M. (2007). *Tourists of history: Memory, kitsch, and consumerism from Oklahoma City to ground zero.* Durham, NC and London: Duke University Press.

Sullivan, J. J. (2010, January). American grotesque. *Gentlemen's Quarterly, 80*(1), 64.

Sullivan, A. (2007, March 2). Coulter in her element. *The Atlantic Online*. Retrieved April 11, 2007, from http://andrewsullivan.theatlantic.com/the_daily_dish/2007/03/coulter_in_her_.html

Swanson, D. (2004, December 20). Media blackout on Bush's war against labor. *Counterpunch*. Retrieved April 14, 2006, from http://www.counterpunch.org/swanson/2202004.html

Taylor, M. L. (2005). *Religion, politics, and the Christian right: Post-9/11 powers and American empire.* Minneapolis, MN: Fortress Press.

Taylor, S. (2007, October 22). Exposing "Islamo-Fascism Awareness Week": David Horowitz can't handle the truth. *Counterpunch*. Retrieved December 4, 2007, from http://www.counterpunch.org/taylor 10222007.html

The Nation. (2005, April 4). The captive mind. Retrieved May 12, 2006, from http://www.thenation.com

The Nation. (2004, June 28). Editorial: The Reagan legacy. *The Nation, 278*(25), 3–5.

The O'Reilly Factor. (2005, February 2). Partial transcript. Retrieved June 3, 2010, from http://www. foxnews.com.story/0,2933,146127,00.html

The O'Reilly Factor. (2003, February 26). Transcript. Retrieved June 3, 2010, from http://www.vdare.com/ pb/worm_review_11.htm

Thernstrom, S. (1990). McCarthyism then and now. *Academic Questions, 4*(1), 14–16.

Toler, D. (1999, March/April). The Right's 'race desk'. *Extra!* Retrieved July 11, 2005, from http:// www.fair.org/index.php?page=1449

Tucker, J. A. (2002, August 22). Albert Jay Nock, forgotten man of the right. Retrieved September 18, 2006, from http://www.lewrockwell.com/tucker/tucker23.html

Vanlandingham, J. (2005, March 23). Capitol bill aims to control leftist profs. *The Independent Florida Alligator*. Retrieved April 22, 2006, from http://www.alligator.org/app/pt2/050323freedom.php

Von Drehle, D. (2009, September 17). Mad man: Is Glenn Beck bad for America? *Time*. Retrieved April 26, 2010, from http://www.time.com

Wallace-Wells, B. (2003, December 12). In the tank: The intellectual decline of AEI. *Washington Monthly*. Retrieved October 24, 2006, from http://www.washingtonmonthly.com/features/2003/0312. wallace-wells.html

Wall Street Journal. (2002, August 30). One faculty indivisible: Even the press corps isn't this uniformly liberal. Retrieved November 9, 2006, from http://www.opinionjournal.com

Walsh, J. (2009, June 10). Can right-wing hate talk lead to murder? Retrieved May 10, 2010, from http:// www.salon.com/opinion/walsh/politics/2009/06/10/von_brunn

Warren, D. (1996). *Radio priest: Charles Coughlin, the father of hate radio.* New York: The Free Press.

Weisberg, J. (1998, January 9). Happy birthday, Heritage Foundation. *Slate*. Retrieved February 14, 2007, from http://slate.msn.com

Weisberg, J. (1992). NAS—Who are these guys, anyways? In P. Aufderheide (Ed.), *Beyond P.C.: Towards a politics of understanding* (pp. 80–88). Minnesota, MN: Graywolf Press.

Whalen, R. (2006, October 16). Revolt of the generals. *The Nation, 283*(12), 11, 13–14, 16, 18.

Wiener, J. (2006, January 26). UCLA's dirty thirty. *The Nation.* Retrieved June 2, 2007, from http://www.thenation.com/doc/20060213/wiener

Wiener, J. (2000, October 2). Hard to muzzle: The return of Lynne Cheney. *The Nation, 271*(9), 13–14, 16–17.

Wilayto, P. (2001, April). The Bradley Foundation: Bush's faith-based initiative. *Z Magazine.* Retrieved October 25, 2006, from http://www.zmag.org/ZMag/articles/apr01wilayto.htm

Wilkinson, F. (2006). Who's your daddy party? *The American Prospect, 17*(6), 32–38.

Williams, H. (2005, January 20). Profiles in chutzpah. *AVA Oregon* 1(2). Retrieved November 17, 2010, from http://www.hartwilliams,com/ava/ava0112.htm

Willis, C. (Ed.). (2004). *The I hate Ann Coulter, Bill O'Reilly, Rush Limbaugh, Michael Savage, Sean Hannity ... reader.* New York: Thunder Mouth Press.

Willis, E. (2006). Escape from freedom: What's the matter with Tom Frank (and the lefties who love him)? *Situations, 1*(2), 5–20. Retrieved December 11, 2006, from http://ojs.gc.cuny.edu/index.php/situations/article/view/30

Willis, E. (2005, September). The pernicious concept of 'balance'. *The Chronicle of Higher Education.* Retrieved May 23, 2008, from http://www.utexas.edu/conferences/africa/ads/1124.html

Wilson, J. K. (2008). *Patriotic correctness: Academic freedom and its enemies.* Boulder, CO: Paradigm Publishers.

Wilson, J. K. (1995). *The myth of political correctness: The conservative attack on higher education.* Durham, NC and London: Duke University Press.

Wilson, J. K. (1994, December). Untitled [Review of Who stole feminism? How women have betrayed women]. *Z Magazine.* Retrieved September 23, 2006, from http://www.zmag.org/zmag/articles/dec94reviews.htm

Winant, G. (2009, May 31). O'Reilly's campaign against murdered doctor. *Salon.com.* Retrieved June 5, 2010, from http://www.salon.com/news/feature/2009/05/31/tiller

Wise, T. (2004, June 10). Reagan, race, and remembrance. *Black Commentator.* Retrieved June 23, 2005, from http://www.blackcommentator.com/94/94wise_reagan_pf.html

Wise, T. (2002, December 16). Making nice with racists: David Horowitz and the soft pedaling of white supremacy. *ZNet.* Retrieved May 10, 2007, from http://www.zmag.org/content/2002-12/16wise.cfm

Wolcott, J. (2004). *Attack poodles and other media mutants: The looting of the news in a time of terror.* New York: Miramax Books.

Wolin, S. (2003, May 19). Inverted totalitarianism. *The Nation.* Retrieved February 4, 2007, from http://www.thenation.com/article/inverted-totalitarianism

Woodward, B. (2002). *Bush at war.* New York: Simon & Schuster.

Woolcock, J. (2005, February 9). Prof. Joseph Woolcock responds to student's allegations. *The Jawa Report.* Retrieved March 24, 2008 from http://mypetjawa.mu.nu/archives/066832.php

Wright, T. (2010, January 20). The rising Tea Baggers could easily become fascist. *Open Salon.* Retrieved April 29, 2010, from http://open.salon.com/blog/tomjwright/2010/01/21/the_rising_tea_baggers_could_easily_become_fascist

Younge, G. (2005, July 11). Racism rebooted: Philadelphia, Mississippi; then and now. *The Nation, 281*(2), 11, 13–14.

Zaitchik, A. (2010, May 6). How Glenn Beck re-invented himself as a crying conservative. Retrieved June 21, 2010, from http://www.alternet.org/story/146752

Zaitchik, A. (2009, September 21–23). The making of Glenn Beck, Parts 1-3. *Salon.* Retrieved April 26, 2010, from http://www.salon.com/news/feature/2009/09/21/glenn_beck

Zaitchik, A. (2009b, September 16). Meet the man who changed Glenn Beck's life. Retrieved June 22, 2010, from http://www.salon.com/news/features/2009/09/16/beck_skousen

Zenike, K. (2010, February 6). Palin assails Obama at Tea Party meeting. *New York Times.* Retrieved April 28, 2010 from http://www.nytimes.com/2010/02/07/US/politics/08palin.html

REFERENCES

Zinn, H. (2000). A flash of the possible. *The Progressive, 64*(1), 20.

Zinn, H. (1991, Spring/Summer). How free is higher education? *Gannett Centre Journal*, 147–154.

Zinsmeister, K. (2002). The one-party campus. *Diversity*. Retrieved November 9, 2006, from http://www.
taemag.com/issues/articleid17443/article_detail.asp

Zipp, J.F. & Fenwick, R. (2006). Is the academy a liberal hegemony?: The political orientations and
educational values of professors. *Public Opinion Quarterly*, 70(3), 304–326.

INDEX